Chapter 1: Yoshimori and Tokine

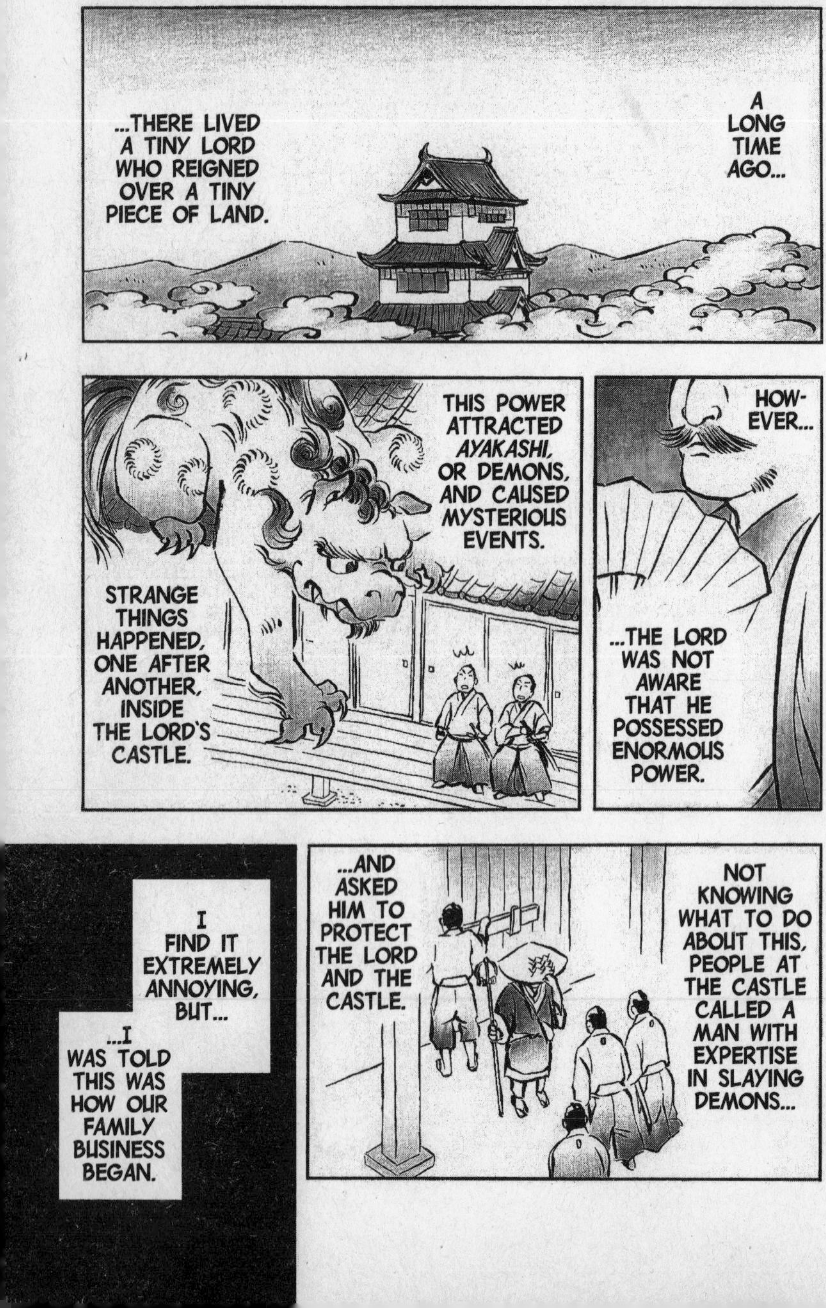
A LONG TIME AGO...
...THERE LIVED A TINY LORD WHO REIGNED OVER A TINY PIECE OF LAND.
HOW-EVER...
...THE LORD WAS NOT AWARE THAT HE POSSESSED ENORMOUS POWER.
THIS POWER ATTRACTED *AYAKASHI*, OR DEMONS, AND CAUSED MYSTERIOUS EVENTS.
STRANGE THINGS HAPPENED, ONE AFTER ANOTHER, INSIDE THE LORD'S CASTLE.
NOT KNOWING WHAT TO DO ABOUT THIS, PEOPLE AT THE CASTLE CALLED A MAN WITH EXPERTISE IN SLAYING DEMONS...
...AND ASKED HIM TO PROTECT THE LORD AND THE CASTLE.
I FIND IT EXTREMELY ANNOYING, BUT...
...I WAS TOLD THIS WAS HOW OUR FAMILY BUSINESS BEGAN.

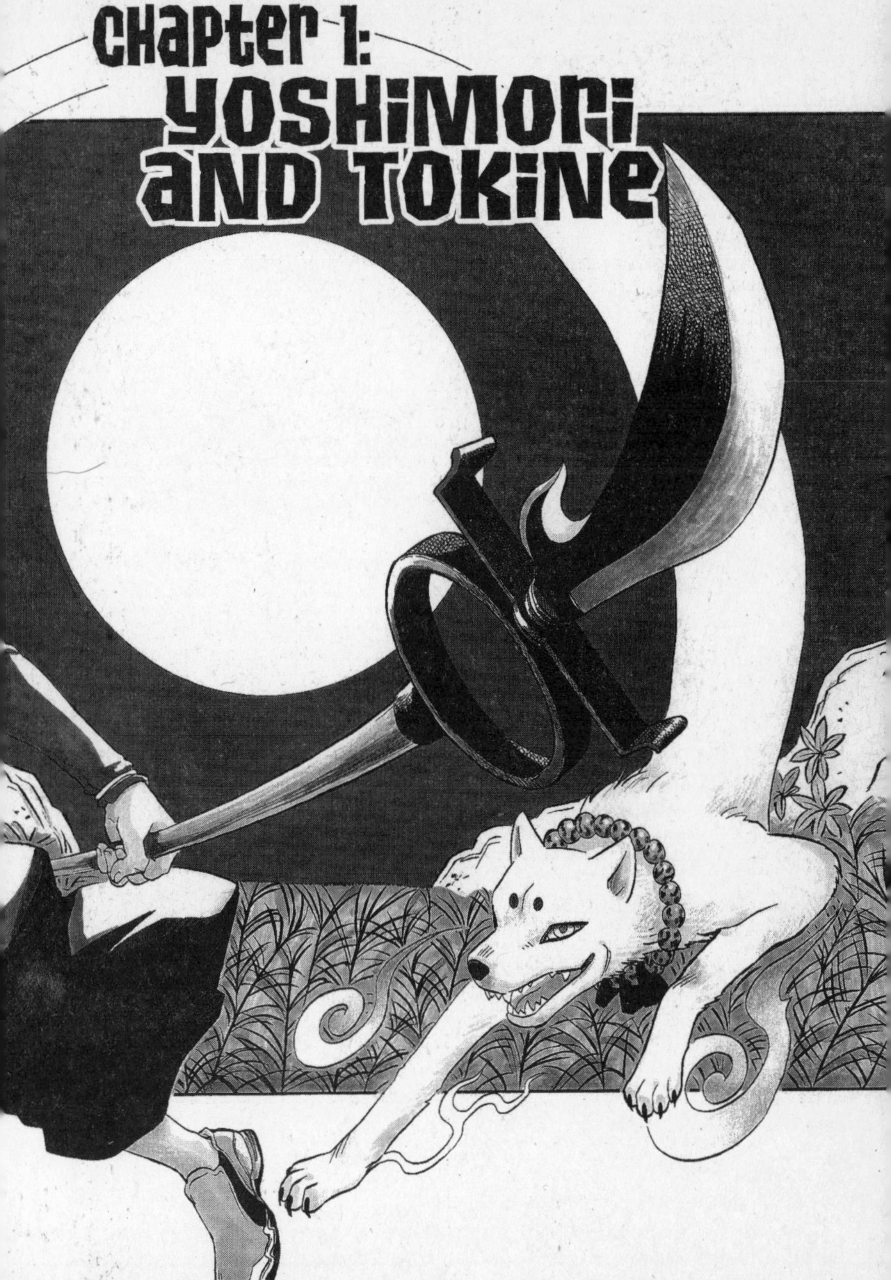
CHAPTER 1:
YOSHIMORI AND TOKINE

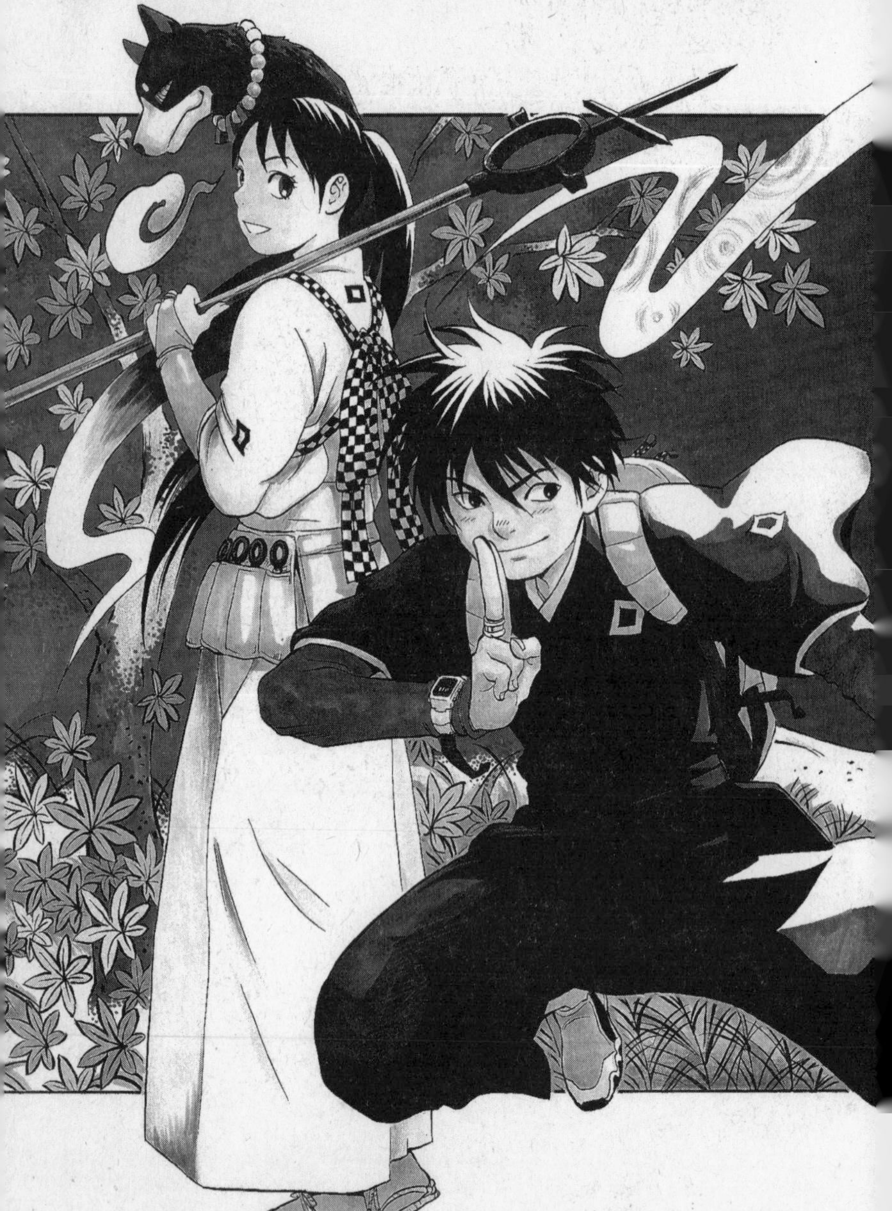

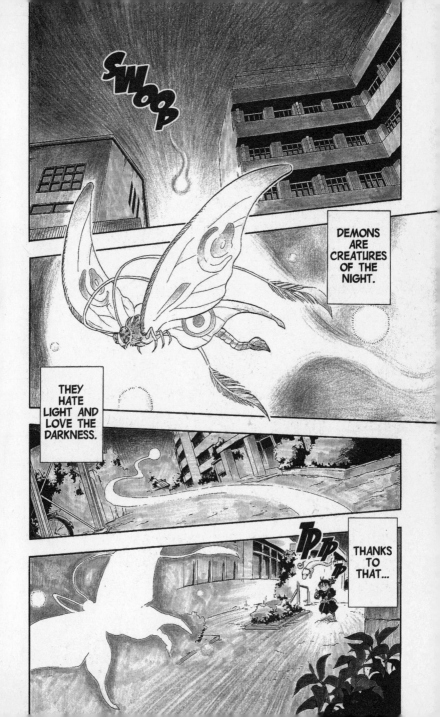

SWOOP

DEMONS ARE CREATURES OF THE NIGHT.

THEY HATE LIGHT AND LOVE THE DARKNESS.

TP. TP. TP.

THANKS TO THAT...

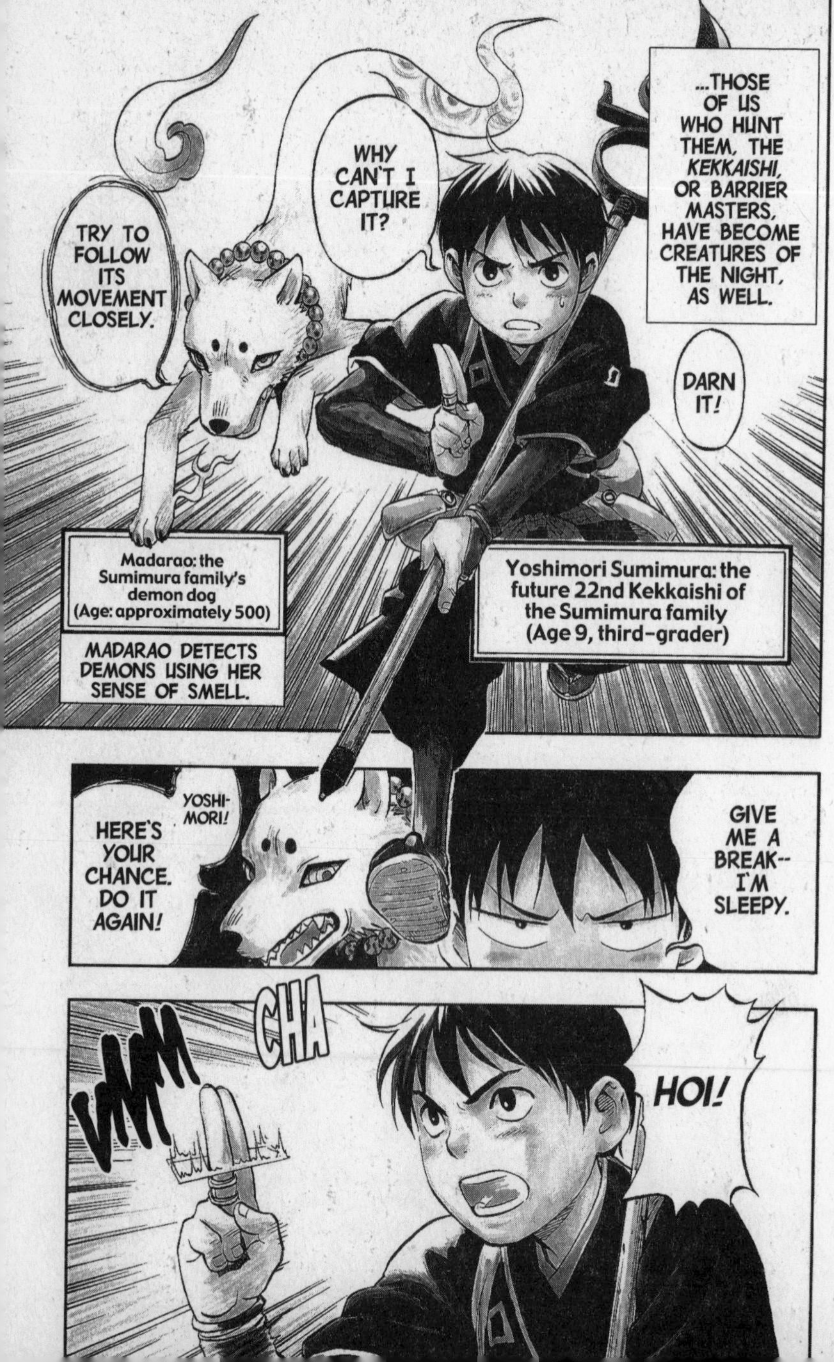
...THOSE OF US WHO HUNT THEM, THE *KEKKAISHI*, OR BARRIER MASTERS, HAVE BECOME CREATURES OF THE NIGHT, AS WELL.
DARN IT!
WHY CAN'T I CAPTURE IT?
TRY TO FOLLOW ITS MOVEMENT CLOSELY.
Yoshimori Sumimura: the future 22nd Kekkaishi of the Sumimura family (Age 9, third-grader)
Madarao: the Sumimura family's demon dog (Age: approximately 500)
MADARAO DETECTS DEMONS USING HER SENSE OF SMELL.
YOSHI-MORI!
HERE'S YOUR CHANCE. DO IT AGAIN!
GIVE ME A BREAK-- I'M SLEEPY.
HOI!
CHA
VMM

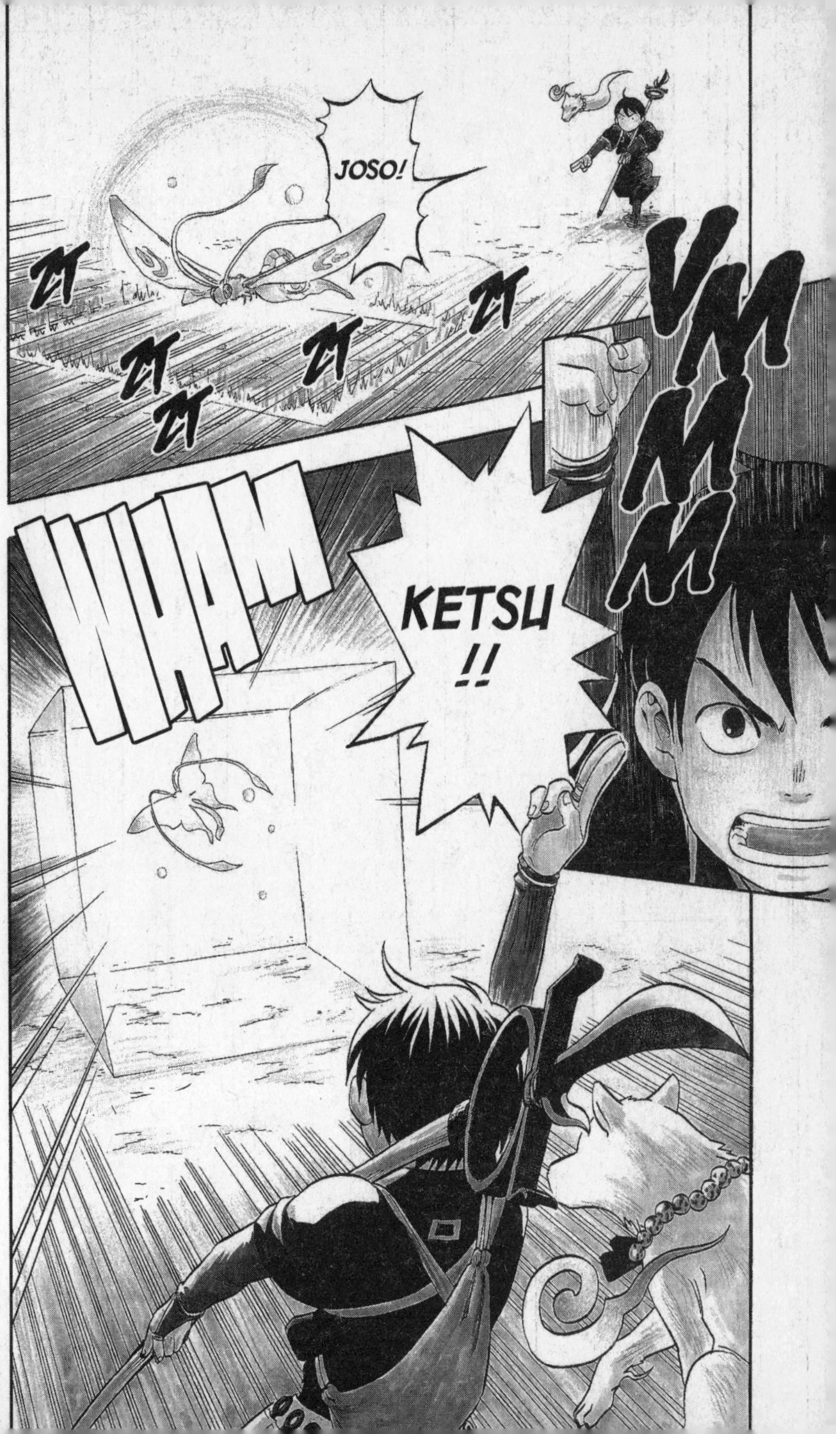
JOSO!
ZT
ZT
ZT
ZT
ZT
VMMM
KETSU!!
WHAM

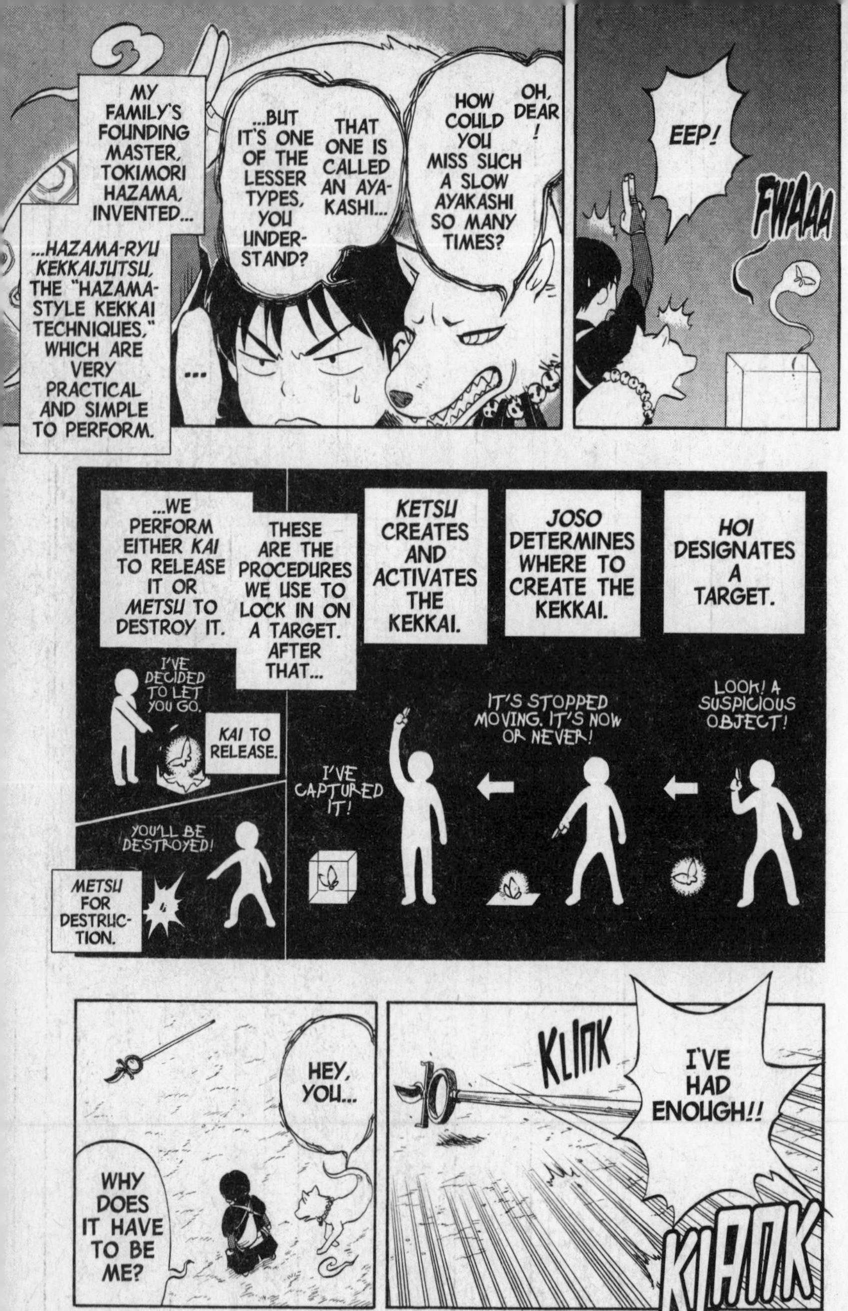
EEP!
FWAAA
OH, DEAR! HOW COULD YOU MISS SUCH A SLOW AYAKASHI SO MANY TIMES?
THAT ONE IS CALLED AN AYA-KASHI... ...BUT IT'S ONE OF THE LESSER TYPES, YOU UNDERSTAND?
...
MY FAMILY'S FOUNDING MASTER, TOKIMORI HAZAMA, INVENTED...
...HAZAMA-RYU KEKKAIJUTSU, THE "HAZAMA-STYLE KEKKAI TECHNIQUES," WHICH ARE VERY PRACTICAL AND SIMPLE TO PERFORM.
HOI DESIGNATES A TARGET.
JOSO DETERMINES WHERE TO CREATE THE KEKKAI.
KETSU CREATES AND ACTIVATES THE KEKKAI.
THESE ARE THE PROCEDURES WE USE TO LOCK IN ON A TARGET. AFTER THAT...
...WE PERFORM EITHER KAI TO RELEASE IT OR METSU TO DESTROY IT.
LOOK! A SUSPICIOUS OBJECT!
IT'S STOPPED MOVING. IT'S NOW OR NEVER!
I'VE CAPTURED IT!
I'VE DECIDED TO LET YOU GO.
KAI TO RELEASE.
YOU'LL BE DESTROYED!
METSU FOR DESTRUCTION.
KLINK
I'VE HAD ENOUGH!!
KLANK
HEY, YOU...
WHY DOES IT HAVE TO BE ME?

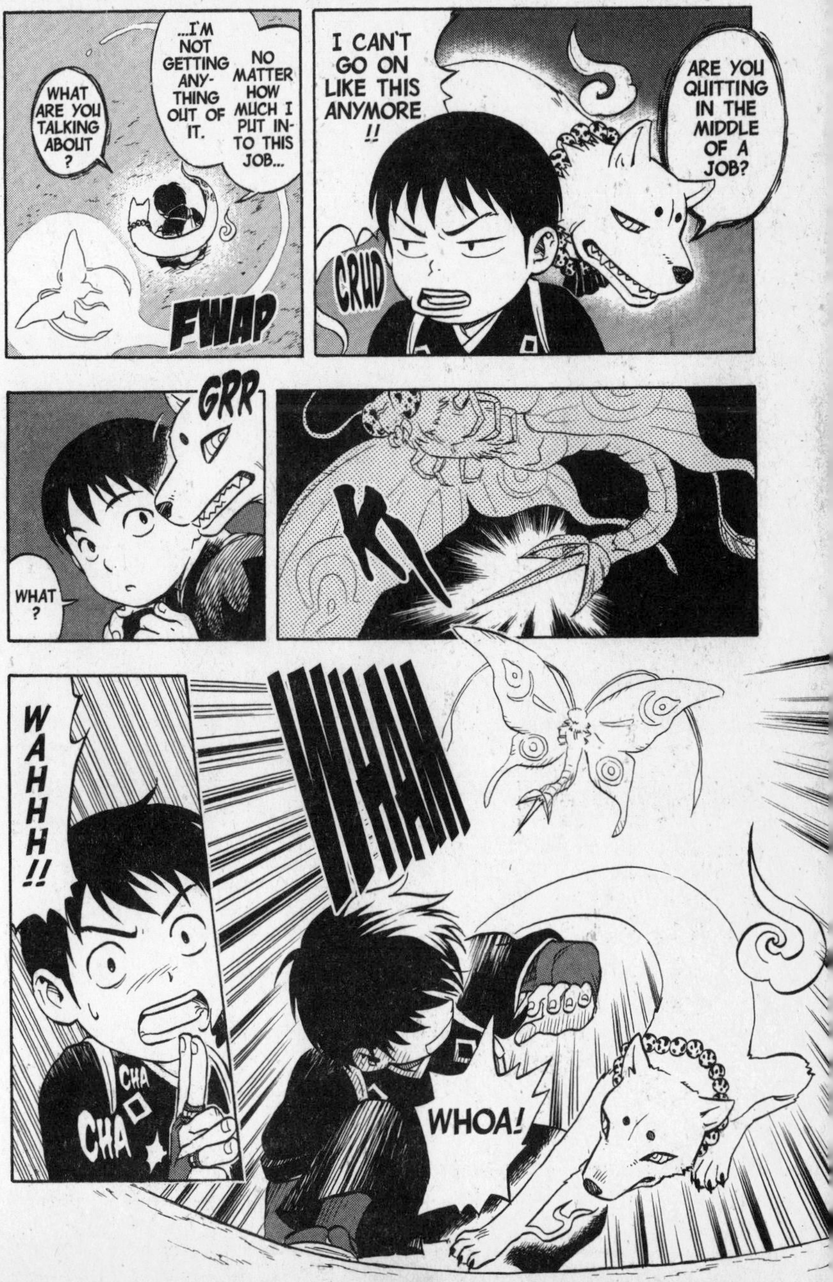
ARE YOU QUITTING IN THE MIDDLE OF A JOB?
I CAN'T GO ON LIKE THIS ANYMORE!!
CRUD
NO MATTER HOW MUCH I PUT IN-TO THIS JOB...
...I'M NOT GETTING ANY-THING OUT OF IT.
WHAT ARE YOU TALKING ABOUT?
FWAP
K
GRR
WHAT?
WHAM
WHOA!
WAHHHH!!
CHA
CHA

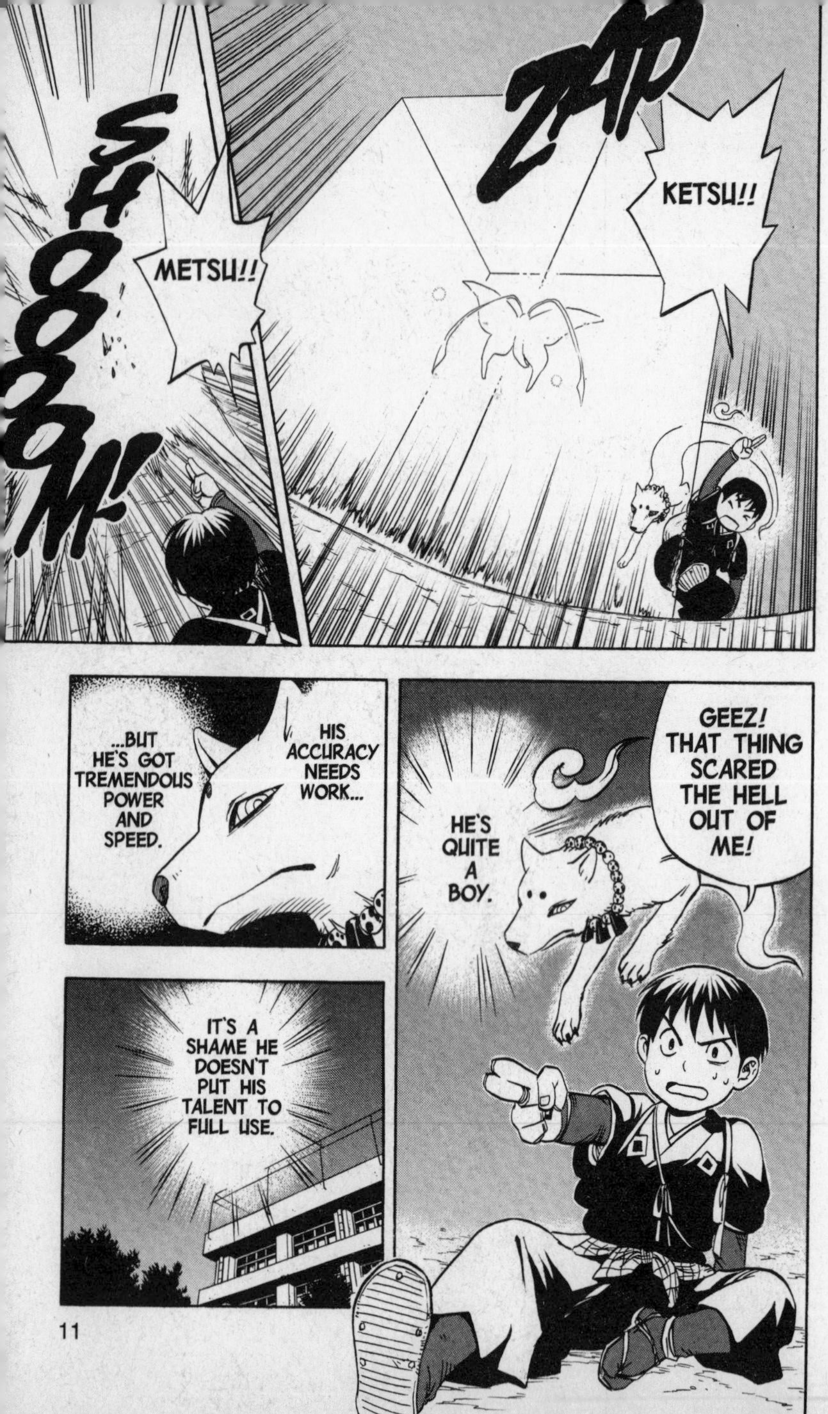
ZAP
KETSU!!
METSU!!
SHOOOOOM!
GEEZ! THAT THING SCARED THE HELL OUT OF ME!
HE'S QUITE A BOY.
HIS ACCURACY NEEDS WORK...
...BUT HE'S GOT TREMENDOUS POWER AND SPEED.
IT'S A SHAME HE DOESN'T PUT HIS TALENT TO FULL USE.

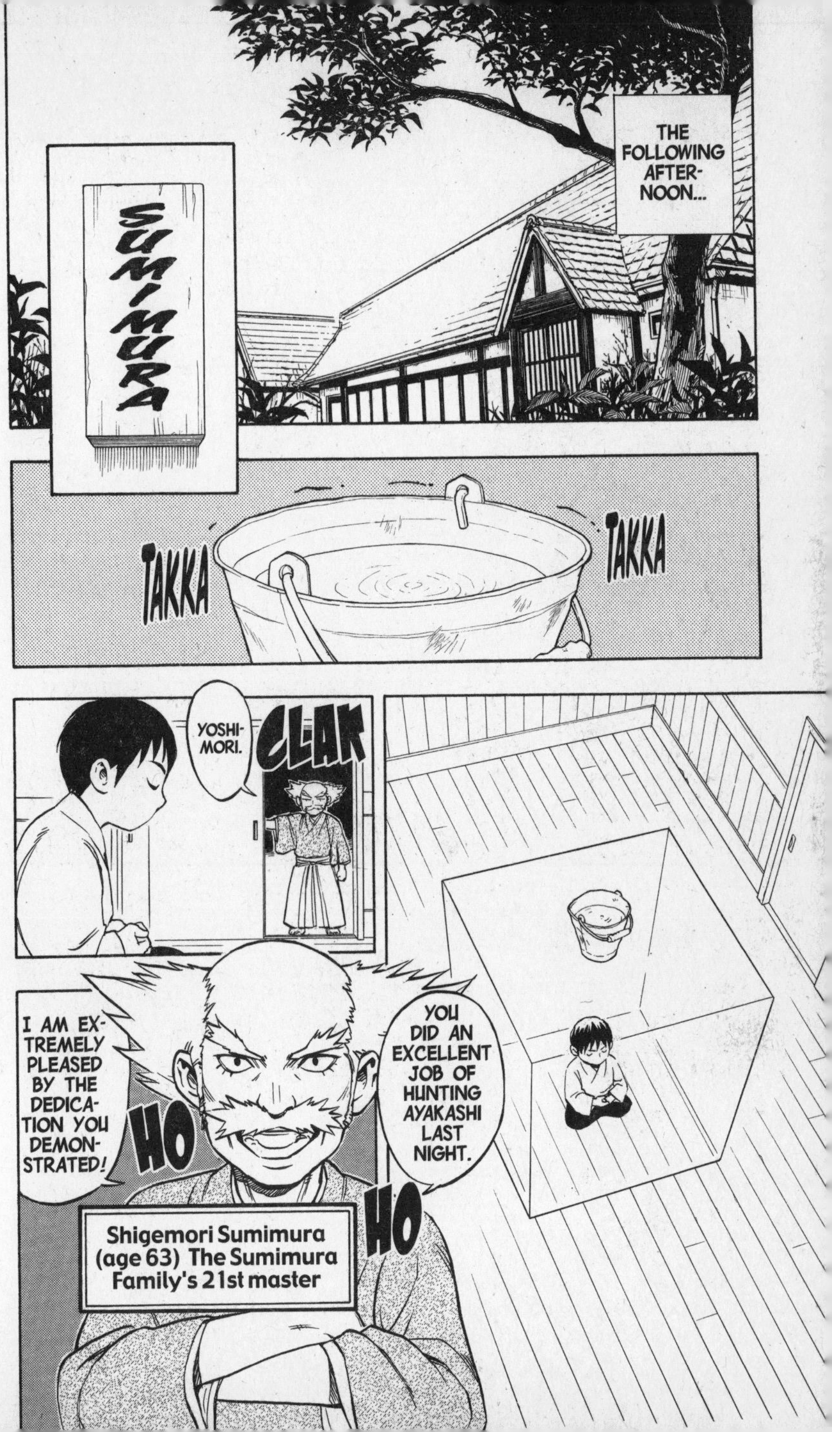
THE FOLLOWING AFTER-NOON...
SUMIMURA
TAKKA
TAKKA
CLAK
YOSHI-MORI.
YOU DID AN EXCELLENT JOB OF HUNTING AYAKASHI LAST NIGHT.
I AM EX-TREMELY PLEASED BY THE DEDICA-TION YOU DEMON-STRATED!
HO
HO
Shigemori Sumimura (age 63) The Sumimura Family's 21st master

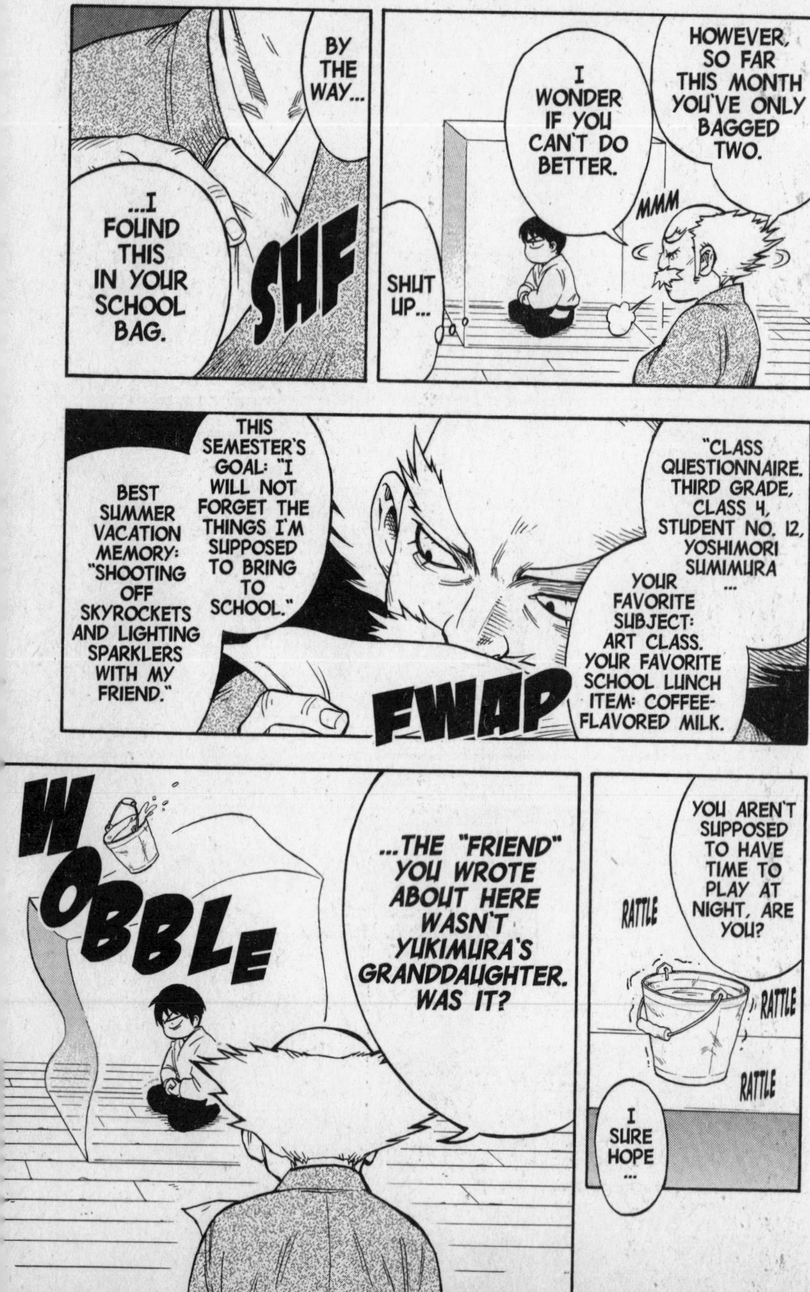
HOWEVER, SO FAR THIS MONTH YOU'VE ONLY BAGGED TWO.
I WONDER IF YOU CAN'T DO BETTER.
MMM
SHUT UP...
BY THE WAY...
...I FOUND THIS IN YOUR SCHOOL BAG.
SHF
"CLASS QUESTIONNAIRE. THIRD GRADE, CLASS 4, STUDENT NO. 12, YOSHIMORI SUMIMURA ...
YOUR FAVORITE SUBJECT: ART CLASS. YOUR FAVORITE SCHOOL LUNCH ITEM: COFFEE-FLAVORED MILK.
FWAP
THIS SEMESTER'S GOAL: "I WILL NOT FORGET THE THINGS I'M SUPPOSED TO BRING TO SCHOOL."
BEST SUMMER VACATION MEMORY: "SHOOTING OFF SKYROCKETS AND LIGHTING SPARKLERS WITH MY FRIEND."
YOU AREN'T SUPPOSED TO HAVE TIME TO PLAY AT NIGHT, ARE YOU?
RATTLE
RATTLE
RATTLE
I SURE HOPE ...
...THE "FRIEND" YOU WROTE ABOUT HERE WASN'T YUKIMURA'S GRANDDAUGHTER. WAS IT?
WOBBLE

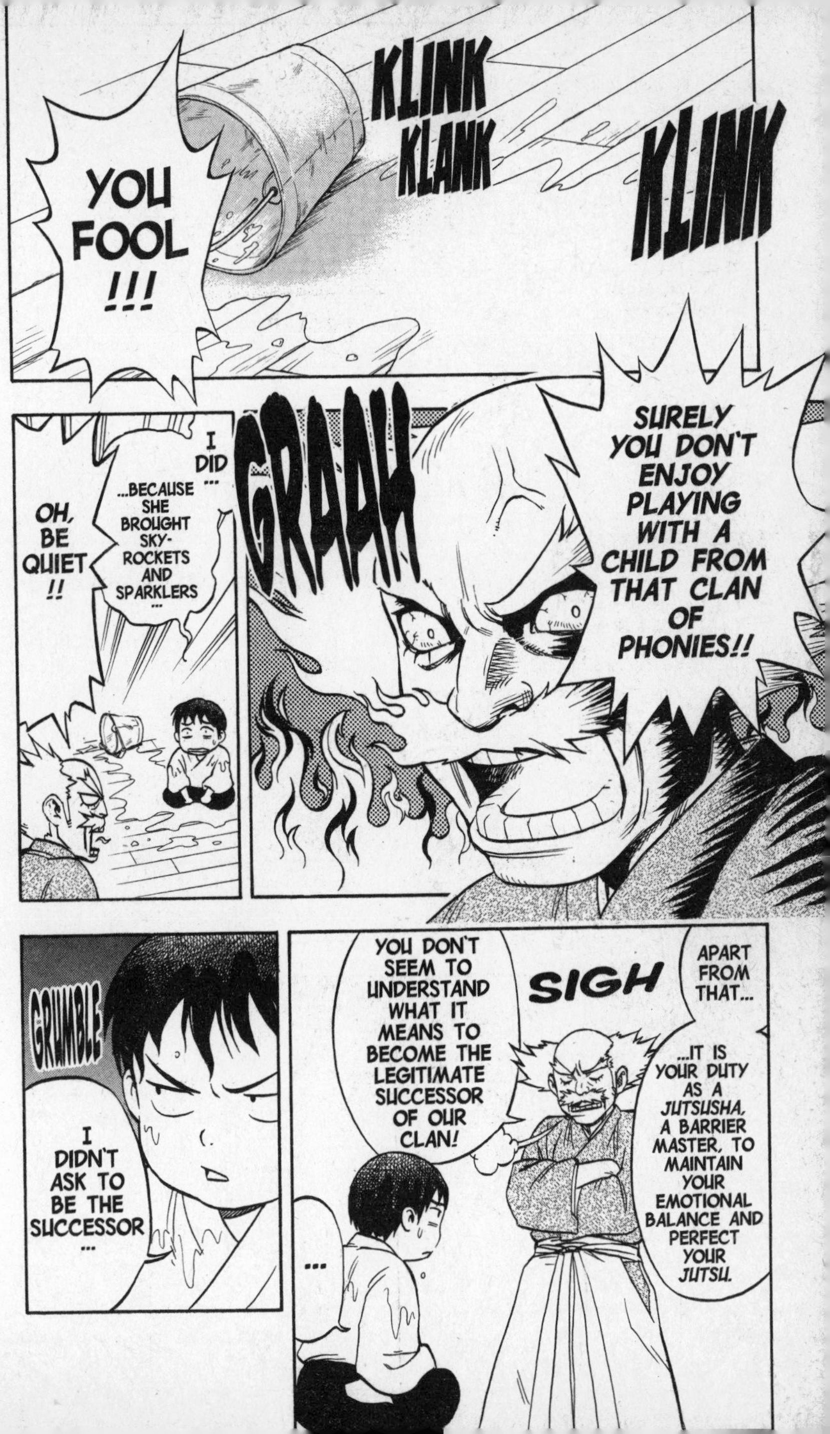
KLINK
KLINK KLANK
YOU FOOL !!!
SURELY YOU DON'T ENJOY PLAYING WITH A CHILD FROM THAT CLAN OF PHONIES!!
GRAAH
I DID ...
...BECAUSE SHE BROUGHT SKY-ROCKETS AND SPARKLERS ...
OH, BE QUIET !!
YOU DON'T SEEM TO UNDERSTAND WHAT IT MEANS TO BECOME THE LEGITIMATE SUCCESSOR OF OUR CLAN!
SIGH
APART FROM THAT...
...IT IS YOUR DUTY AS A JUTSUSHA, A BARRIER MASTER, TO MAINTAIN YOUR EMOTIONAL BALANCE AND PERFECT YOUR JUTSU.
...
GRUMBLE
I DIDN'T ASK TO BE THE SUCCESSOR ...

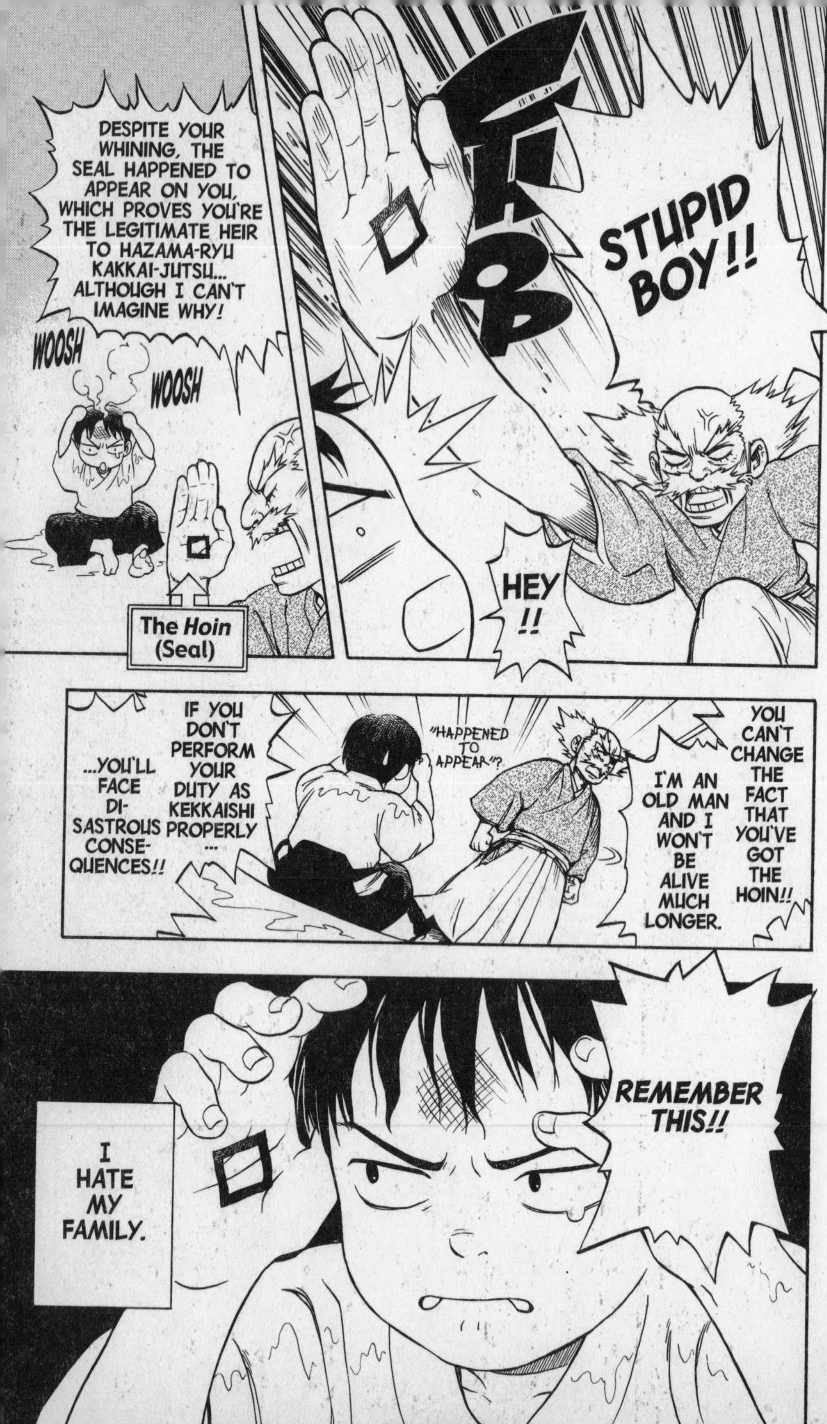
STUPID BOY!!
HEY!!
DESPITE YOUR WHINING, THE SEAL HAPPENED TO APPEAR ON YOU, WHICH PROVES YOU'RE THE LEGITIMATE HEIR TO HAZAMA-RYU KAKKAI-JUTSU... ALTHOUGH I CAN'T IMAGINE WHY!
WOOSH
WOOSH
The Hoin (Seal)
YOU CAN'T CHANGE THE FACT THAT YOU'VE GOT THE HOIN!!
I'M AN OLD MAN AND I WON'T BE ALIVE MUCH LONGER.
"HAPPENED TO APPEAR"?
IF YOU DON'T PERFORM YOUR DUTY AS KEKKAISHI PROPERLY...
...YOU'LL FACE DI-SASTROUS CONSE-QUENCES!!
REMEMBER THIS!!
I HATE MY FAMILY.

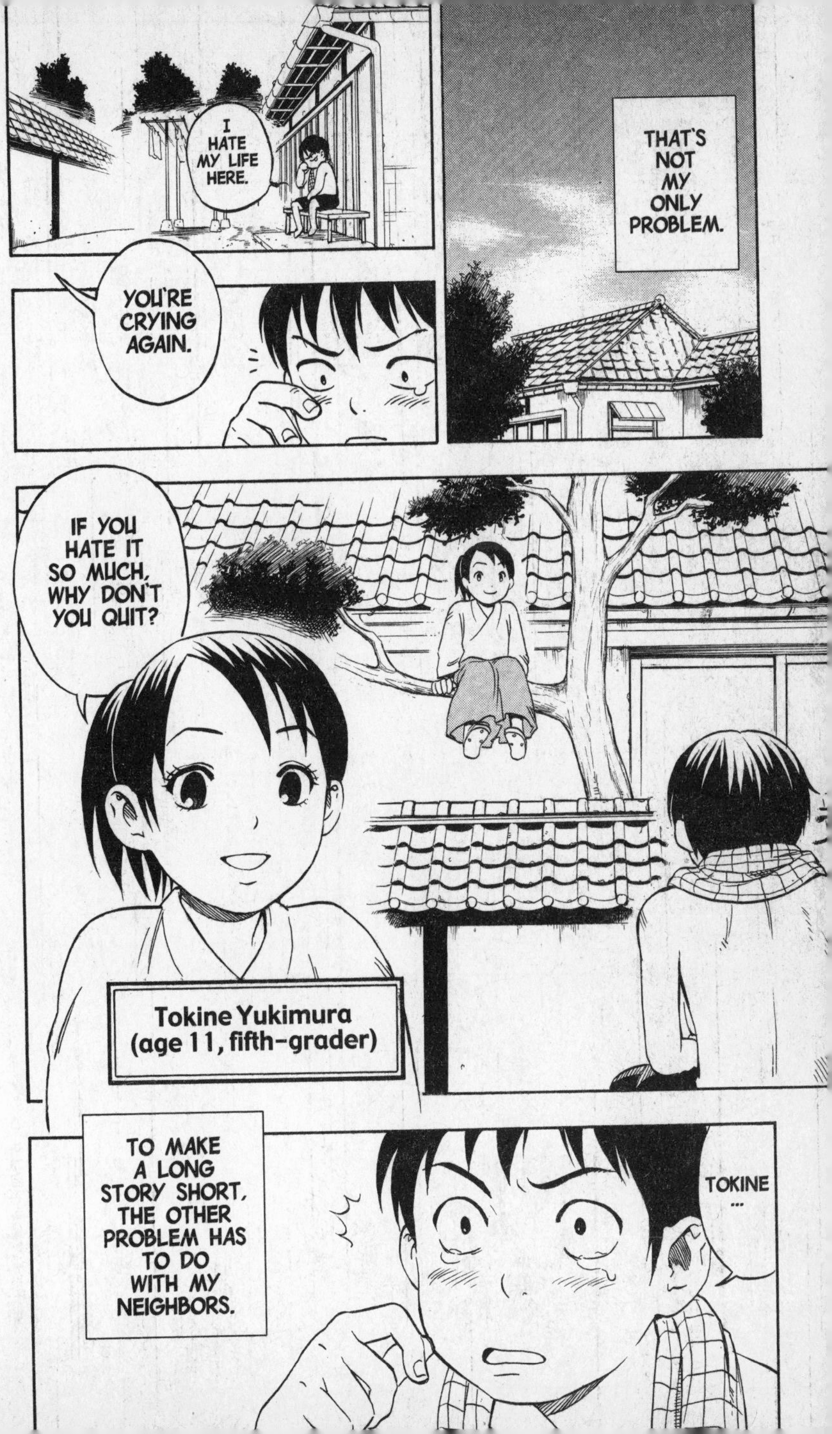
THAT'S NOT MY ONLY PROBLEM.
I HATE MY LIFE HERE.
YOU'RE CRYING AGAIN.
IF YOU HATE IT SO MUCH, WHY DON'T YOU QUIT?
Tokine Yukimura (age 11, fifth-grader)
TOKINE ...
TO MAKE A LONG STORY SHORT, THE OTHER PROBLEM HAS TO DO WITH MY NEIGHBORS.

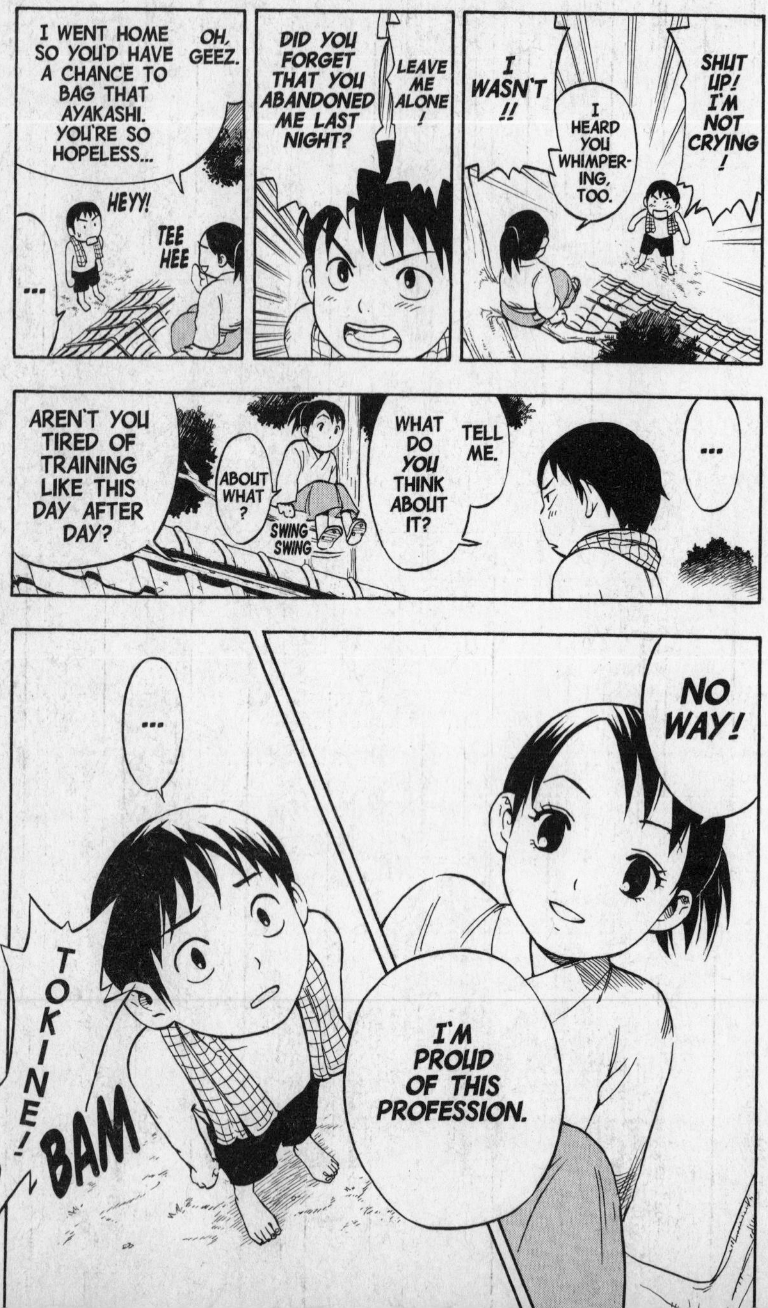
OH, GEEZ.
I WENT HOME SO YOU'D HAVE A CHANCE TO BAG THAT AYAKASHI. YOU'RE SO HOPELESS...
HEYY!
TEE HEE
...
DID YOU FORGET THAT YOU ABANDONED ME LAST NIGHT?
LEAVE ME ALONE!
I WASN'T!!
I HEARD YOU WHIMPERING, TOO.
SHUT UP! I'M NOT CRYING!
AREN'T YOU TIRED OF TRAINING LIKE THIS DAY AFTER DAY?
ABOUT WHAT?
SWING SWING
TELL ME.
WHAT DO YOU THINK ABOUT IT?
...
...
NO WAY!
I'M PROUD OF THIS PROFESSION.
TOKINE!
BAM

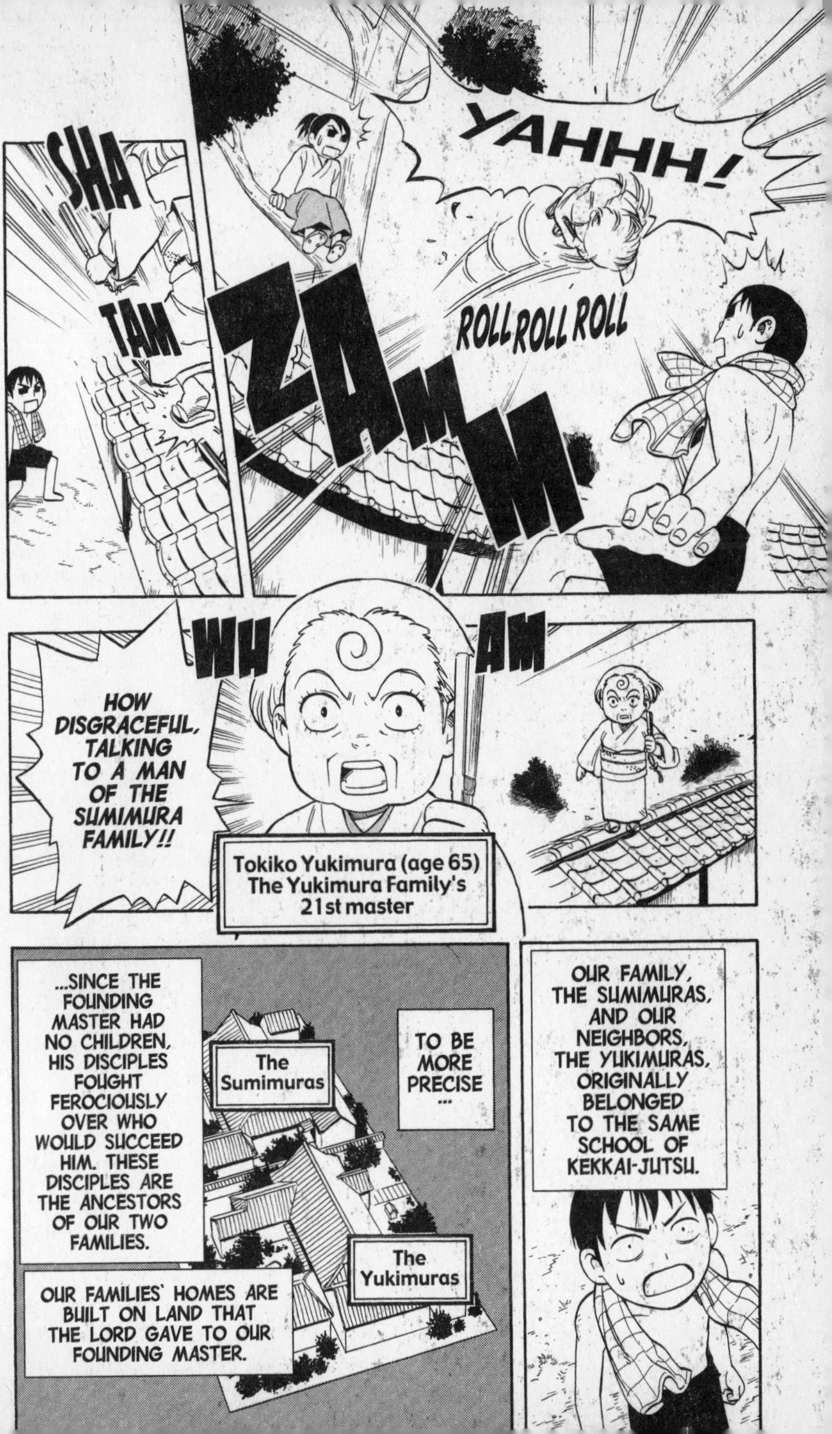

YAHHH!
ROLL ROLL ROLL
ZAMM
SHA
TAM
WHAM
HOW DISGRACEFUL, TALKING TO A MAN OF THE SUMIMURA FAMILY!!
Tokiko Yukimura (age 65)
The Yukimura Family's
21st master
OUR FAMILY, THE SUMIMURAS, AND OUR NEIGHBORS, THE YUKIMURAS, ORIGINALLY BELONGED TO THE SAME SCHOOL OF KEKKAI-JUTSU.
TO BE MORE PRECISE ...
...SINCE THE FOUNDING MASTER HAD NO CHILDREN, HIS DISCIPLES FOUGHT FEROCIOUSLY OVER WHO WOULD SUCCEED HIM. THESE DISCIPLES ARE THE ANCESTORS OF OUR TWO FAMILIES.
The Sumimuras
The Yukimuras
OUR FAMILIES' HOMES ARE BUILT ON LAND THAT THE LORD GAVE TO OUR FOUNDING MASTER.

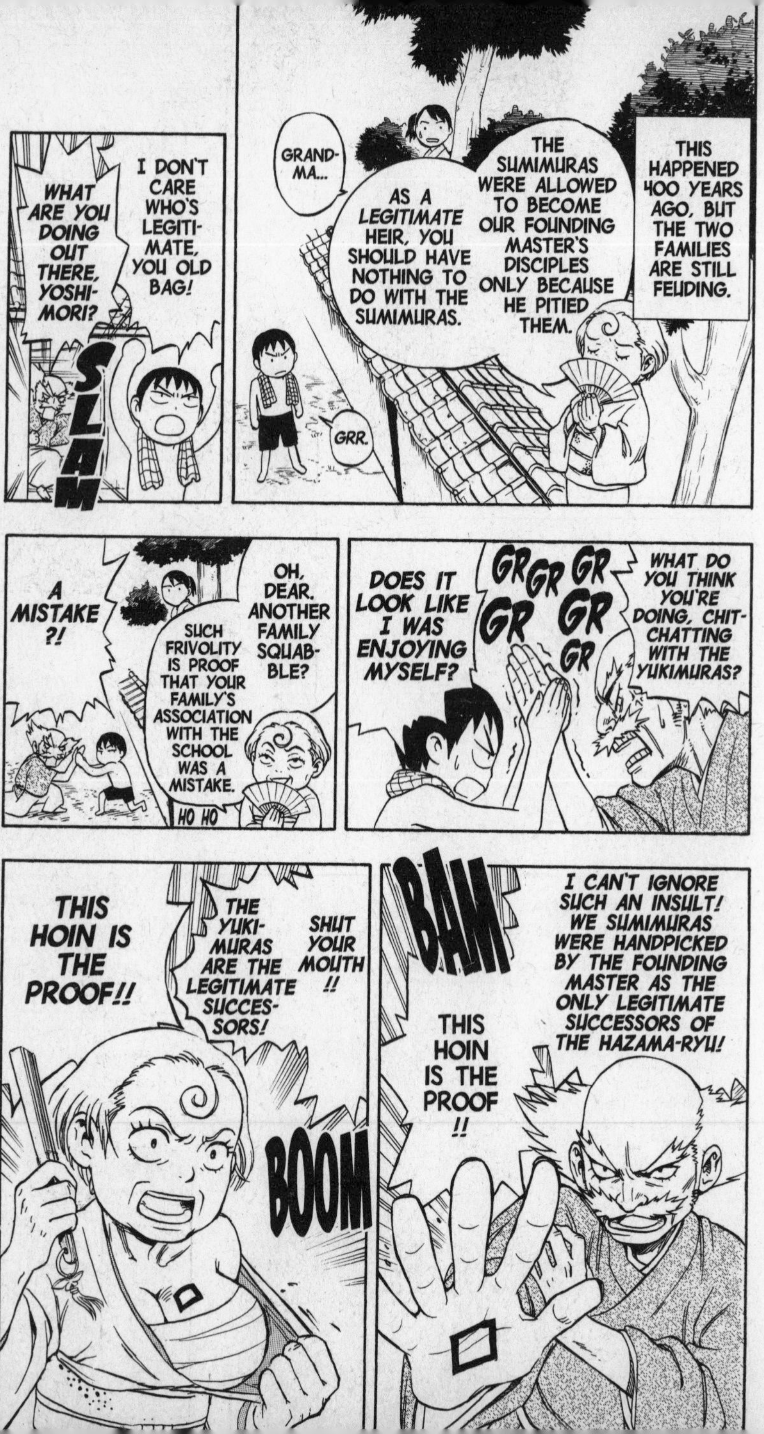
THIS HAPPENED 400 YEARS AGO, BUT THE TWO FAMILIES ARE STILL FEUDING.
THE SUMIMURAS WERE ALLOWED TO BECOME OUR FOUNDING MASTER'S DISCIPLES ONLY BECAUSE HE PITIED THEM.
AS A LEGITIMATE HEIR, YOU SHOULD HAVE NOTHING TO DO WITH THE SUMIMURAS.
GRAND-MA...
GRR.
I DON'T CARE WHO'S LEGITI-MATE, YOU OLD BAG!
WHAT ARE YOU DOING OUT THERE, YOSHI-MORI?
SLAM
WHAT DO YOU THINK YOU'RE DOING, CHIT-CHATTING WITH THE YUKIMURAS?
GR GR GR GR GR GR
DOES IT LOOK LIKE I WAS ENJOYING MYSELF?
OH, DEAR. ANOTHER FAMILY SQUAB-BLE?
SUCH FRIVOLITY IS PROOF THAT YOUR FAMILY'S ASSOCIATION WITH THE SCHOOL WAS A MISTAKE.
HO HO
A MISTAKE ?!
I CAN'T IGNORE SUCH AN INSULT! WE SUMIMURAS WERE HANDPICKED BY THE FOUNDING MASTER AS THE ONLY LEGITIMATE SUCCESSORS OF THE HAZAMA-RYU!
BAM
THIS HOIN IS THE PROOF !!
SHUT YOUR MOUTH !!
THE YUKI-MURAS ARE THE LEGITIMATE SUCCES-SORS!
THIS HOIN IS THE PROOF!!
BOOM

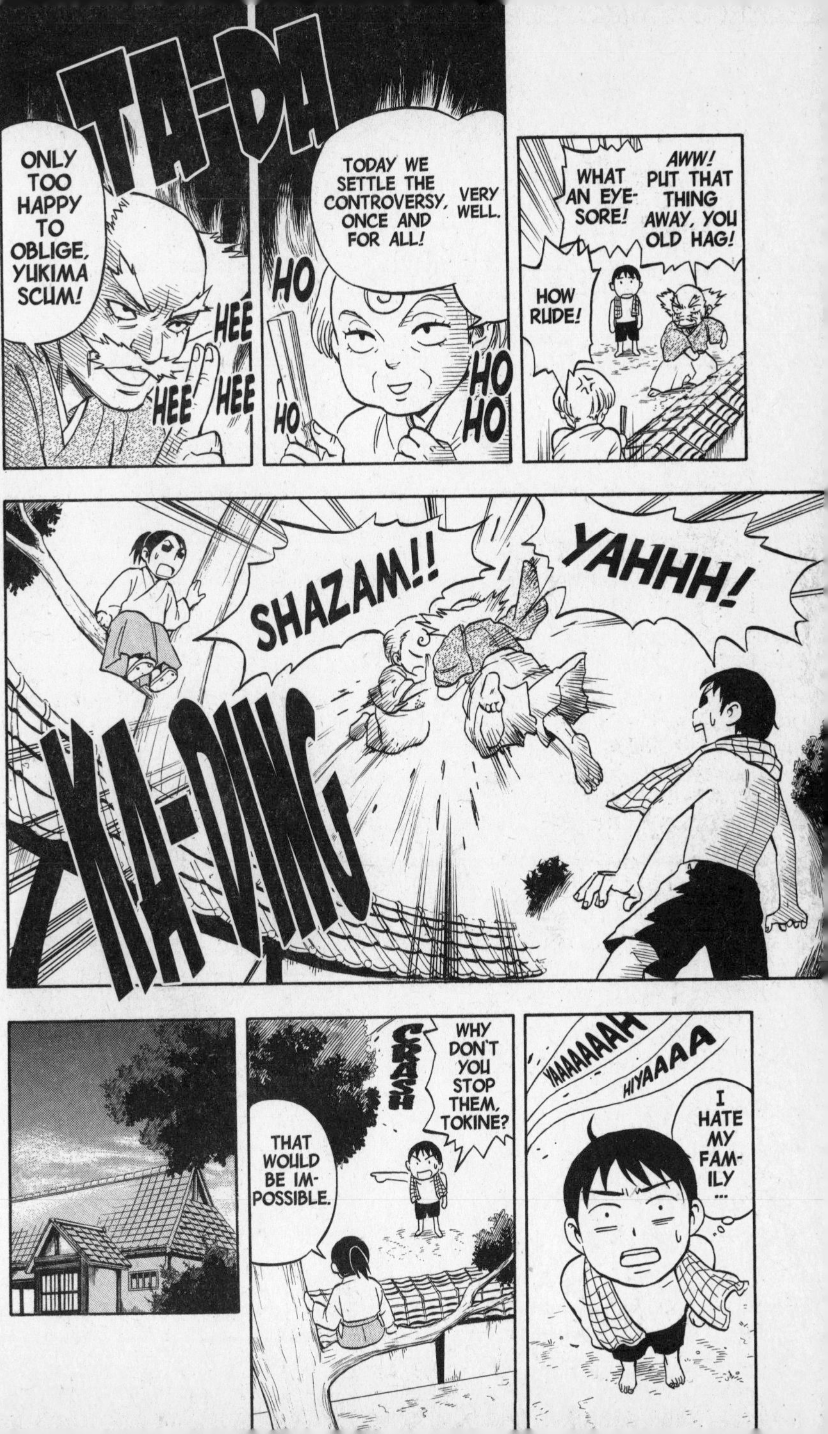
AWW! PUT THAT THING AWAY, YOU OLD HAG!
WHAT AN EYE-SORE!
HOW RUDE!
VERY WELL.
TODAY WE SETTLE THE CONTROVERSY, ONCE AND FOR ALL!
HO HO
HO HO
TA-DA
ONLY TOO HAPPY TO OBLIGE, YUKIMA SCUM!
HEE HEE
HEE HEE
YAHHH!
SHAZAM!!
KA-DING
YAAAAAAAH
HIYAAAA
I HATE MY FAM-ILY...
WHY DON'T YOU STOP THEM, TOKINE?
CRASH
THAT WOULD BE IM-POSSIBLE.

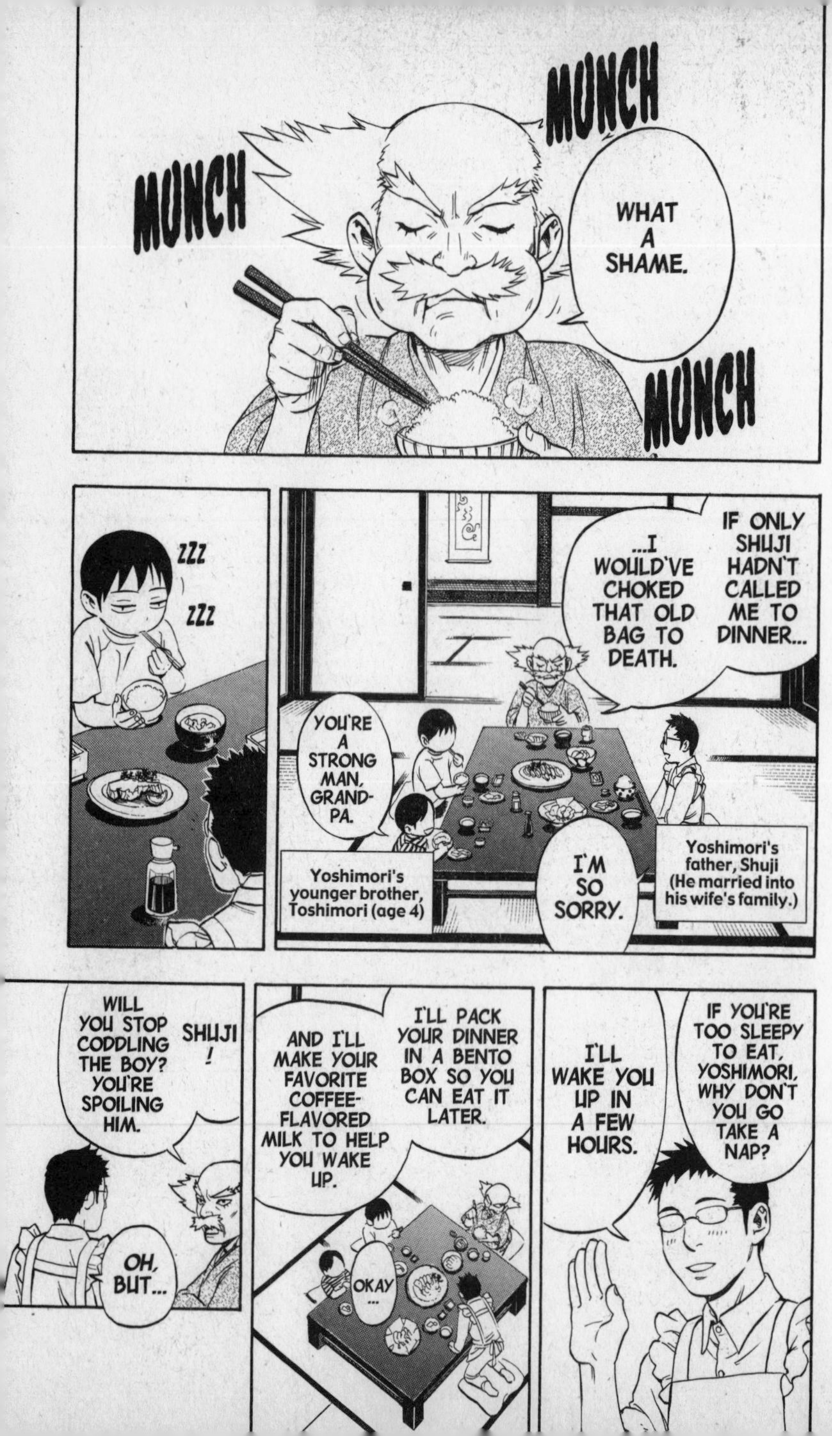
MUNCH
WHAT A SHAME.
MUNCH
MUNCH
IF ONLY SHUJI HADN'T CALLED ME TO DINNER...
...I WOULD'VE CHOKED THAT OLD BAG TO DEATH.
YOU'RE A STRONG MAN, GRANDPA.
Yoshimori's father, Shuji (He married into his wife's family.)
I'M SO SORRY.
Yoshimori's younger brother, Toshimori (age 4)
ZZZ
ZZZ
IF YOU'RE TOO SLEEPY TO EAT, YOSHIMORI, WHY DON'T YOU GO TAKE A NAP?
I'LL WAKE YOU UP IN A FEW HOURS.
I'LL PACK YOUR DINNER IN A BENTO BOX SO YOU CAN EAT IT LATER.
AND I'LL MAKE YOUR FAVORITE COFFEE-FLAVORED MILK TO HELP YOU WAKE UP.
OKAY...
SHUJI!
WILL YOU STOP CODDLING THE BOY? YOU'RE SPOILING HIM.
OH, BUT...

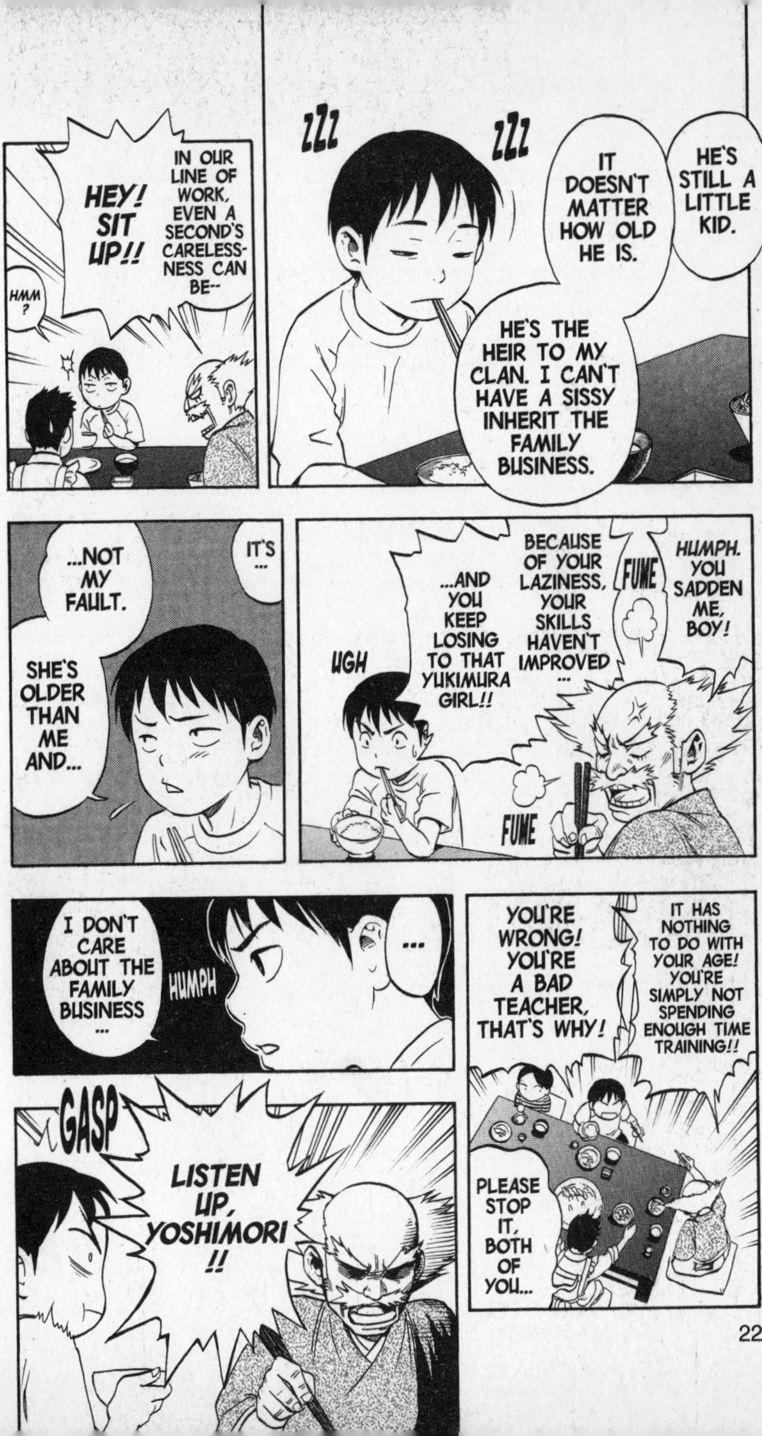
HE'S STILL A LITTLE KID.
IT DOESN'T MATTER HOW OLD HE IS.
ZZZ
ZZZ
HE'S THE HEIR TO MY CLAN. I CAN'T HAVE A SISSY INHERIT THE FAMILY BUSINESS.
IN OUR LINE OF WORK, EVEN A SECOND'S CARELESSNESS CAN BE--
HEY! SIT UP!!
HMM?
HUMPH. YOU SADDEN ME, BOY!
FUME
BECAUSE OF YOUR LAZINESS, YOUR SKILLS HAVEN'T IMPROVED...
...AND YOU KEEP LOSING TO THAT YUKIMURA GIRL!!
UGH
FUME
IT'S...
...NOT MY FAULT.
SHE'S OLDER THAN ME AND...
IT HAS NOTHING TO DO WITH YOUR AGE! YOU'RE SIMPLY NOT SPENDING ENOUGH TIME TRAINING!!
YOU'RE WRONG! YOU'RE A BAD TEACHER, THAT'S WHY!
PLEASE STOP IT, BOTH OF YOU...
...
HUMPH
I DON'T CARE ABOUT THE FAMILY BUSINESS...
GASP
LISTEN UP, YOSHIMORI!!

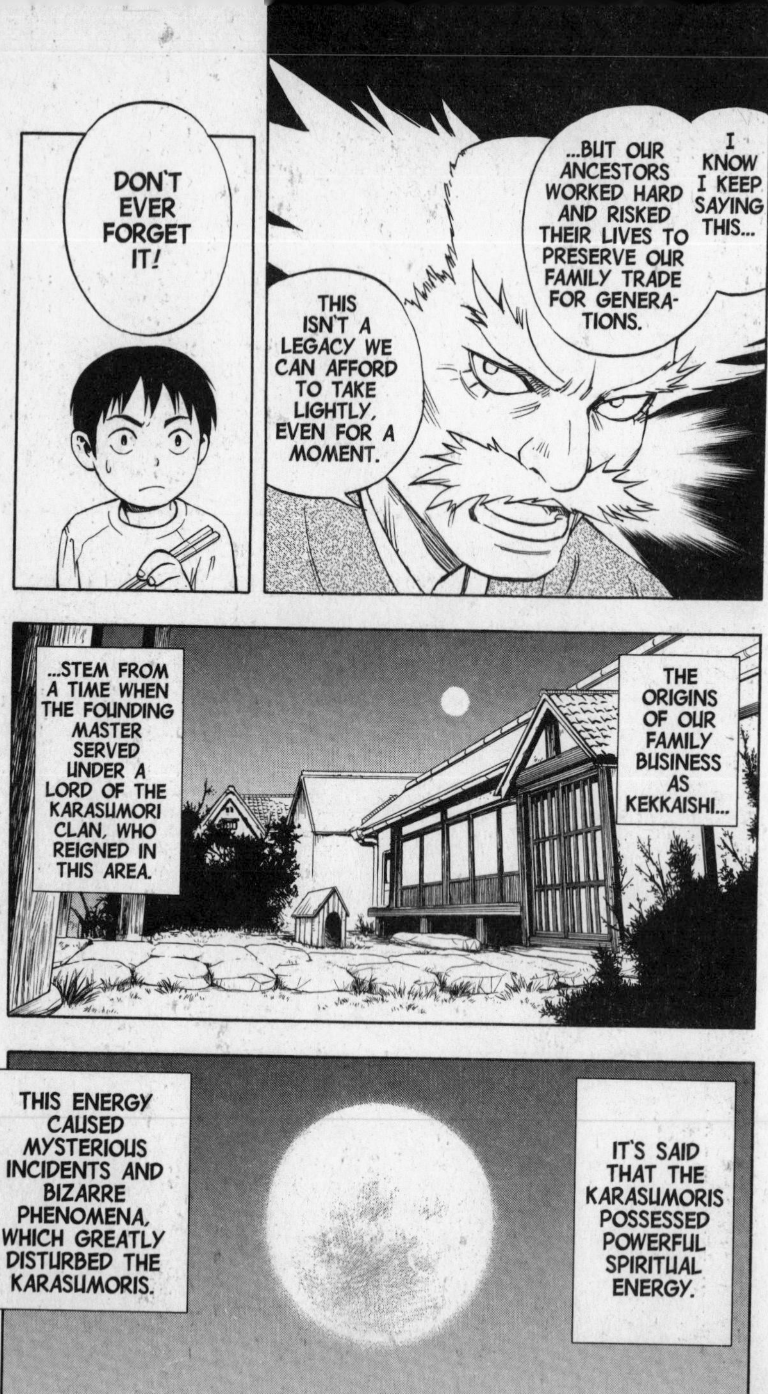
I KNOW I KEEP SAYING THIS...
...BUT OUR ANCESTORS WORKED HARD AND RISKED THEIR LIVES TO PRESERVE OUR FAMILY TRADE FOR GENERA-TIONS.
THIS ISN'T A LEGACY WE CAN AFFORD TO TAKE LIGHTLY, EVEN FOR A MOMENT.
DON'T EVER FORGET IT!
THE ORIGINS OF OUR FAMILY BUSINESS AS KEKKAISHI...
...STEM FROM A TIME WHEN THE FOUNDING MASTER SERVED UNDER A LORD OF THE KARASUMORI CLAN, WHO REIGNED IN THIS AREA.
IT'S SAID THAT THE KARASUMORIS POSSESSED POWERFUL SPIRITUAL ENERGY.
THIS ENERGY CAUSED MYSTERIOUS INCIDENTS AND BIZARRE PHENOMENA, WHICH GREATLY DISTURBED THE KARASUMORIS.

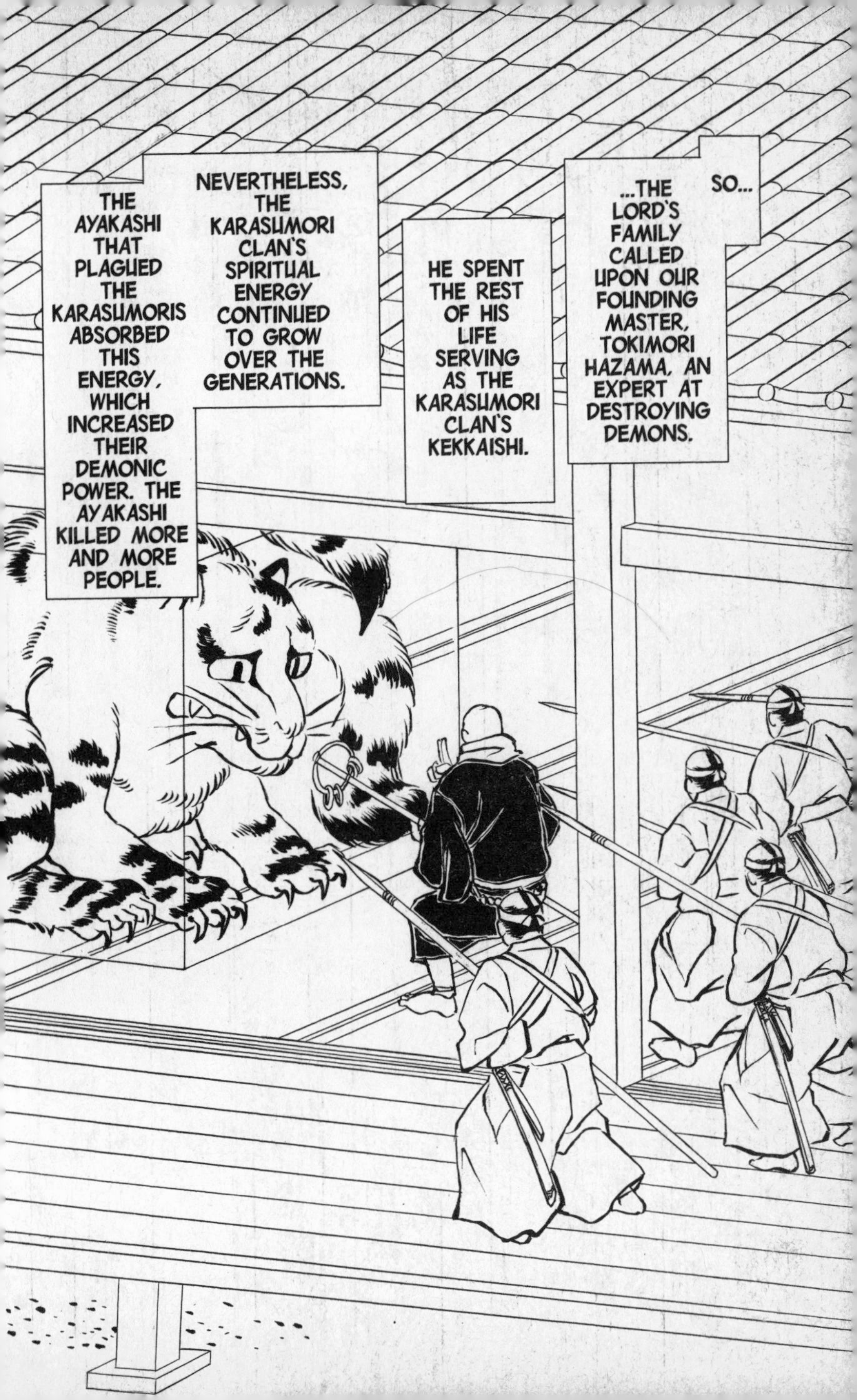
SO...
...THE LORD'S FAMILY CALLED UPON OUR FOUNDING MASTER, TOKIMORI HAZAMA, AN EXPERT AT DESTROYING DEMONS.
HE SPENT THE REST OF HIS LIFE SERVING AS THE KARASUMORI CLAN'S KEKKAISHI.
NEVERTHELESS, THE KARASUMORI CLAN'S SPIRITUAL ENERGY CONTINUED TO GROW OVER THE GENERATIONS.
THE AYAKASHI THAT PLAGUED THE KARASUMORIS ABSORBED THIS ENERGY, WHICH INCREASED THEIR DEMONIC POWER. THE AYAKASHI KILLED MORE AND MORE PEOPLE.

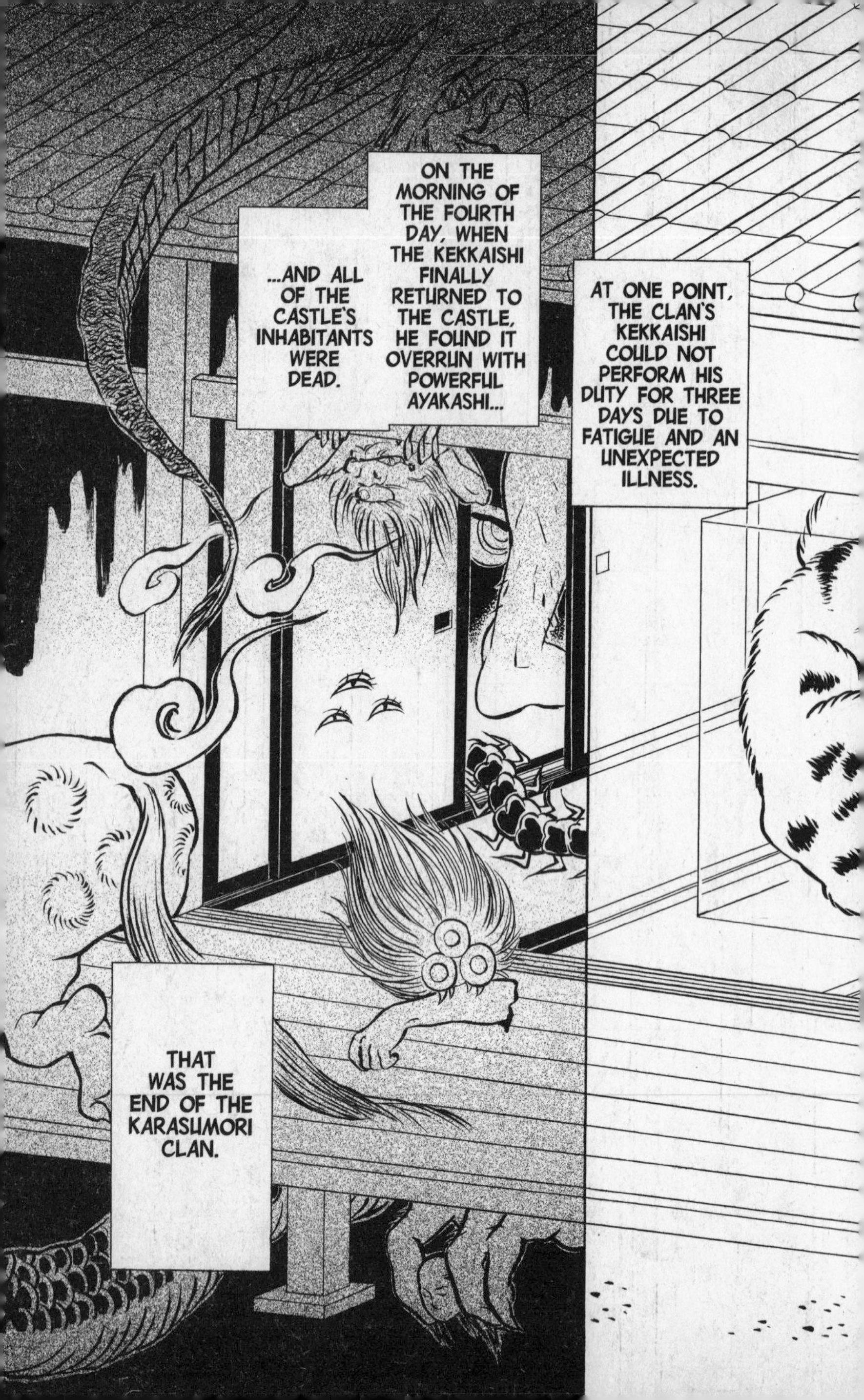
AT ONE POINT, THE CLAN'S KEKKAISHI COULD NOT PERFORM HIS DUTY FOR THREE DAYS DUE TO FATIGUE AND AN UNEXPECTED ILLNESS.
ON THE MORNING OF THE FOURTH DAY, WHEN THE KEKKAISHI FINALLY RETURNED TO THE CASTLE, HE FOUND IT OVERRUN WITH POWERFUL AYAKASHI...
...AND ALL OF THE CASTLE'S INHABITANTS WERE DEAD.
THAT WAS THE END OF THE KARASUMORI CLAN.

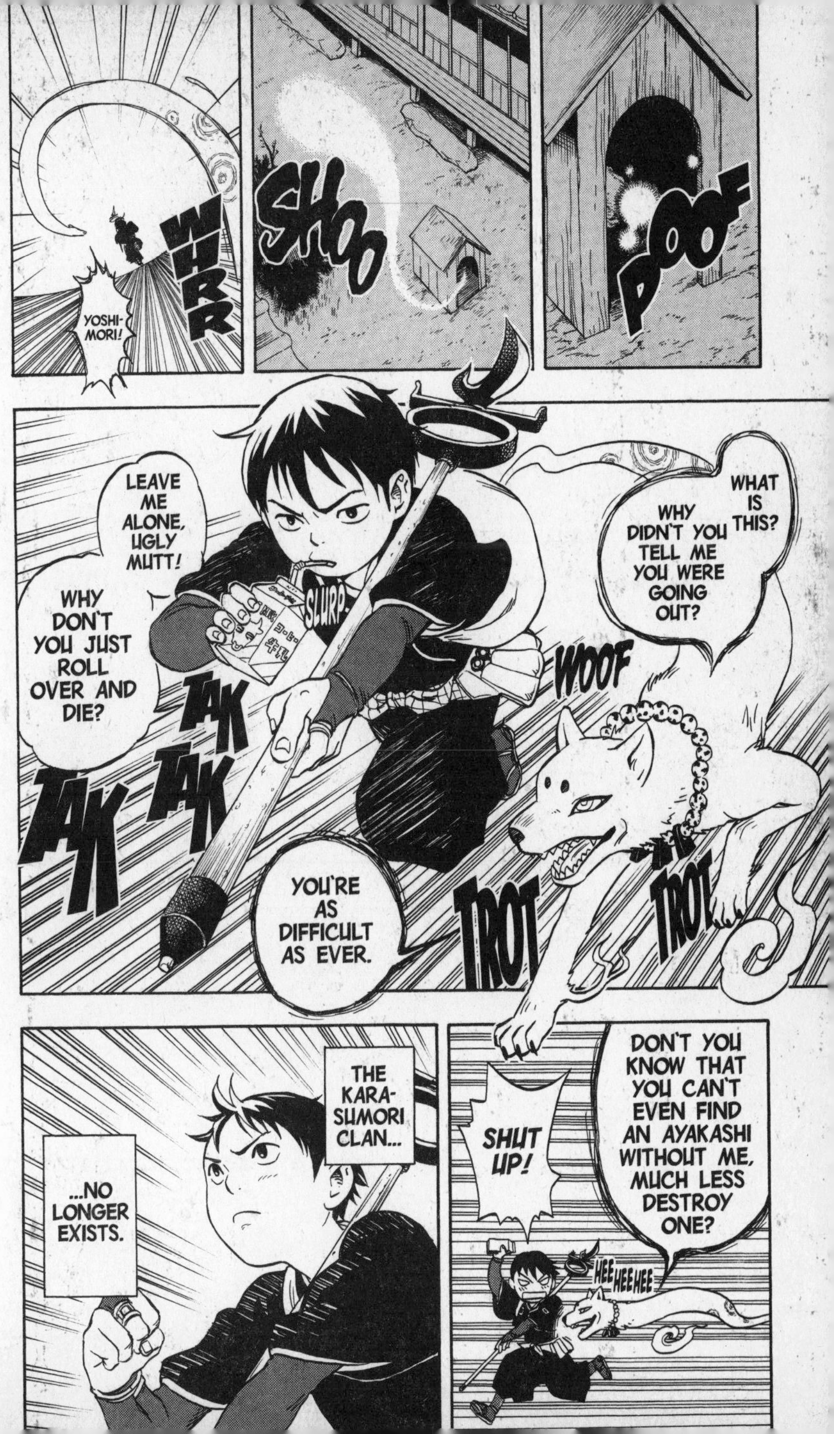
POOF
SHOO
WHRR
YOSHI-MORI!
WHAT IS THIS?
WHY DIDN'T YOU TELL ME YOU WERE GOING OUT?
WOOF
LEAVE ME ALONE, UGLY MUTT!
WHY DON'T YOU JUST ROLL OVER AND DIE?
SLURP
TROT TROT
YOU'RE AS DIFFICULT AS EVER.
TAK TAK TAK
DON'T YOU KNOW THAT YOU CAN'T EVEN FIND AN AYAKASHI WITHOUT ME, MUCH LESS DESTROY ONE?
SHUT UP!
HEE HEE HEE
THE KARA-SUMORI CLAN...
...NO LONGER EXISTS.

THEIR SPIRITUAL POWER, HOWEVER, IS STILL ALIVE AND KICKING.
A day later
+Karasumori Power
IF YOU LEAVE THE SMALL AYAKASHI ALONE, THEY WILL EVOLVE INTO SOMETHING VERY DANGEROUS.
THEREFORE, ACCORDING TO GRANDPA, MY FAMILY RECEIVES PAYMENT FROM A SHADOWY RESIDENTS' ASSOCIATION...
...AND CONTINUES TO PLY THE FAMILY TRADE EVERY SINGLE DAY.
A SMALL SHRINE DEDICATED TO THE SOULS OF THE KARASUMORI CLAN--THE SOURCE OF THEIR SPIRITUAL ENERGY--IS LOCATED...
ALLEY-OOP.
...DEEP UNDERGROUND...
...BENEATH MY SCHOOL...
...WHERE THE CASTLE ONCE STOOD.
Private School
Karasumori Academy of Junior and Senior High Schools
Entrance to High School Building
Entrance to Junior High School Building This Way
UH.
TOKINE!
DID YOU NOTICE ANYTHING OUT OF THE ORDINARY?
TK
TK
TK

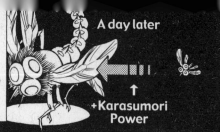

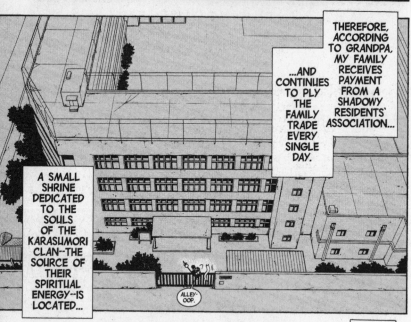

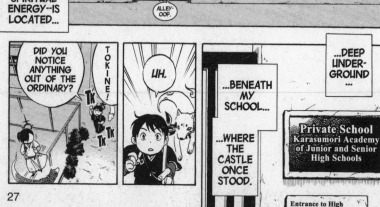

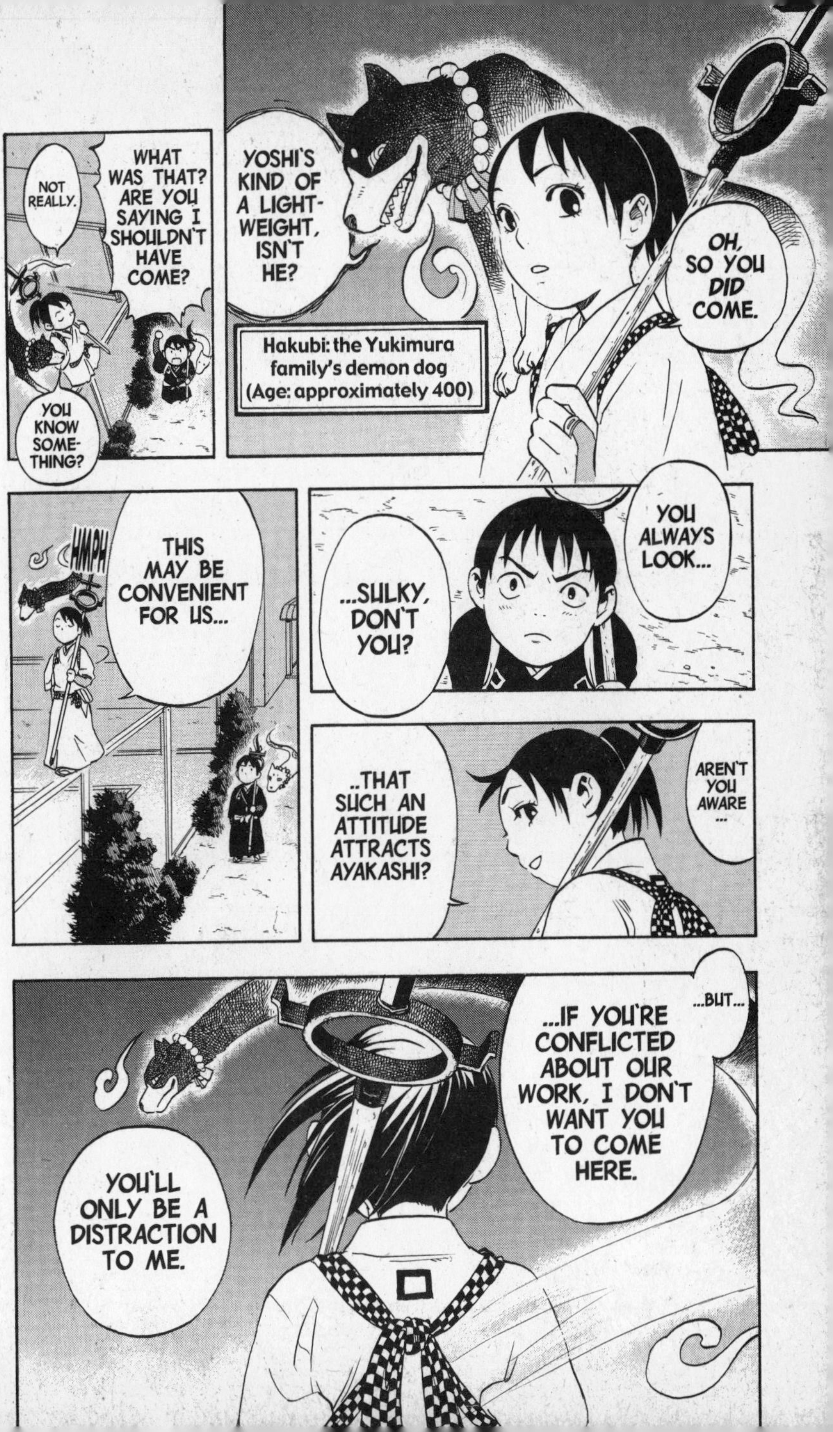
OH, SO YOU DID COME.
YOSHI'S KIND OF A LIGHT-WEIGHT, ISN'T HE?
Hakubi: the Yukimura family's demon dog (Age: approximately 400)
WHAT WAS THAT? ARE YOU SAYING I SHOULDN'T HAVE COME?
NOT REALLY.
YOU KNOW SOME-THING?
YOU ALWAYS LOOK...
...SULKY, DON'T YOU?
AREN'T YOU AWARE...
..THAT SUCH AN ATTITUDE ATTRACTS AYAKASHI?
HMPH
THIS MAY BE CONVENIENT FOR US...
...BUT...
...IF YOU'RE CONFLICTED ABOUT OUR WORK, I DON'T WANT YOU TO COME HERE.
YOU'LL ONLY BE A DISTRACTION TO ME.

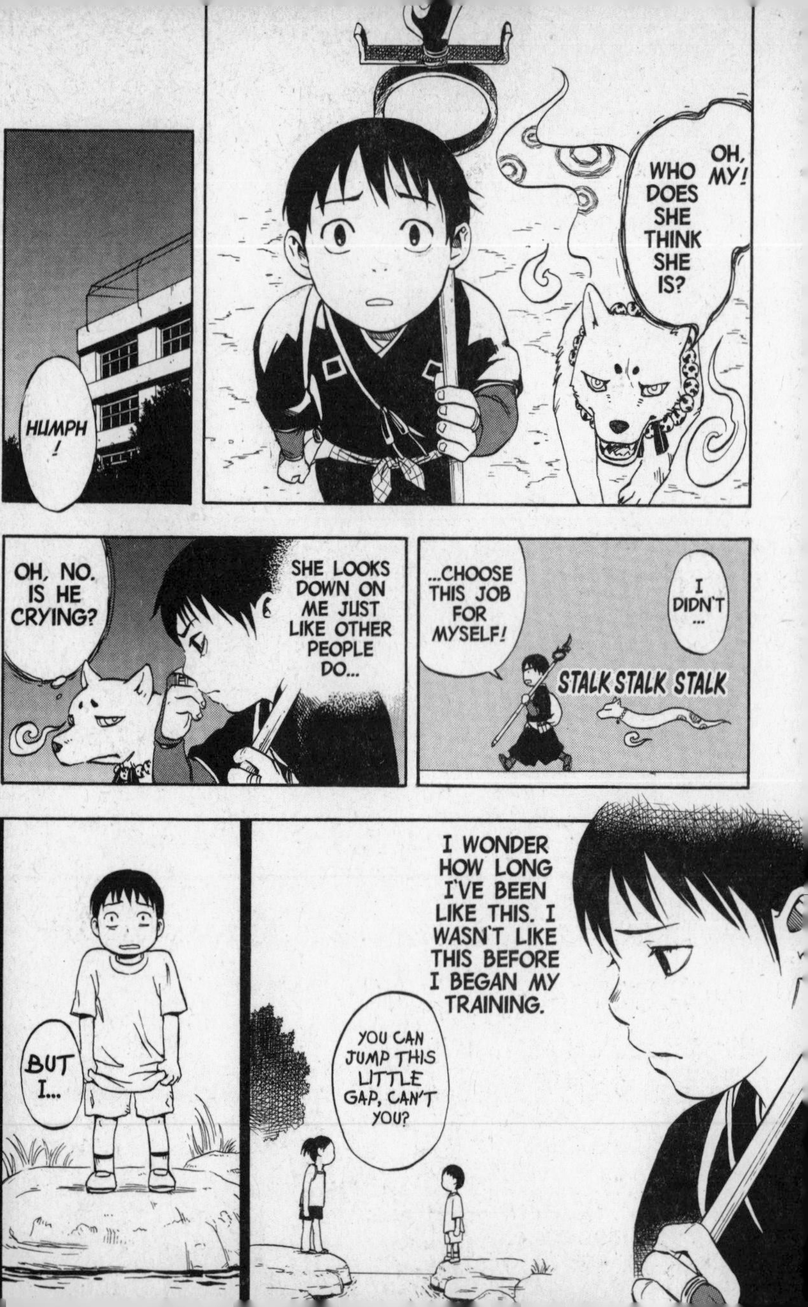
OH, MY! WHO DOES SHE THINK SHE IS?
HUMPH!
I DIDN'T ...
...CHOOSE THIS JOB FOR MYSELF!
STALK STALK STALK
SHE LOOKS DOWN ON ME JUST LIKE OTHER PEOPLE DO...
OH, NO. IS HE CRYING?
I WONDER HOW LONG I'VE BEEN LIKE THIS. I WASN'T LIKE THIS BEFORE I BEGAN MY TRAINING.
YOU CAN JUMP THIS LITTLE GAP, CAN'T YOU?
BUT I...

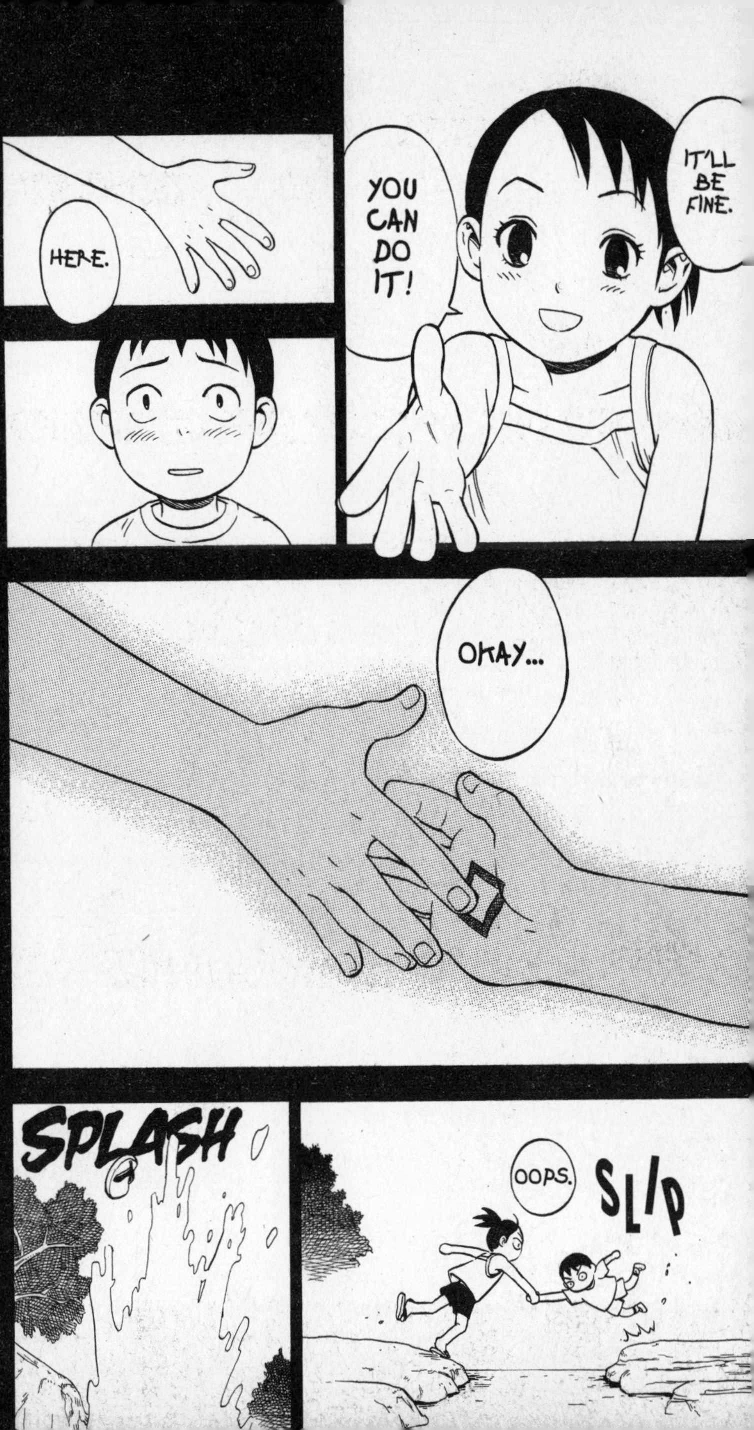
IT'LL BE FINE.
YOU CAN DO IT!
HERE.
OKAY...
OOPS.
SLIP
SPLASH

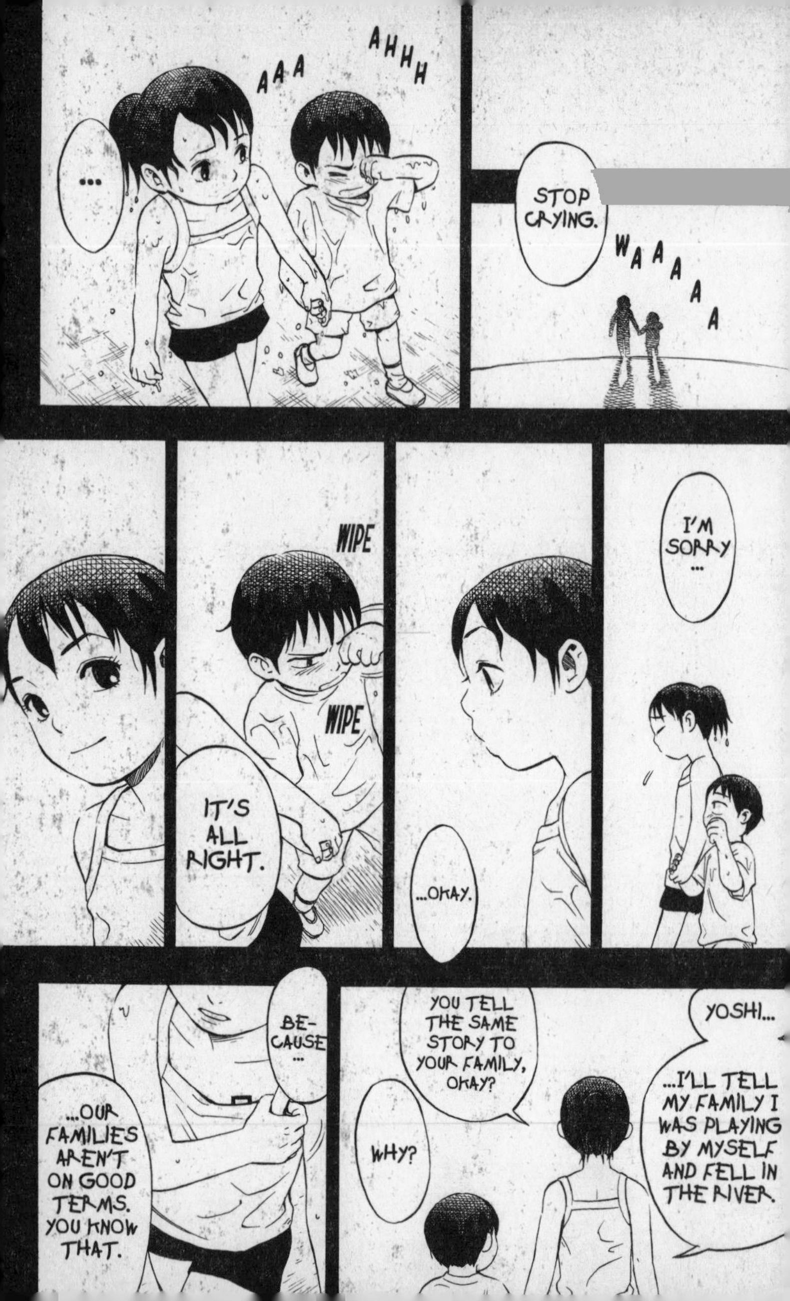
STOP CRYING.
WAAAAA
AHHHH
AAA
...
I'M SORRY ...
...OKAY.
WIPE
WIPE
IT'S ALL RIGHT.
YOSHI...
...I'LL TELL MY FAMILY I WAS PLAYING BY MYSELF AND FELL IN THE RIVER.
YOU TELL THE SAME STORY TO YOUR FAMILY, OKAY?
WHY?
BE-CAUSE ...
...OUR FAMILIES AREN'T ON GOOD TERMS. YOU KNOW THAT.

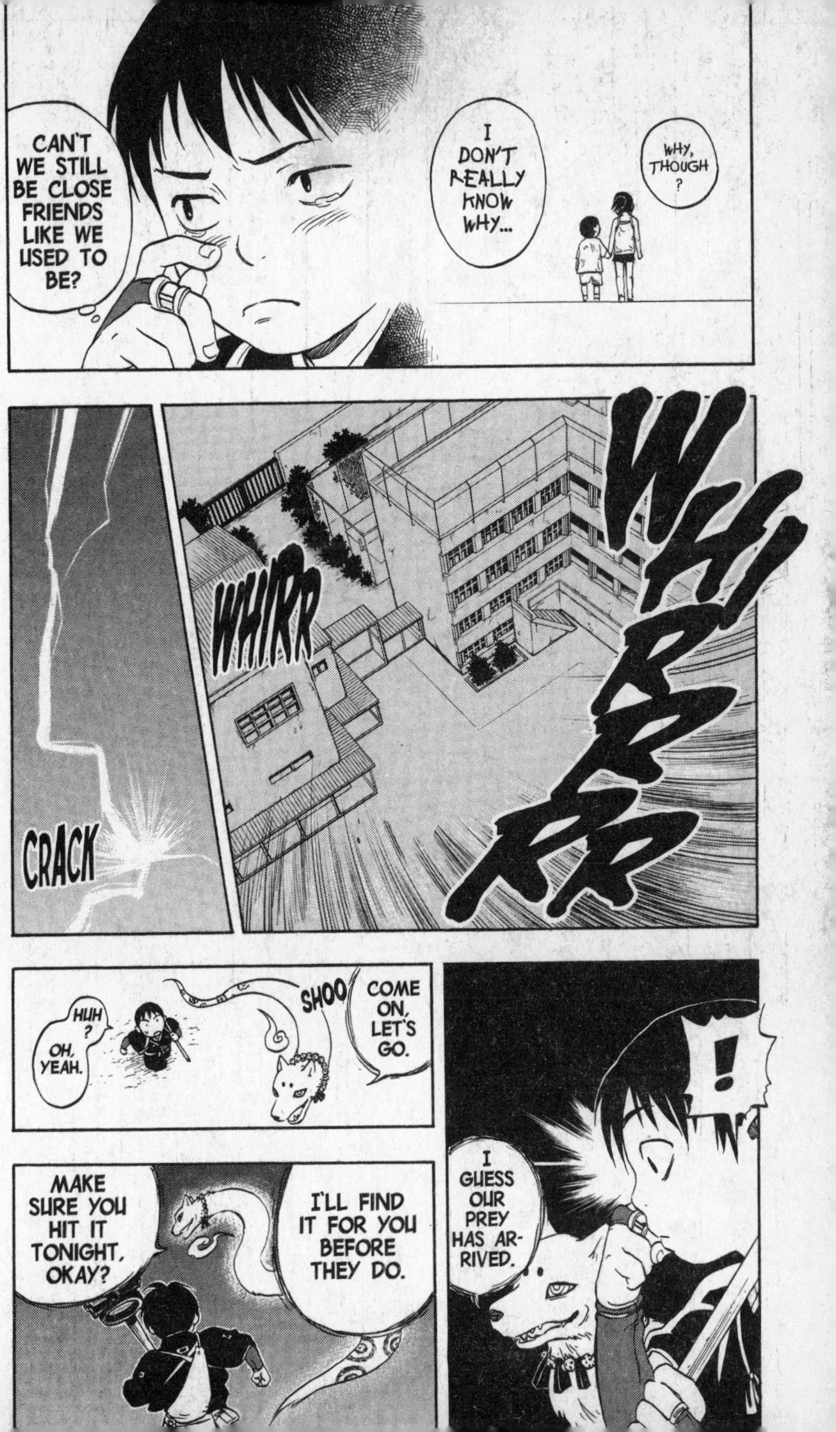
WHY, THOUGH?
I DON'T REALLY KNOW WHY...
CAN'T WE STILL BE CLOSE FRIENDS LIKE WE USED TO BE?
WHIRRRR
WHIRR
CRACK
!
I GUESS OUR PREY HAS AR-RIVED.
COME ON, LET'S GO.
SHOO
HUH? OH, YEAH.
I'LL FIND IT FOR YOU BEFORE THEY DO.
MAKE SURE YOU HIT IT TONIGHT, OKAY?

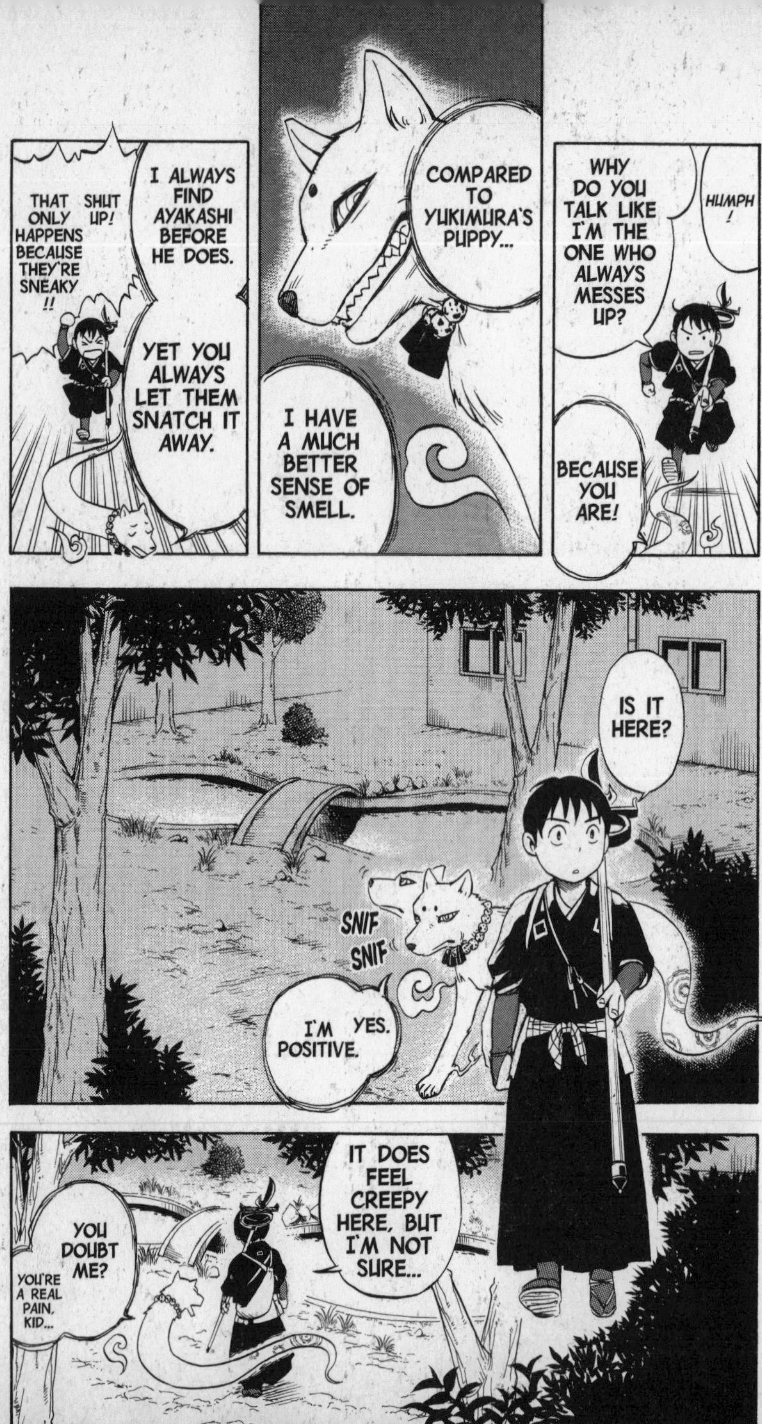
HUMPH!
WHY DO YOU TALK LIKE I'M THE ONE WHO ALWAYS MESSES UP?
BECAUSE YOU ARE!
COMPARED TO YUKIMURA'S PUPPY...
I HAVE A MUCH BETTER SENSE OF SMELL.
I ALWAYS FIND AYAKASHI BEFORE HE DOES.
YET YOU ALWAYS LET THEM SNATCH IT AWAY.
SHUT UP!
THAT ONLY HAPPENS BECAUSE THEY'RE SNEAKY!!
IS IT HERE?
SNIF
SNIF
YES.
I'M POSITIVE.
IT DOES FEEL CREEPY HERE, BUT I'M NOT SURE...
YOU DOUBT ME?
YOU'RE A REAL PAIN, KID...

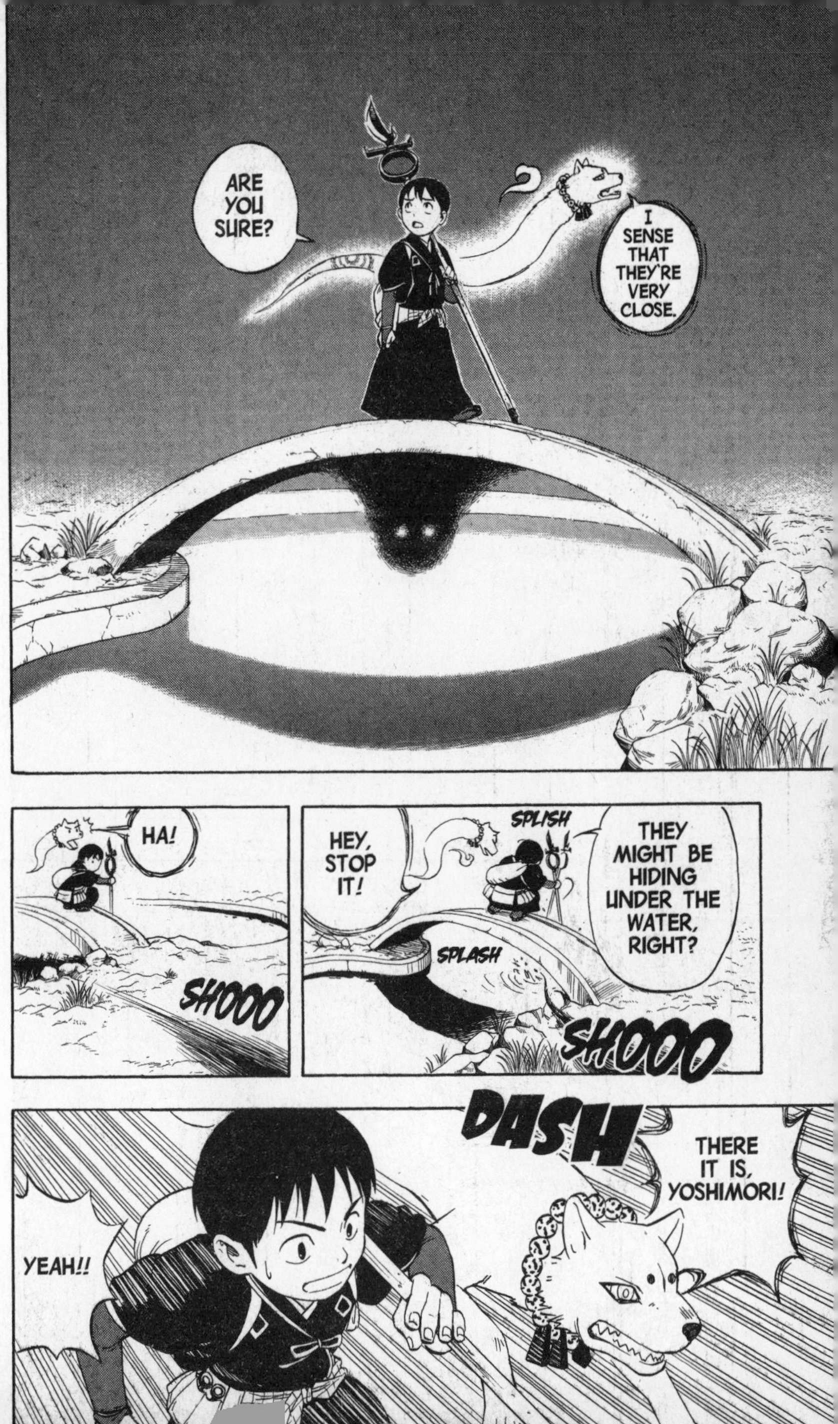
I SENSE THAT THEY'RE VERY CLOSE.
ARE YOU SURE?
SPLISH
THEY MIGHT BE HIDING UNDER THE WATER, RIGHT?
HEY, STOP IT!
SPLASH
SHOOO
HA!
SHOOO
DASH
THERE IT IS, YOSHIMORI!
YEAH!!

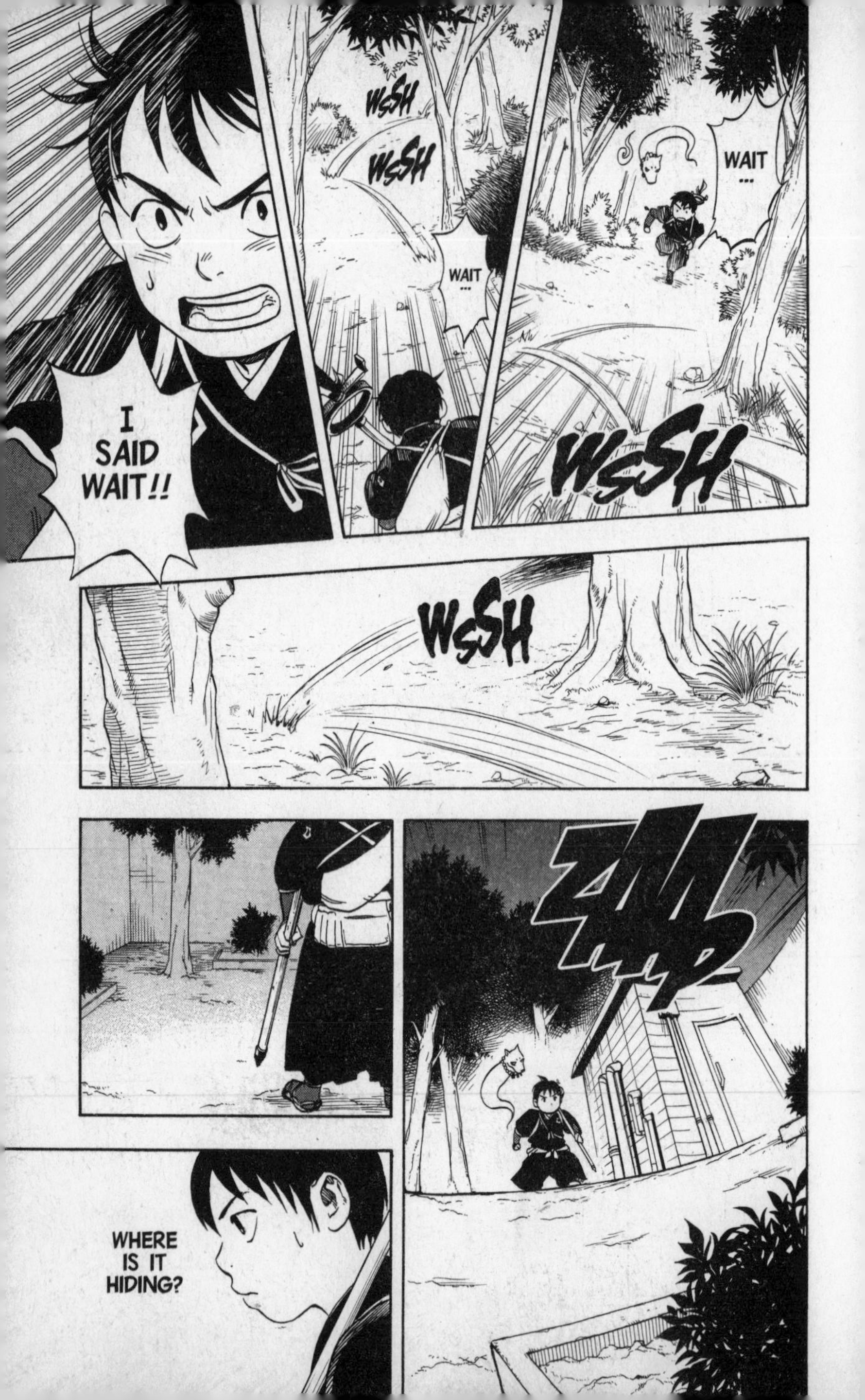
WAIT ...
WSSH
WSSH
WSSH
WAIT ...
I SAID WAIT!!
WSSH
WHERE IS IT HIDING?

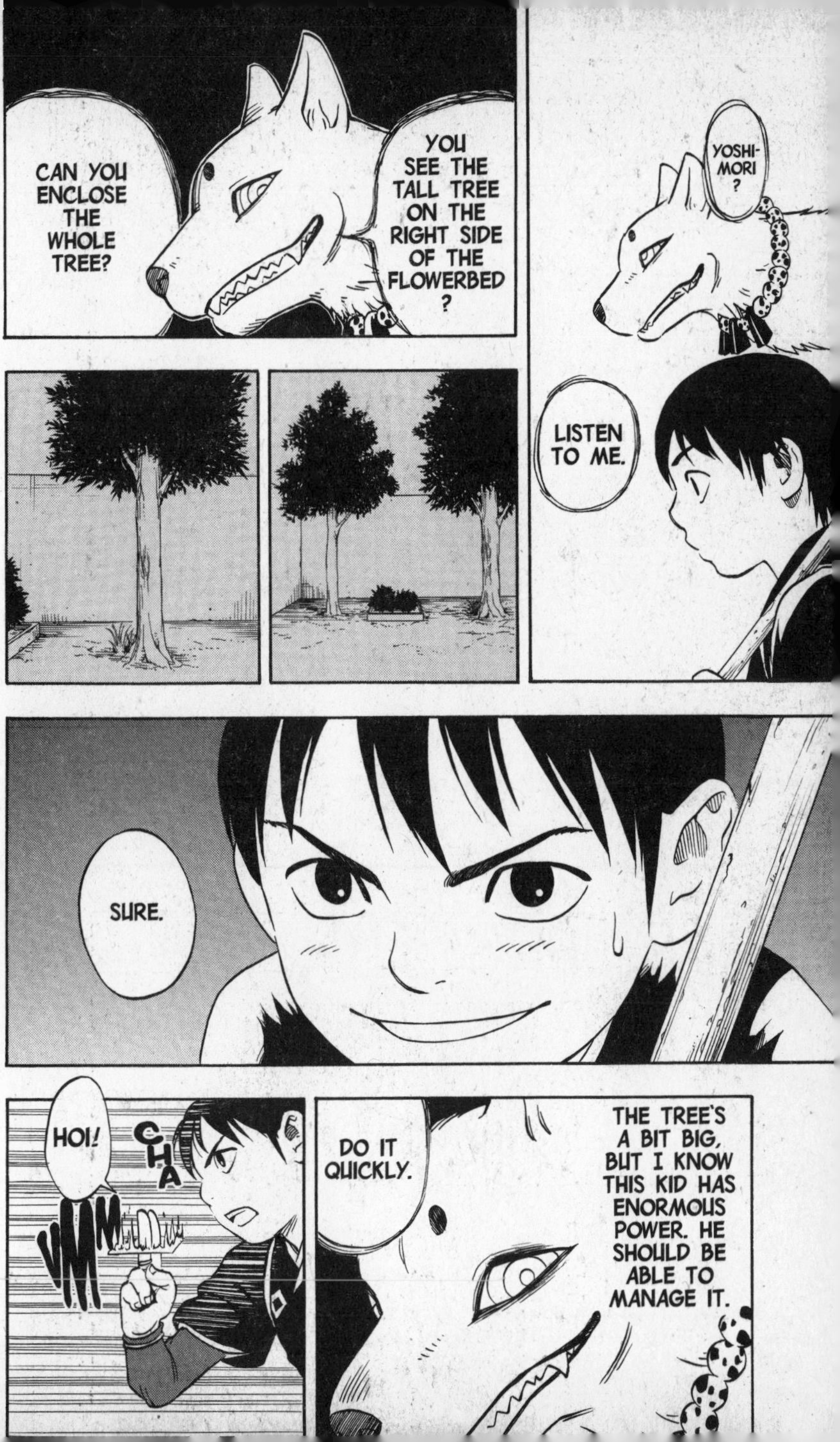
YOSHI-MORI?
LISTEN TO ME.
YOU SEE THE TALL TREE ON THE RIGHT SIDE OF THE FLOWERBED?
CAN YOU ENCLOSE THE WHOLE TREE?
SURE.
THE TREE'S A BIT BIG, BUT I KNOW THIS KID HAS ENORMOUS POWER. HE SHOULD BE ABLE TO MANAGE IT.
DO IT QUICKLY.
HOI!
CHA
VMM

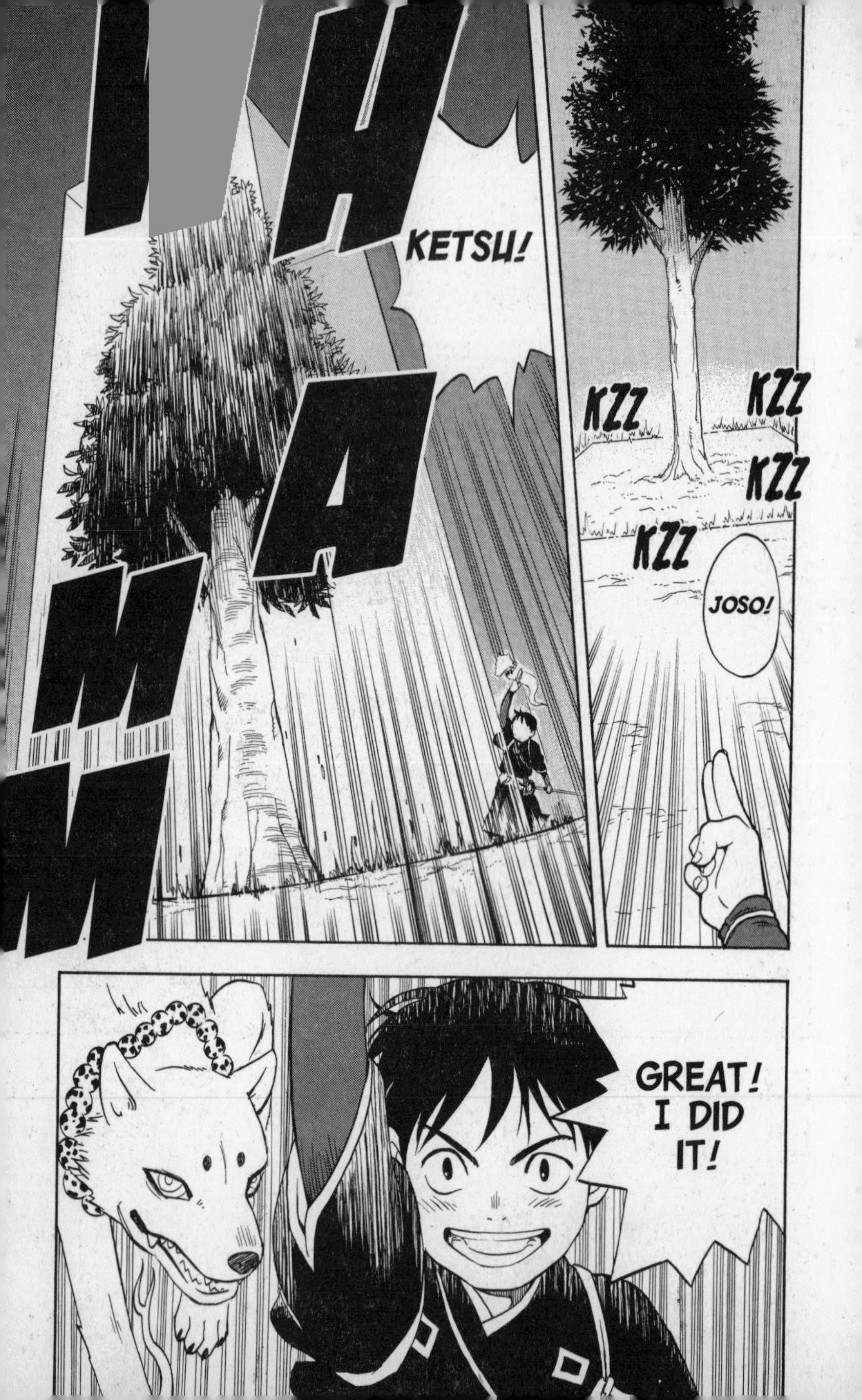
KZZ
KZZ
KZZ
KZZ
JOSO!
KETSU!
GREAT! I DID IT!

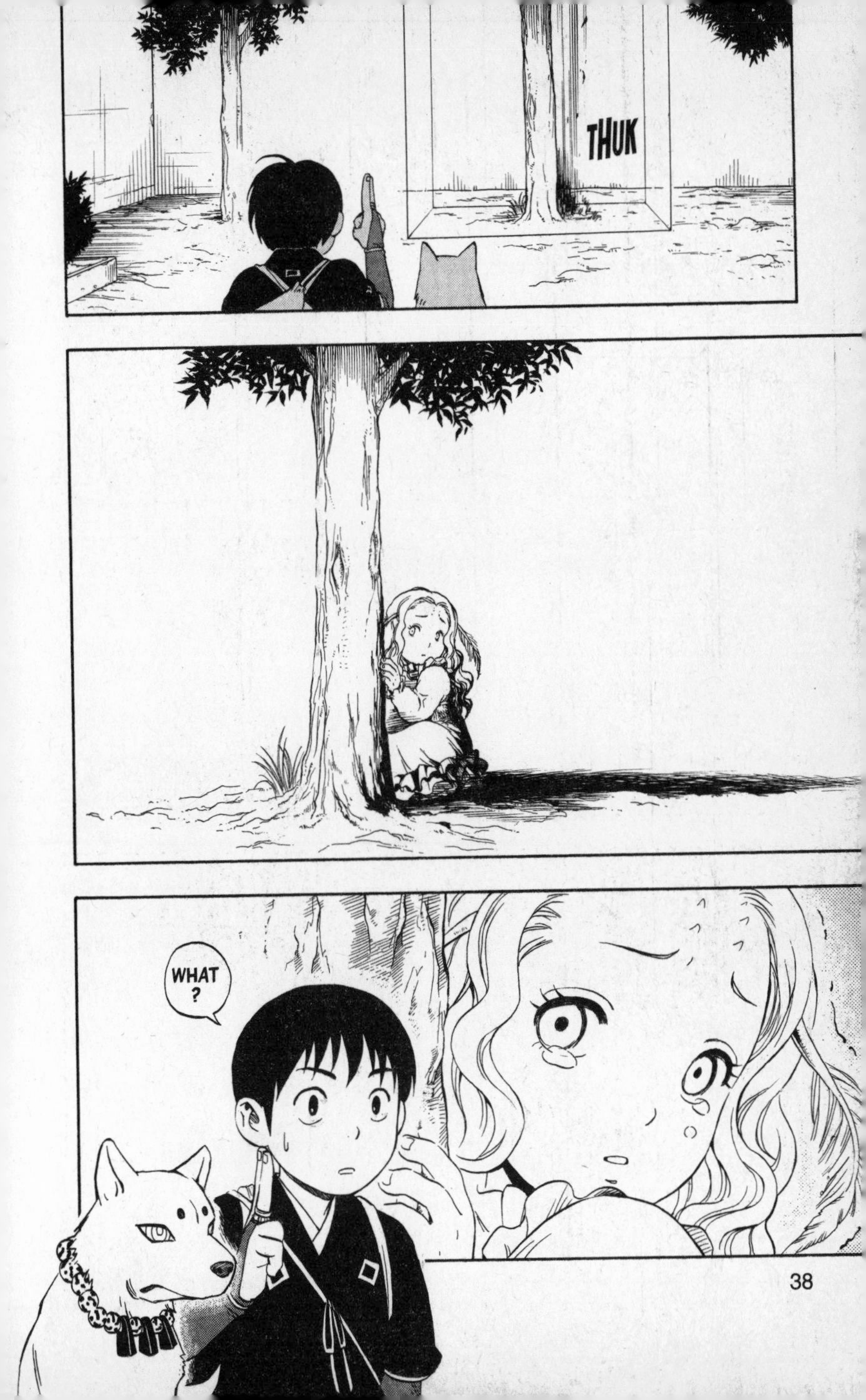
THUK
WHAT ?

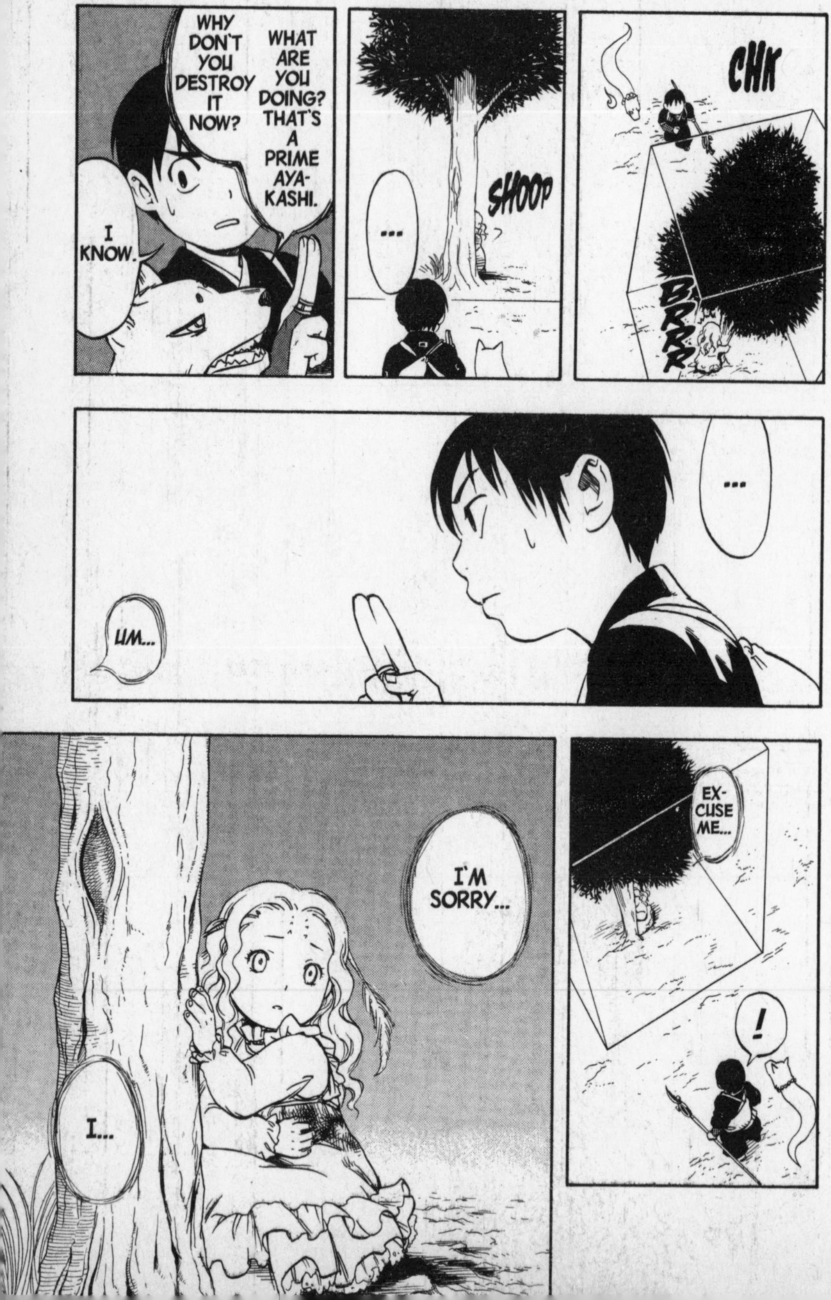
CHK
BRRR
SHOOP
...
WHAT ARE YOU DOING? THAT'S A PRIME AYA-KASHI.
WHY DON'T YOU DESTROY IT NOW?
I KNOW.
...
UM...
EX-CUSE ME...
!
I'M SORRY...
I...

BUT ...

...I'M LEAVING RIGHT AWAY.

I WAS TOLD...

...MY WOUND WOULD HEAL FASTER IF I CAME HERE.

...BUT THIS IS MY JOB.

SO PLEASE ...

I'M SORRY...

...I UNDER-STAND...

OOH ...

HEY!

I'M SORRY TO CAUSE YOU TROUBLE.

40

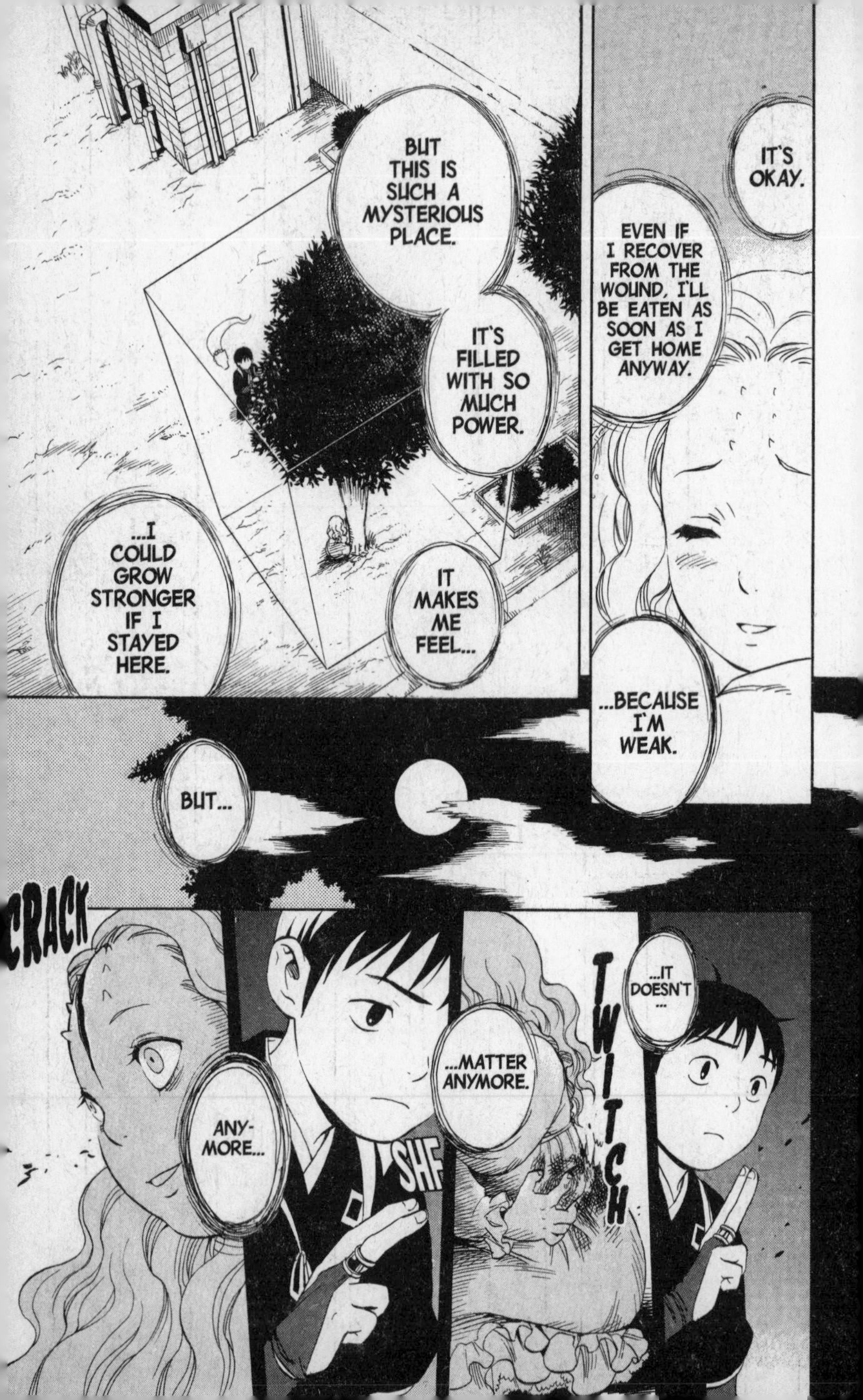
IT'S OKAY.
EVEN IF I RECOVER FROM THE WOUND, I'LL BE EATEN AS SOON AS I GET HOME ANYWAY.
...BECAUSE I'M WEAK.
BUT THIS IS SUCH A MYSTERIOUS PLACE.
IT'S FILLED WITH SO MUCH POWER.
IT MAKES ME FEEL...
...I COULD GROW STRONGER IF I STAYED HERE.
BUT...
...IT DOESN'T ...
TWITCH
...MATTER ANYMORE.
SHF
ANY-MORE...
CRACK

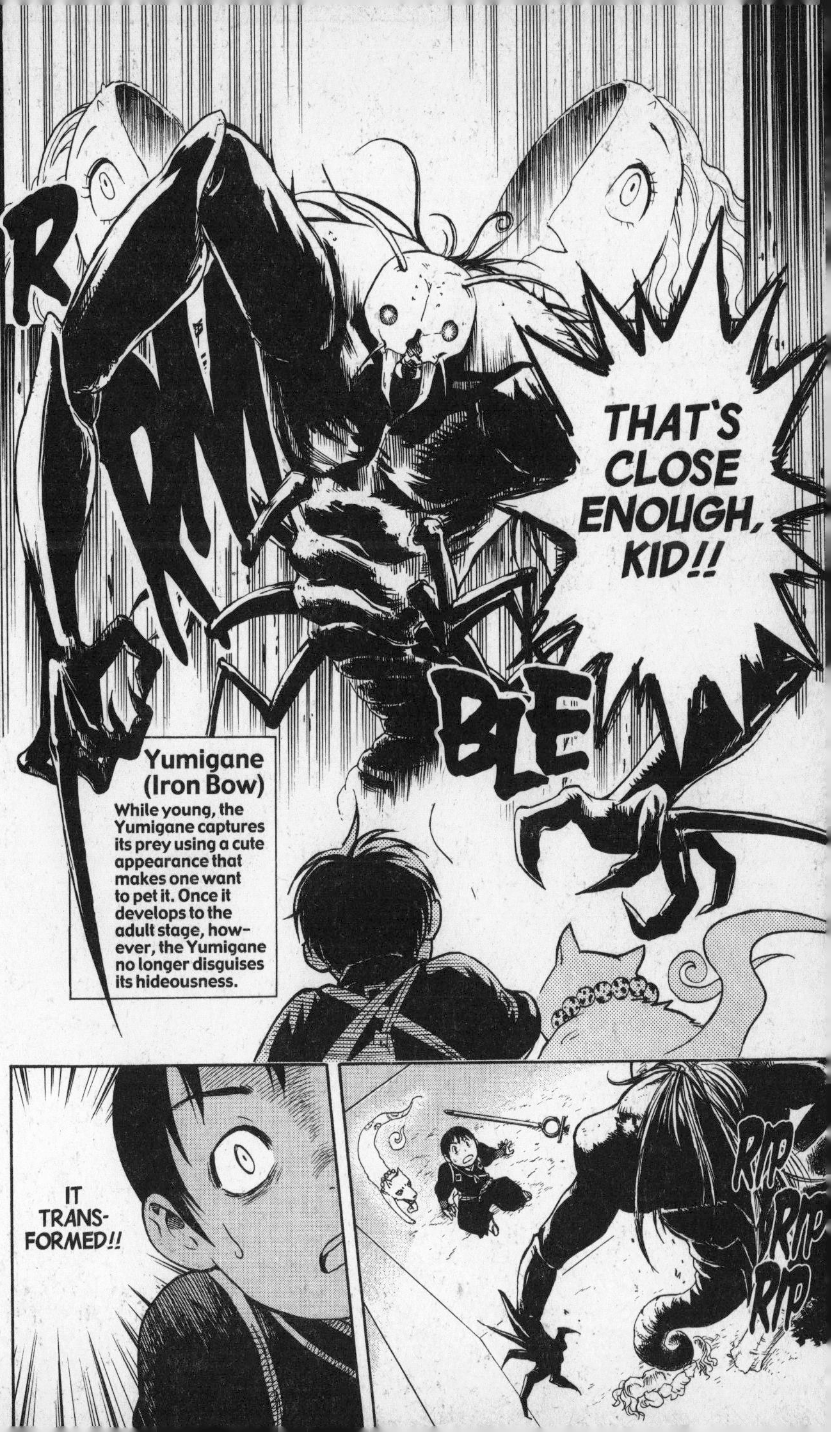
R
RUM
BLE
THAT'S CLOSE ENOUGH, KID!!
Yumigane (Iron Bow)
While young, the Yumigane captures its prey using a cute appearance that makes one want to pet it. Once it develops to the adult stage, however, the Yumigane no longer disguises its hideousness.
RIP RIP RIP
IT TRANS-FORMED!!

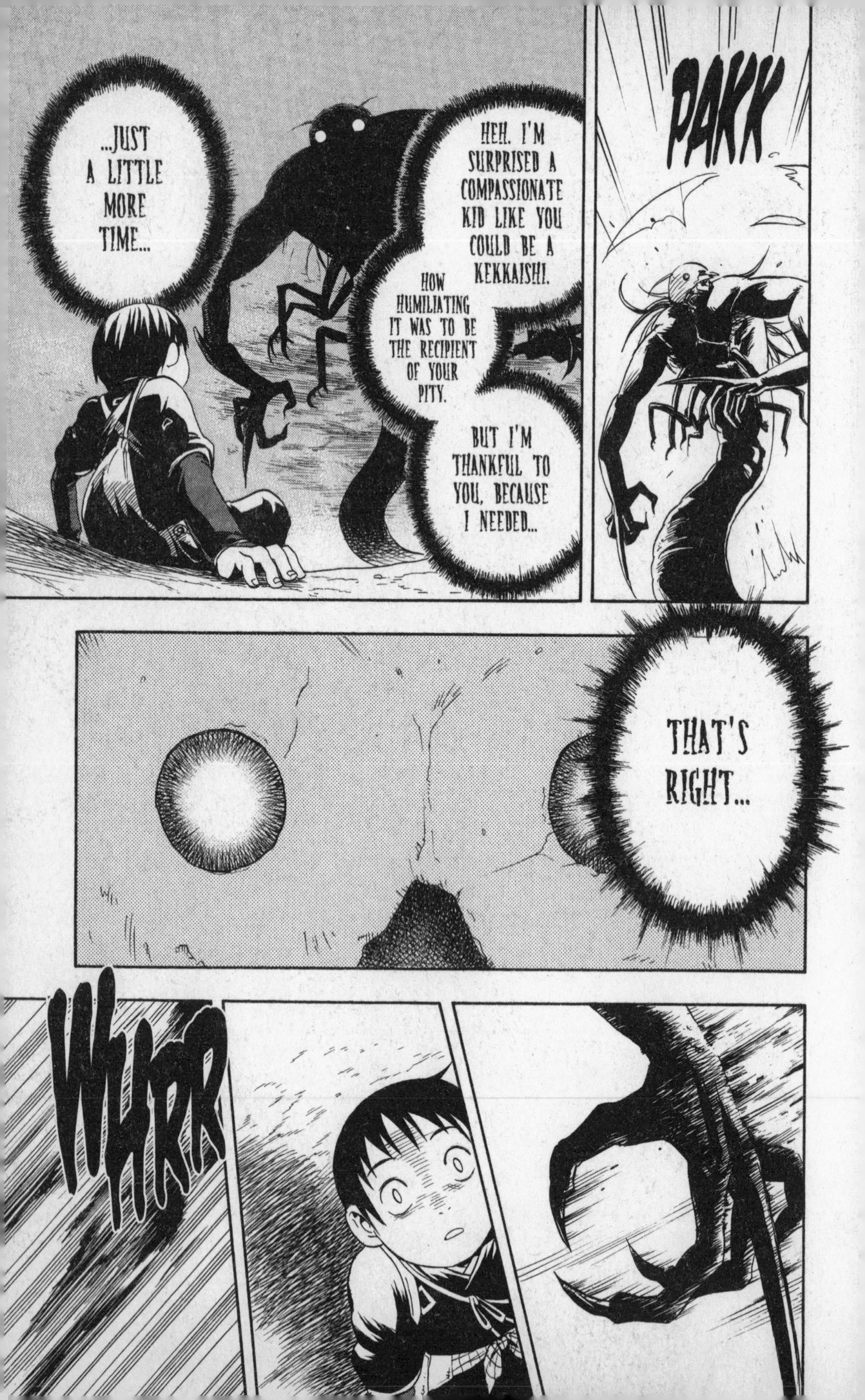
PAKK
HEH. I'M SURPRISED A COMPASSIONATE KID LIKE YOU COULD BE A KEKKAISHI.
HOW HUMILIATING IT WAS TO BE THE RECIPIENT OF YOUR PITY.
BUT I'M THANKFUL TO YOU, BECAUSE I NEEDED...
...JUST A LITTLE MORE TIME...
THAT'S RIGHT...
WHRR

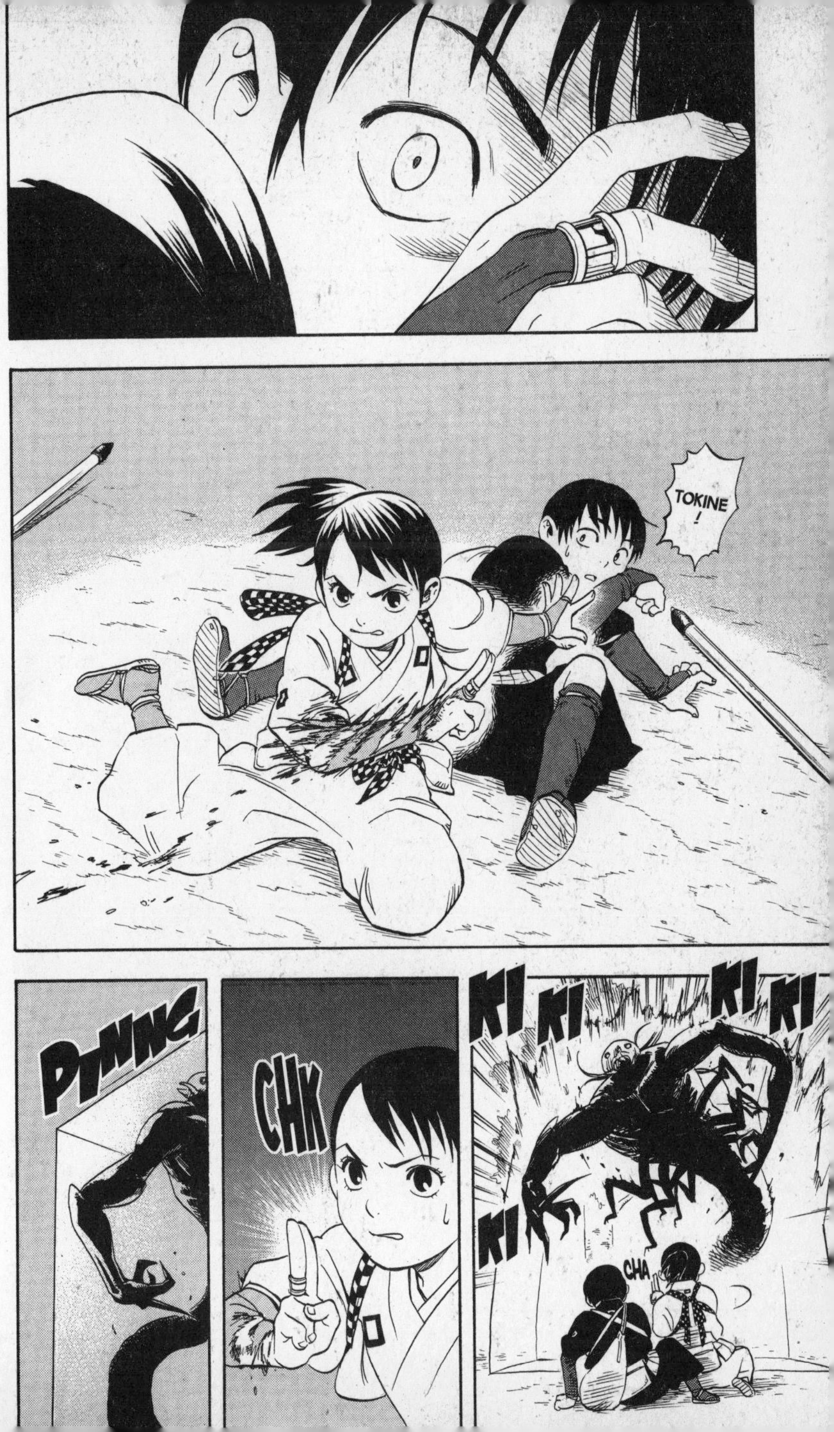
TOKINE!
KI KI KI KI KI
CHA
CHK
PTWNG

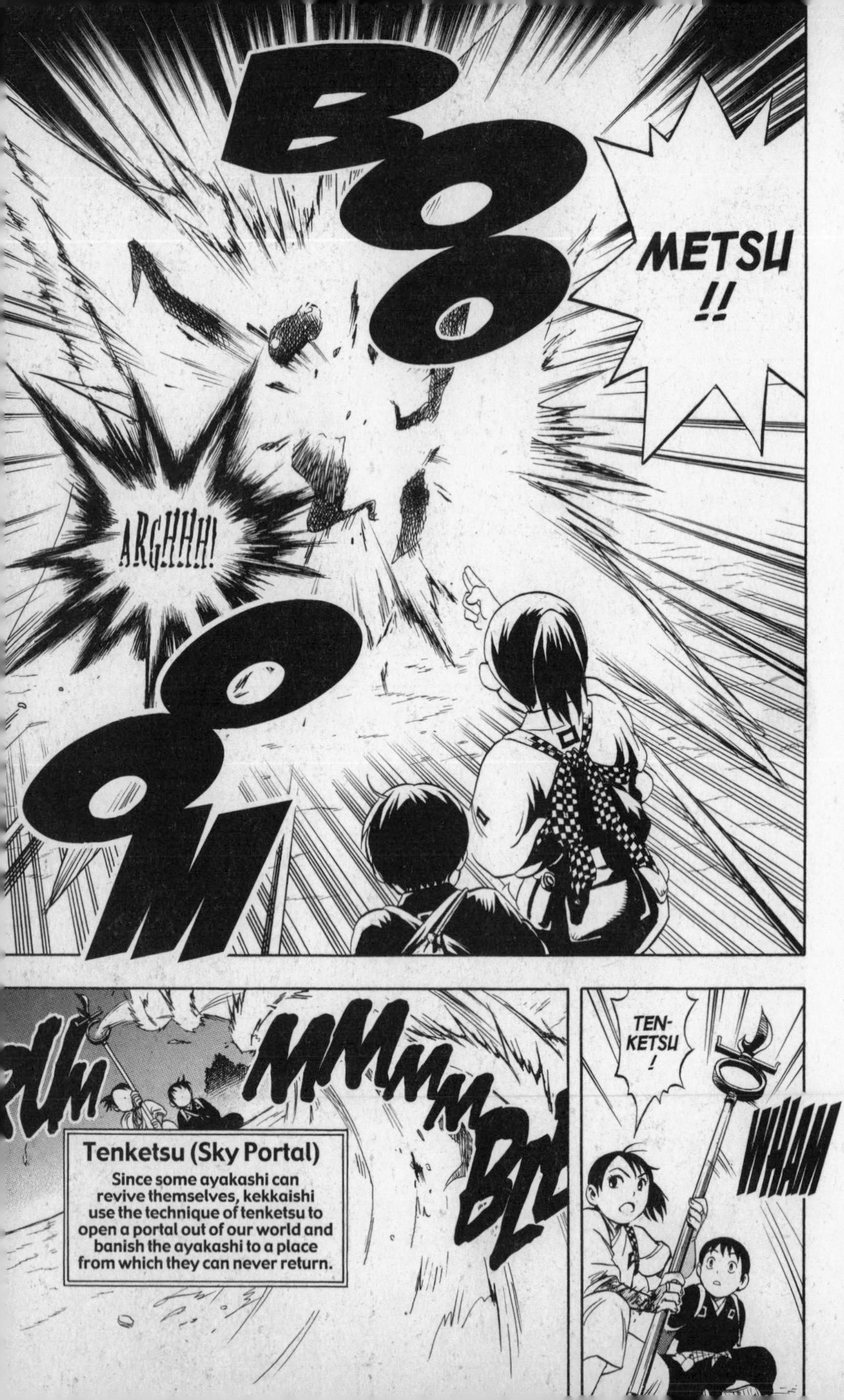
BOOOOM
METSU !!
ARGHHH!
TEN-KETSU !
WHAM
Tenketsu (Sky Portal)
Since some ayakashi can revive themselves, kekkaishi use the technique of tenketsu to open a portal out of our world and banish the ayakashi to a place from which they can never return.

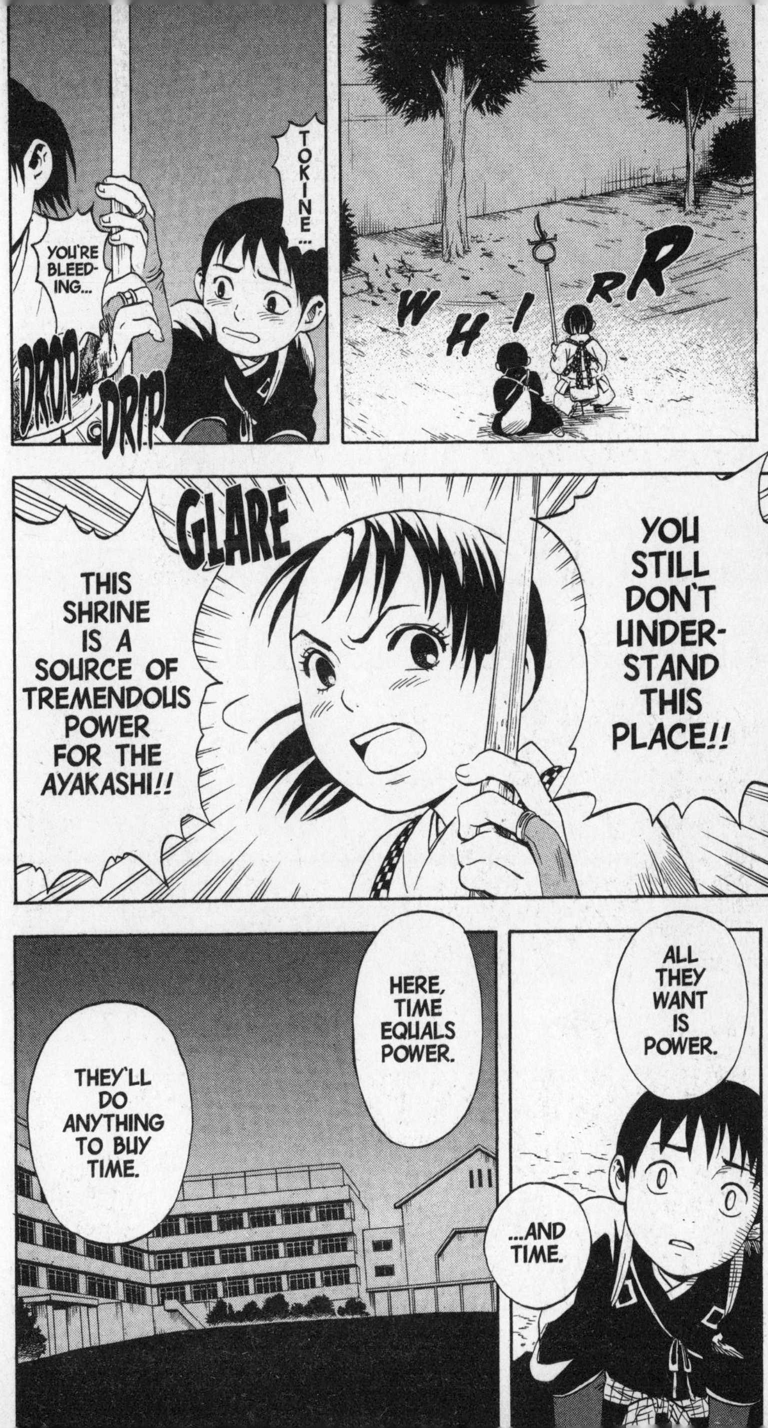
WHIRR
TOKINE...
YOU'RE BLEEDING...
DROP
DRIP
YOU STILL DON'T UNDERSTAND THIS PLACE!!
GLARE
THIS SHRINE IS A SOURCE OF TREMENDOUS POWER FOR THE AYAKASHI!!
ALL THEY WANT IS POWER.
...AND TIME.
HERE, TIME EQUALS POWER.
THEY'LL DO ANYTHING TO BUY TIME.

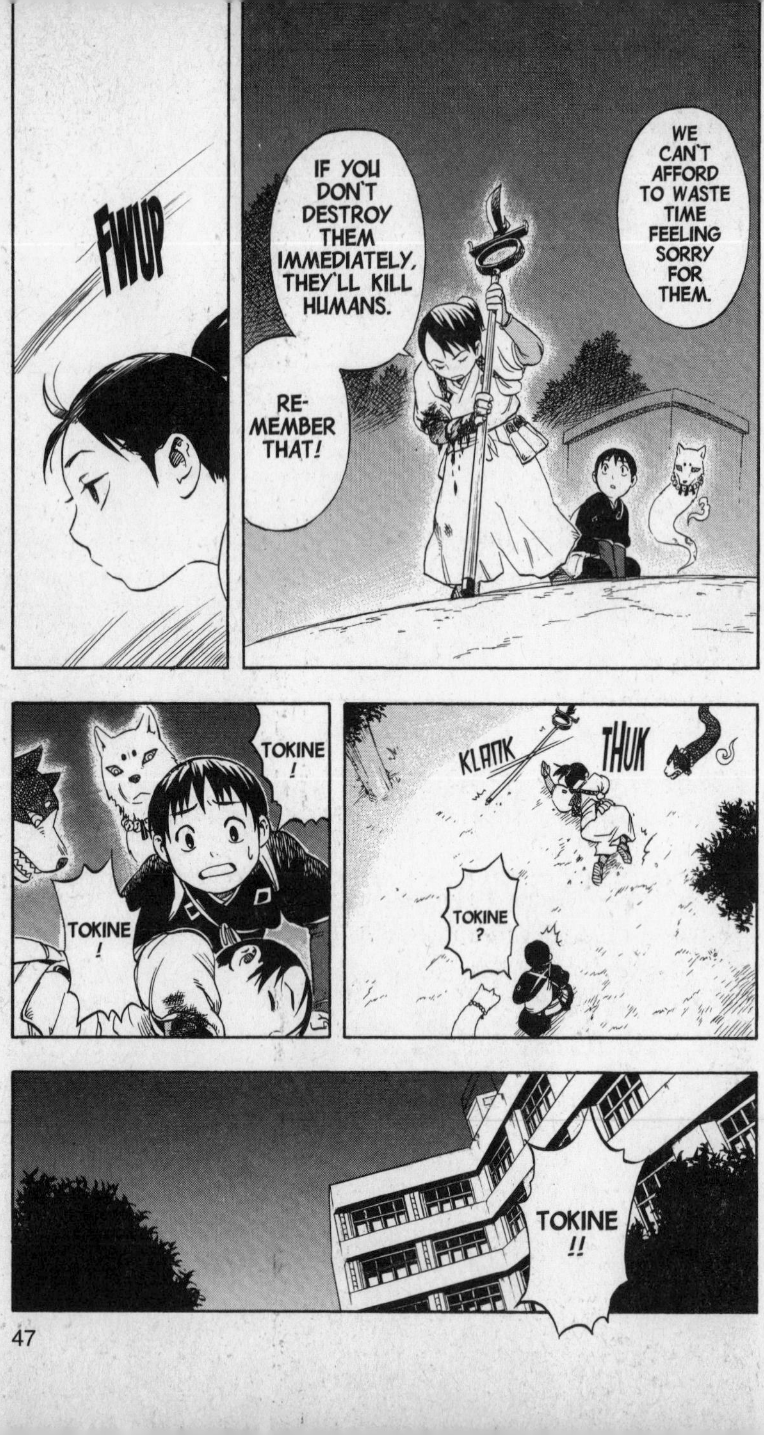
WE CAN'T AFFORD TO WASTE TIME FEELING SORRY FOR THEM.
IF YOU DON'T DESTROY THEM IMMEDIATELY, THEY'LL KILL HUMANS.
RE-MEMBER THAT!
FWUP
THUK
KLANK
TOKINE?
TOKINE!
TOKINE!
TOKINE!!

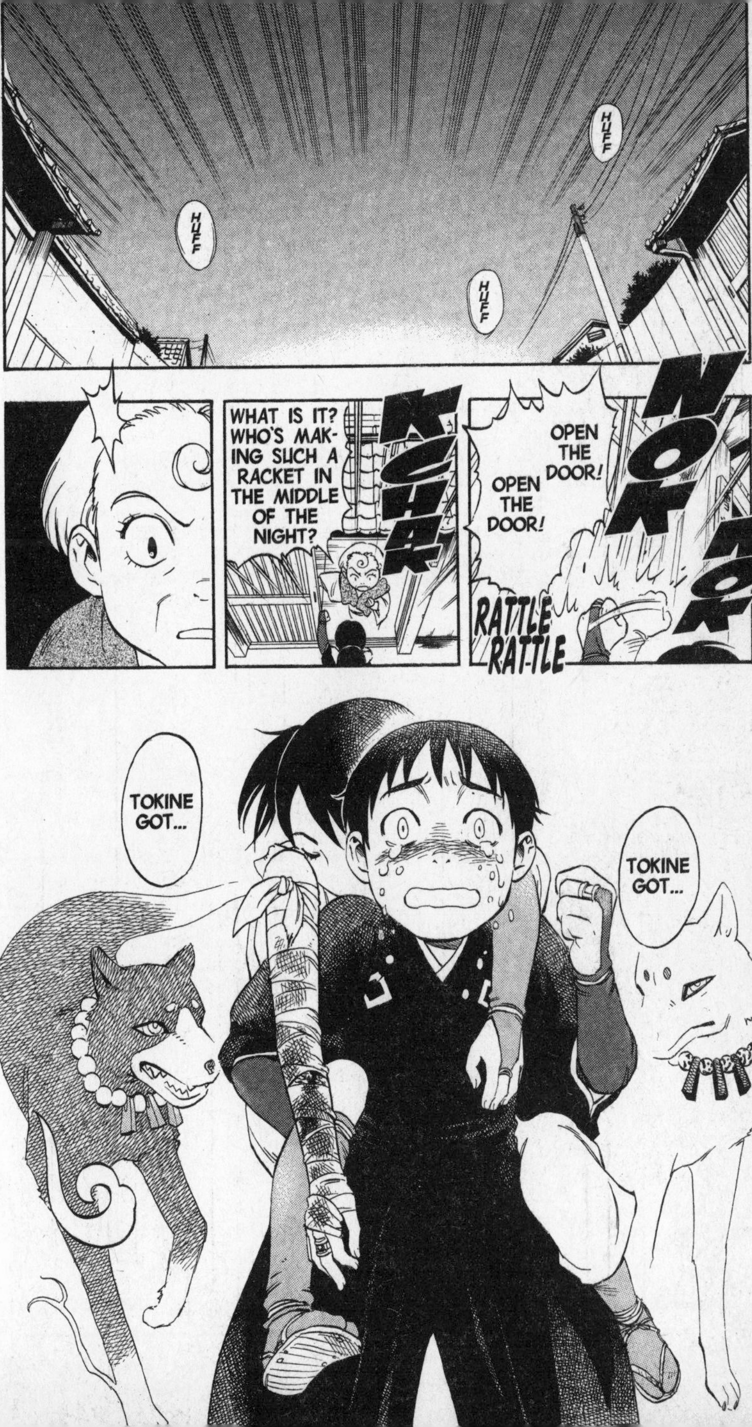
HUFF
HUFF
HUFF
NOK
NOK
OPEN THE DOOR!
OPEN THE DOOR!
RATTLE RATTLE
KCHAK
WHAT IS IT? WHO'S MAKING SUCH A RACKET IN THE MIDDLE OF THE NIGHT?
TOKINE GOT...
TOKINE GOT...

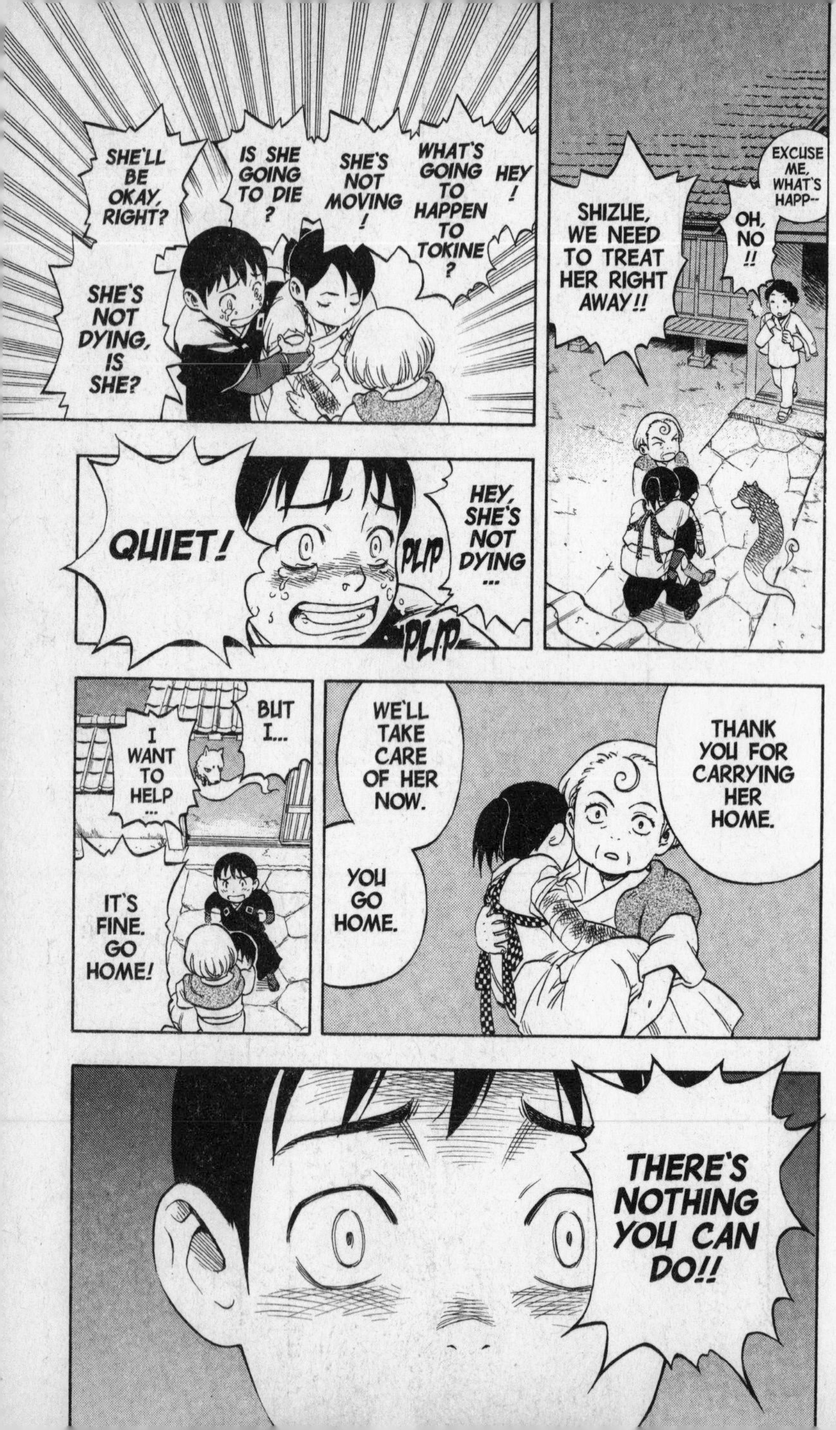
EXCUSE ME, WHAT'S HAPP--
OH, NO!!
SHIZUE, WE NEED TO TREAT HER RIGHT AWAY!!
HEY!
WHAT'S GOING TO HAPPEN TO TOKINE?
SHE'S NOT MOVING!
IS SHE GOING TO DIE?
SHE'LL BE OKAY, RIGHT?
SHE'S NOT DYING, IS SHE?
HEY, SHE'S NOT DYING...
PLIP
PLIP
QUIET!
THANK YOU FOR CARRYING HER HOME.
WE'LL TAKE CARE OF HER NOW.
YOU GO HOME.
BUT I...
I WANT TO HELP...
IT'S FINE. GO HOME!
THERE'S NOTHING YOU CAN DO!!

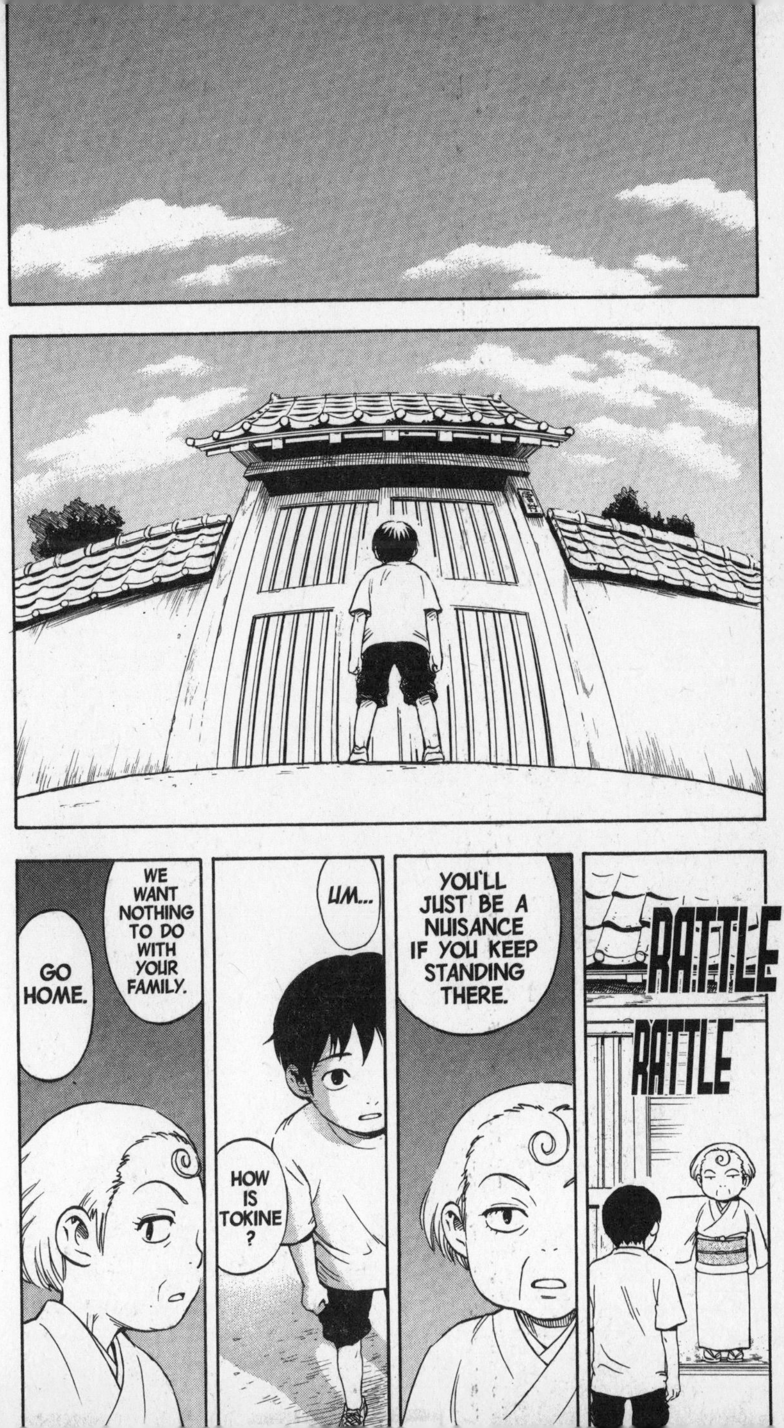
RATTLE
RATTLE
YOU'LL JUST BE A NUISANCE IF YOU KEEP STANDING THERE.
UM...
HOW IS TOKINE?
WE WANT NOTHING TO DO WITH YOUR FAMILY.
GO HOME.

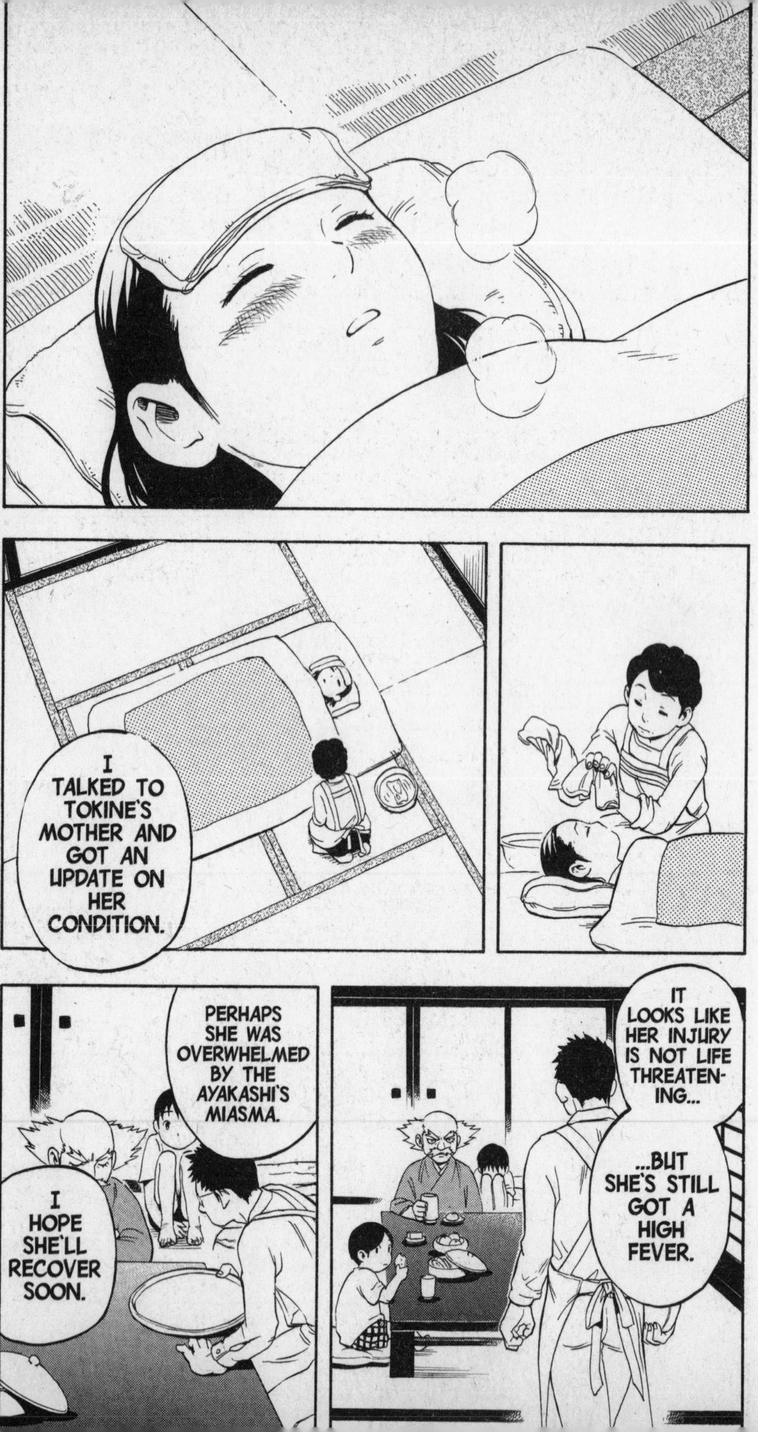
I TALKED TO TOKINE'S MOTHER AND GOT AN UPDATE ON HER CONDITION.
IT LOOKS LIKE HER INJURY IS NOT LIFE THREATENING...
...BUT SHE'S STILL GOT A HIGH FEVER.
PERHAPS SHE WAS OVERWHELMED BY THE AYAKASHI'S MIASMA.
I HOPE SHE'LL RECOVER SOON.

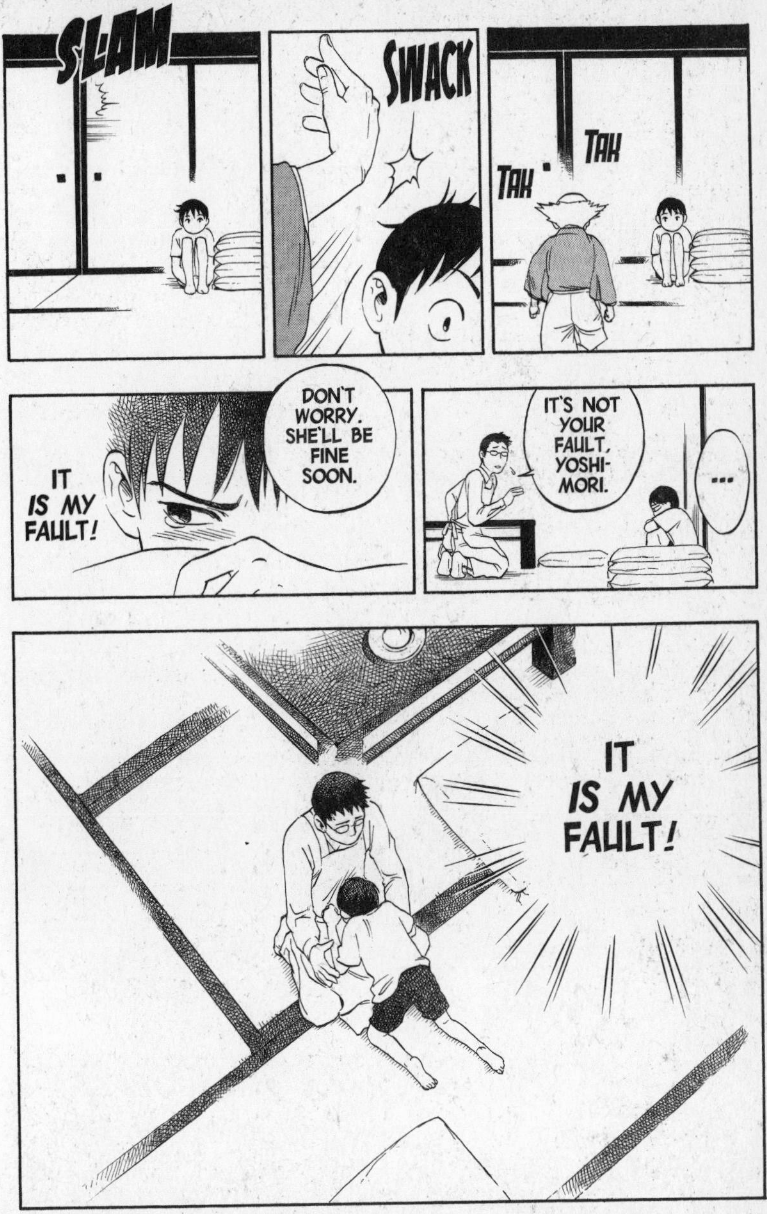
TAK
TAK
SWACK
SLAM
IT'S NOT YOUR FAULT, YOSHIMORI.
...
DON'T WORRY. SHE'LL BE FINE SOON.
IT IS MY FAULT!
IT IS MY FAULT!

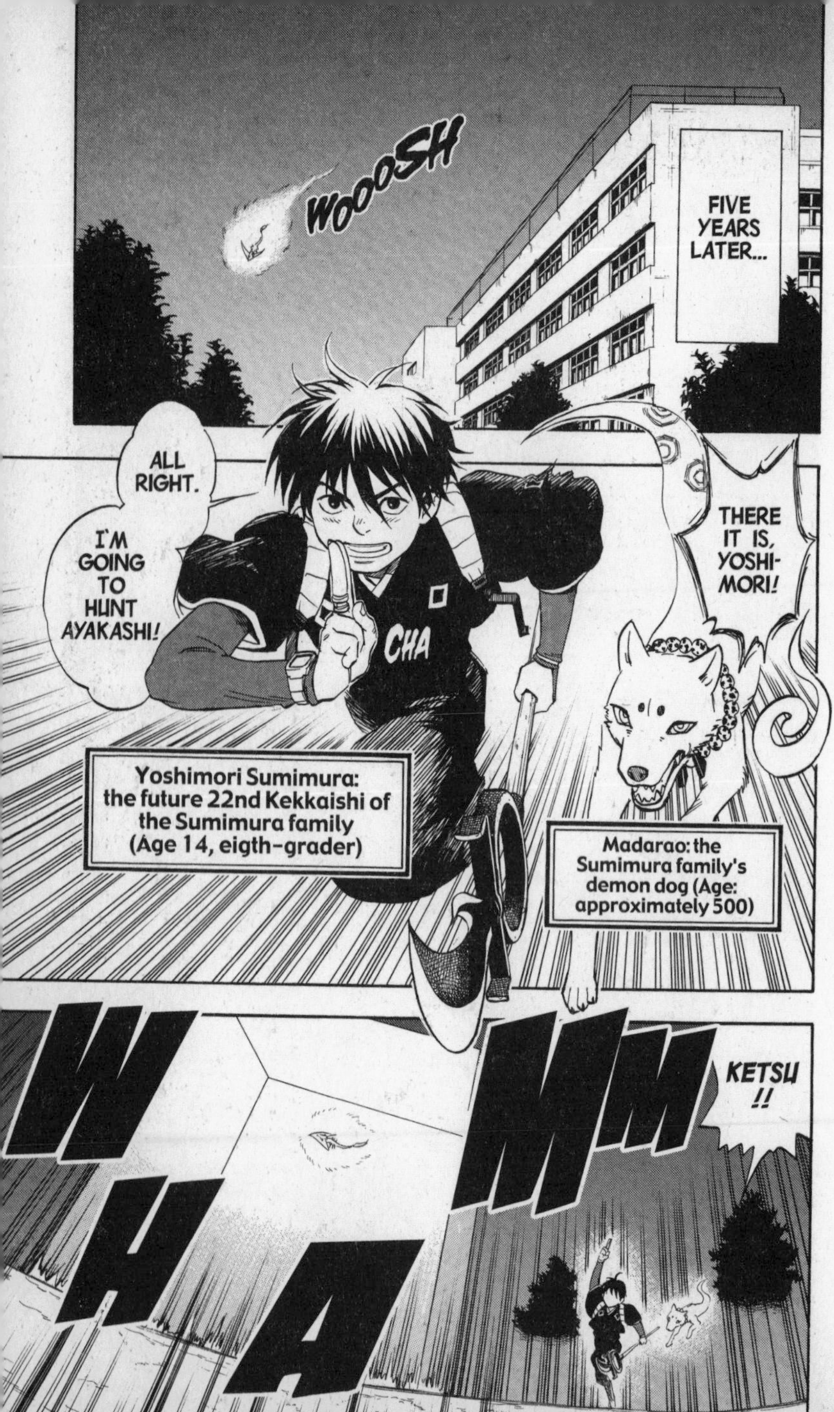
FIVE YEARS LATER...
WOOOSH
THERE IT IS, YOSHI-MORI!
ALL RIGHT. I'M GOING TO HUNT AYAKASHI!
Madarao: the Sumimura family's demon dog (Age: approximately 500)
Yoshimori Sumimura: the future 22nd Kekkaishi of the Sumimura family (Age 14, eigth-grader)
KETSU !!

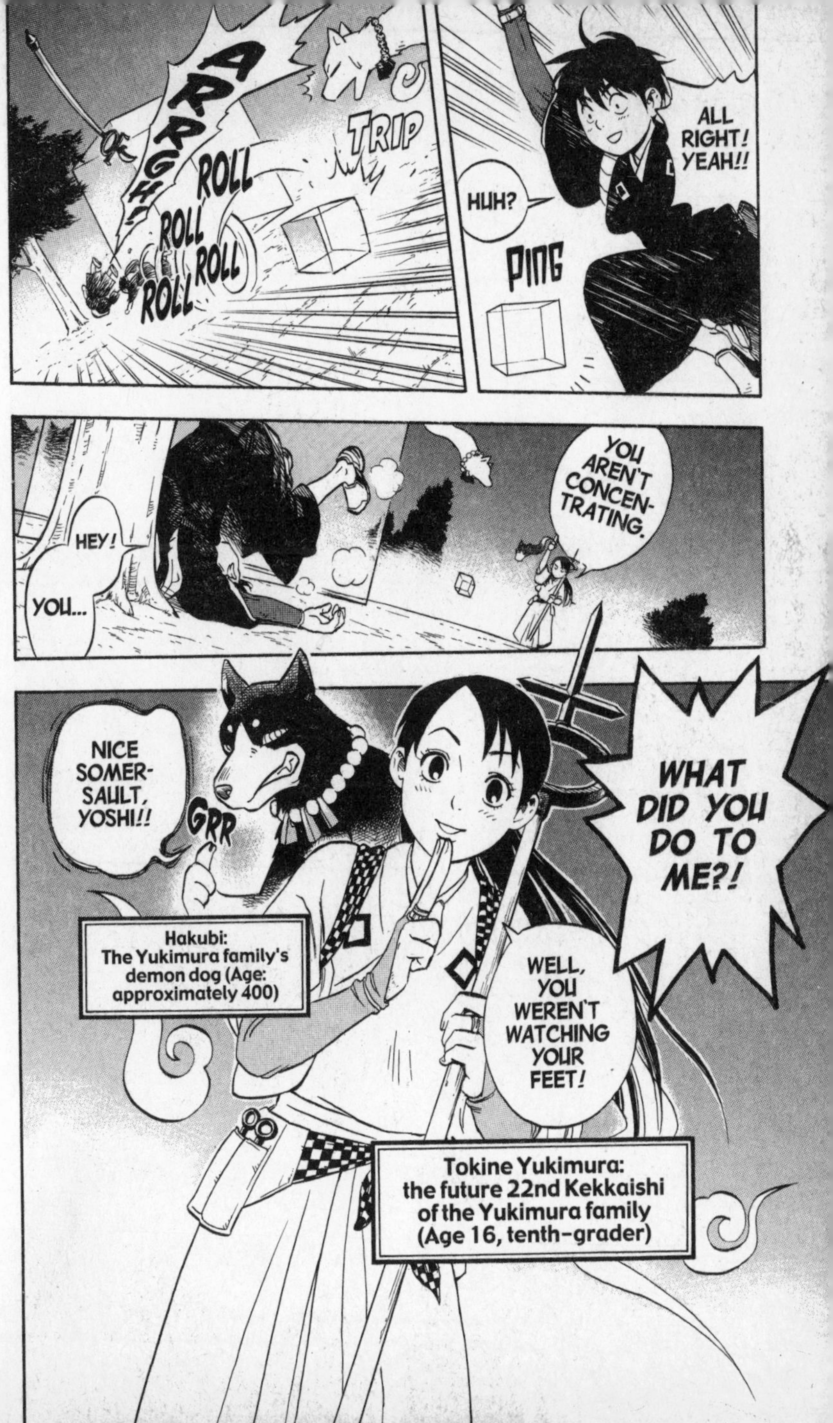
ALL RIGHT! YEAH!!
HUH?
PING
TRIP
ARRGH!
ROLL ROLL ROLL ROLL
YOU AREN'T CONCEN-TRATING.
HEY!
YOU...
WHAT DID YOU DO TO ME?!
WELL, YOU WEREN'T WATCHING YOUR FEET!
NICE SOMER-SAULT, YOSHI!!
GRR
Hakubi: The Yukimura family's demon dog (Age: approximately 400)
Tokine Yukimura: the future 22nd Kekkaishi of the Yukimura family (Age 16, tenth-grader)

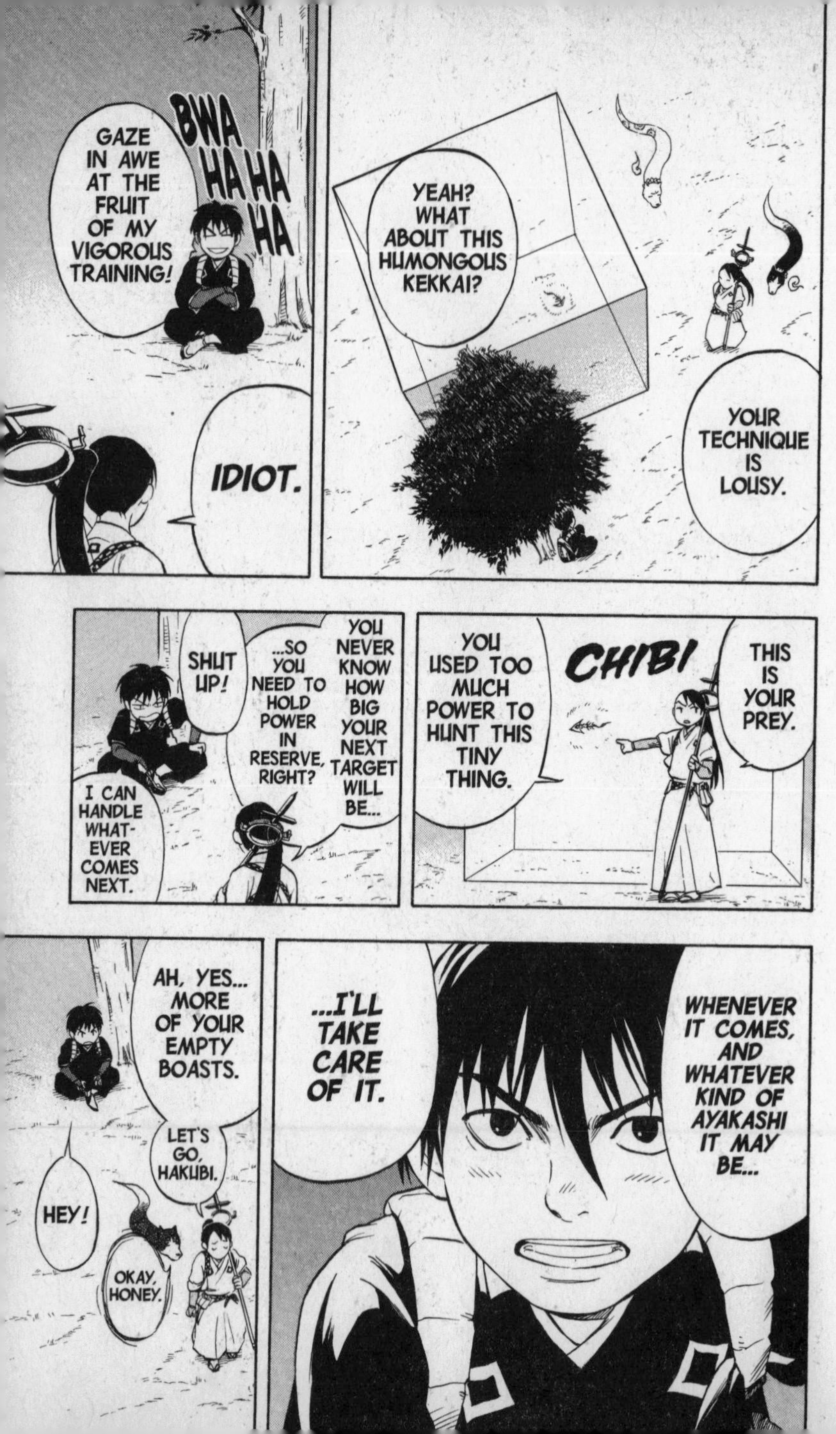
YOUR TECHNIQUE IS LOUSY.
YEAH? WHAT ABOUT THIS HUMONGOUS KEKKAI?
GAZE IN AWE AT THE FRUIT OF MY VIGOROUS TRAINING!
BWA HA HA HA HA
IDIOT.
THIS IS YOUR PREY.
CHIBI
YOU USED TOO MUCH POWER TO HUNT THIS TINY THING.
YOU NEVER KNOW HOW BIG YOUR NEXT TARGET WILL BE...
...SO YOU NEED TO HOLD POWER IN RESERVE, RIGHT?
SHUT UP!
I CAN HANDLE WHATEVER COMES NEXT.
WHENEVER IT COMES, AND WHATEVER KIND OF AYAKASHI IT MAY BE...
...I'LL TAKE CARE OF IT.
AH, YES... MORE OF YOUR EMPTY BOASTS.
LET'S GO, HAKUBI.
OKAY, HONEY.
HEY!

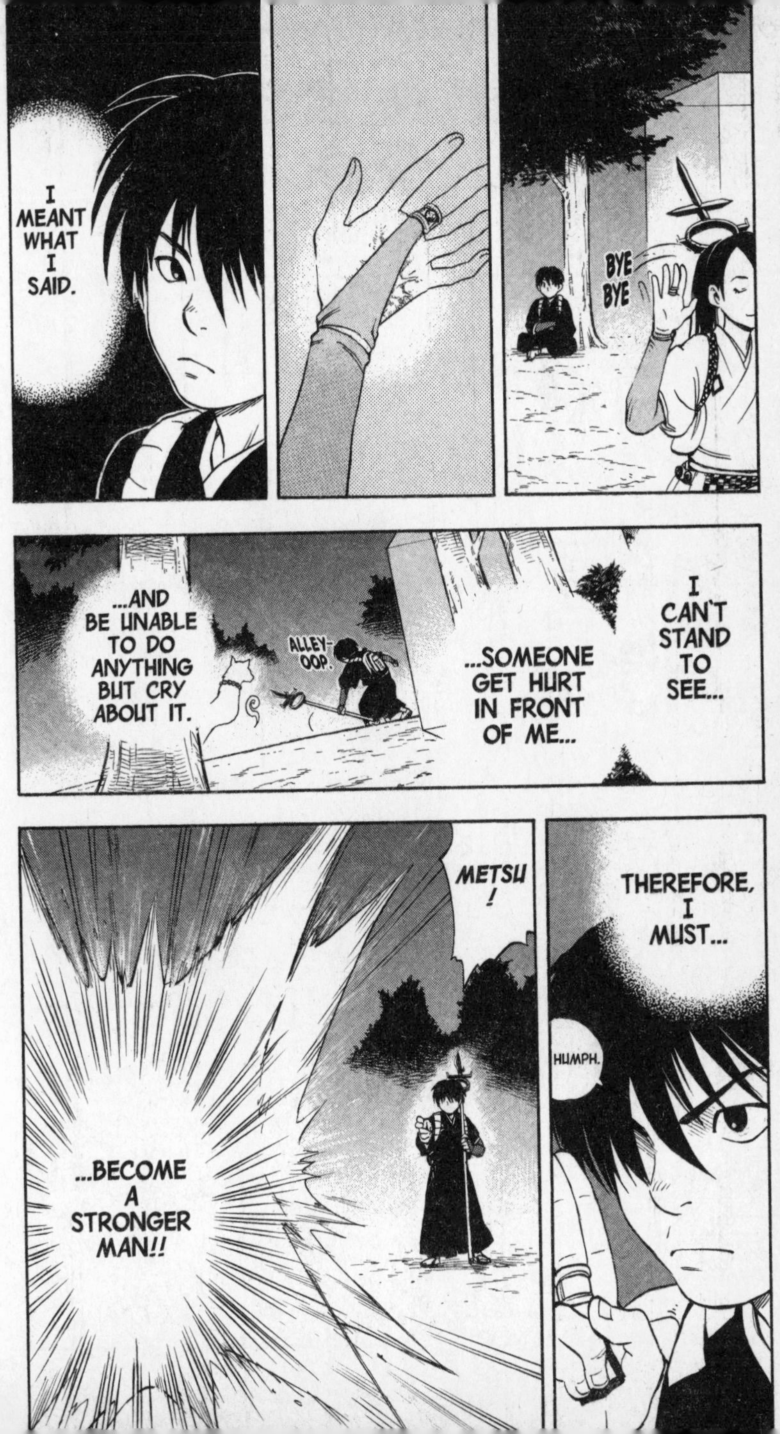
BYE BYE
I MEANT WHAT I SAID.
I CAN'T STAND TO SEE...
...SOMEONE GET HURT IN FRONT OF ME...
ALLEY-OOP.
...AND BE UNABLE TO DO ANYTHING BUT CRY ABOUT IT.
THEREFORE, I MUST...
HUMPH.
METSU!
...BECOME A STRONGER MAN!!

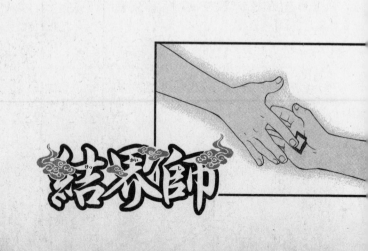
結界師

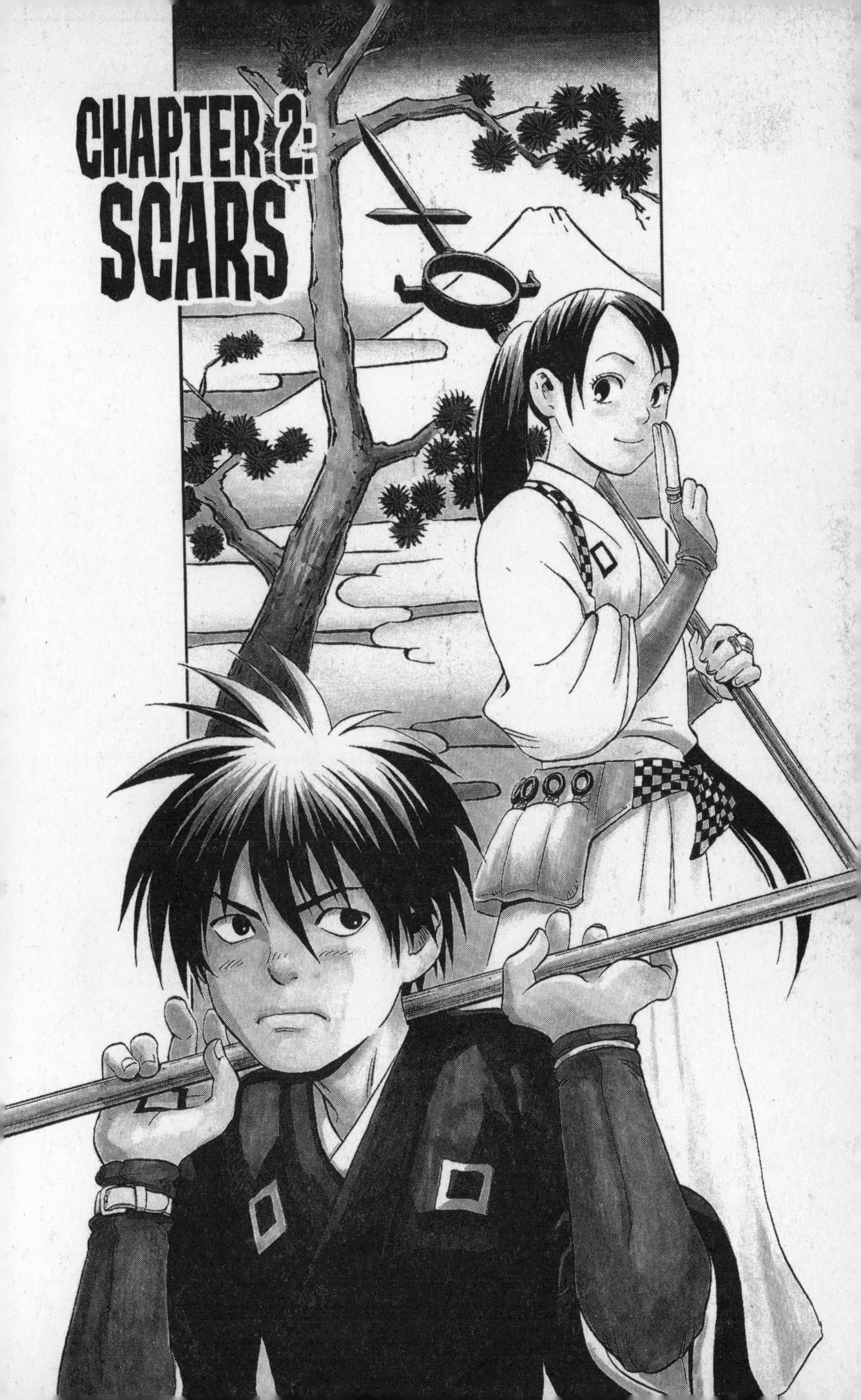
CHAPTER 2:
SCARS

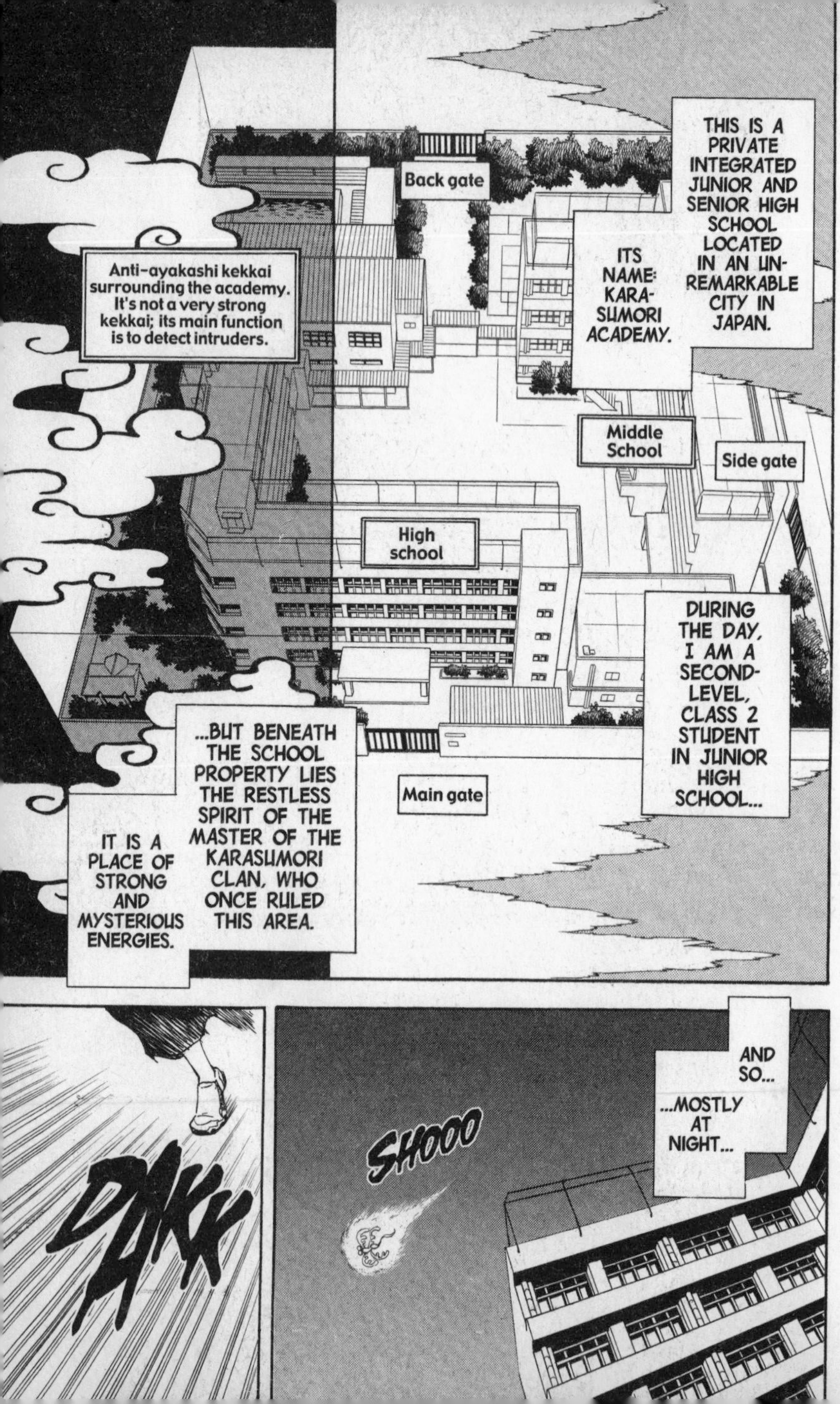
THIS IS A PRIVATE INTEGRATED JUNIOR AND SENIOR HIGH SCHOOL LOCATED IN AN UNREMARKABLE CITY IN JAPAN.
ITS NAME: KARASUMORI ACADEMY.
Back gate
Anti-ayakashi kekkai surrounding the academy. It's not a very strong kekkai; its main function is to detect intruders.
Middle School
Side gate
High school
Main gate
DURING THE DAY, I AM A SECOND-LEVEL, CLASS 2 STUDENT IN JUNIOR HIGH SCHOOL...
...BUT BENEATH THE SCHOOL PROPERTY LIES THE RESTLESS SPIRIT OF THE MASTER OF THE KARASUMORI CLAN, WHO ONCE RULED THIS AREA.
IT IS A PLACE OF STRONG AND MYSTERIOUS ENERGIES.
AND SO...
...MOSTLY AT NIGHT...
SHOOO
DAKK

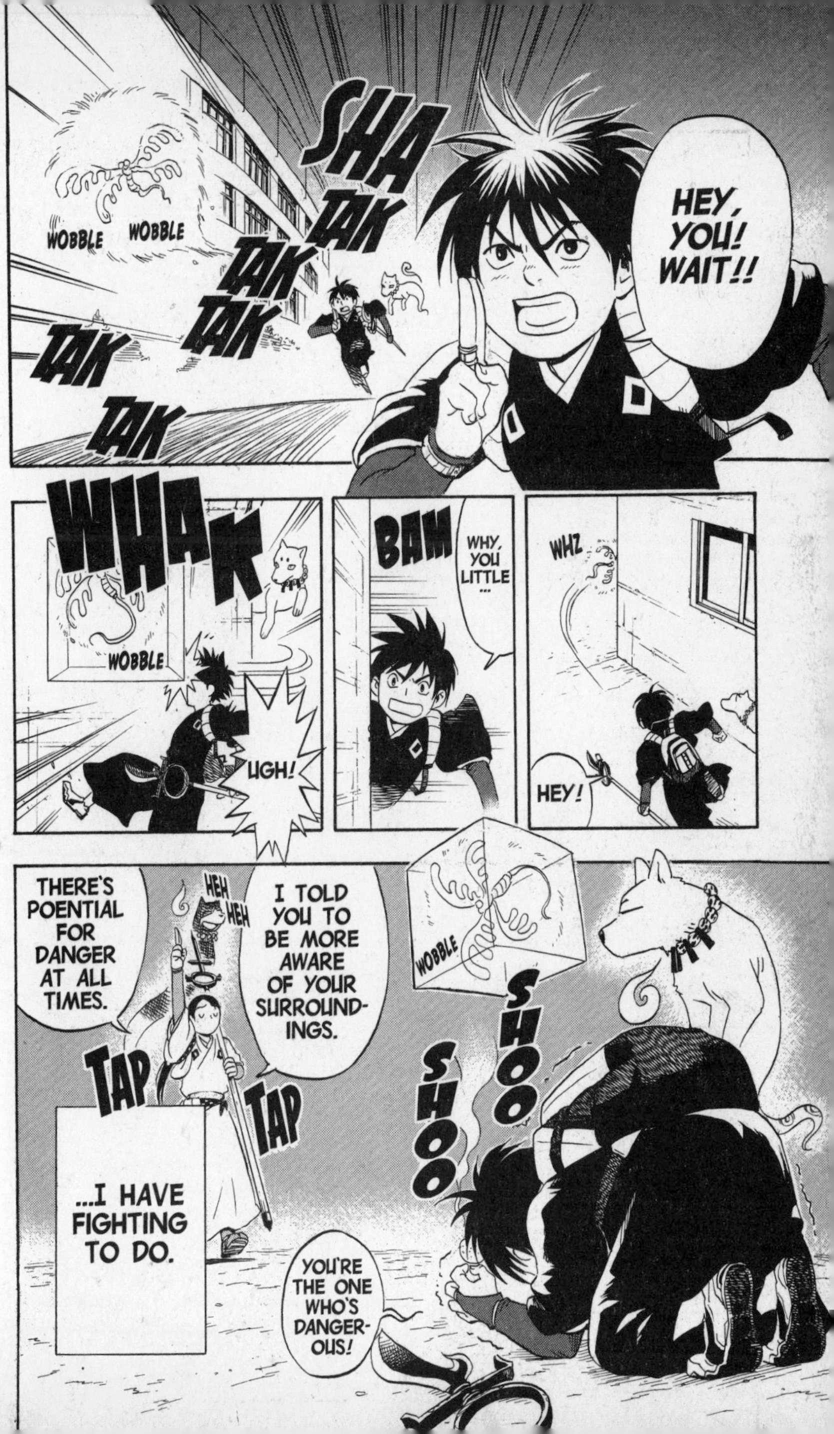
HEY, YOU! WAIT!!
SHA
TAK
TAK
TAK
TAK
TAK
WOBBLE
WOBBLE
WHZ
HEY!
BAM
WHY, YOU LITTLE ...
WHAK
WOBBLE
UGH!
WOBBLE
SHOO
SHOO
I TOLD YOU TO BE MORE AWARE OF YOUR SURROUND-INGS.
HEH HEH
THERE'S POENTIAL FOR DANGER AT ALL TIMES.
TAP
TAP
YOU'RE THE ONE WHO'S DANGER-OUS!
...I HAVE FIGHTING TO DO.

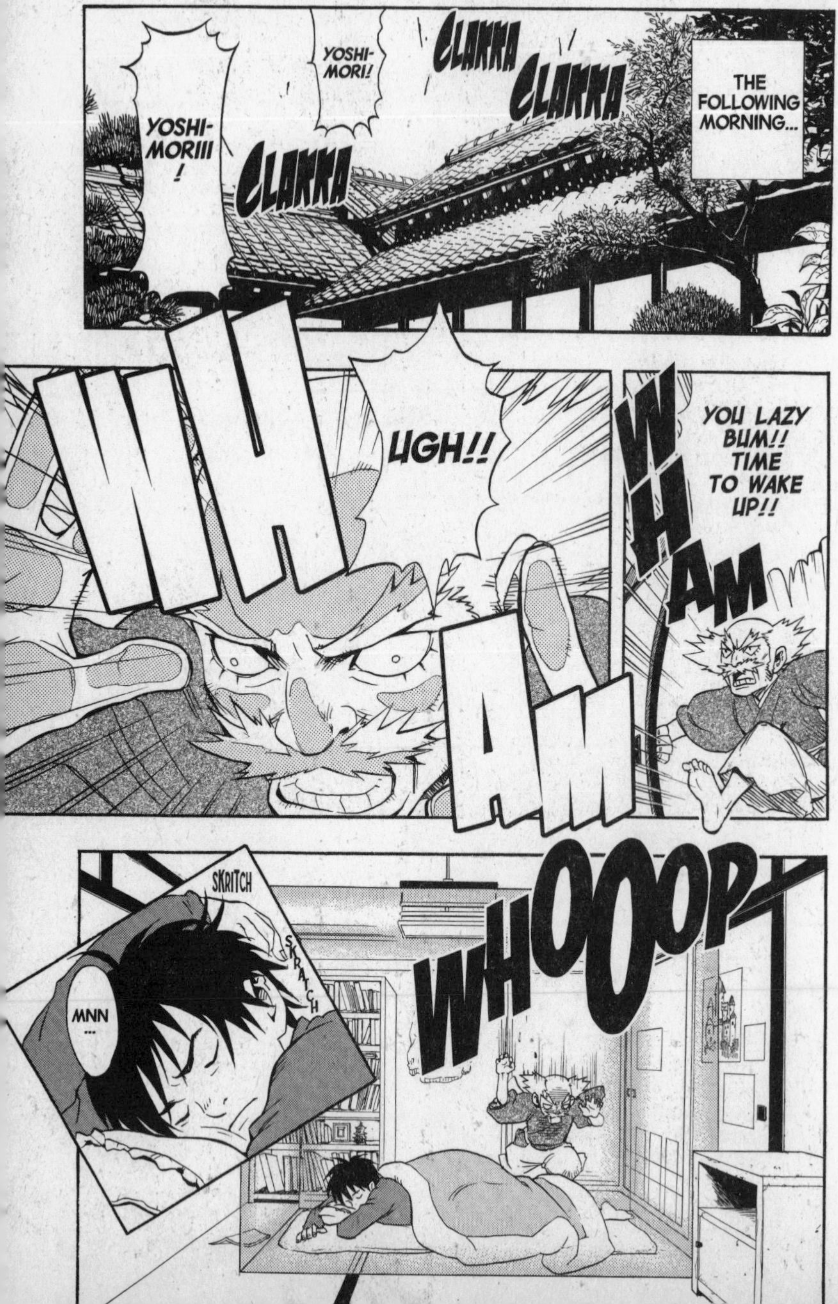
THE FOLLOWING MORNING...
CLARRA
CLARRA
YOSHI-MORI!
CLARRA
YOSHI-MORIII!
YOU LAZY BUM!! TIME TO WAKE UP!!
WHAM
UGH!!
WHAM
WHOOOP
SKRITCH
SKRATCH
MNN...

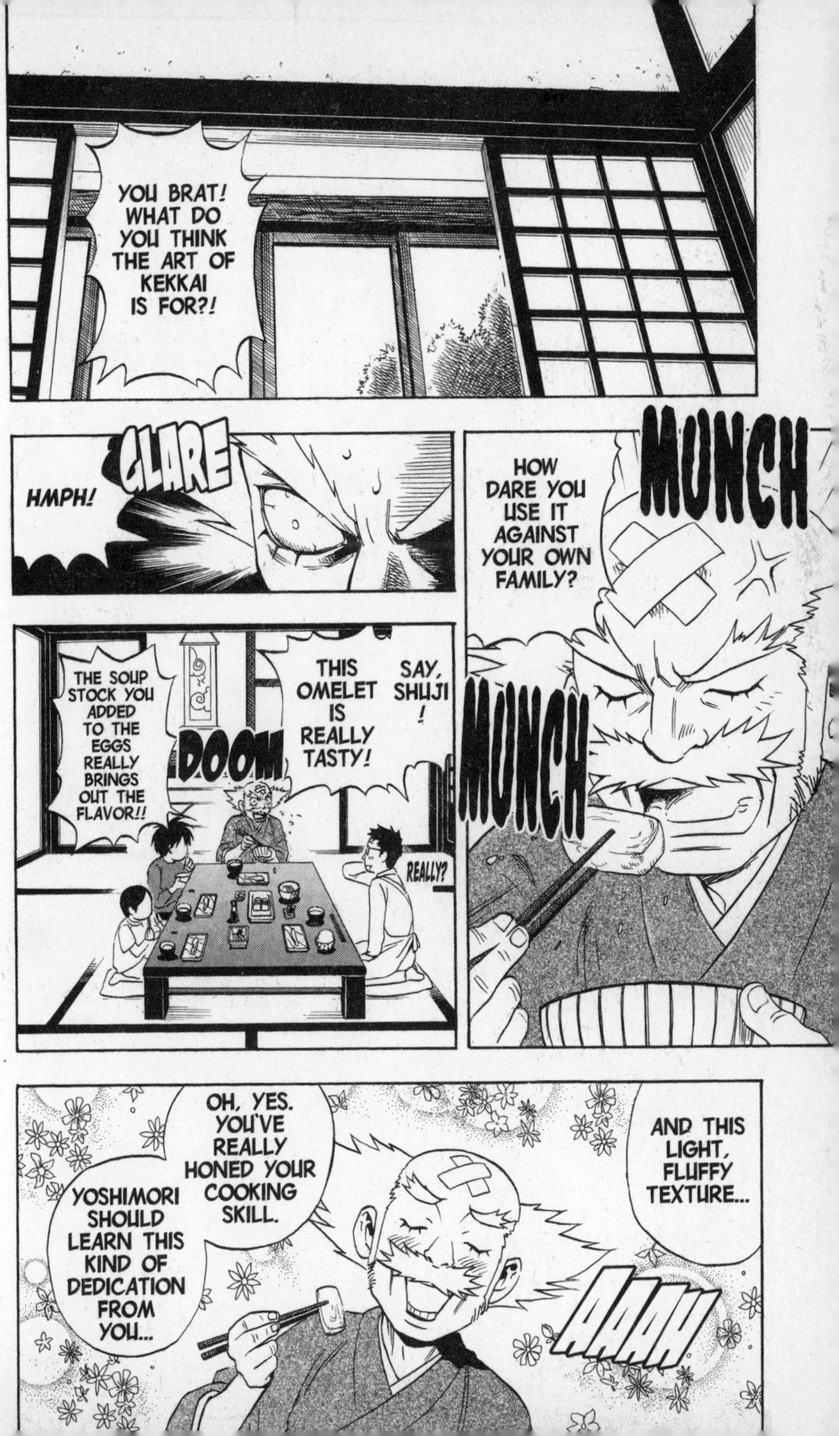
YOU BRAT! WHAT DO YOU THINK THE ART OF KEKKAI IS FOR?!
MUNCH
HOW DARE YOU USE IT AGAINST YOUR OWN FAMILY?
MUNCH
GLARE
HMPH!
SAY, SHUJI!
THIS OMELET IS REALLY TASTY!
DOOM
THE SOUP STOCK YOU ADDED TO THE EGGS REALLY BRINGS OUT THE FLAVOR!!
REALLY?
AND THIS LIGHT, FLUFFY TEXTURE...
AAAH
OH, YES. YOU'VE REALLY HONED YOUR COOKING SKILL.
YOSHIMORI SHOULD LEARN THIS KIND OF DEDICATION FROM YOU...

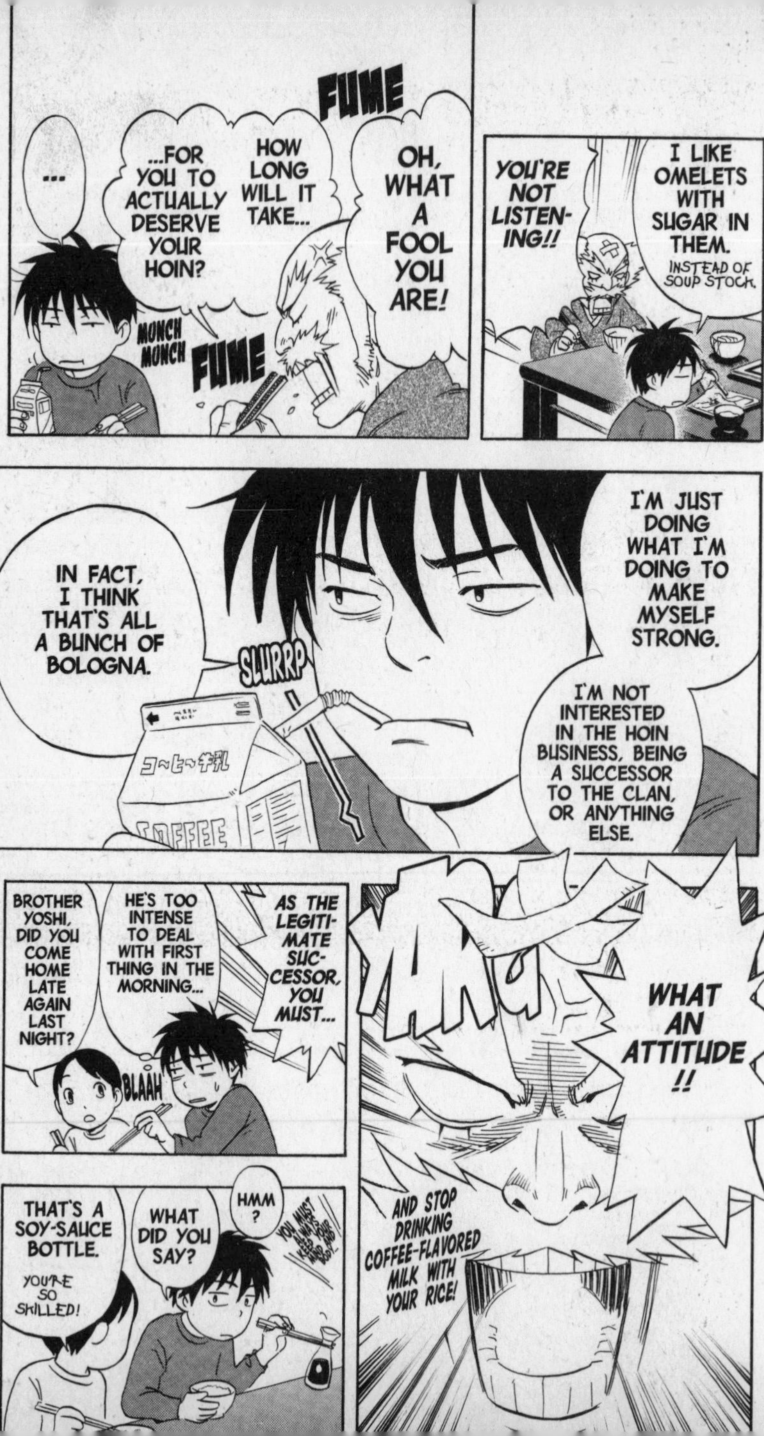
I LIKE OMELETS WITH SUGAR IN THEM.
INSTEAD OF SOUP STOCK.
YOU'RE NOT LISTEN-ING!!
FUME
OH, WHAT A FOOL YOU ARE!
HOW LONG WILL IT TAKE...
...FOR YOU TO ACTUALLY DESERVE YOUR HOIN?
...
MUNCH MUNCH
FUME
I'M JUST DOING WHAT I'M DOING TO MAKE MYSELF STRONG.
I'M NOT INTERESTED IN THE HOIN BUSINESS, BEING A SUCCESSOR TO THE CLAN, OR ANYTHING ELSE.
IN FACT, I THINK THAT'S ALL A BUNCH OF BOLOGNA.
SLURRP
コ~ヒ~牛乳
COFFEE
WHAT AN ATTITUDE !!
AND STOP DRINKING COFFEE-FLAVORED MILK WITH YOUR RICE!
AS THE LEGITI-MATE SUC-CESSOR, YOU MUST...
HE'S TOO INTENSE TO DEAL WITH FIRST THING IN THE MORNING...
BROTHER YOSHI, DID YOU COME HOME LATE AGAIN LAST NIGHT?
BLAAH
HMM ?
YOU MUST ALWAYS KEEP YOUR MIND AND BODY...
WHAT DID YOU SAY?
THAT'S A SOY-SAUCE BOTTLE.
YOU'RE SO SKILLED!

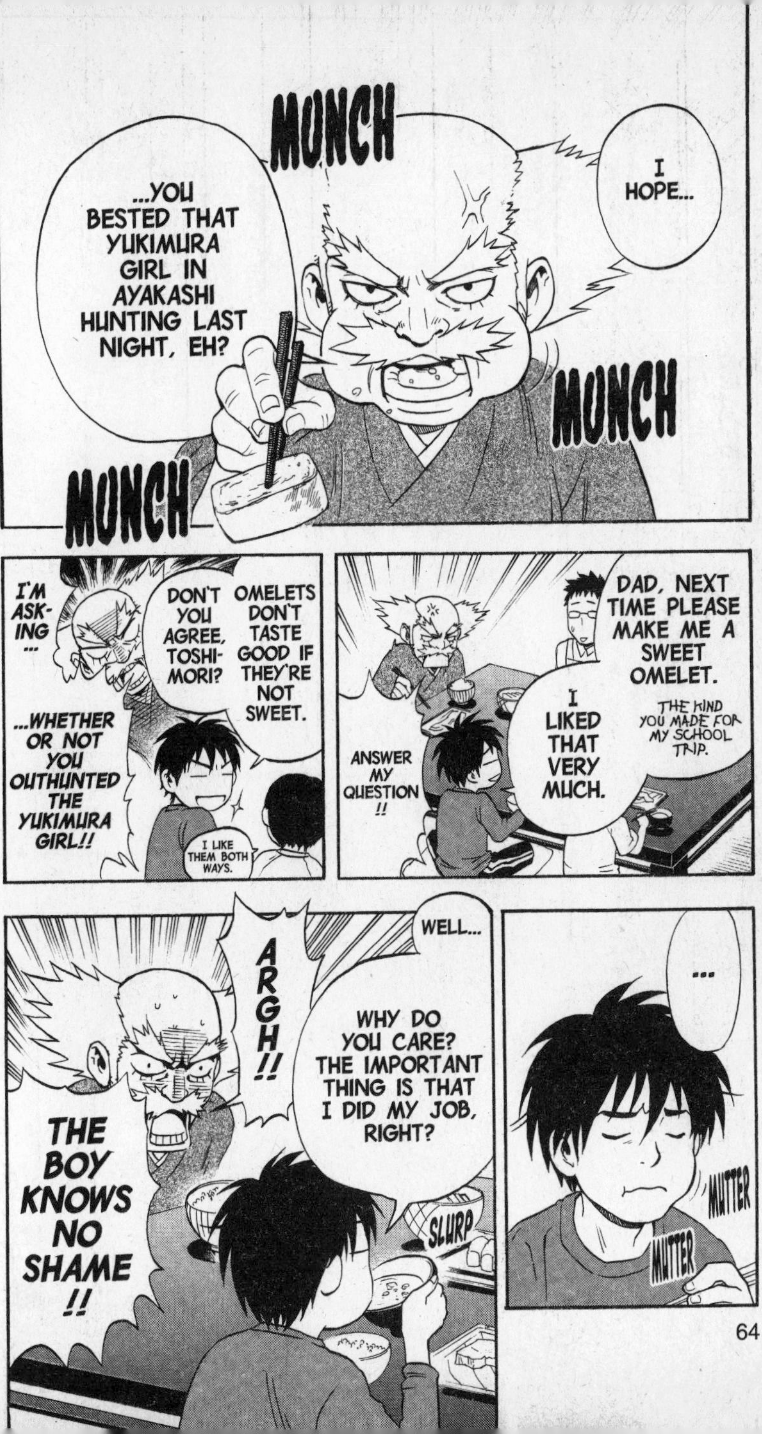
I HOPE...
...YOU BESTED THAT YUKIMURA GIRL IN AYAKASHI HUNTING LAST NIGHT, EH?
MUNCH
MUNCH
MUNCH
DAD, NEXT TIME PLEASE MAKE ME A SWEET OMELET.
THE KIND YOU MADE FOR MY SCHOOL TRIP.
I LIKED THAT VERY MUCH.
ANSWER MY QUESTION!!
OMELETS DON'T TASTE GOOD IF THEY'RE NOT SWEET.
DON'T YOU AGREE, TOSHI-MORI?
I LIKE THEM BOTH WAYS.
I'M ASK-ING...
...WHETHER OR NOT YOU OUTHUNTED THE YUKIMURA GIRL!!
...
MUTTER
MUTTER
WELL...
WHY DO YOU CARE? THE IMPORTANT THING IS THAT I DID MY JOB, RIGHT?
ARGH!!
SLURP
THE BOY KNOWS NO SHAME!!

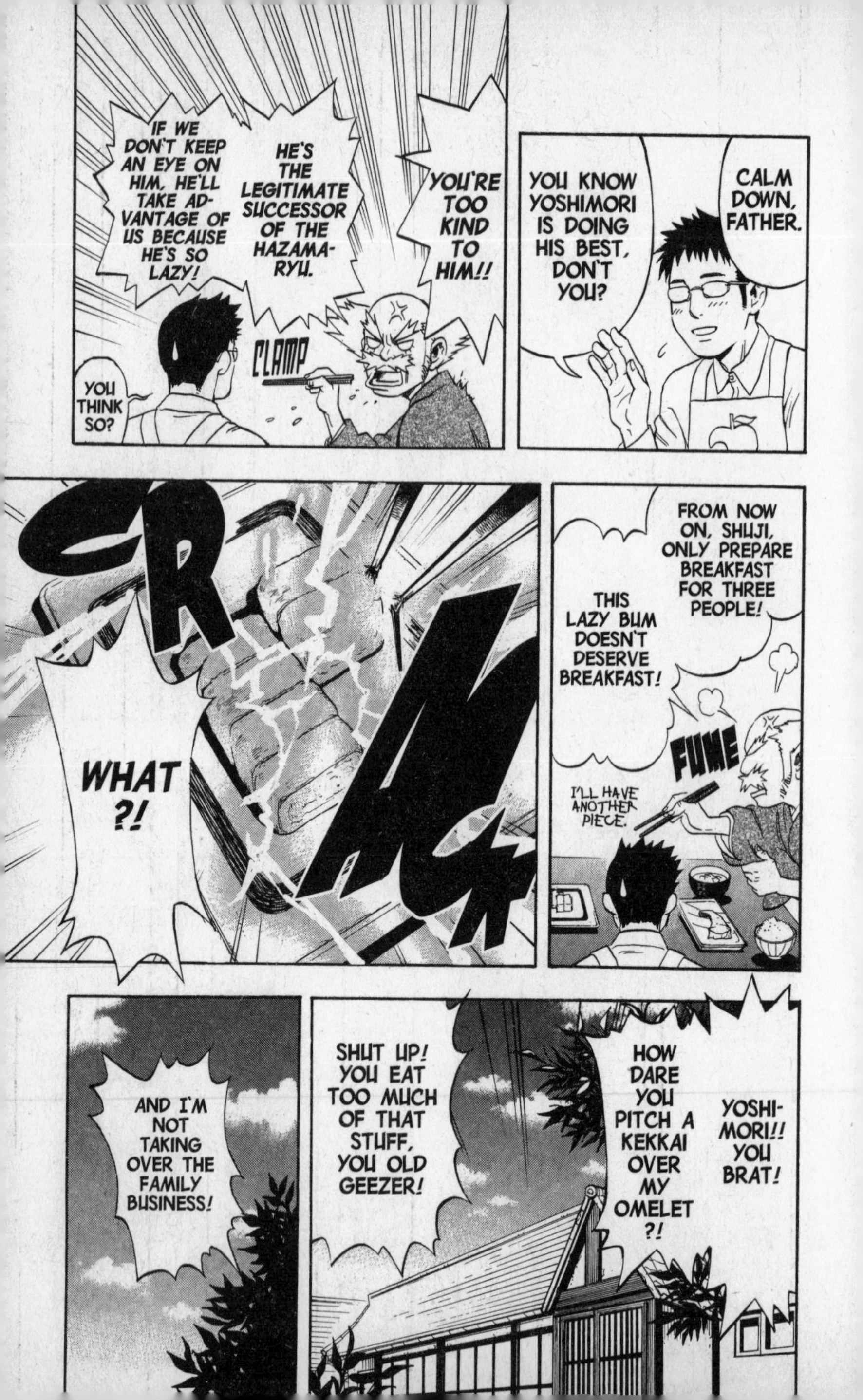
CALM DOWN, FATHER.
YOU KNOW YOSHIMORI IS DOING HIS BEST, DON'T YOU?
YOU'RE TOO KIND TO HIM!!
HE'S THE LEGITIMATE SUCCESSOR OF THE HAZAMA-RYU.
IF WE DON'T KEEP AN EYE ON HIM, HE'LL TAKE ADVANTAGE OF US BECAUSE HE'S SO LAZY!
CLAMP
YOU THINK SO?
FROM NOW ON, SHUJI, ONLY PREPARE BREAKFAST FOR THREE PEOPLE!
THIS LAZY BUM DOESN'T DESERVE BREAKFAST!
FUME
I'LL HAVE ANOTHER PIECE.
WHAT ?!
YOSHIMORI!! YOU BRAT!
HOW DARE YOU PITCH A KEKKAI OVER MY OMELET ?!
SHUT UP! YOU EAT TOO MUCH OF THAT STUFF, YOU OLD GEEZER!
AND I'M NOT TAKING OVER THE FAMILY BUSINESS!

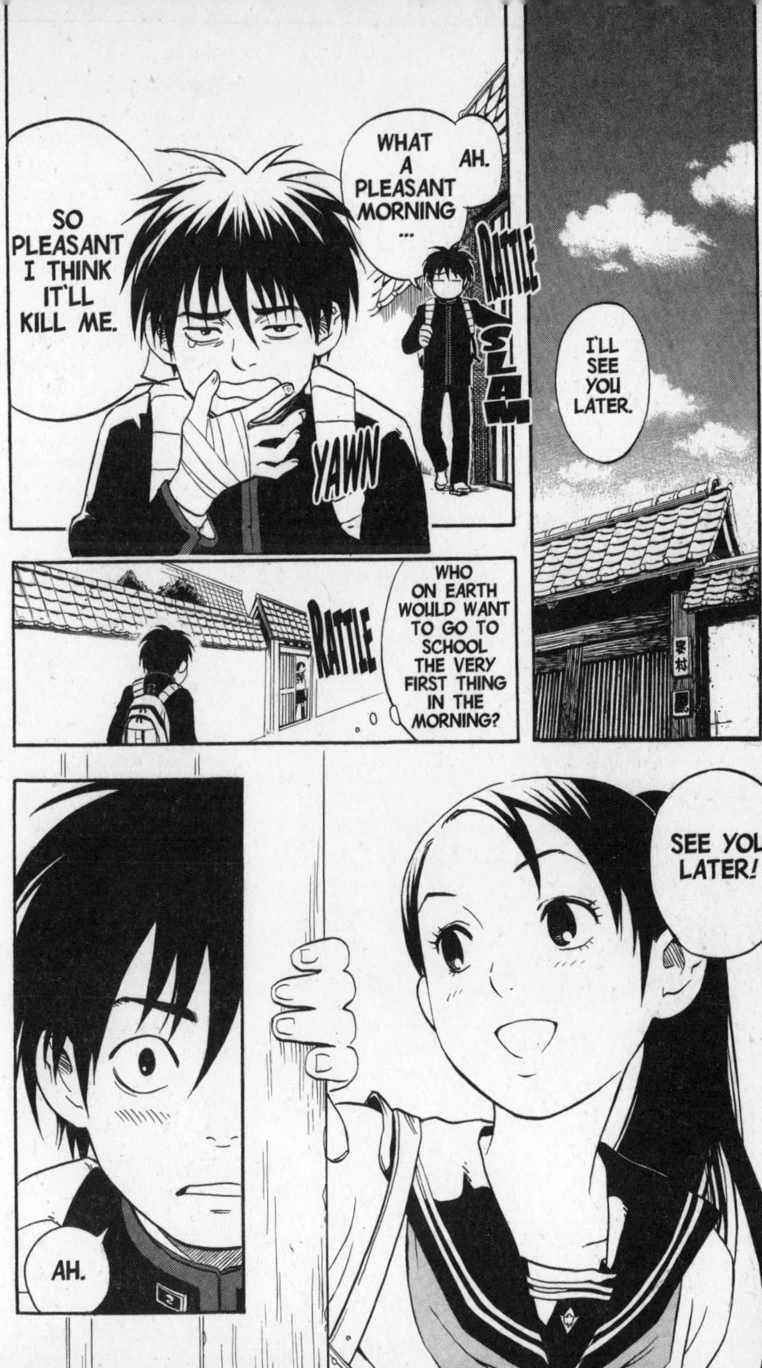
I'LL SEE YOU LATER.
AH. WHAT A PLEASANT MORNING ...
RATTLE
SLAM
SO PLEASANT I THINK IT'LL KILL ME.
YAWN
WHO ON EARTH WOULD WANT TO GO TO SCHOOL THE VERY FIRST THING IN THE MORNING?
RATTLE
SEE YOU LATER!
AH.

YOU LOOK SULKY AS USUAL.

SHE SIGHED WHEN SHE SAW MY FACE!!

IT BRINGS ME DOWN.

...

UH.

AH.

HEY.

STEP STEP STEP

STEP STEP

RIGHT NOW YOU'RE THE ONE TALKING TO ME. IS THAT ACCEPTABLE?

OR, DOES THE RULE NOT APPLY WHEN WE'RE ON THE WAY TO SCHOOL?

OKAY, FINE. JUST DON'T TALK TO ME DURING THE DAY, ALL RIGHT?

THEY'RE THE SAME. THEY STAND ON THE SAME GROUNDS.

YOUR JUNIOR HIGH AND MY HIGH SCHOOL ARE NOT THE SAME. THEY'RE IN DIFFERENT BUILDINGS.

I CAN'T HELP IT. WE ATTEND THE SAME SCHOOL.

STOP FOLLOWING ME, KID!

67

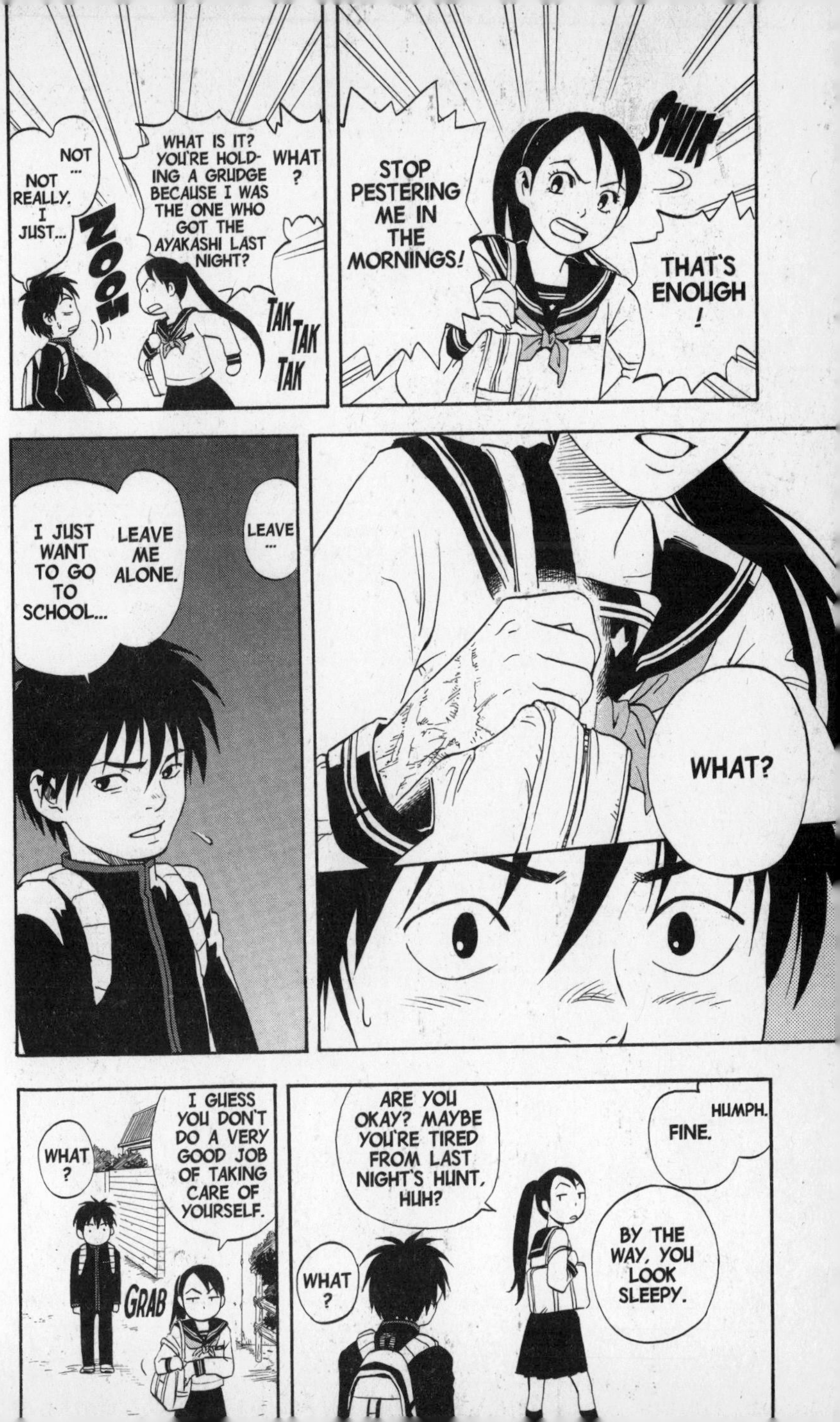
SHIK
STOP PESTERING ME IN THE MORNINGS!
THAT'S ENOUGH!
WHAT?
WHAT IS IT? YOU'RE HOLDING A GRUDGE BECAUSE I WAS THE ONE WHO GOT THE AYAKASHI LAST NIGHT?
NOT... NOT REALLY. I JUST...
NOOM
TAK TAK TAK
WHAT?
LEAVE...
LEAVE ME ALONE.
I JUST WANT TO GO TO SCHOOL...
HUMPH. FINE.
BY THE WAY, YOU LOOK SLEEPY.
ARE YOU OKAY? MAYBE YOU'RE TIRED FROM LAST NIGHT'S HUNT, HUH?
WHAT?
I GUESS YOU DON'T DO A VERY GOOD JOB OF TAKING CARE OF YOURSELF.
WHAT?
GRAB

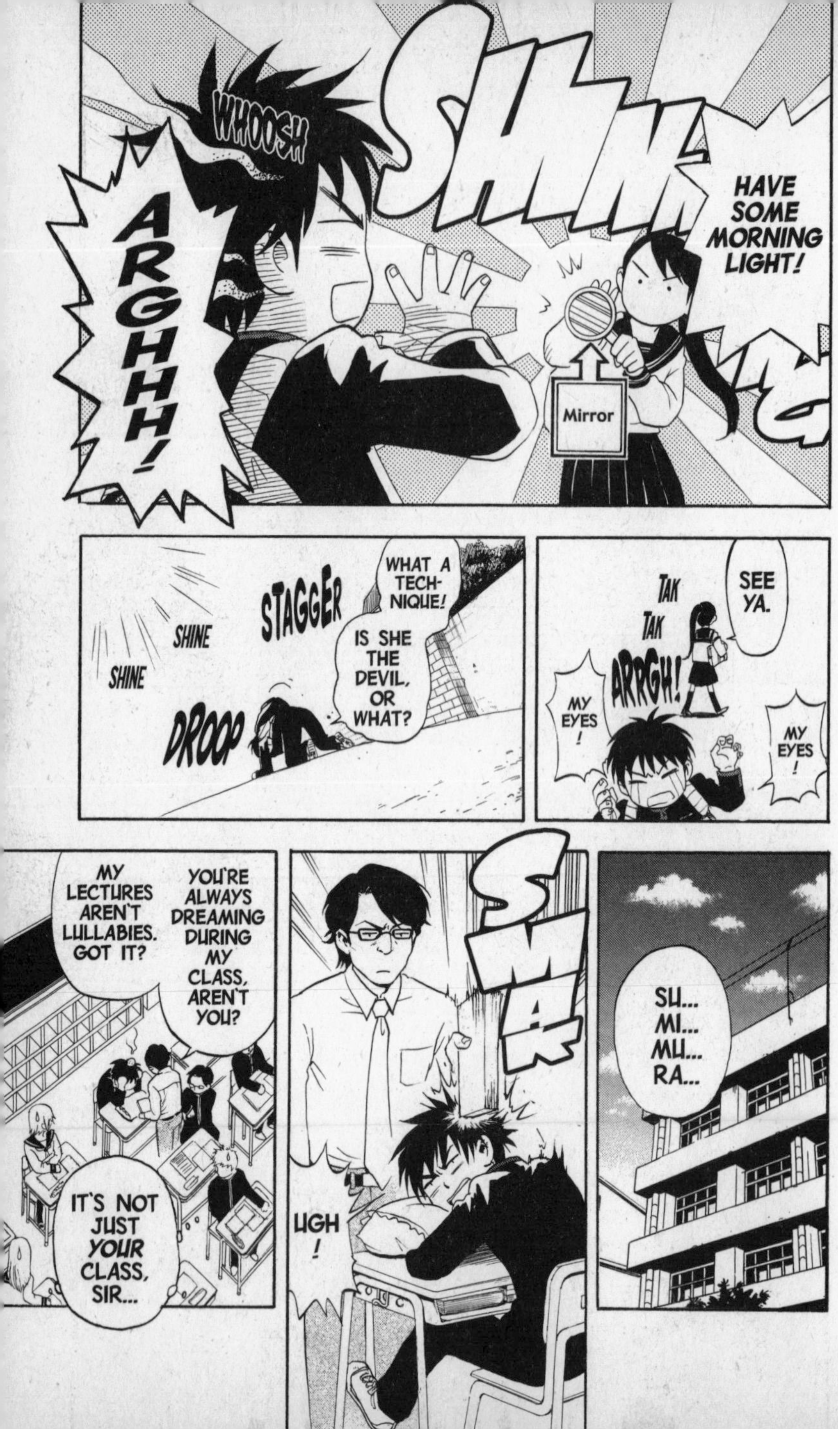
HAVE SOME MORNING LIGHT!
Mirror
WHOOSH
ARGHHH!
SEE YA.
TAK TAK
ARRGH!
MY EYES!
MY EYES!
WHAT A TECHNIQUE!
IS SHE THE DEVIL, OR WHAT?
STAGGER
SHINE
SHINE
DROOP
SU... MI... MU... RA...
SMAK
UGH!
YOU'RE ALWAYS DREAMING DURING MY CLASS, AREN'T YOU?
MY LECTURES AREN'T LULLABIES. GOT IT?
IT'S NOT JUST *YOUR* CLASS, SIR...

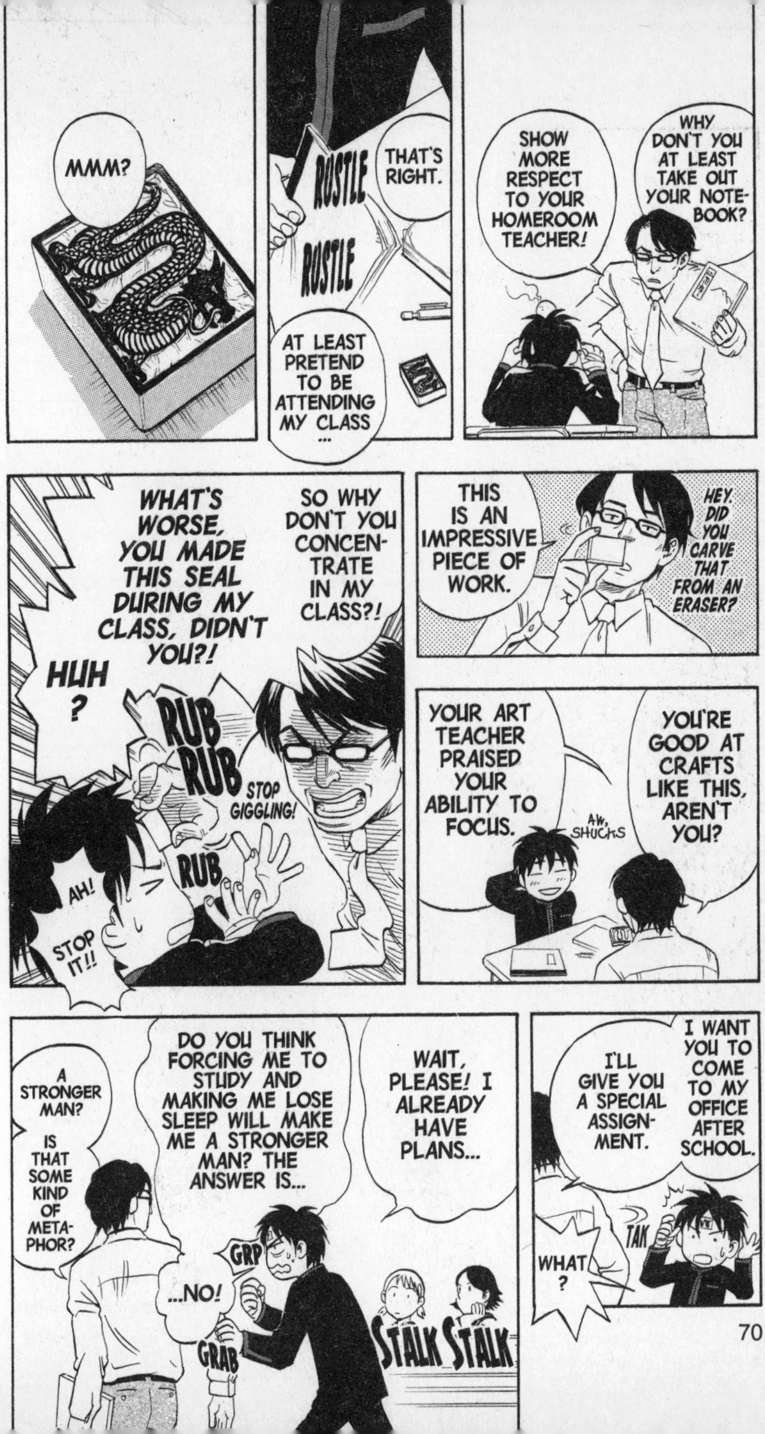
WHY DON'T YOU AT LEAST TAKE OUT YOUR NOTE-BOOK?
SHOW MORE RESPECT TO YOUR HOMEROOM TEACHER!
THAT'S RIGHT.
RUSTLE
RUSTLE
AT LEAST PRETEND TO BE ATTENDING MY CLASS ...
MMM?
HEY. DID YOU CARVE THAT FROM AN ERASER?
THIS IS AN IMPRESSIVE PIECE OF WORK.
YOU'RE GOOD AT CRAFTS LIKE THIS, AREN'T YOU?
AW, SHUCKS
YOUR ART TEACHER PRAISED YOUR ABILITY TO FOCUS.
SO WHY DON'T YOU CONCEN-TRATE IN MY CLASS?!
WHAT'S WORSE, YOU MADE THIS SEAL DURING MY CLASS, DIDN'T YOU?!
HUH ?
RUB RUB
STOP GIGGLING!
RUB
AH!
STOP IT!!
I WANT YOU TO COME TO MY OFFICE AFTER SCHOOL.
I'LL GIVE YOU A SPECIAL ASSIGN-MENT.
TAK
WHAT ?
WAIT, PLEASE! I ALREADY HAVE PLANS...
STALK STALK
DO YOU THINK FORCING ME TO STUDY AND MAKING ME LOSE SLEEP WILL MAKE ME A STRONGER MAN? THE ANSWER IS...
GRP
GRAB
...NO!
A STRONGER MAN?
IS THAT SOME KIND OF META-PHOR?

I TOLD YOU TO PREPARE THIS PROBLEM, DIDN'T I?

WHAT'S WRONG?

I'M SORRY...

CLOP

CLOP

HOW ABOUT YOU, MISS YUKIMURA?

SURE.

HUH?

IS IT SUPPOSED TO BE MY TURN?

WELL DONE, MISS YUKIMURA!

YOU'RE AS FLAWLESS AS YOUR EQUATIONS.

WOW

TAP

TAP

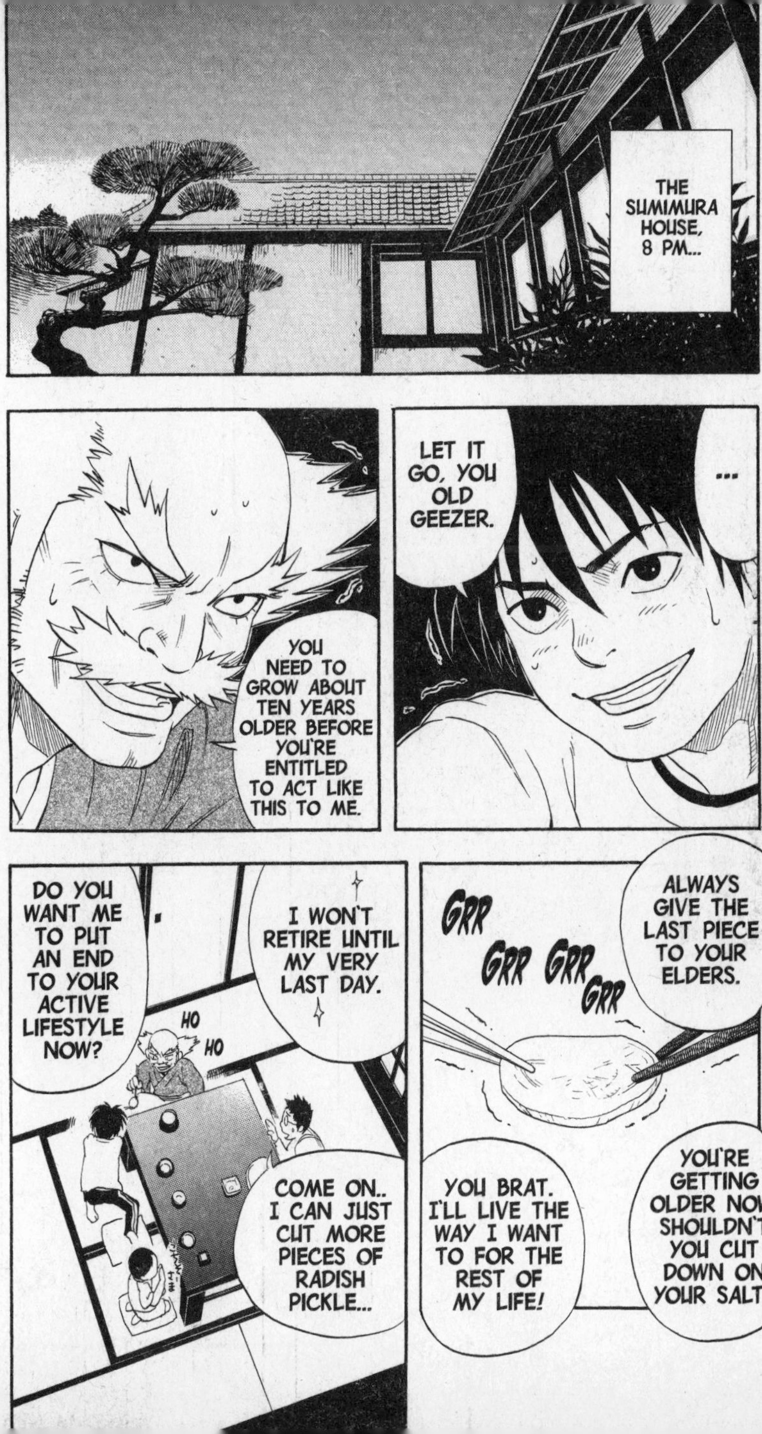
THE SUMIMURA HOUSE, 8 PM...
...
LET IT GO, YOU OLD GEEZER.
YOU NEED TO GROW ABOUT TEN YEARS OLDER BEFORE YOU'RE ENTITLED TO ACT LIKE THIS TO ME.
ALWAYS GIVE THE LAST PIECE TO YOUR ELDERS.
GRR GRR GRR GRR
YOU'RE GETTING OLDER NOW. SHOULDN'T YOU CUT DOWN ON YOUR SALT?
YOU BRAT. I'LL LIVE THE WAY I WANT TO FOR THE REST OF MY LIFE!
I WON'T RETIRE UNTIL MY VERY LAST DAY.
DO YOU WANT ME TO PUT AN END TO YOUR ACTIVE LIFESTYLE NOW?
HO HO
COME ON.. I CAN JUST CUT MORE PIECES OF RADISH PICKLE...

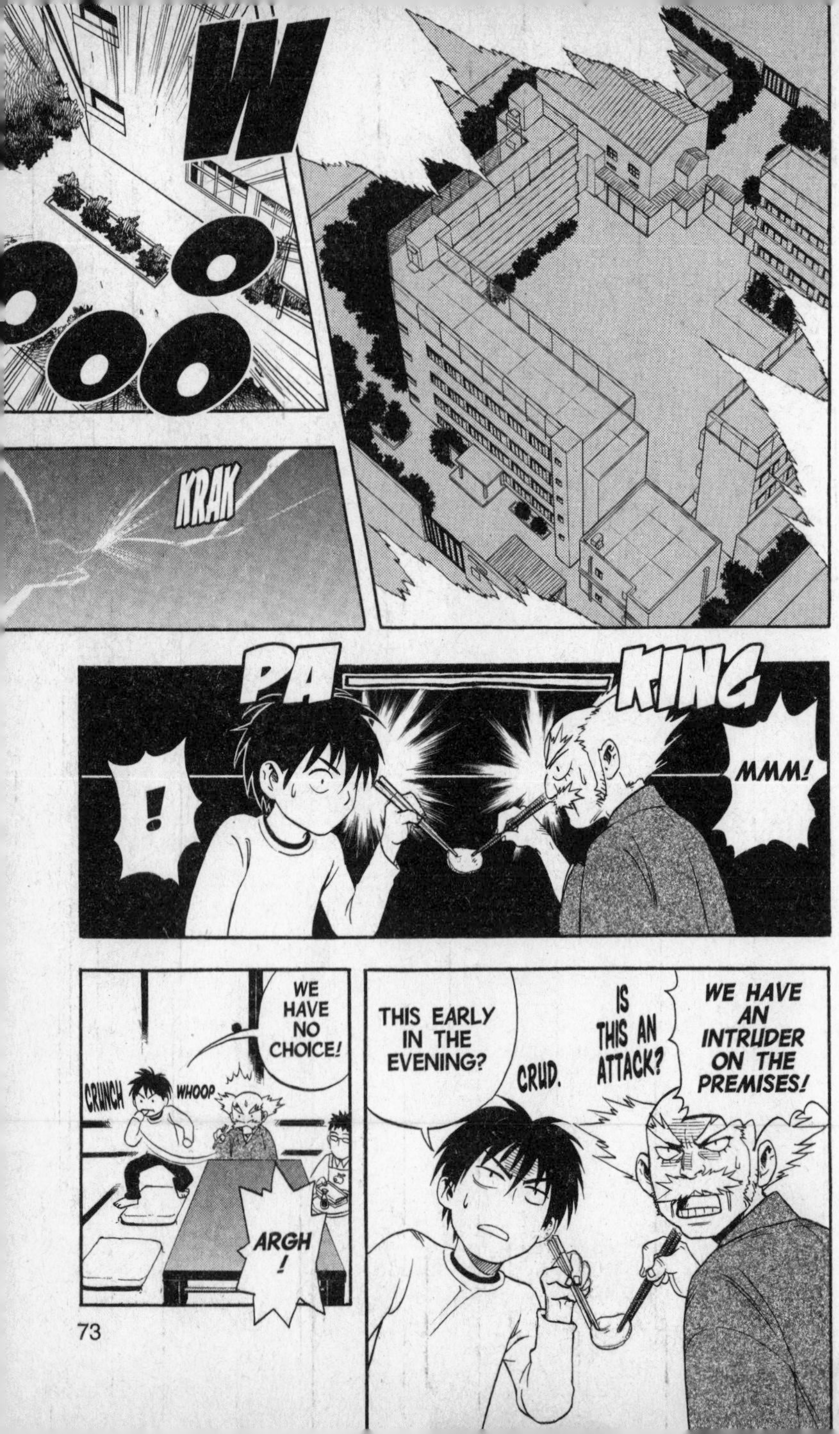
WOOOOO
KRAK
MMM!
PA—KING
!
WE HAVE AN INTRUDER ON THE PREMISES!
IS THIS AN ATTACK?
CRUD.
THIS EARLY IN THE EVENING?
WE HAVE NO CHOICE!
WHOOP
CRUNCH
ARGH!

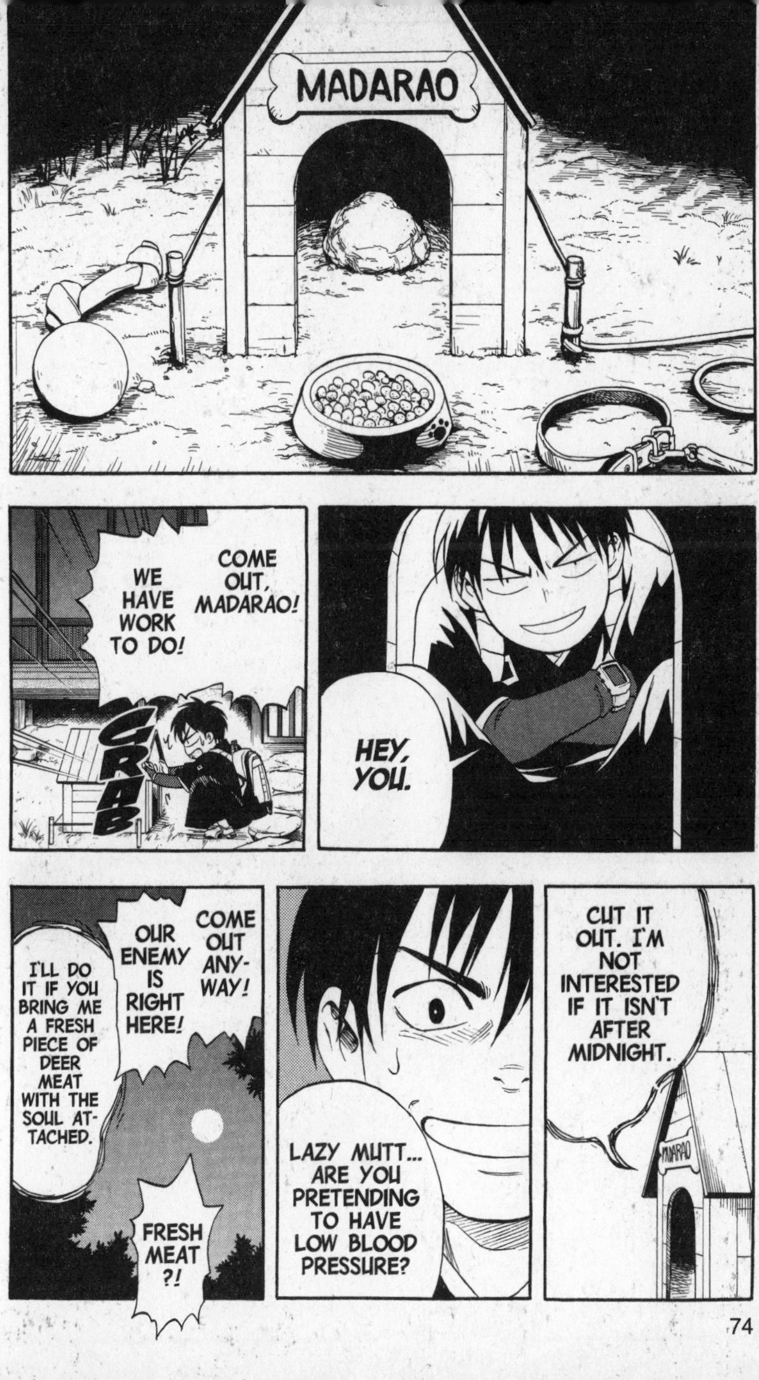
MADARAO
HEY, YOU.
COME OUT, MADARAO!
WE HAVE WORK TO DO!
GRAB
CUT IT OUT. I'M NOT INTERESTED IF IT ISN'T AFTER MIDNIGHT.
LAZY MUTT... ARE YOU PRETENDING TO HAVE LOW BLOOD PRESSURE?
COME OUT ANY-WAY!
OUR ENEMY IS RIGHT HERE!
I'LL DO IT IF YOU BRING ME A FRESH PIECE OF DEER MEAT WITH THE SOUL AT-TACHED.
FRESH MEAT ?!

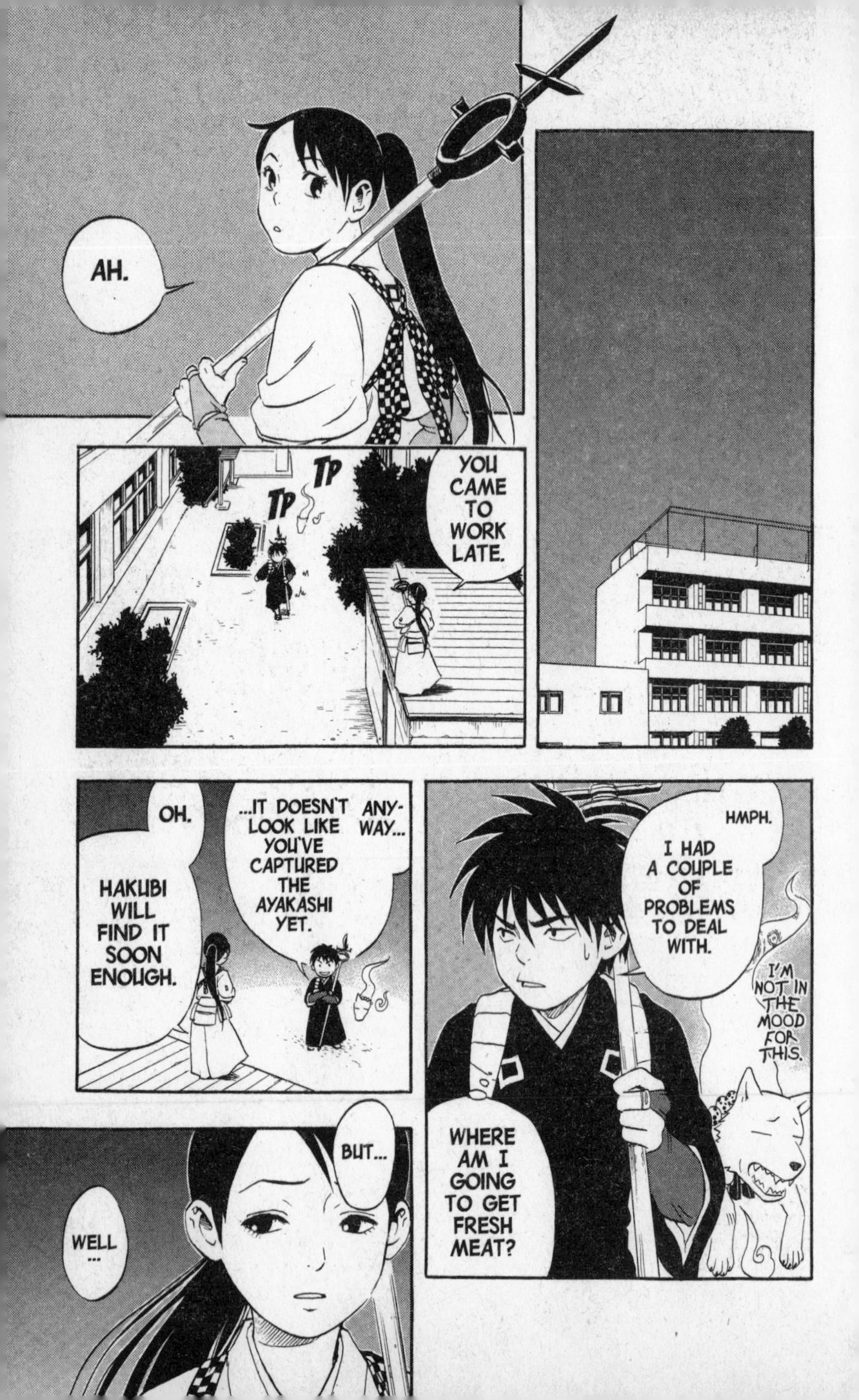
AH.
TP
TP
YOU CAME TO WORK LATE.
HMPH.
I HAD A COUPLE OF PROBLEMS TO DEAL WITH.
I'M NOT IN THE MOOD FOR THIS.
WHERE AM I GOING TO GET FRESH MEAT?
ANYWAY...
...IT DOESN'T LOOK LIKE YOU'VE CAPTURED THE AYAKASHI YET.
OH.
HAKUBI WILL FIND IT SOON ENOUGH.
BUT...
WELL...

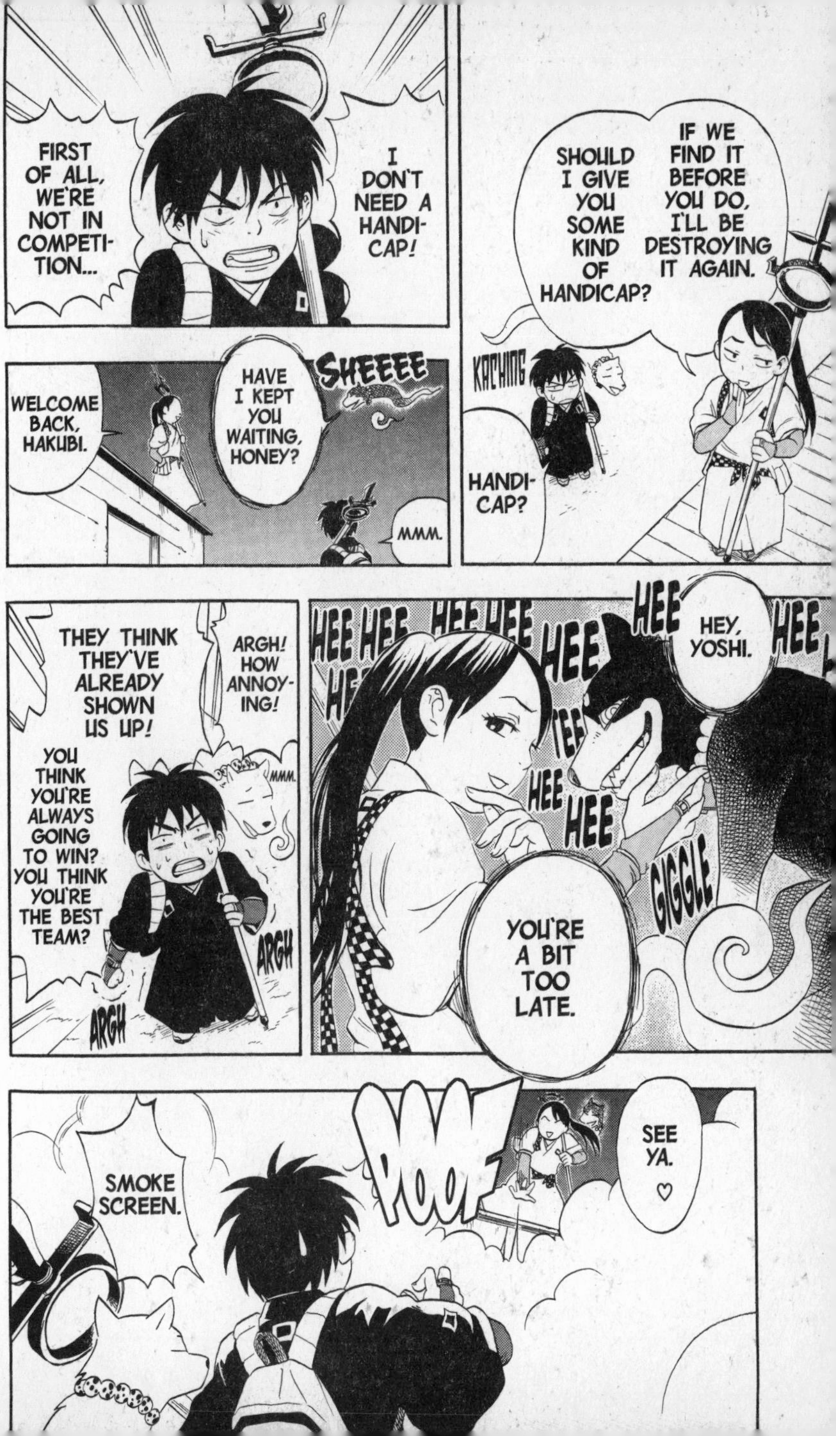

IF WE FIND IT BEFORE YOU DO, I'LL BE DESTROYING IT AGAIN.
SHOULD I GIVE YOU SOME KIND OF HANDICAP?
KACHING
HANDI-CAP?
I DON'T NEED A HANDI-CAP!
FIRST OF ALL, WE'RE NOT IN COMPETITI-TION...
SHEEEE
HAVE I KEPT YOU WAITING, HONEY?
WELCOME BACK, HAKUBI.
MMM.
HEE HEE HEE HEE HEE HEE HEE
HEY, YOSHI.
HEE HEE HEE
YOU'RE A BIT TOO LATE.
GIGGLE
ARGH! HOW ANNOY-ING!
THEY THINK THEY'VE ALREADY SHOWN US UP!
MMM.
YOU THINK YOU'RE ALWAYS GOING TO WIN? YOU THINK YOU'RE THE BEST TEAM?
ARGH
ARGH
SEE YA. ♡
POOF
SMOKE SCREEN.

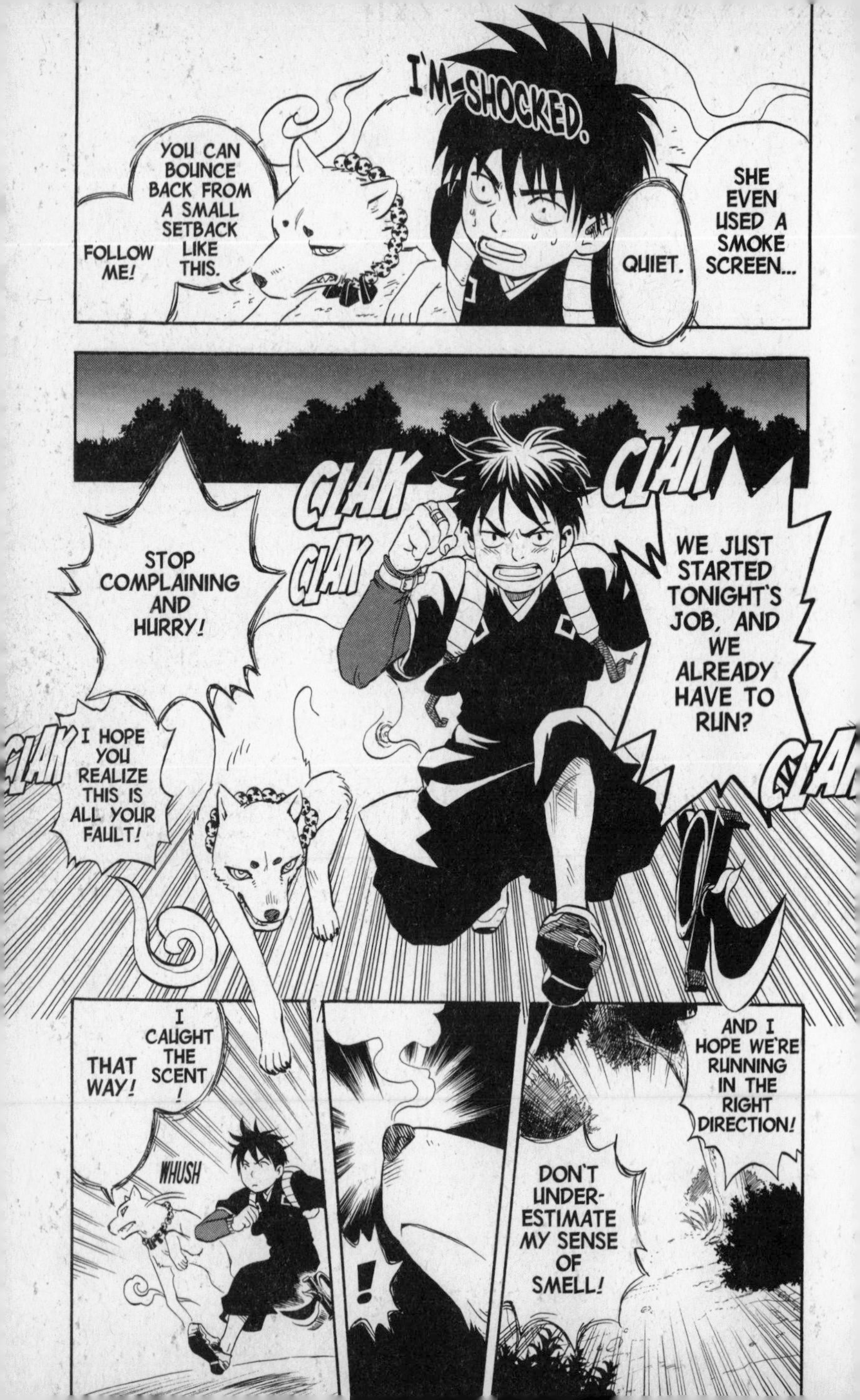
SHE EVEN USED A SMOKE SCREEN...
I'M SHOCKED.
QUIET.
YOU CAN BOUNCE BACK FROM A SMALL SETBACK LIKE THIS.
FOLLOW ME!
CLAK
WE JUST STARTED TONIGHT'S JOB, AND WE ALREADY HAVE TO RUN?
CLAK
CLAK
STOP COMPLAINING AND HURRY!
CLAK
I HOPE YOU REALIZE THIS IS ALL YOUR FAULT!
AND I HOPE WE'RE RUNNING IN THE RIGHT DIRECTION!
DON'T UNDER-ESTIMATE MY SENSE OF SMELL!
!
I CAUGHT THE SCENT!
THAT WAY!
WHUSH

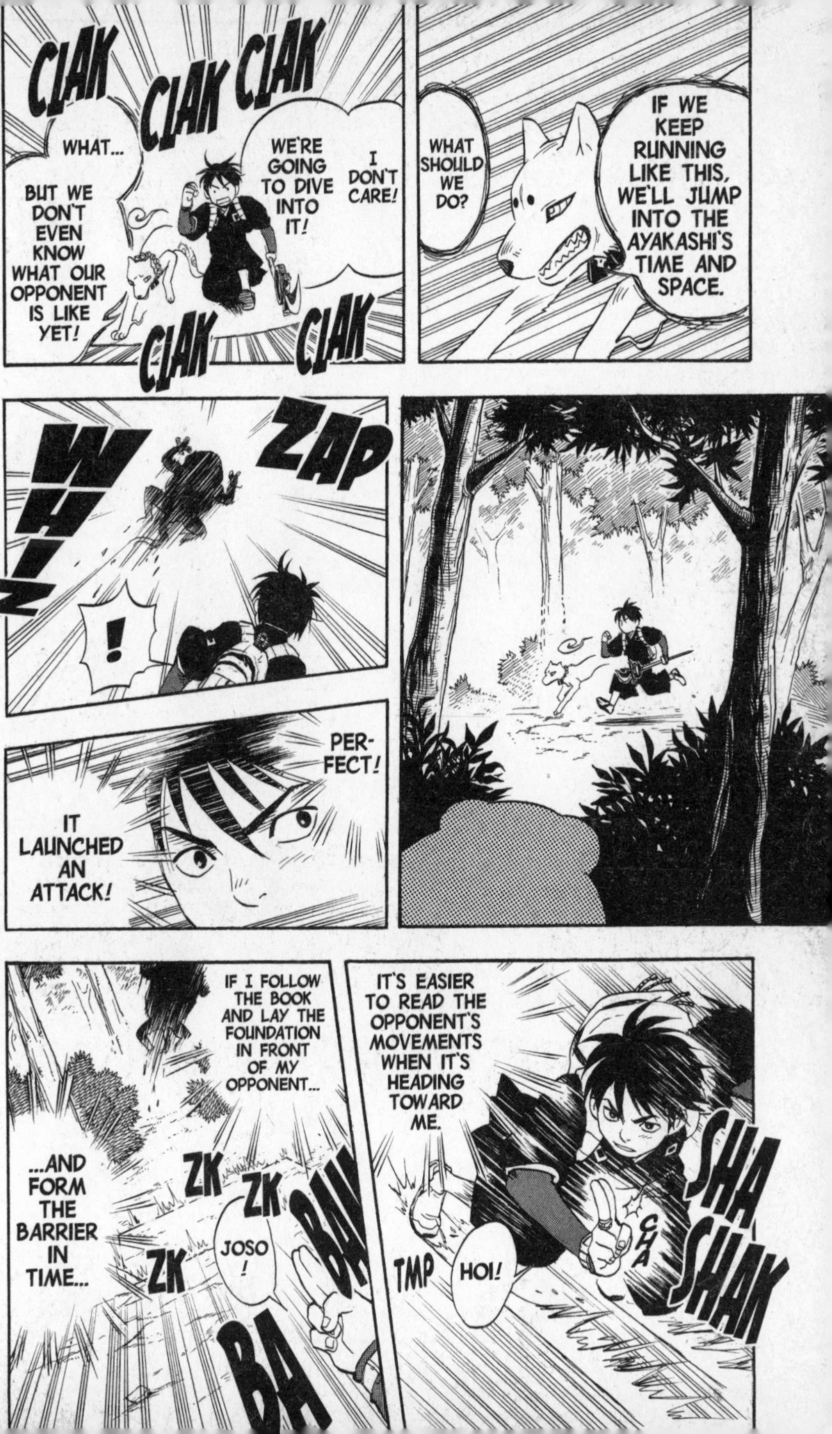
WHAT SHOULD WE DO?
IF WE KEEP RUNNING LIKE THIS, WE'LL JUMP INTO THE AYAKASHI'S TIME AND SPACE.
CLAK CLAK CLAK
WHAT... BUT WE DON'T EVEN KNOW WHAT OUR OPPONENT IS LIKE YET!
I DON'T CARE!
WE'RE GOING TO DIVE INTO IT!
CLAK CLAK
ZAP
WHIZ
!
PER-FECT!
IT LAUNCHED AN ATTACK!
IT'S EASIER TO READ THE OPPONENT'S MOVEMENTS WHEN IT'S HEADING TOWARD ME.
SHA SHAK
CHA
HOI!
TMP
IF I FOLLOW THE BOOK AND LAY THE FOUNDATION IN FRONT OF MY OPPONENT...
...AND FORM THE BARRIER IN TIME...
ZK ZK ZK
JOSO!
BA BAN

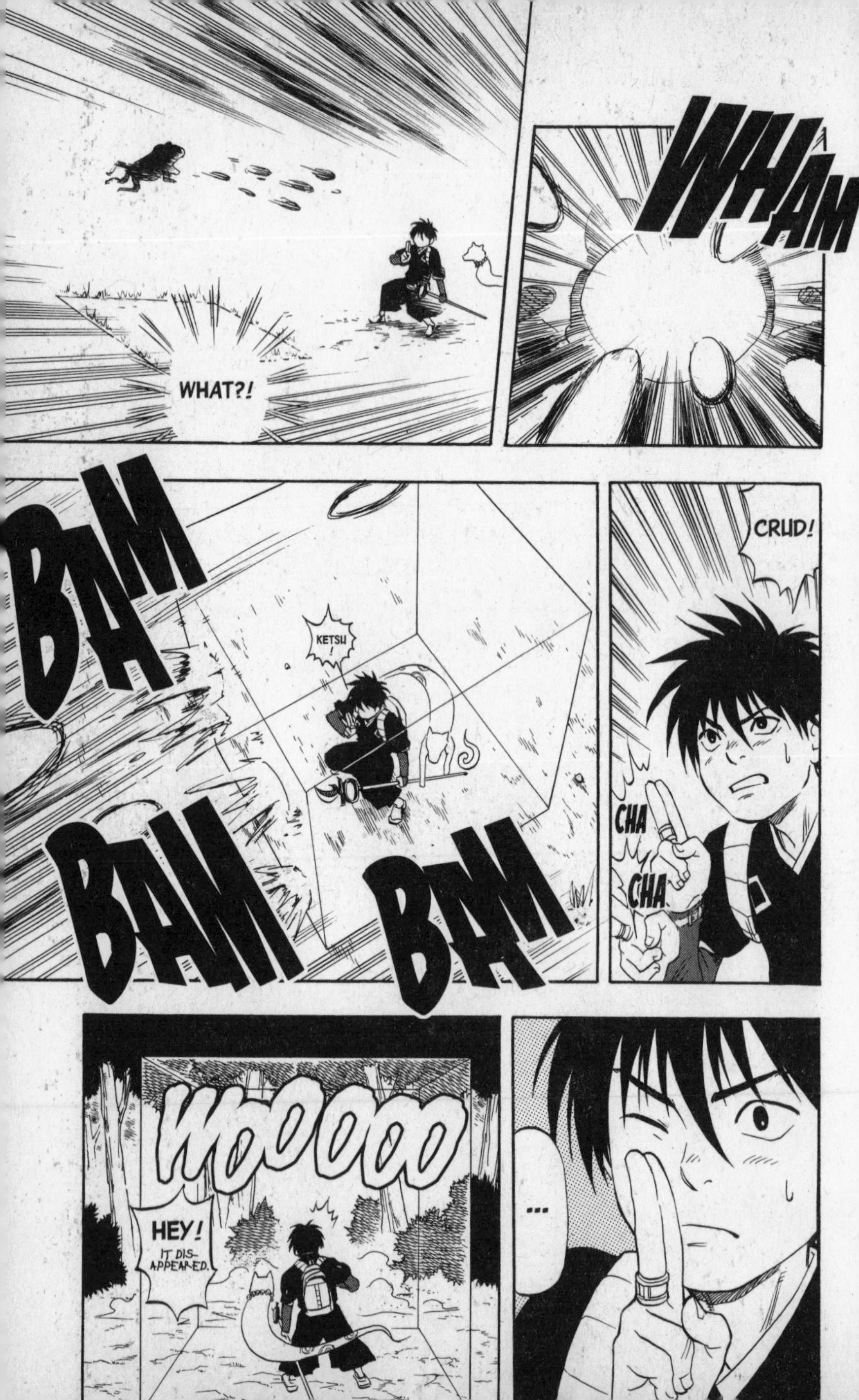
WHAM
WHAT?!
CRUD!
CHA
CHA
BAM
KETSU!
BAM
BAM
...
WOOOOO
HEY!
IT DIS-APPEARED.

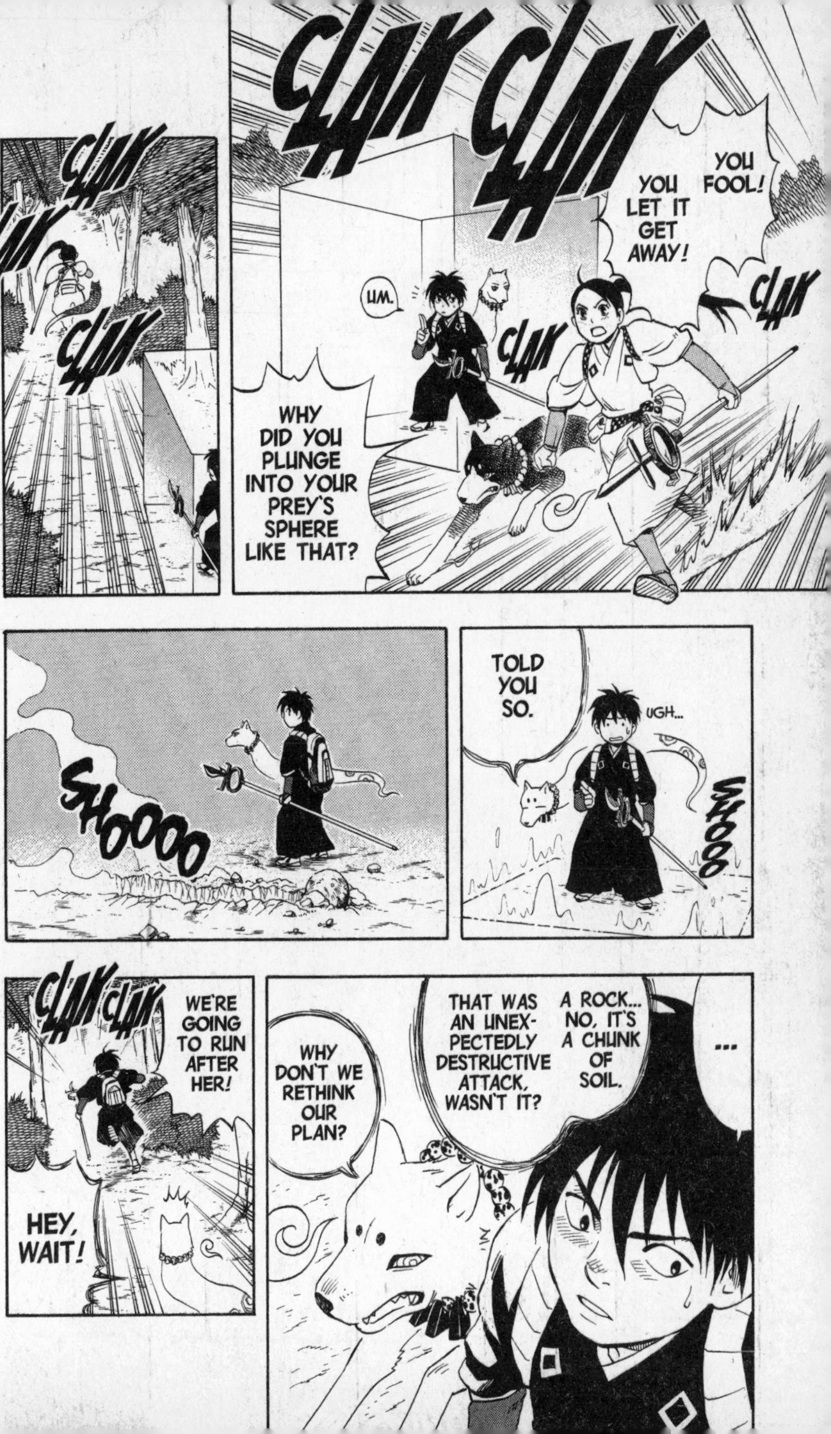
CLAK CLAK
YOU FOOL!
YOU LET IT GET AWAY!
UM.
CLAK
CLAK
WHY DID YOU PLUNGE INTO YOUR PREY'S SPHERE LIKE THAT?
CLAK
CLAK
CLAK
TOLD YOU SO.
UGH...
SHOOO
SHOOOO
...
A ROCK... NO, IT'S A CHUNK OF SOIL.
THAT WAS AN UNEX-PECTEDLY DESTRUCTIVE ATTACK, WASN'T IT?
WHY DON'T WE RETHINK OUR PLAN?
CLAK CLAK
WE'RE GOING TO RUN AFTER HER!
HEY, WAIT!

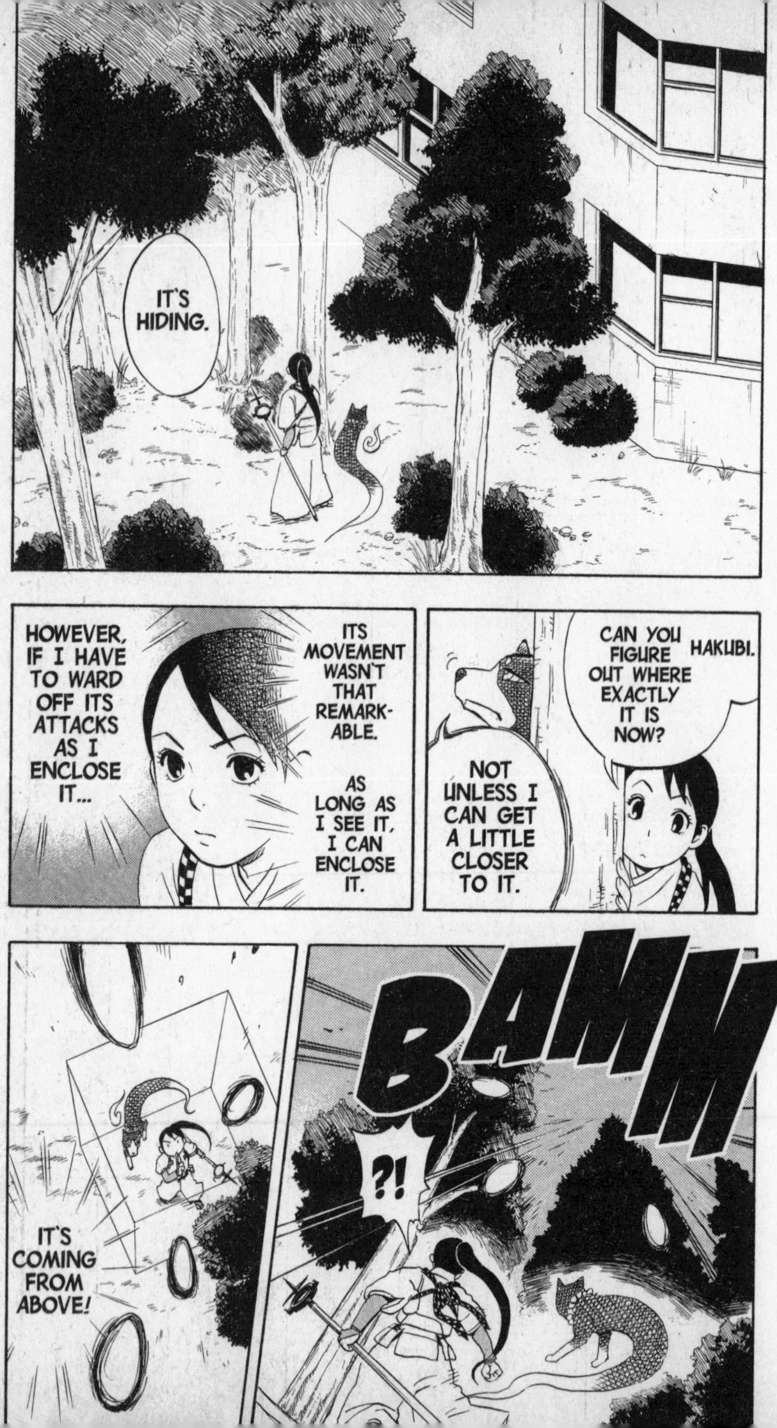
IT'S HIDING.
HAKUBI. CAN YOU FIGURE OUT WHERE EXACTLY IT IS NOW?
NOT UNLESS I CAN GET A LITTLE CLOSER TO IT.
ITS MOVEMENT WASN'T THAT REMARKABLE.
AS LONG AS I SEE IT, I CAN ENCLOSE IT.
HOWEVER, IF I HAVE TO WARD OFF ITS ATTACKS AS I ENCLOSE IT...
BAMM
?!
IT'S COMING FROM ABOVE!

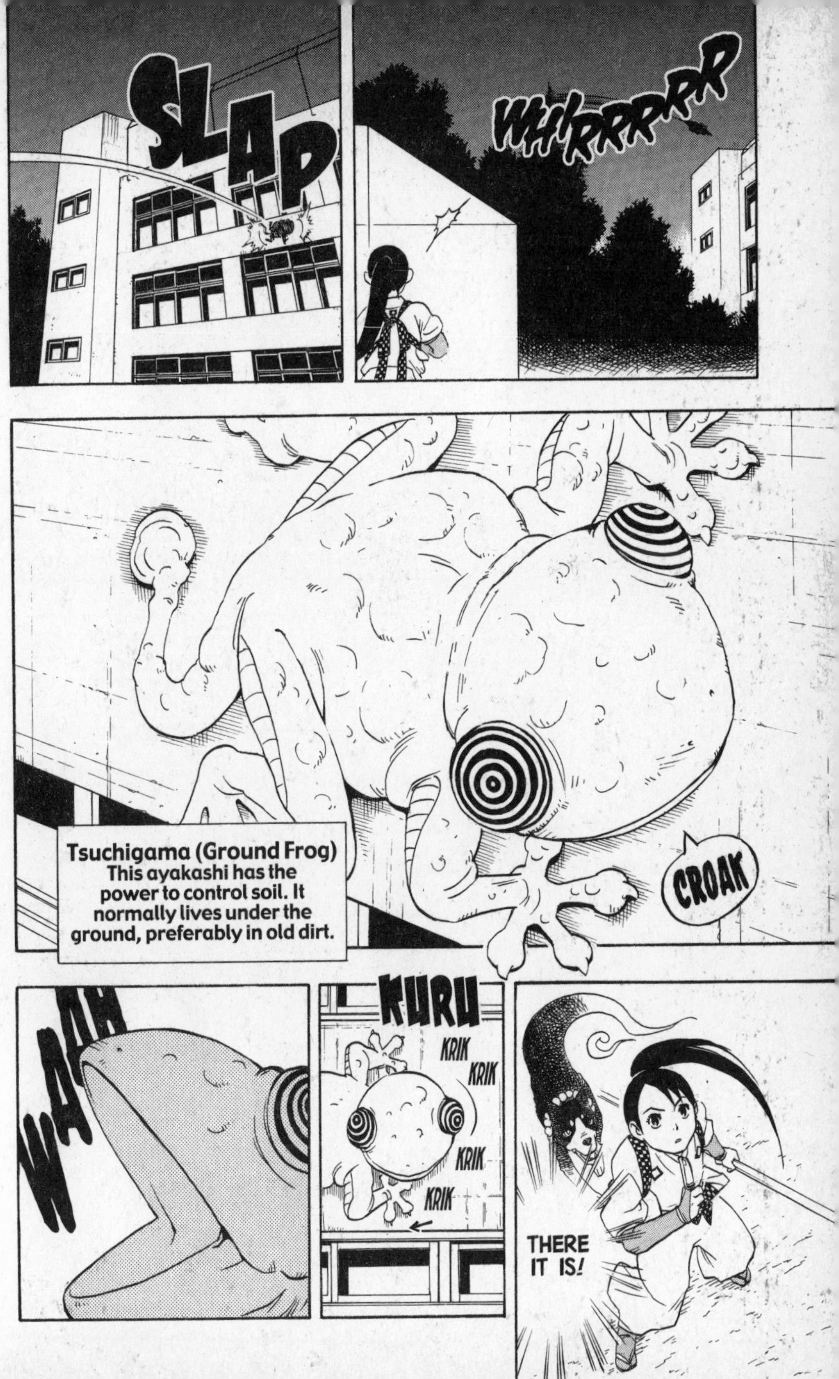
WHIRRRRRR
SLAP
Tsuchigama (Ground Frog)
This ayakashi has the power to control soil. It normally lives under the ground, preferably in old dirt.
CROAK
THERE IT IS!
KURU
KRIK
KRIK
KRIK
KRIK
WAAH

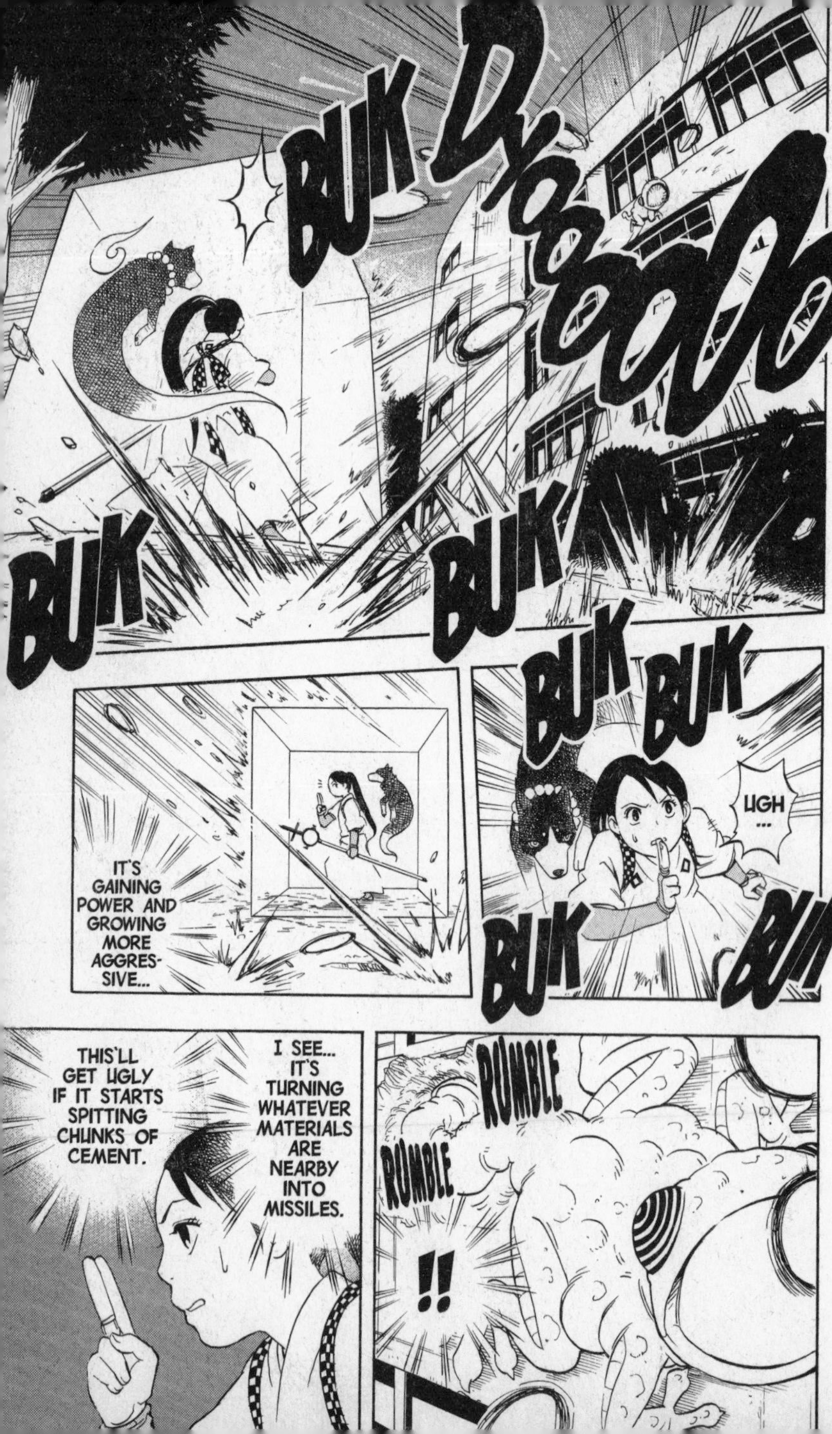
BUK
BUK
BUK
BUK
BUK
UGH...
BUK
BUK
IT'S GAINING POWER AND GROWING MORE AGGRES-SIVE...
RUMBLE
RUMBLE
!!
I SEE... IT'S TURNING WHATEVER MATERIALS ARE NEARBY INTO MISSILES.
THIS'LL GET UGLY IF IT STARTS SPITTING CHUNKS OF CEMENT.

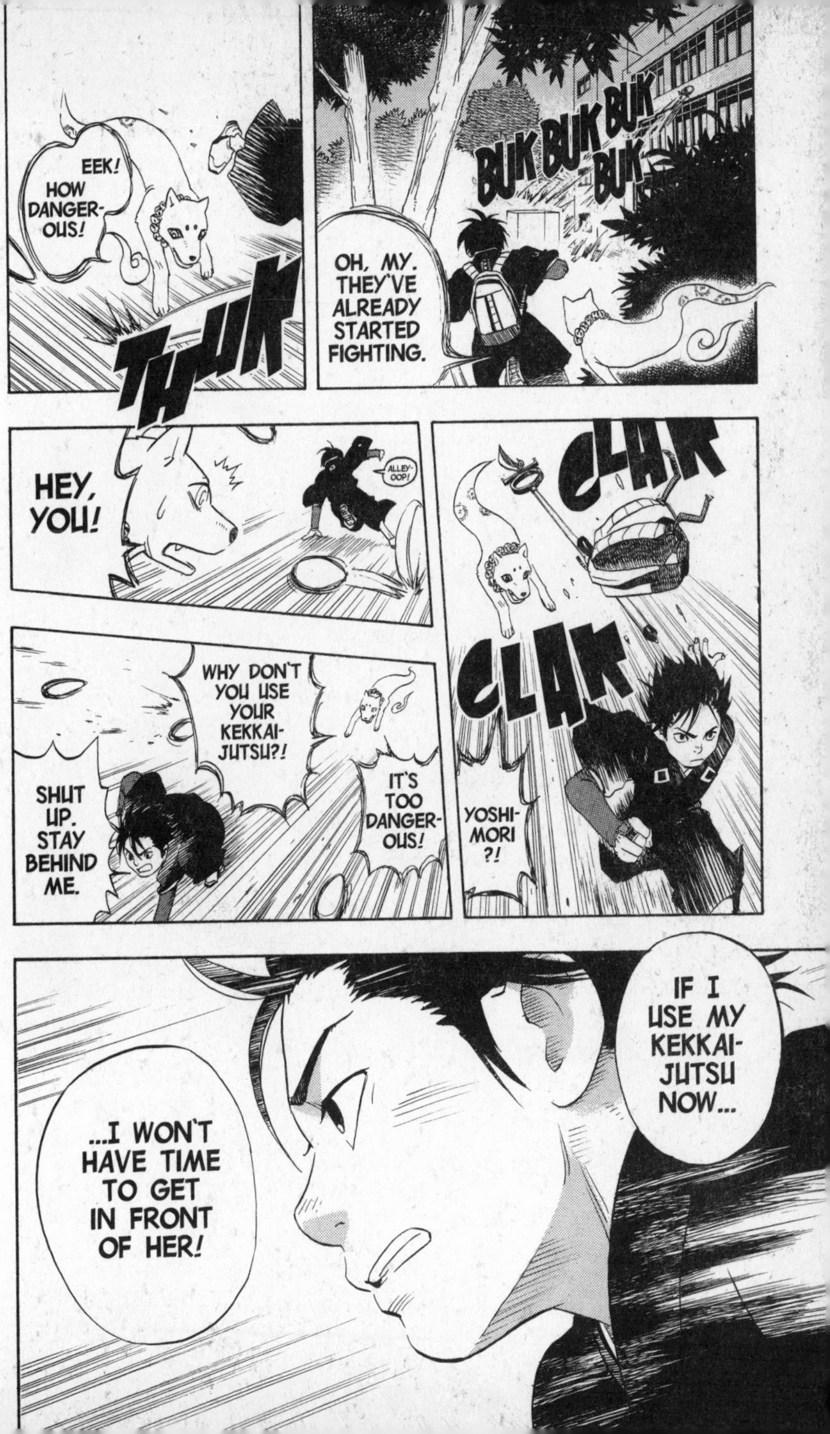
BUK BUK BUK BUK
OH, MY. THEY'VE ALREADY STARTED FIGHTING.
EEK! HOW DANGER-OUS!
THUK
CLAK
CLAK
YOSHI-MORI?!
HEY, YOU!
ALLEY-OOP!
WHY DON'T YOU USE YOUR KEKKAI-JUTSU?!
IT'S TOO DANGER-OUS!
SHUT UP. STAY BEHIND ME.
IF I USE MY KEKKAI-JUTSU NOW...
...I WON'T HAVE TIME TO GET IN FRONT OF HER!

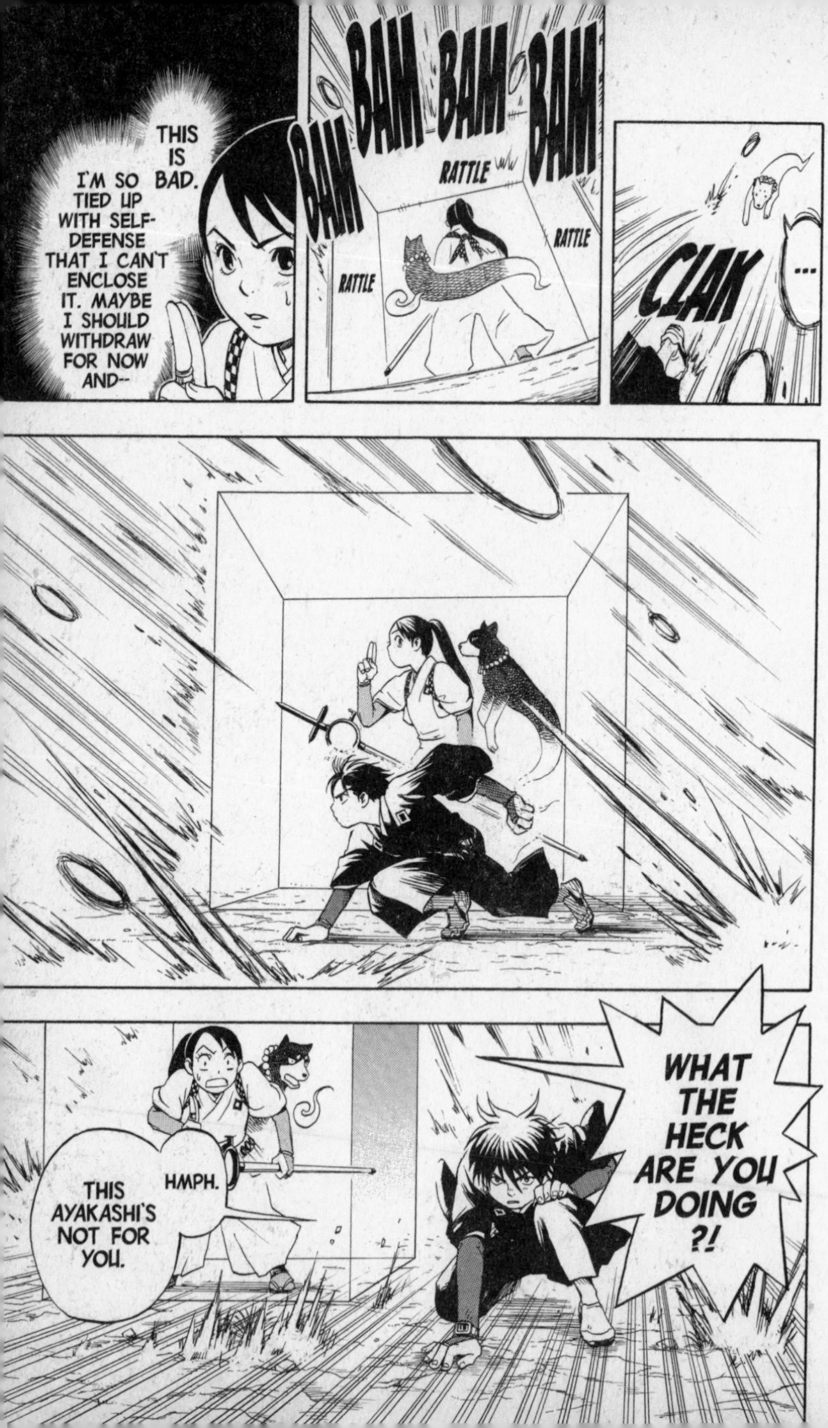
CLAK
...
BAM BAM BAM BAM
RATTLE
RATTLE
RATTLE
THIS IS BAD.
I'M SO TIED UP WITH SELF-DEFENSE THAT I CAN'T ENCLOSE IT. MAYBE I SHOULD WITHDRAW FOR NOW AND--
WHAT THE HECK ARE YOU DOING?!
HMPH.
THIS AYAKASHI'S NOT FOR YOU.

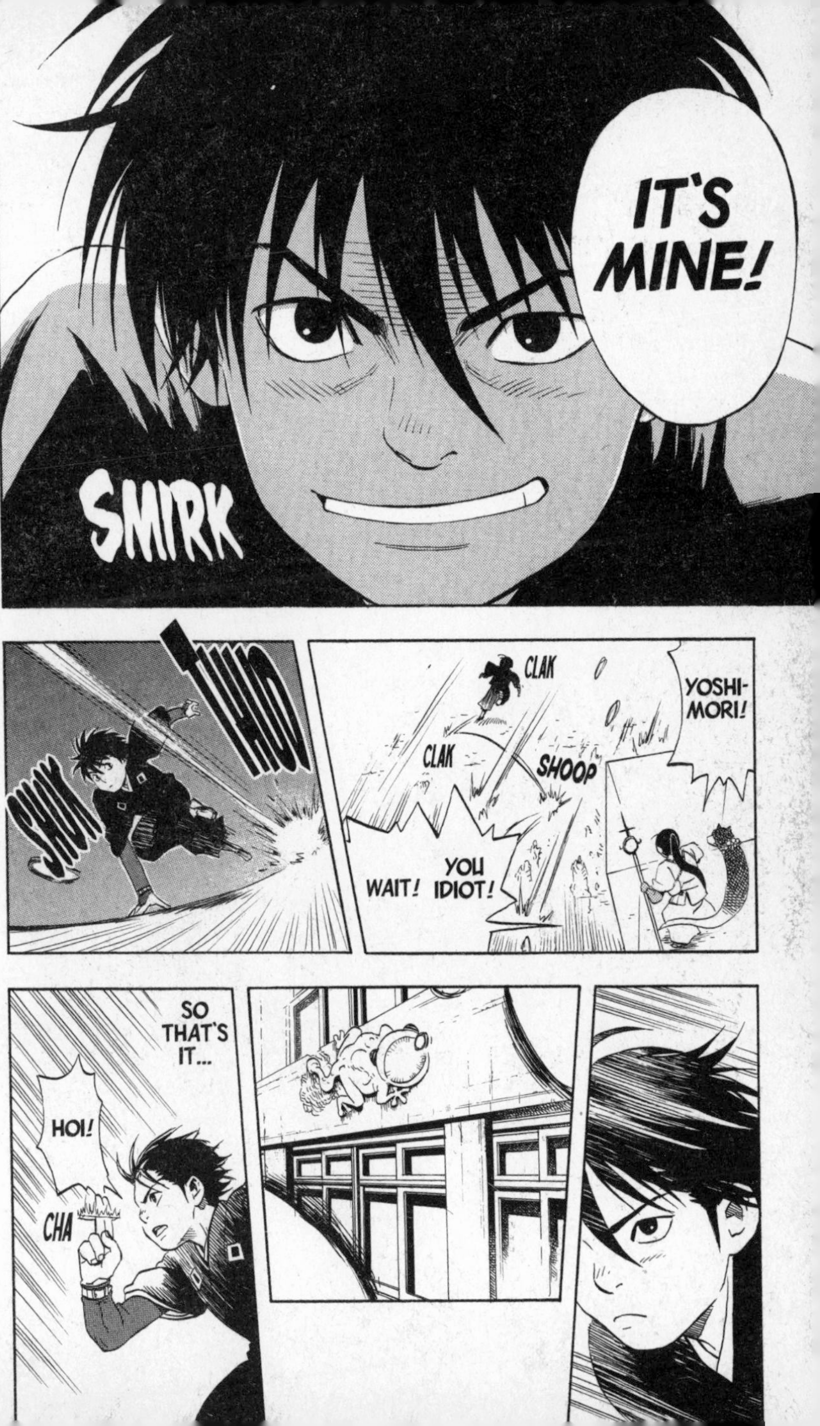
IT'S MINE!
SMIRK
YOSHI-MORI!
CLAK
CLAK
SHOOP
YOU IDIOT!
WAIT!
THUD
SHOK
SO THAT'S IT...
HOI!
CHA

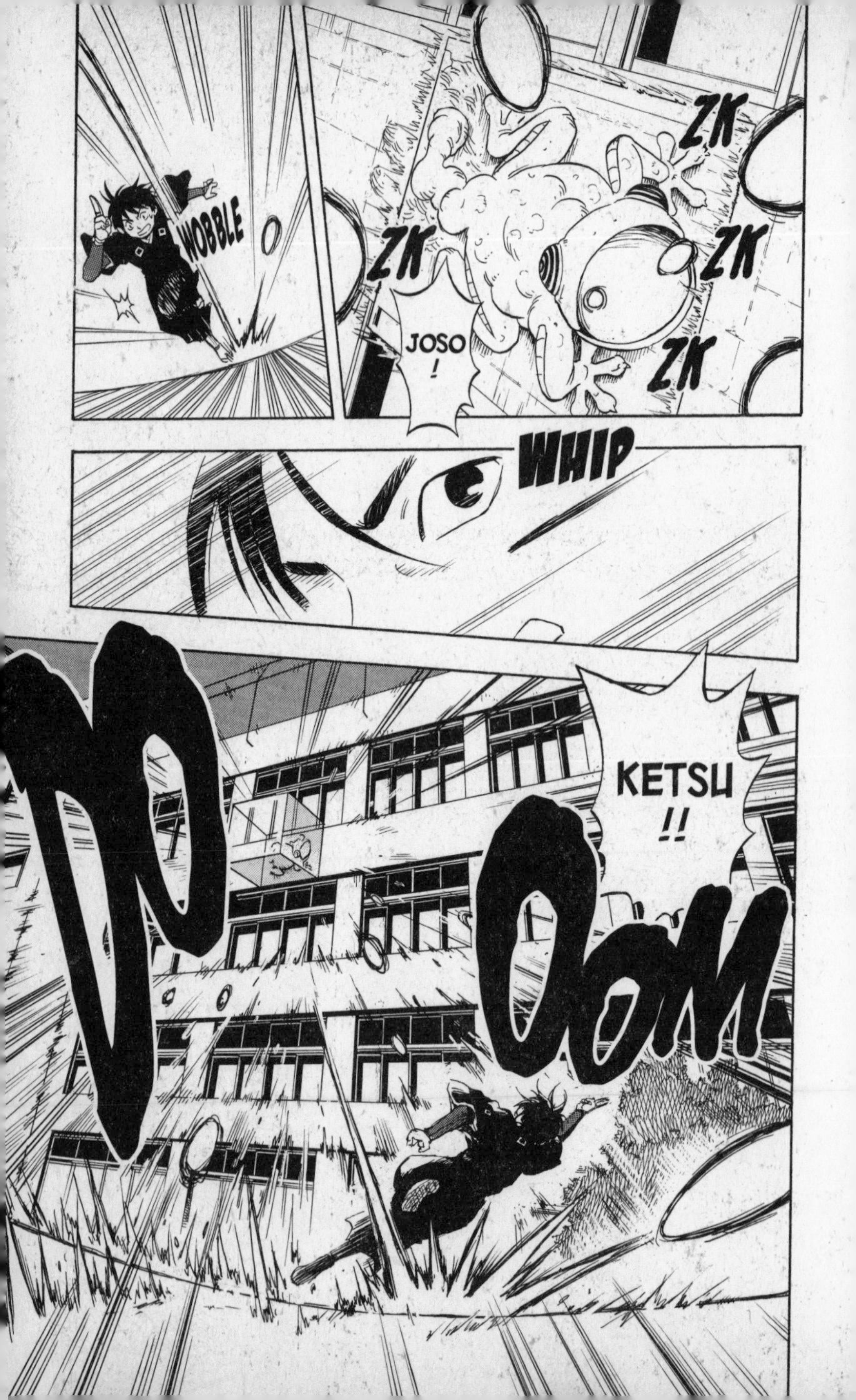
ZK
ZK
ZK
ZK
ZK
JOSO!
WOBBLE
WHIP
KETSU!!
DOOM

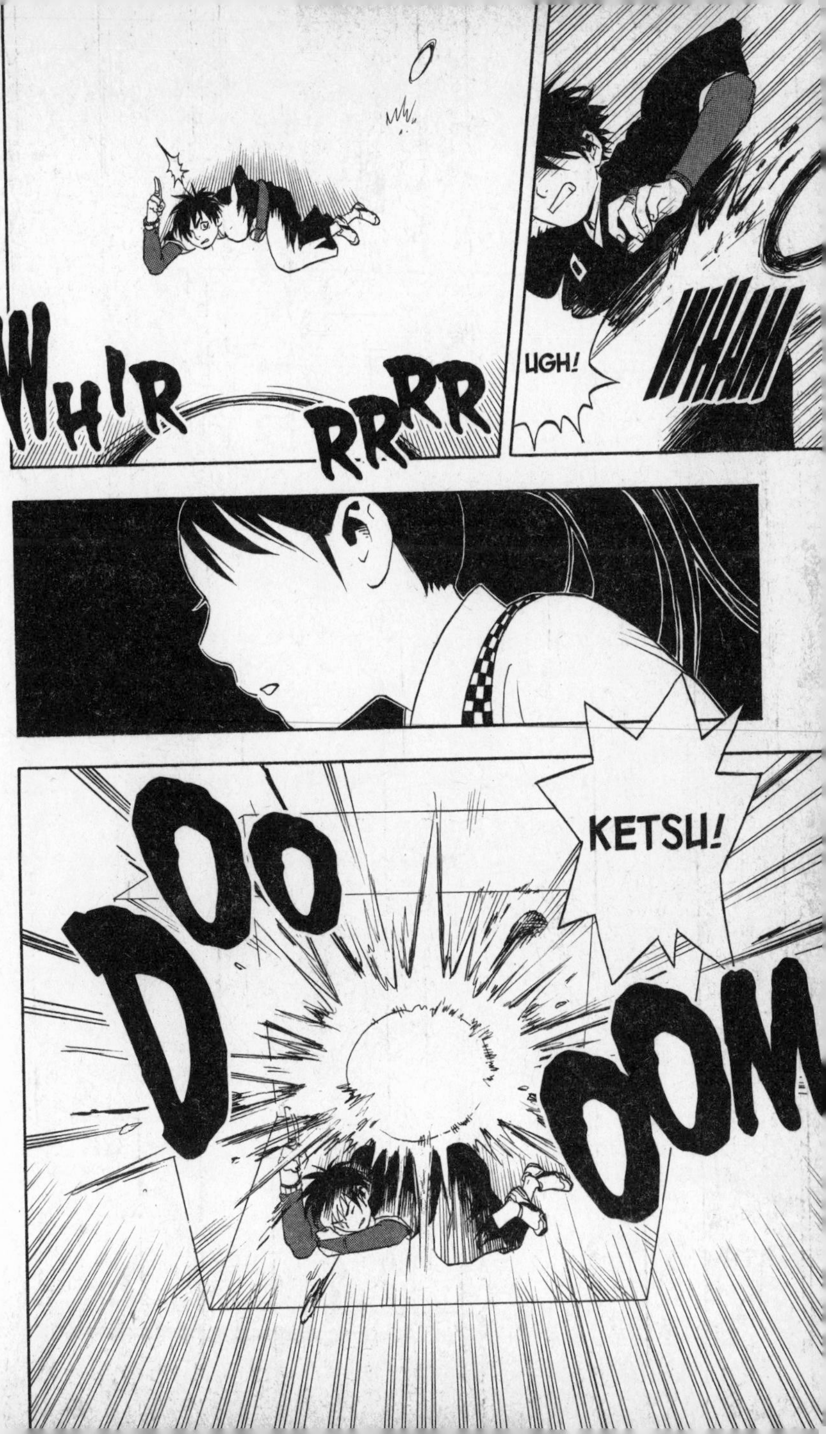
UGH!
WHAM
WHIR RRRR
KETSU!
DOO OOM

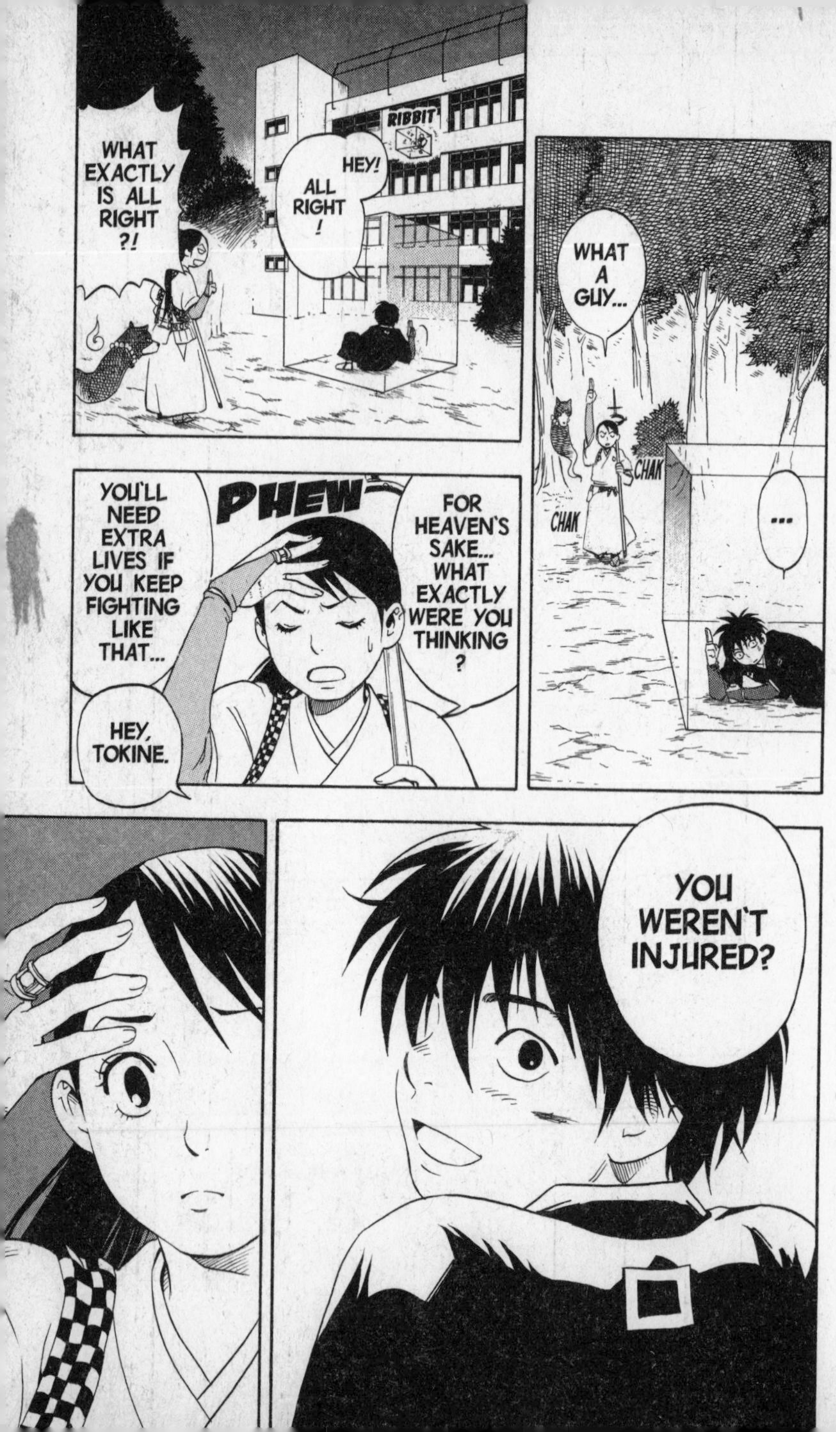
RIBBIT
HEY! ALL RIGHT!
WHAT EXACTLY IS ALL RIGHT ?!
WHAT A GUY...
CHAK
CHAK
...
PHEW
FOR HEAVEN'S SAKE... WHAT EXACTLY WERE YOU THINKING ?
YOU'LL NEED EXTRA LIVES IF YOU KEEP FIGHTING LIKE THAT...
HEY, TOKINE.
YOU WEREN'T INJURED?

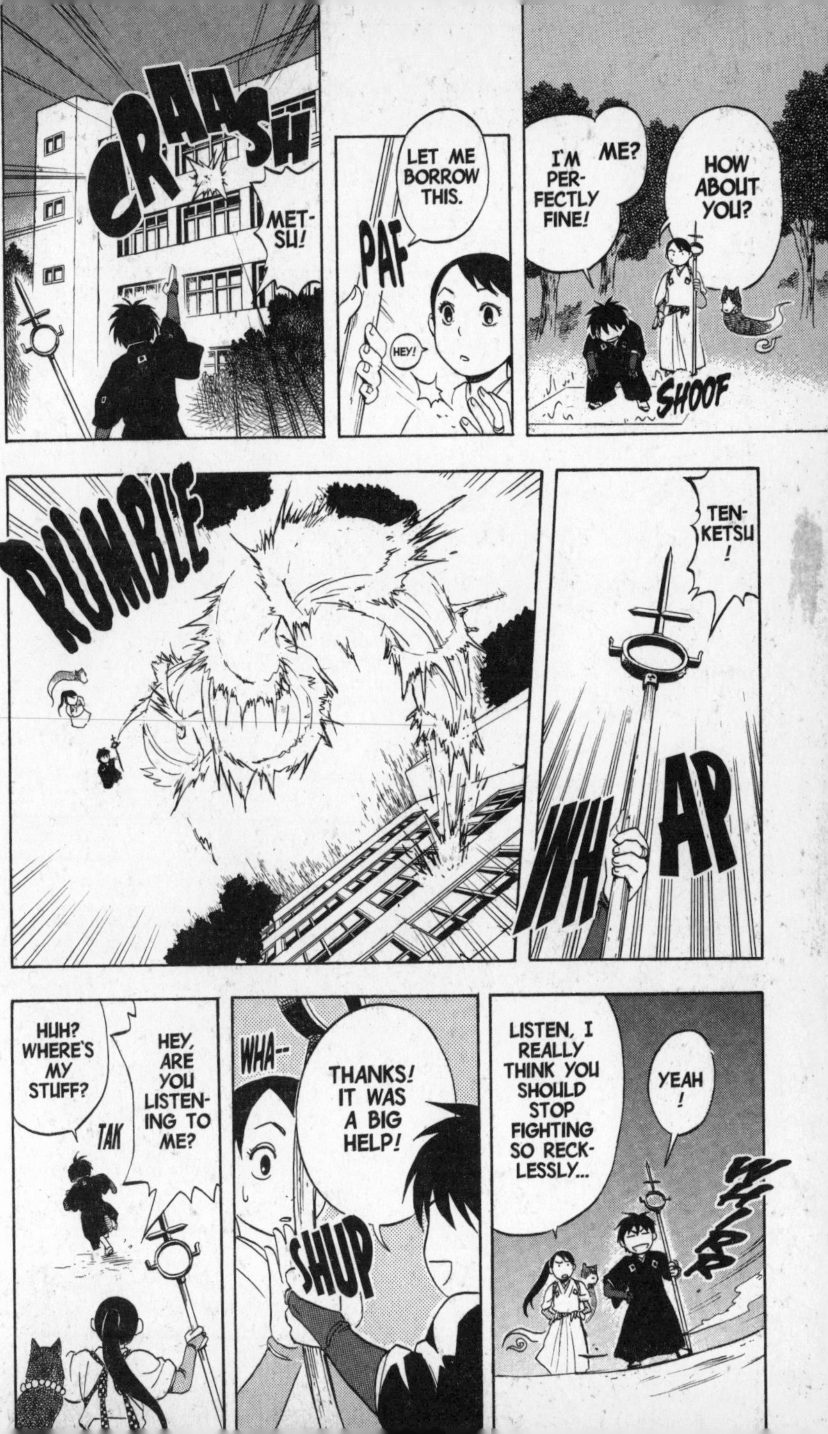
HOW ABOUT YOU?
ME?
I'M PER-FECTLY FINE!
SHOOF
LET ME BORROW THIS.
PAF
HEY!
CRAAASH
MET-SU!
TEN-KETSU!
WHAP
RUMBLE
YEAH!
LISTEN, I REALLY THINK YOU SHOULD STOP FIGHTING SO RECK-LESSLY...
THANKS! IT WAS A BIG HELP!
WHA--
SHUP
HEY, ARE YOU LISTEN-ING TO ME?
HUH? WHERE'S MY STUFF?
TAK

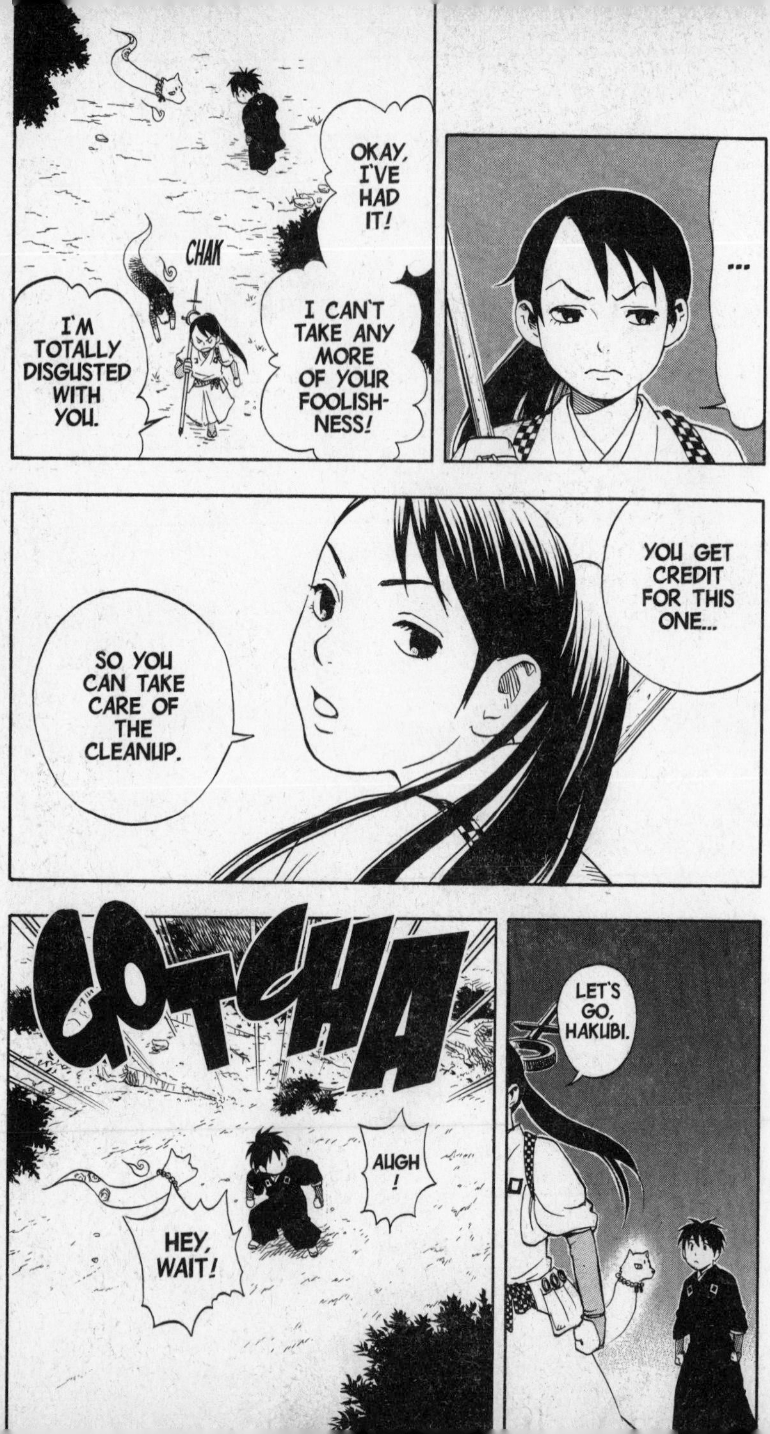
...
OKAY, I'VE HAD IT!
I CAN'T TAKE ANY MORE OF YOUR FOOLISHNESS!
CHAK
I'M TOTALLY DISGUSTED WITH YOU.
YOU GET CREDIT FOR THIS ONE...
SO YOU CAN TAKE CARE OF THE CLEANUP.
LET'S GO, HAKUBI.
GOTCHA
AUGH!
HEY, WAIT!

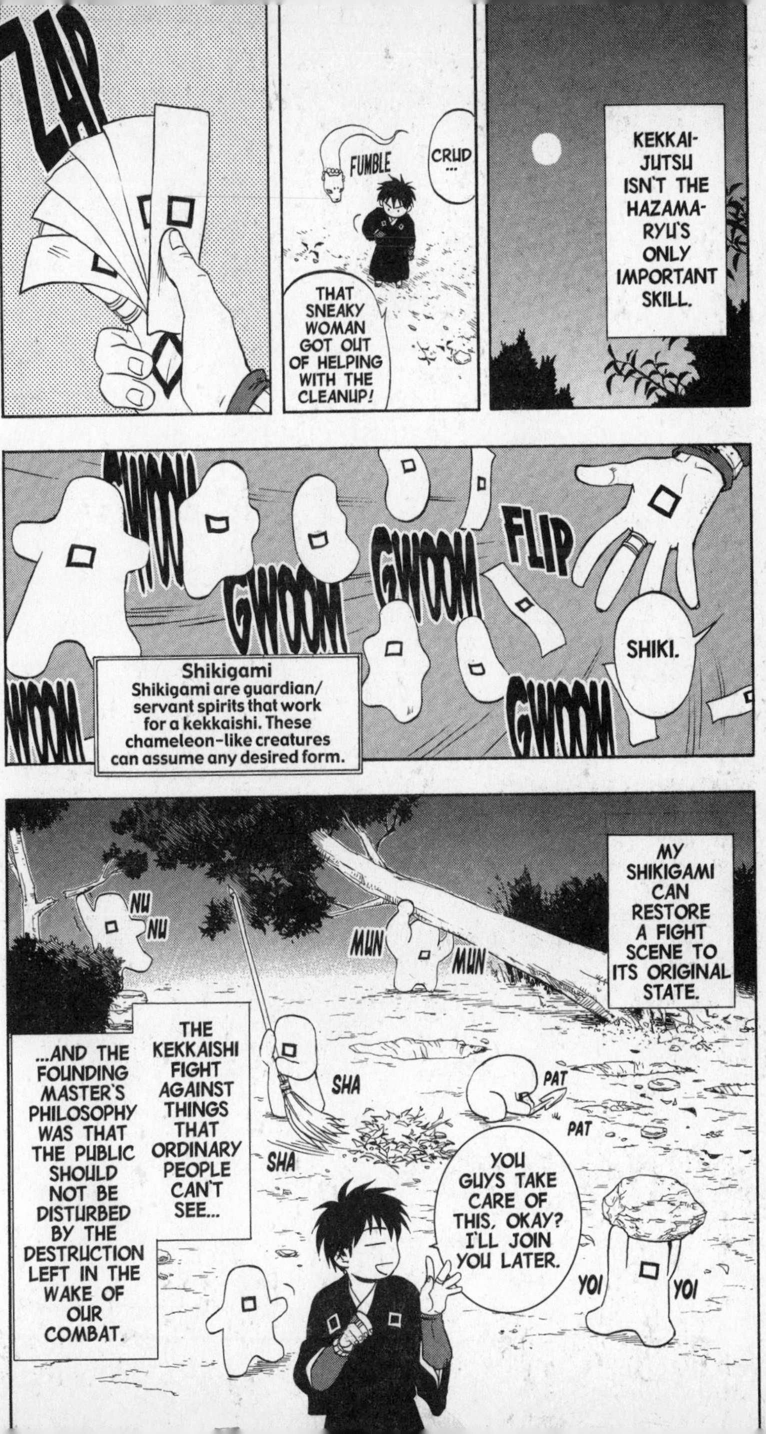
KEKKAI-JUTSU ISN'T THE HAZAMA-RYU'S ONLY IMPORTANT SKILL.
CRUD...
FUMBLE
THAT SNEAKY WOMAN GOT OUT OF HELPING WITH THE CLEANUP!
ZAP
SHIKI.
FLIP
GWOOM
GWOOM
GWOOM
GWOOM
GWOOM
Shikigami
Shikigami are guardian/servant spirits that work for a kekkaishi. These chameleon-like creatures can assume any desired form.
MY SHIKIGAMI CAN RESTORE A FIGHT SCENE TO ITS ORIGINAL STATE.
MUN
MUN
NU
NU
PAT
PAT
SHA
SHA
YOI
YOI
YOU GUYS TAKE CARE OF THIS, OKAY? I'LL JOIN YOU LATER.
THE KEKKAISHI FIGHT AGAINST THINGS THAT ORDINARY PEOPLE CAN'T SEE...
...AND THE FOUNDING MASTER'S PHILOSOPHY WAS THAT THE PUBLIC SHOULD NOT BE DISTURBED BY THE DESTRUCTION LEFT IN THE WAKE OF OUR COMBAT.

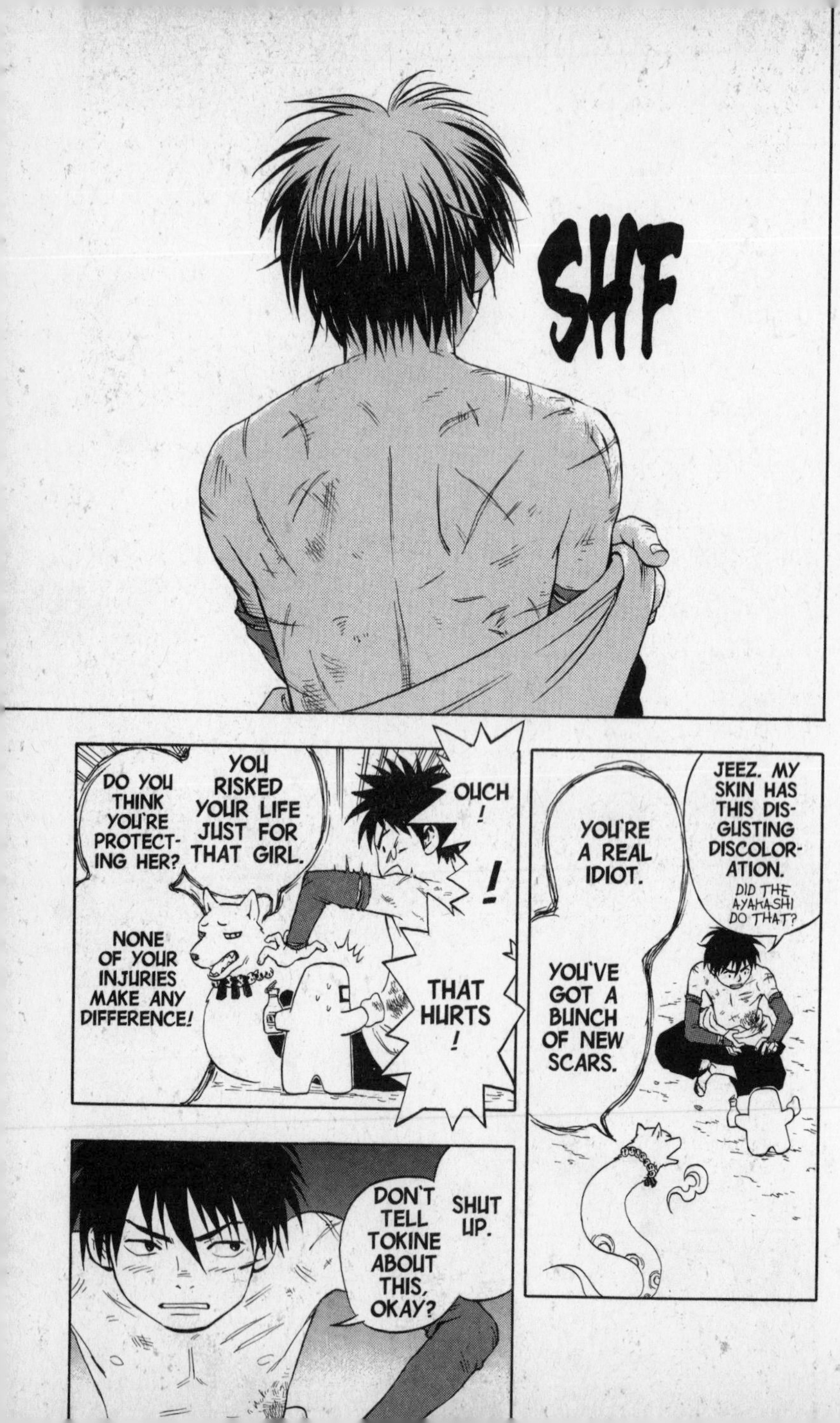
SHF
JEEZ. MY SKIN HAS THIS DISGUSTING DISCOLORATION.
DID THE AYAKASHI DO THAT?
YOU'RE A REAL IDIOT.
YOU'VE GOT A BUNCH OF NEW SCARS.
OUCH!
YOU RISKED YOUR LIFE JUST FOR THAT GIRL.
DO YOU THINK YOU'RE PROTECTING HER?
!
THAT HURTS!
NONE OF YOUR INJURIES MAKE ANY DIFFERENCE!
SHUT UP.
DON'T TELL TOKINE ABOUT THIS, OKAY?

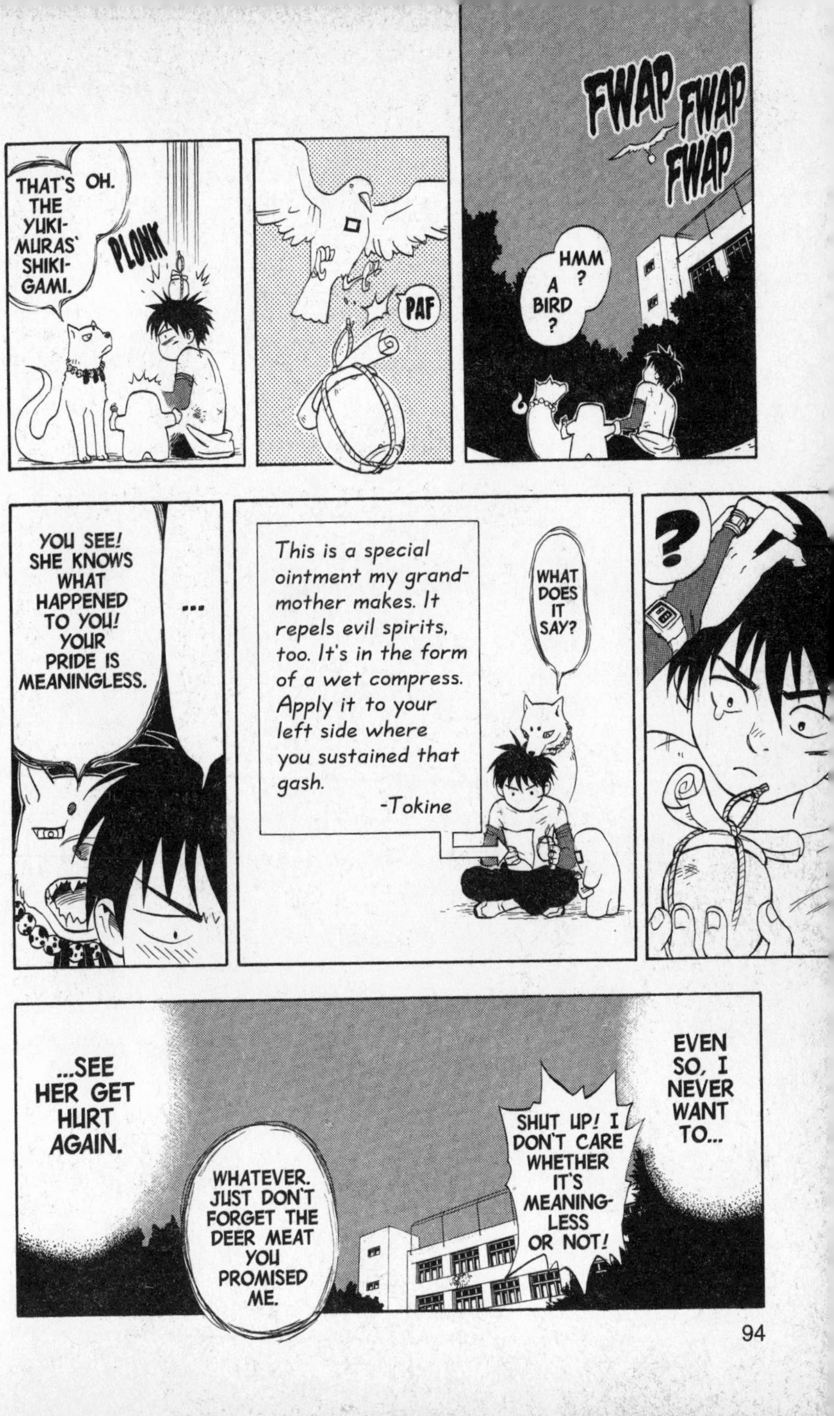
FWAP FWAP FWAP FWAP
HMM? A BIRD?
PAF
PLONK
THAT'S OH. THE YUKIMURAS' SHIKIGAMI.
?
WHAT DOES IT SAY?
This is a special ointment my grandmother makes. It repels evil spirits, too. It's in the form of a wet compress. Apply it to your left side where you sustained that gash. -Tokine
...
YOU SEE! SHE KNOWS WHAT HAPPENED TO YOU! YOUR PRIDE IS MEANINGLESS.
SHUT UP! I DON'T CARE WHETHER IT'S MEANINGLESS OR NOT!
WHATEVER. JUST DON'T FORGET THE DEER MEAT YOU PROMISED ME.
EVEN SO, I NEVER WANT TO...
...SEE HER GET HURT AGAIN.

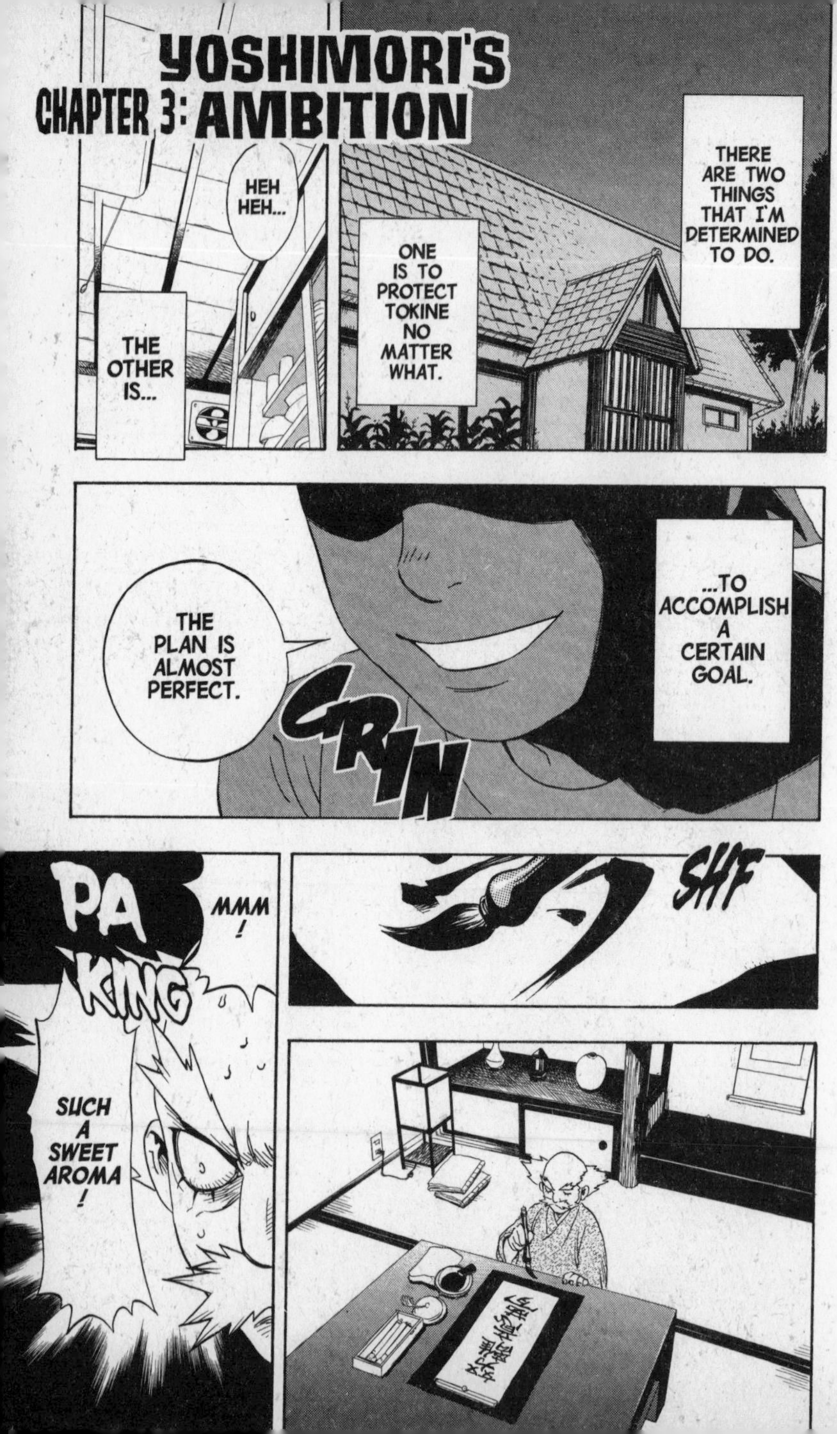
CHAPTER 3: YOSHIMORI'S AMBITION
THERE ARE TWO THINGS THAT I'M DETERMINED TO DO.
ONE IS TO PROTECT TOKINE NO MATTER WHAT.
HEH HEH...
THE OTHER IS...
...TO ACCOMPLISH A CERTAIN GOAL.
THE PLAN IS ALMOST PERFECT.
GRIN
SHF
PA KING
MMM!
SUCH A SWEET AROMA!

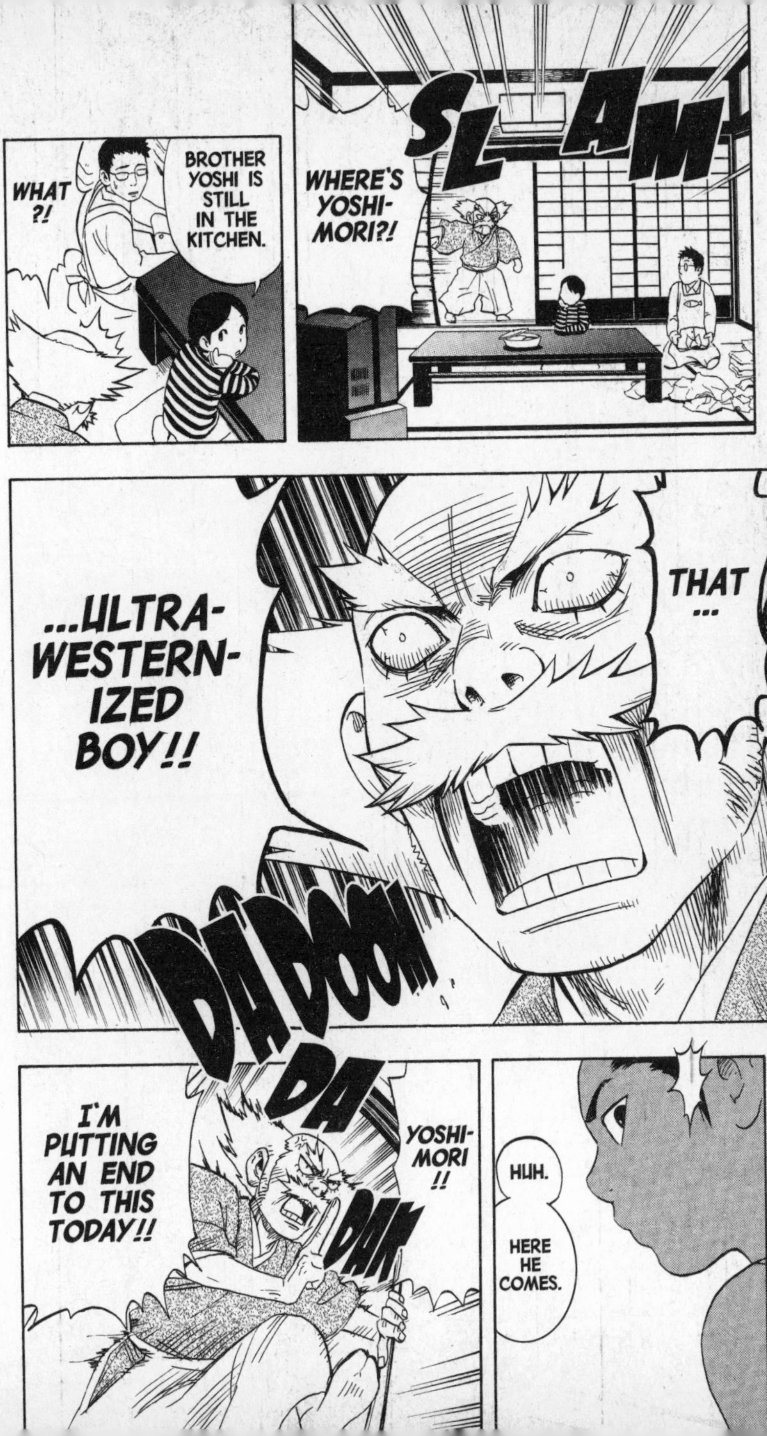
SLAM
WHERE'S YOSHIMORI?!
BROTHER YOSHI IS STILL IN THE KITCHEN.
WHAT?!
THAT...
...ULTRA-WESTERNIZED BOY!!
DADOOM
HUH.
HERE HE COMES.
DA
DAN
YOSHIMORI!!
I'M PUTTING AN END TO THIS TODAY!!

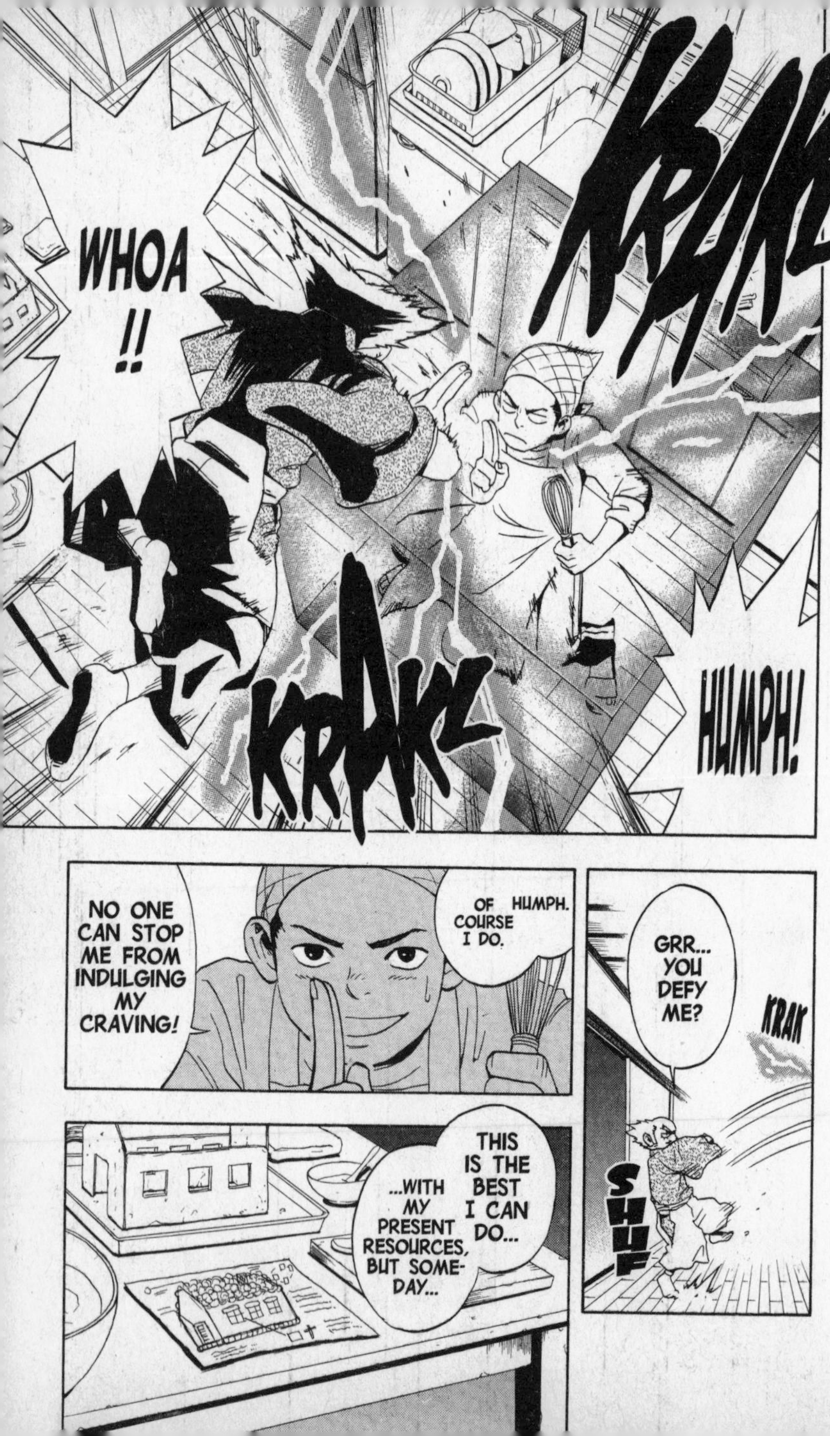
KRAK
WHOA !!
HUMPH!
KRAKL
GRR... YOU DEFY ME?
KRAK
SHUF
HUMPH. OF COURSE I DO.
NO ONE CAN STOP ME FROM INDULGING MY CRAVING!
THIS IS THE BEST I CAN DO...
...WITH MY PRESENT RESOURCES, BUT SOME-DAY...

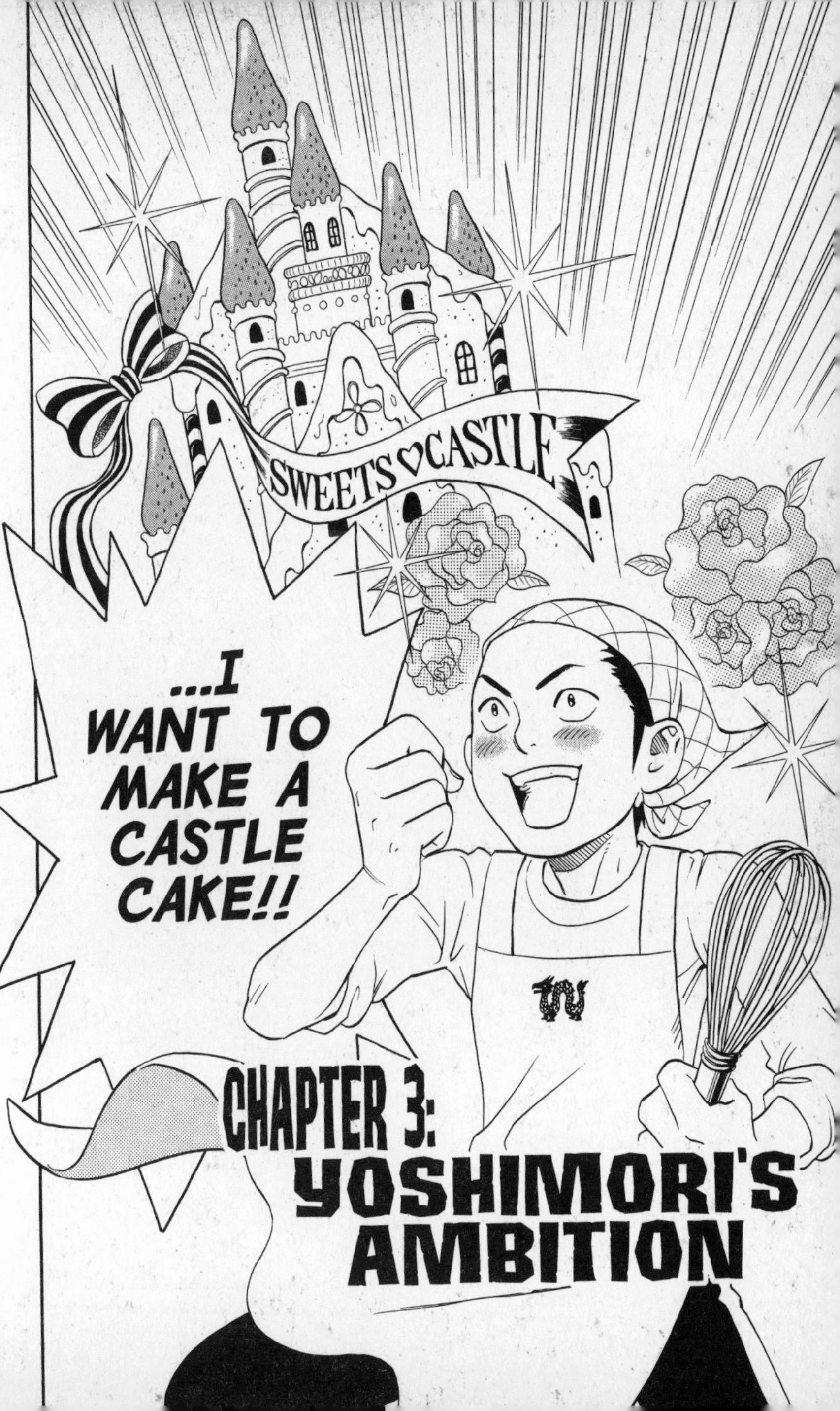
SWEETS♡CASTLE
...I WANT TO MAKE A CASTLE CAKE!!
CHAPTER 3:
YOSHIMORI'S AMBITION

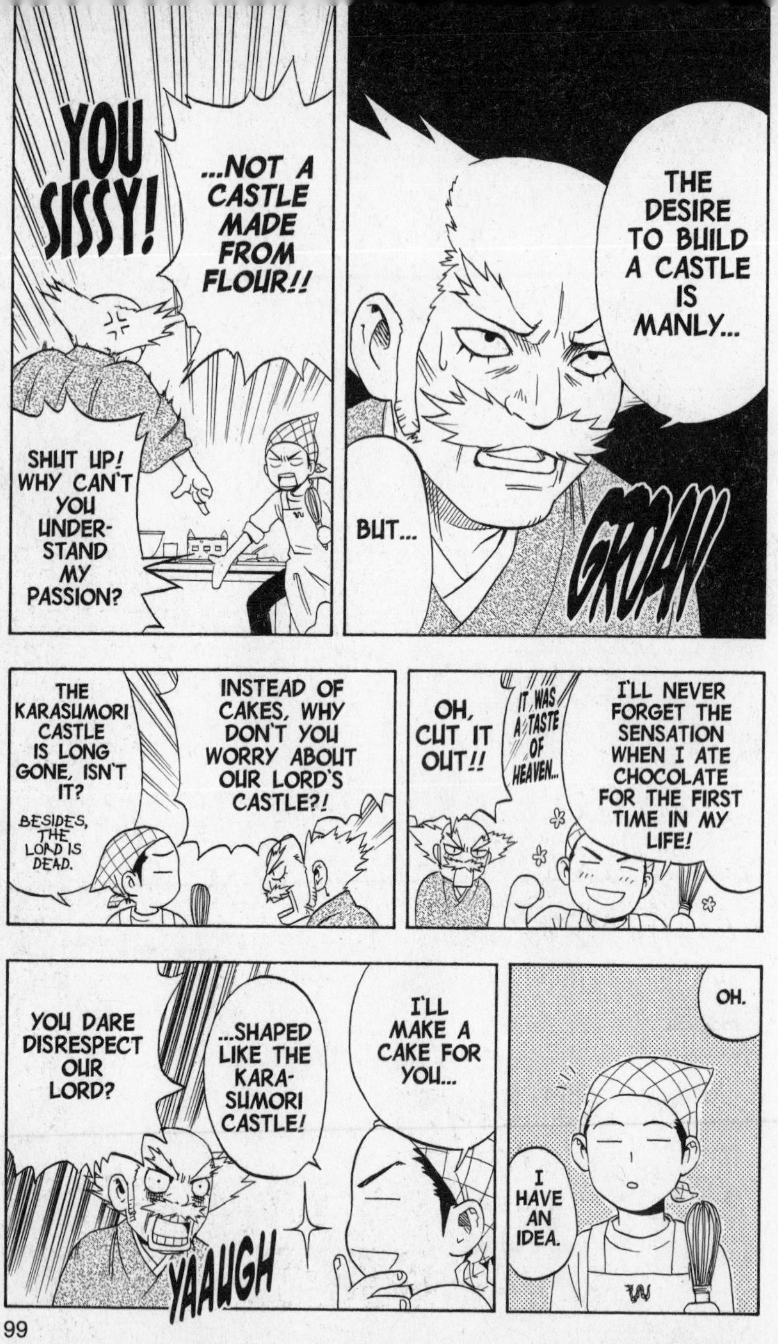
THE DESIRE TO BUILD A CASTLE IS MANLY...
BUT...
GROAN
...NOT A CASTLE MADE FROM FLOUR!!
YOU SISSY!
SHUT UP! WHY CAN'T YOU UNDER-STAND MY PASSION?
I'LL NEVER FORGET THE SENSATION WHEN I ATE CHOCOLATE FOR THE FIRST TIME IN MY LIFE!
IT WAS A TASTE OF HEAVEN...
OH, CUT IT OUT!!
INSTEAD OF CAKES, WHY DON'T YOU WORRY ABOUT OUR LORD'S CASTLE?!
THE KARASUMORI CASTLE IS LONG GONE, ISN'T IT?
BESIDES, THE LORD IS DEAD.
OH.
I HAVE AN IDEA.
I'LL MAKE A CAKE FOR YOU...
...SHAPED LIKE THE KARA-SUMORI CASTLE!
YOU DARE DISRESPECT OUR LORD?
YAAUGH

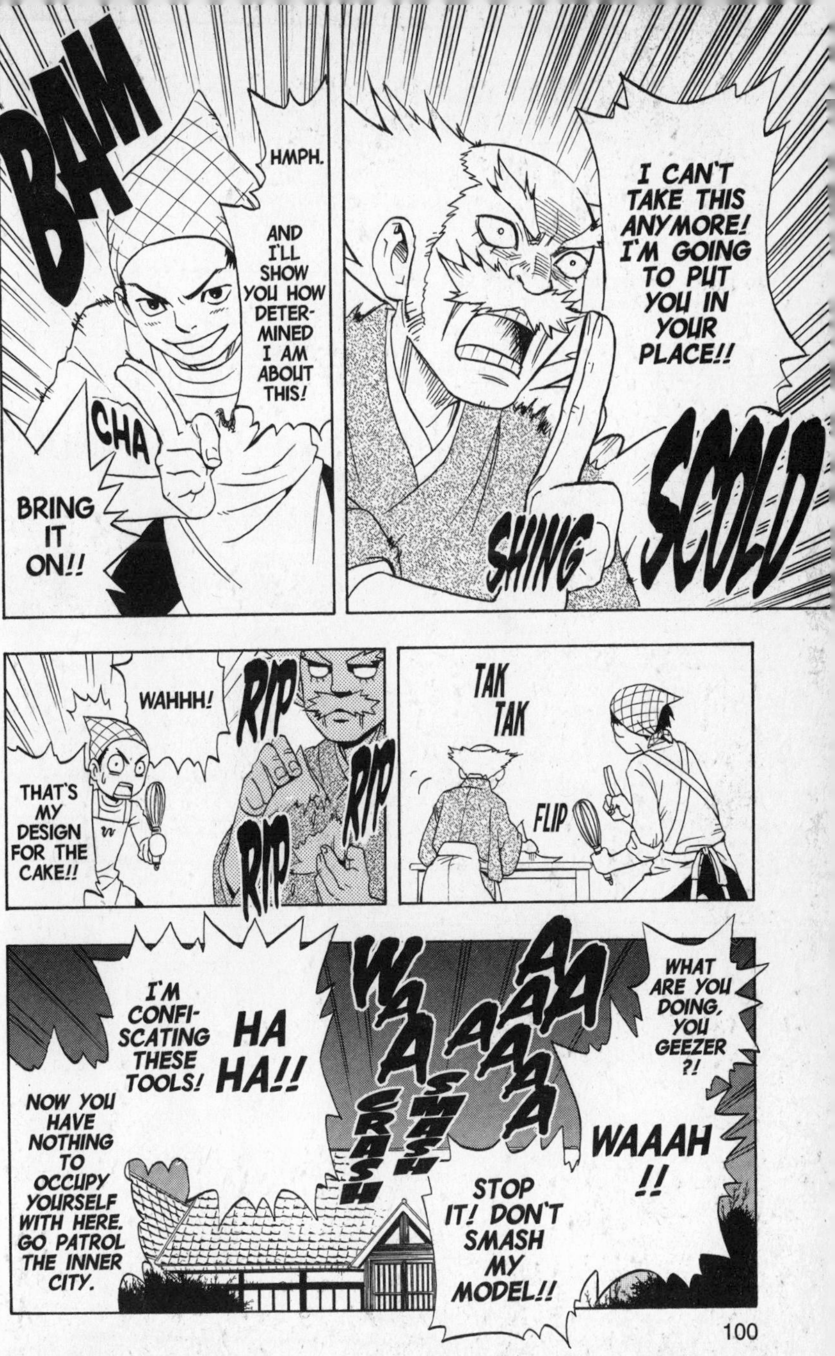
I CAN'T TAKE THIS ANYMORE! I'M GOING TO PUT YOU IN YOUR PLACE!!
SCOLD
SHING
BAM
HMPH.
AND I'LL SHOW YOU HOW DETER-MINED I AM ABOUT THIS!
CHA
BRING IT ON!!
TAK TAK
FLIP
WAHHH!
RIP
RIP
RIP
THAT'S MY DESIGN FOR THE CAKE!!
WHAT ARE YOU DOING, YOU GEEZER?!
WAAAH!!
AAAAAAAA
WAAA
SMASH
CRASH
STOP IT! DON'T SMASH MY MODEL!!
HA HA!!
I'M CONFI-SCATING THESE TOOLS!
NOW YOU HAVE NOTHING TO OCCUPY YOURSELF WITH HERE. GO PATROL THE INNER CITY.

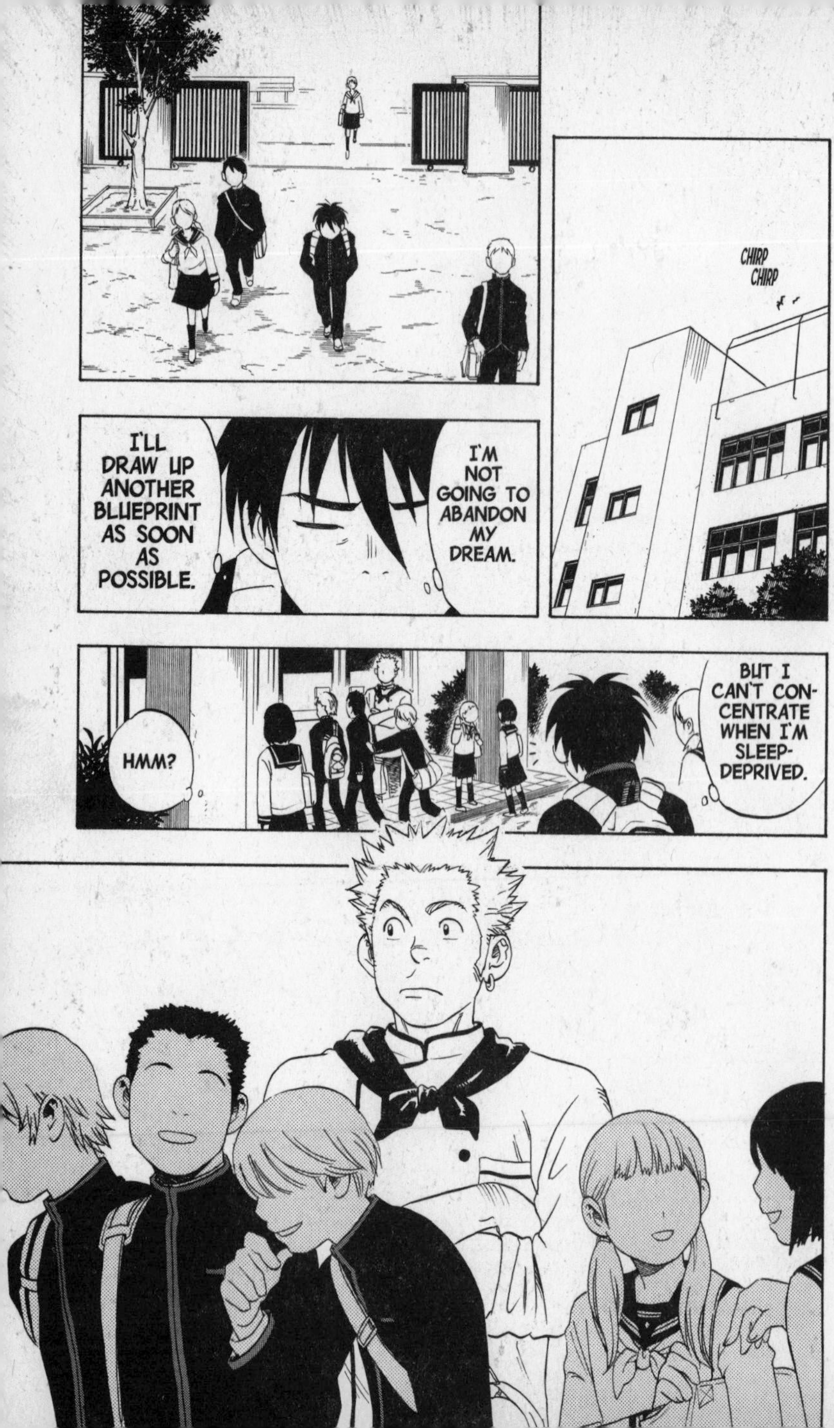
CHIRP CHIRP
I'M NOT GOING TO ABANDON MY DREAM.
I'LL DRAW UP ANOTHER BLUEPRINT AS SOON AS POSSIBLE.
BUT I CAN'T CONCENTRATE WHEN I'M SLEEP-DEPRIVED.
HMM?

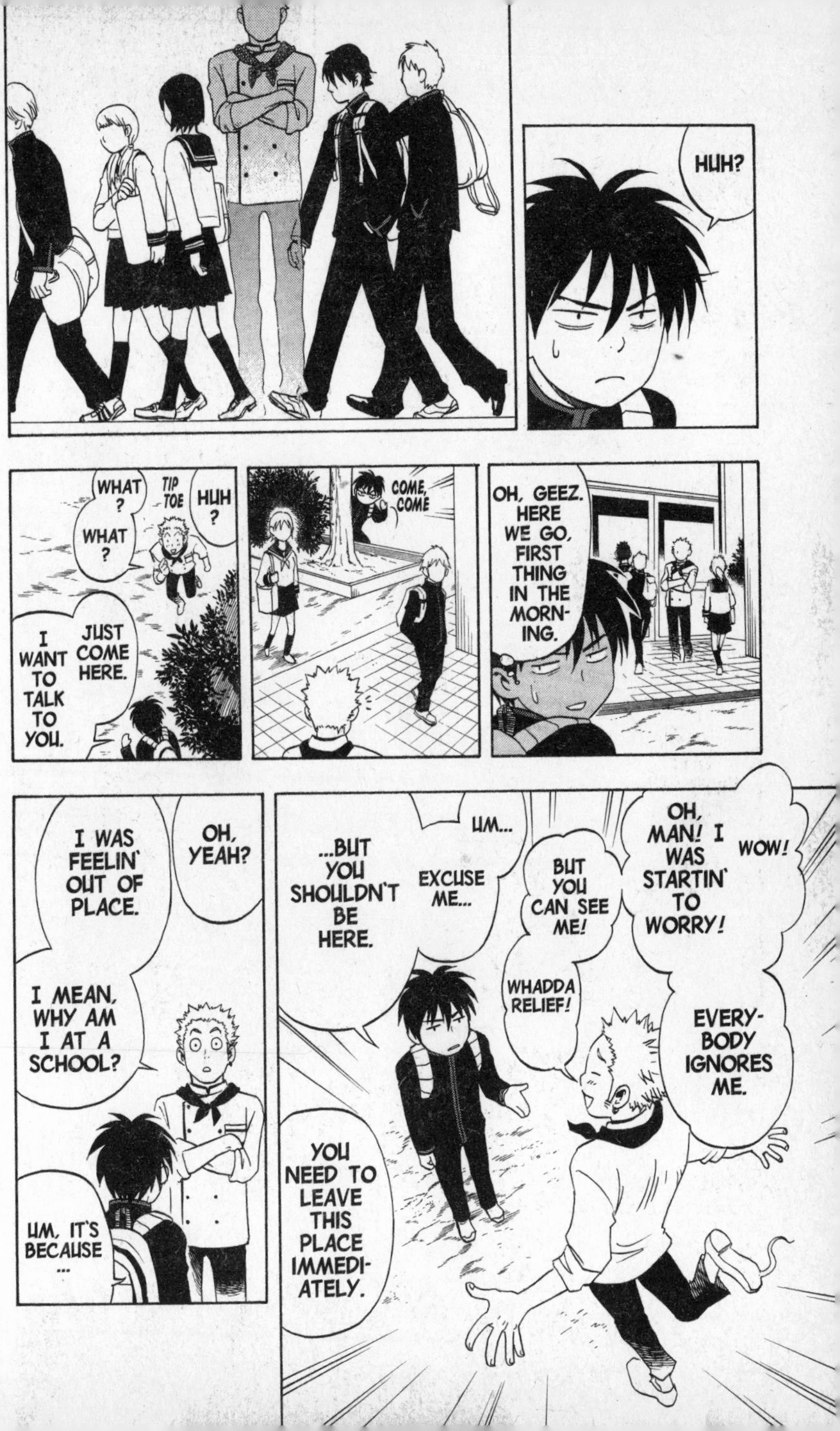
HUH?
OH, GEEZ. HERE WE GO, FIRST THING IN THE MORNING.
COME, COME
HUH?
TIP TOE
WHAT? WHAT?
JUST COME HERE.
I WANT TO TALK TO YOU.
WOW!
OH, MAN! I WAS STARTIN' TO WORRY!
BUT YOU CAN SEE ME!
WHADDA RELIEF!
EVERY-BODY IGNORES ME.
UM...
EXCUSE ME...
...BUT YOU SHOULDN'T BE HERE.
YOU NEED TO LEAVE THIS PLACE IMMEDI-ATELY.
OH, YEAH?
I WAS FEELIN' OUT OF PLACE.
I MEAN, WHY AM I AT A SCHOOL?
UM, IT'S BECAUSE ...

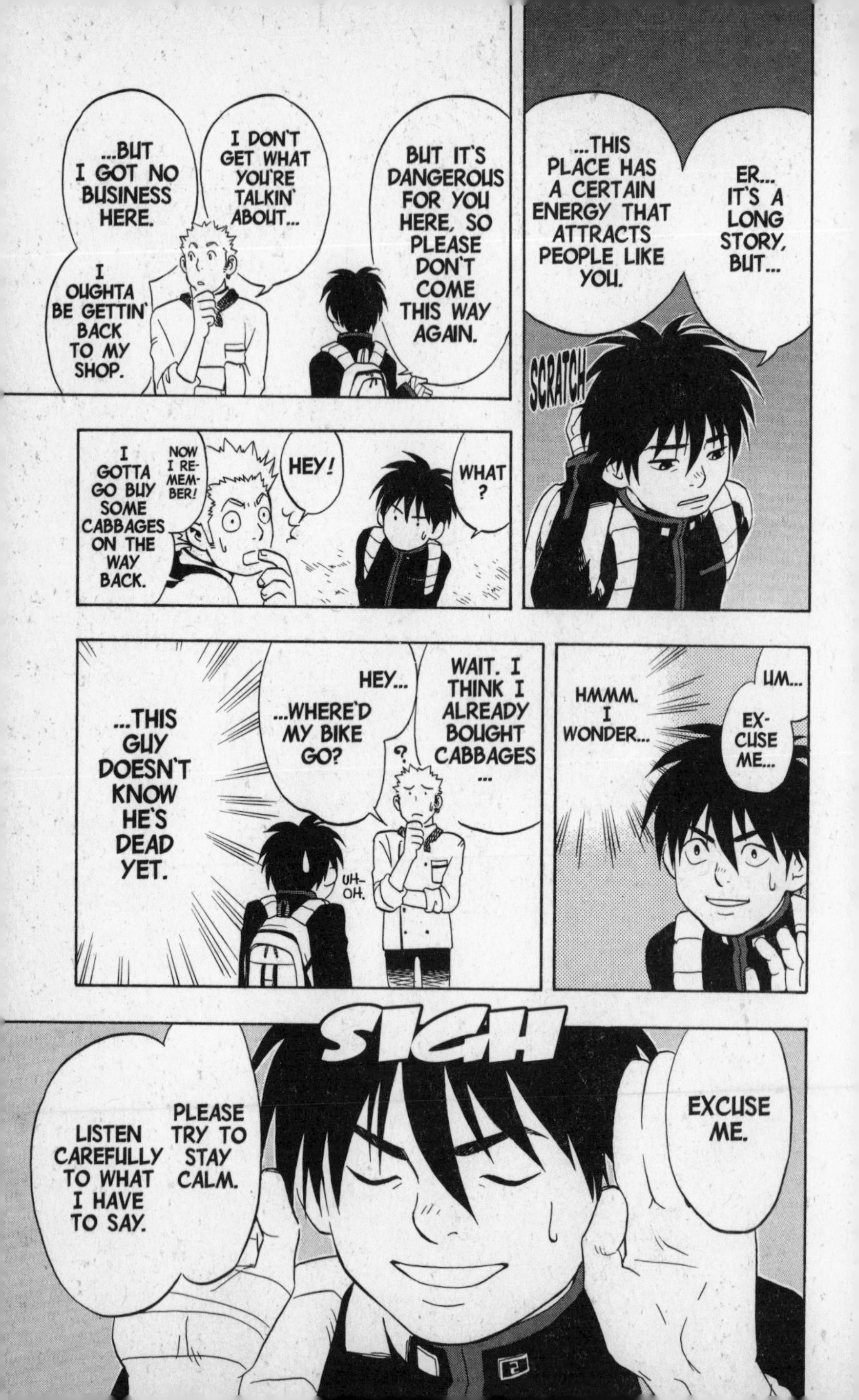
ER... IT'S A LONG STORY, BUT...
...THIS PLACE HAS A CERTAIN ENERGY THAT ATTRACTS PEOPLE LIKE YOU.
SCRATCH
BUT IT'S DANGEROUS FOR YOU HERE, SO PLEASE DON'T COME THIS WAY AGAIN.
I DON'T GET WHAT YOU'RE TALKIN' ABOUT...
...BUT I GOT NO BUSINESS HERE.
I OUGHTA BE GETTIN' BACK TO MY SHOP.
WHAT ?
HEY!
NOW I RE-MEM-BER!
I GOTTA GO BUY SOME CABBAGES ON THE WAY BACK.
UM...
EX-CUSE ME...
HMMM. I WONDER...
WAIT. I THINK I ALREADY BOUGHT CABBAGES ...
HEY...
...WHERE'D MY BIKE GO?
?
UH-OH.
...THIS GUY DOESN'T KNOW HE'S DEAD YET.
SIGH
EXCUSE ME.
PLEASE TRY TO STAY CALM.
LISTEN CAREFULLY TO WHAT I HAVE TO SAY.

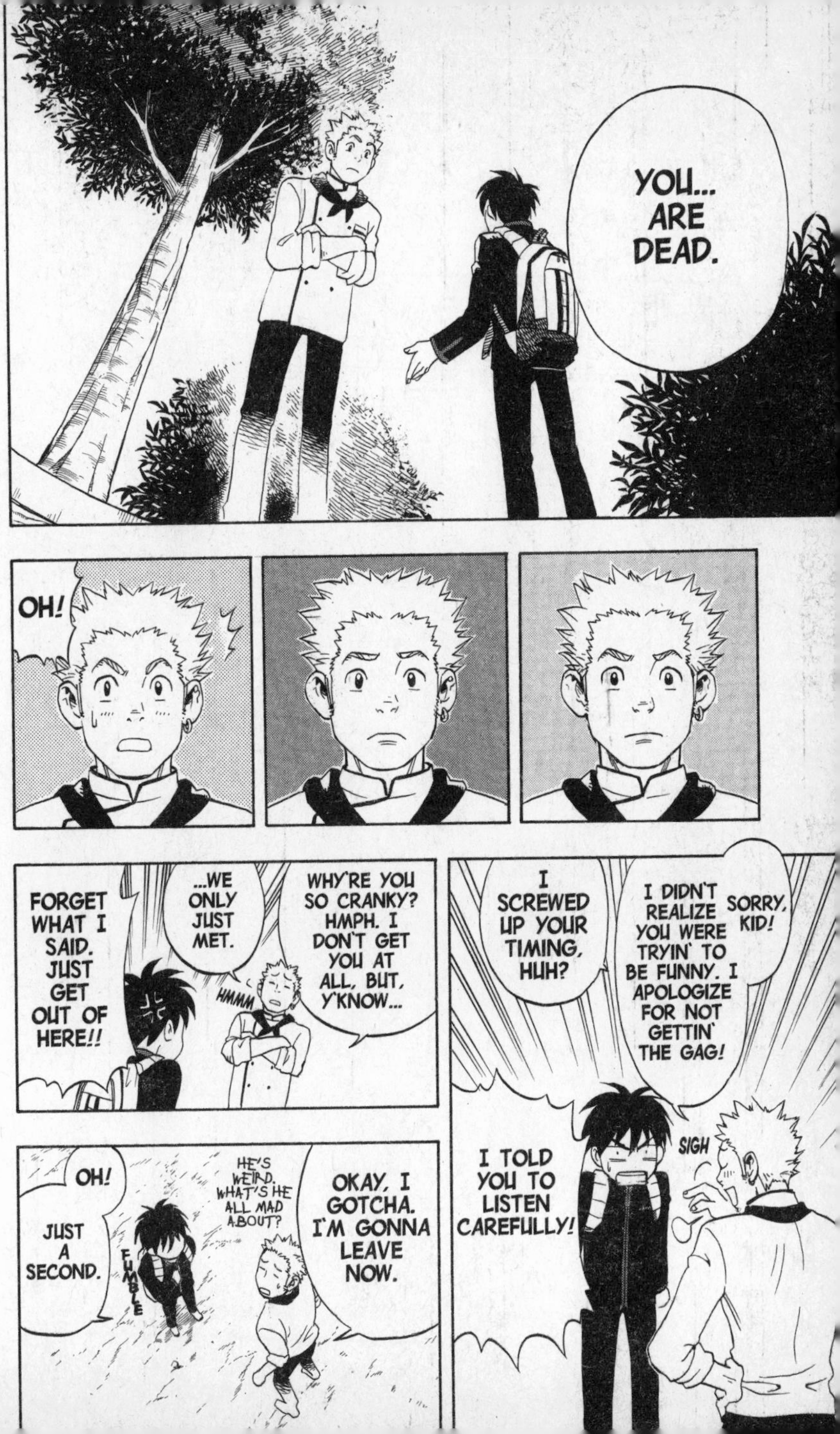
YOU... ARE DEAD.
OH!
SORRY, KID!
I DIDN'T REALIZE YOU WERE TRYIN' TO BE FUNNY. I APOLOGIZE FOR NOT GETTIN' THE GAG!
I SCREWED UP YOUR TIMING, HUH?
SIGH
I TOLD YOU TO LISTEN CAREFULLY!
WHY'RE YOU SO CRANKY? HMPH. I DON'T GET YOU AT ALL, BUT, Y'KNOW...
HMMM
...WE ONLY JUST MET.
FORGET WHAT I SAID. JUST GET OUT OF HERE!!
OKAY, I GOTCHA. I'M GONNA LEAVE NOW.
HE'S WEIRD. WHAT'S HE ALL MAD ABOUT?
FUMBLE
OH!
JUST A SECOND.

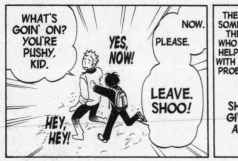

PLEASE GO TO THIS PLACE.
THERE'S SOMEONE THERE WHO CAN HELP YOU WITH YOUR PROBLEM.
SHE CAN GIVE YOU ADVICE.
NOW.
PLEASE.
LEAVE. SHOO!
YES, NOW!
WHAT'S GOIN' ON? YOU'RE PUSHY, KID.
HEY, HEY!
DING DONG DING
BUZZ
BUZZ
CLIK
BYE-BYE
TAK
SEE YA.
I WANTED TO FINISH MY NEW CAKE DESIGN...
CLICK
...BUT I ENDED UP SLEEPING THROUGH ALL MY CLASSES.
AND I'M STILL SO SLEEPY...
I NEED SOMETHING TO MOTIVATE MYSELF...

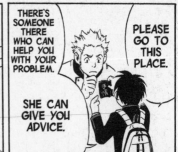

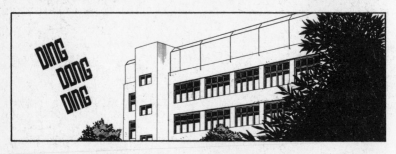

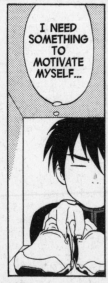

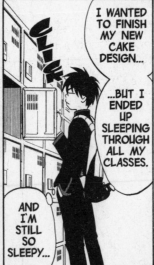

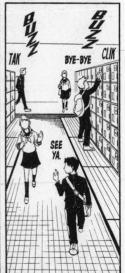

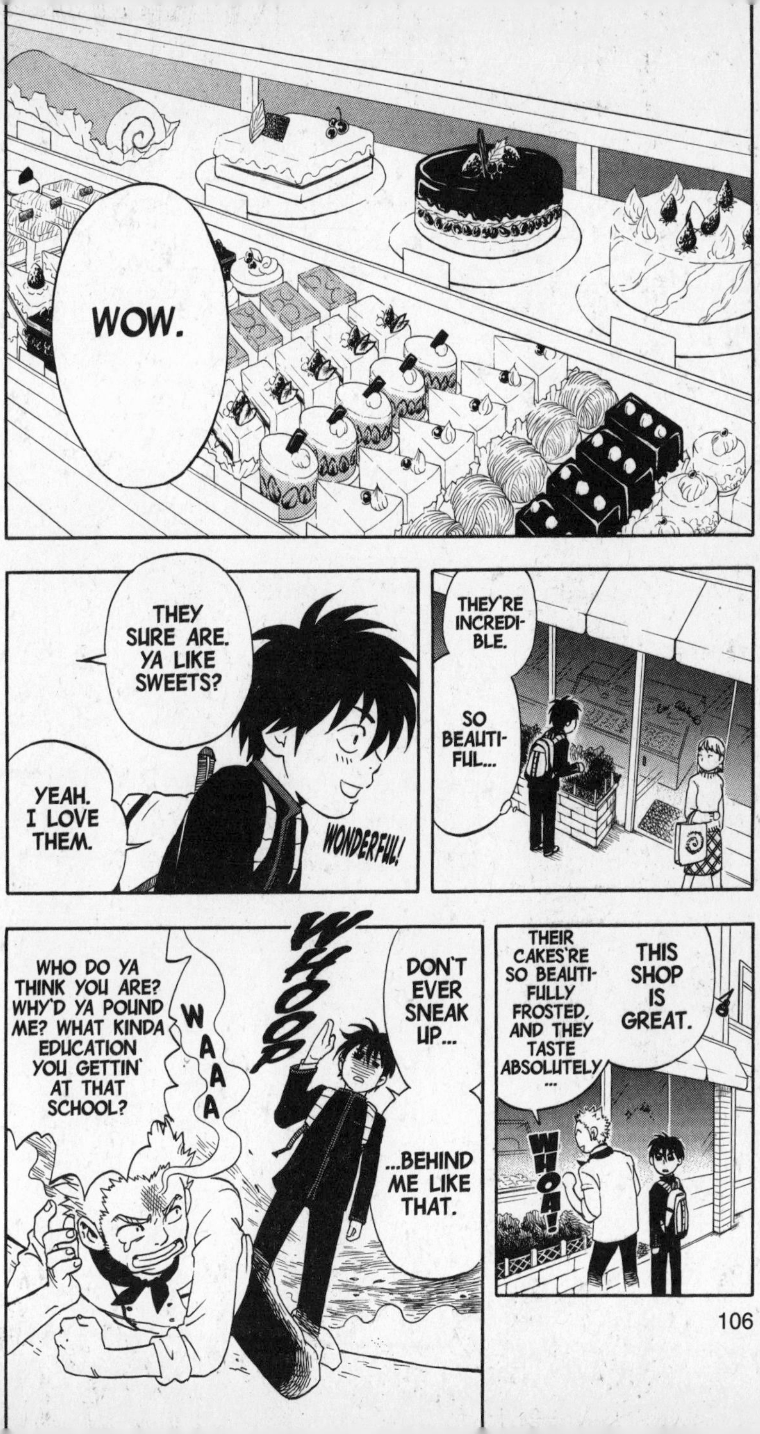
WOW.
THEY'RE INCREDI-BLE.
SO BEAUTI-FUL...
THEY SURE ARE. YA LIKE SWEETS?
YEAH. I LOVE THEM.
WONDERFUL!
THIS SHOP IS GREAT.
THEIR CAKES'RE SO BEAUTI-FULLY FROSTED, AND THEY TASTE ABSOLUTELY...
WHOA!
WHOOP
DON'T EVER SNEAK UP...
...BEHIND ME LIKE THAT.
WAAAA
WHO DO YA THINK YOU ARE? WHY'D YA POUND ME? WHAT KINDA EDUCATION YOU GETTIN' AT THAT SCHOOL?

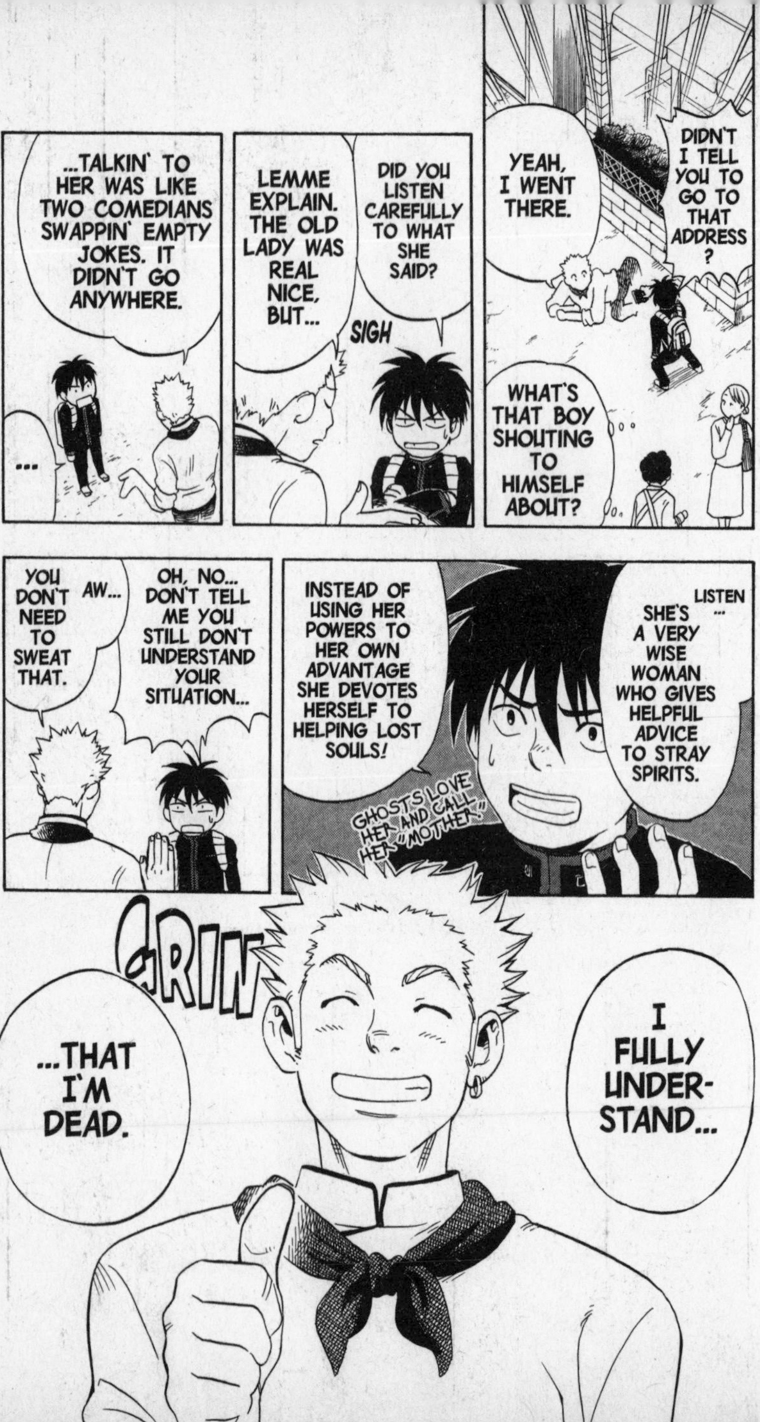
DIDN'T I TELL YOU TO GO TO THAT ADDRESS?
YEAH, I WENT THERE.
WHAT'S THAT BOY SHOUTING TO HIMSELF ABOUT?
DID YOU LISTEN CAREFULLY TO WHAT SHE SAID?
SIGH
LEMME EXPLAIN. THE OLD LADY WAS REAL NICE, BUT...
...TALKIN' TO HER WAS LIKE TWO COMEDIANS SWAPPIN' EMPTY JOKES. IT DIDN'T GO ANYWHERE.
...
LISTEN...
SHE'S A VERY WISE WOMAN WHO GIVES HELPFUL ADVICE TO STRAY SPIRITS.
INSTEAD OF USING HER POWERS TO HER OWN ADVANTAGE SHE DEVOTES HERSELF TO HELPING LOST SOULS!
GHOSTS LOVE HER AND CALL HER "MOTHER."
OH, NO... DON'T TELL ME YOU STILL DON'T UNDERSTAND YOUR SITUATION...
AW...
YOU DON'T NEED TO SWEAT THAT.
GRIN
I FULLY UNDER-STAND...
...THAT I'M DEAD.

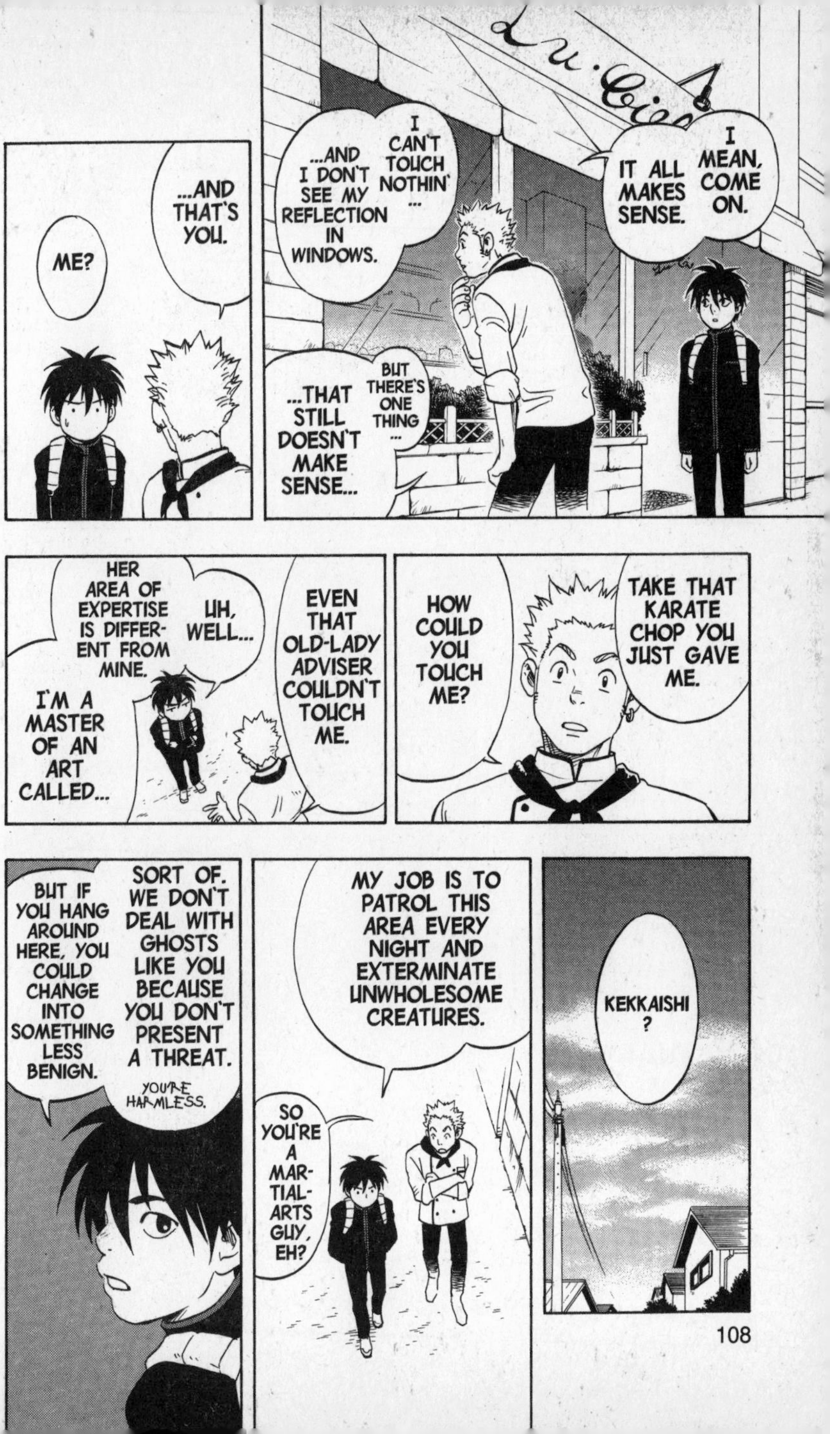
I MEAN, COME ON.
IT ALL MAKES SENSE.
I CAN'T TOUCH NOTHIN'...
...AND I DON'T SEE MY REFLECTION IN WINDOWS.
BUT THERE'S ONE THING...
...THAT STILL DOESN'T MAKE SENSE...
...AND THAT'S YOU.
ME?
TAKE THAT KARATE CHOP YOU JUST GAVE ME.
HOW COULD YOU TOUCH ME?
EVEN THAT OLD-LADY ADVISER COULDN'T TOUCH ME.
UH, WELL...
HER AREA OF EXPERTISE IS DIFFER-ENT FROM MINE.
I'M A MASTER OF AN ART CALLED...
KEKKAISHI?
MY JOB IS TO PATROL THIS AREA EVERY NIGHT AND EXTERMINATE UNWHOLESOME CREATURES.
SO YOU'RE A MAR-TIAL-ARTS GUY, EH?
SORT OF. WE DON'T DEAL WITH GHOSTS LIKE YOU BECAUSE YOU DON'T PRESENT A THREAT.
YOU'RE HARMLESS.
BUT IF YOU HANG AROUND HERE, YOU COULD CHANGE INTO SOMETHING LESS BENIGN.

...I'LL HAVE TO TERMINATE YOU.

IF YOU DO...

REALLY? DO YOU KNOW WHAT I'D TURN INTO?

IDIOT! DON'T TRY IT, OKAY?

I BET I COULD DO AMAZING THINGS.

HO HO

DO YOU KNOW WHAT MY VERY LAST WORD WAS?

IT WAS "CABBAGE!"

BIKE

DON'T YOU THINK THAT STINKS?

I DON'T CARE!

DON'T YOU GET IT? YOU'RE ALREADY DEAD!!

HANG ON HERE! I CAN'T JUST LIE BACK AND DIE!

EEK!

I CAN'T HELP YOU, I JUST ERADICATE AYAKASHI, PERIOD!

KREEK KREEK

GRAB

WHAT?

NOW PLEASE REST IN PEACE.

...A PATISSIER.

I WAS...

IF ONLY I'D SAID "STRAW-BERRIES!" OR SOMETHIN' LIKE THAT.

IT DOESN'T MAKE ANY DIFFER-ENCE, DOES IT?

RIGHT?

YEAH, IT DOES! A HUGE DIFFERENCE!

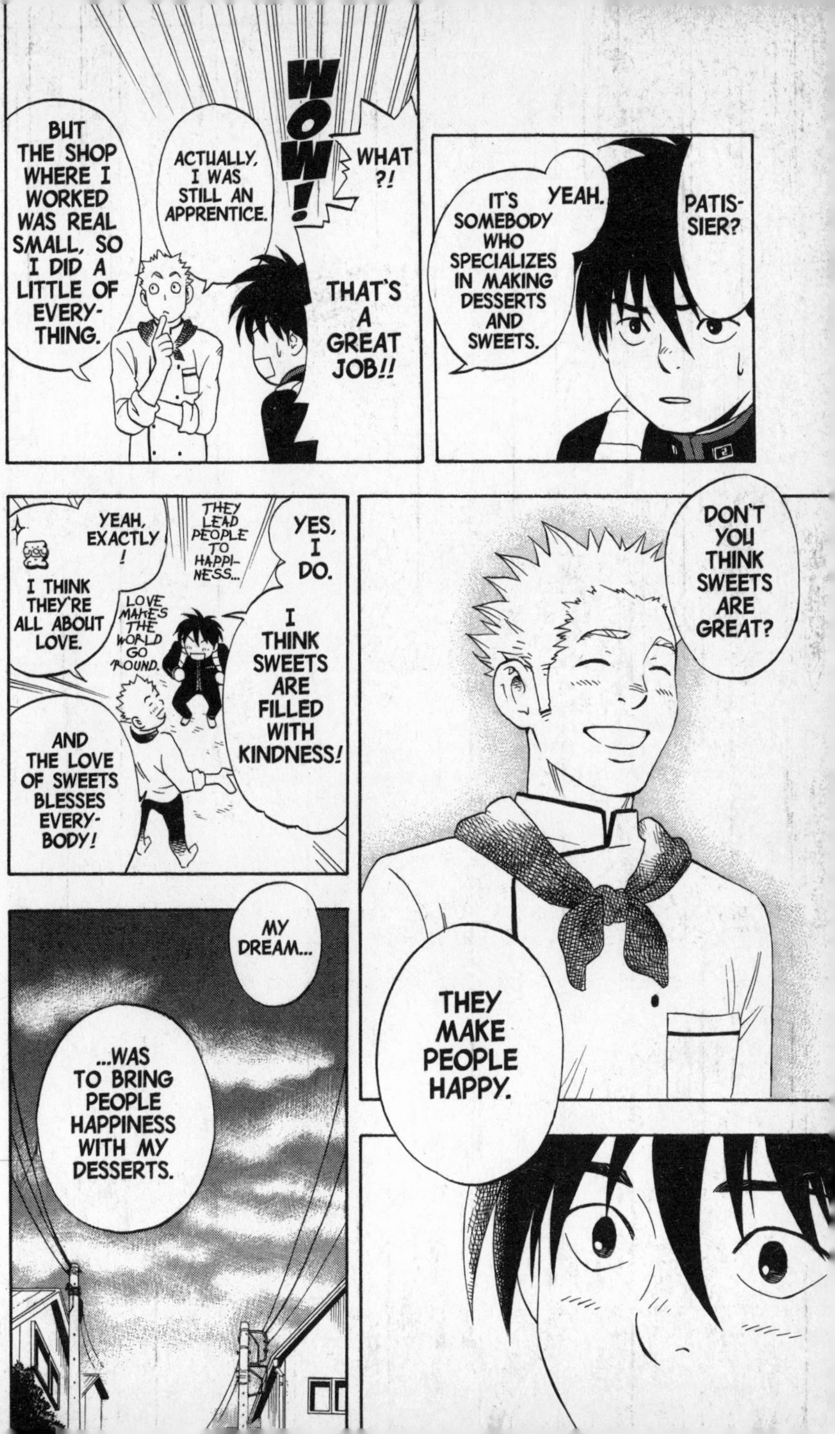
PATIS-SIER?
YEAH.
IT'S SOMEBODY WHO SPECIALIZES IN MAKING DESSERTS AND SWEETS.
WOW!
WHAT ?!
THAT'S A GREAT JOB!!
ACTUALLY, I WAS STILL AN APPRENTICE.
BUT THE SHOP WHERE I WORKED WAS REAL SMALL, SO I DID A LITTLE OF EVERY-THING.
DON'T YOU THINK SWEETS ARE GREAT?
THEY MAKE PEOPLE HAPPY.
YES, I DO.
I THINK SWEETS ARE FILLED WITH KINDNESS!
THEY LEAD PEOPLE TO HAPPI-NESS...
YEAH, EXACTLY!
I THINK THEY'RE ALL ABOUT LOVE.
LOVE MAKES THE WORLD GO 'ROUND.
AND THE LOVE OF SWEETS BLESSES EVERY-BODY!
MY DREAM...
...WAS TO BRING PEOPLE HAPPINESS WITH MY DESSERTS.

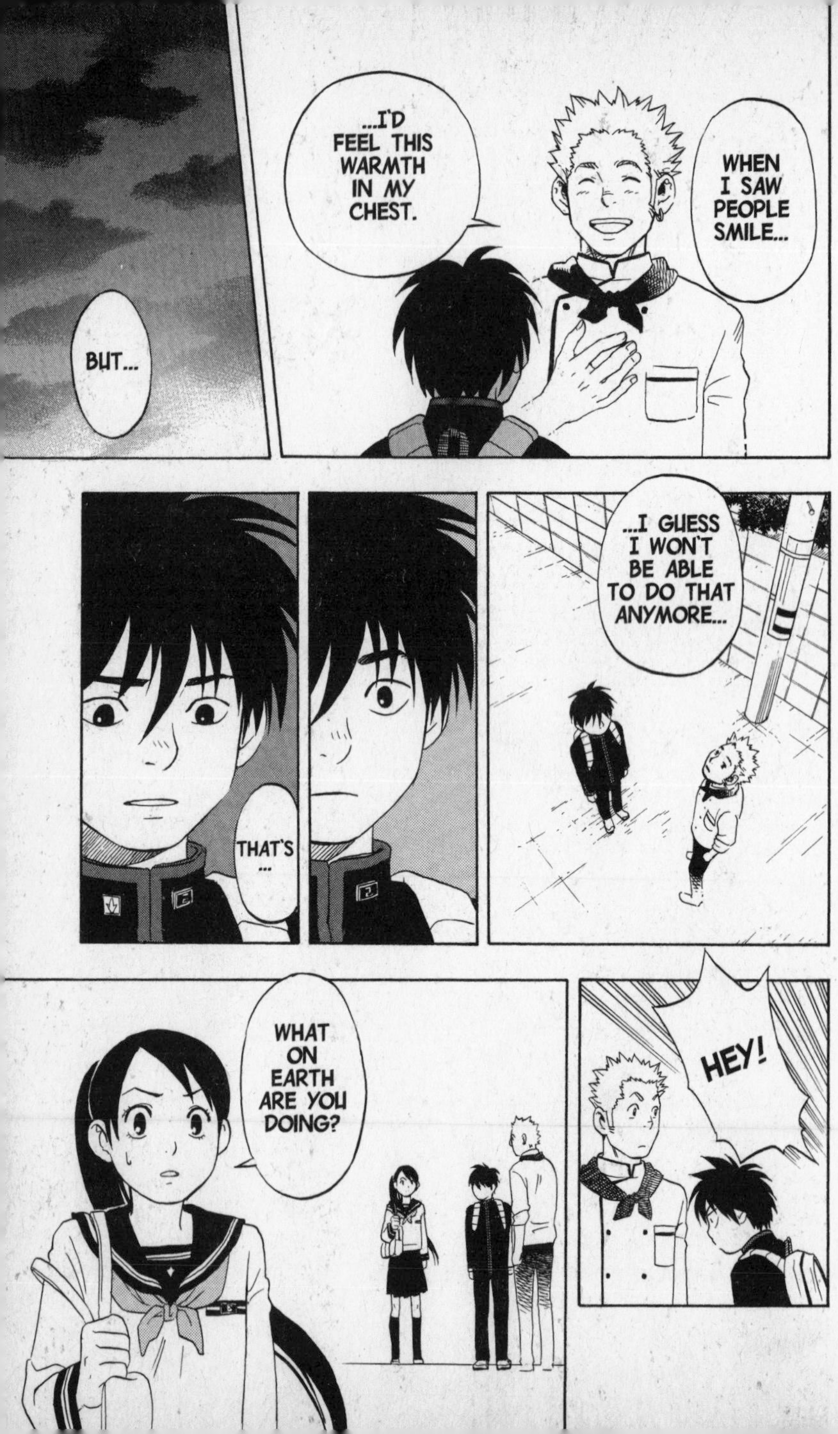
WHEN I SAW PEOPLE SMILE...
...I'D FEEL THIS WARMTH IN MY CHEST.
BUT...
...I GUESS I WON'T BE ABLE TO DO THAT ANYMORE...
THAT'S ...
HEY!
WHAT ON EARTH ARE YOU DOING?

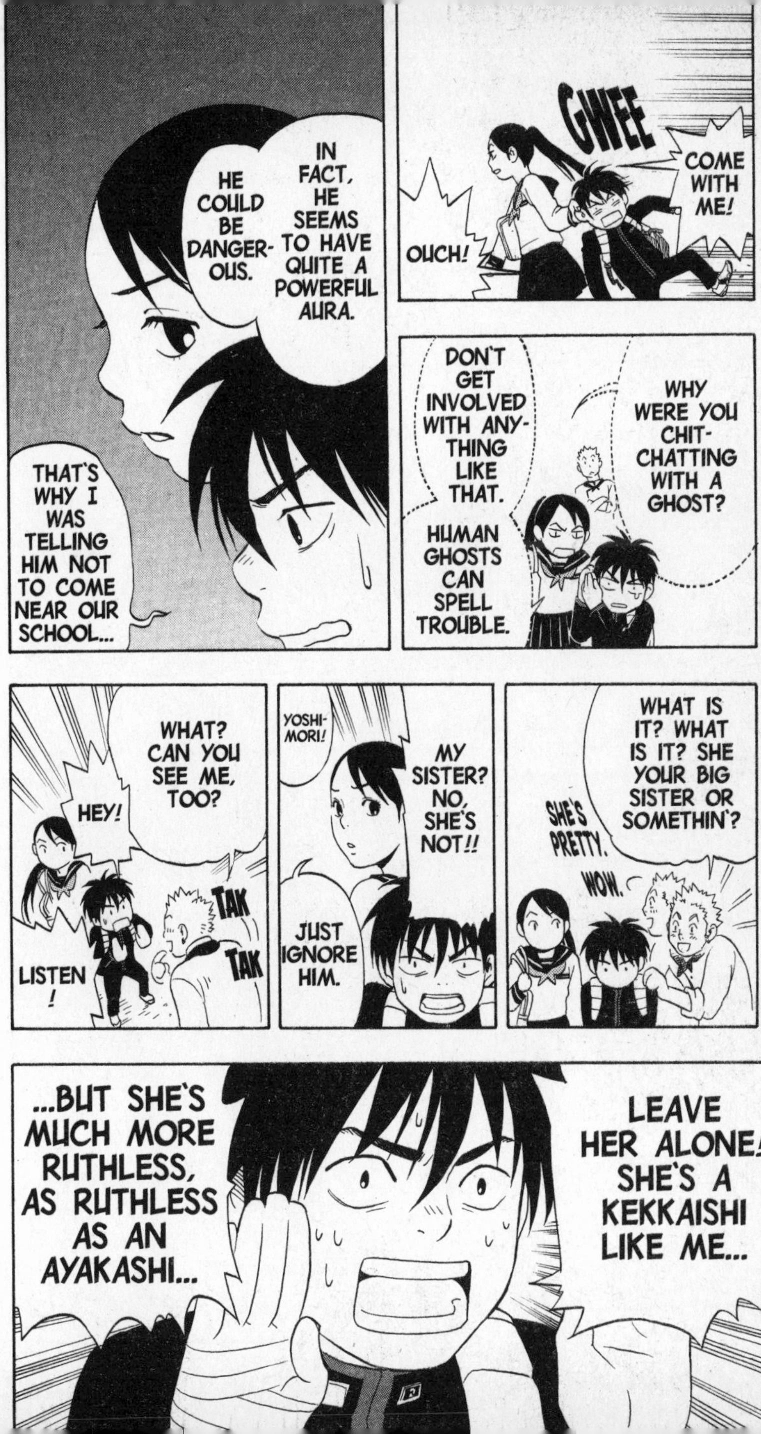
GWEE
COME WITH ME!
OUCH!
WHY WERE YOU CHIT-CHATTING WITH A GHOST?
DON'T GET INVOLVED WITH ANYTHING LIKE THAT.
HUMAN GHOSTS CAN SPELL TROUBLE.
IN FACT, HE SEEMS TO HAVE QUITE A POWERFUL AURA.
HE COULD BE DANGEROUS.
THAT'S WHY I WAS TELLING HIM NOT TO COME NEAR OUR SCHOOL...
WHAT IS IT? WHAT IS IT? SHE YOUR BIG SISTER OR SOMETHIN'?
SHE'S PRETTY.
WOW.
MY SISTER? NO, SHE'S NOT!!
YOSHIMORI!
JUST IGNORE HIM.
WHAT? CAN YOU SEE ME, TOO?
HEY!
TAK
TAK
LISTEN!
LEAVE HER ALONE! SHE'S A KEKKAISHI LIKE ME...
...BUT SHE'S MUCH MORE RUTHLESS, AS RUTHLESS AS AN AYAKASHI...

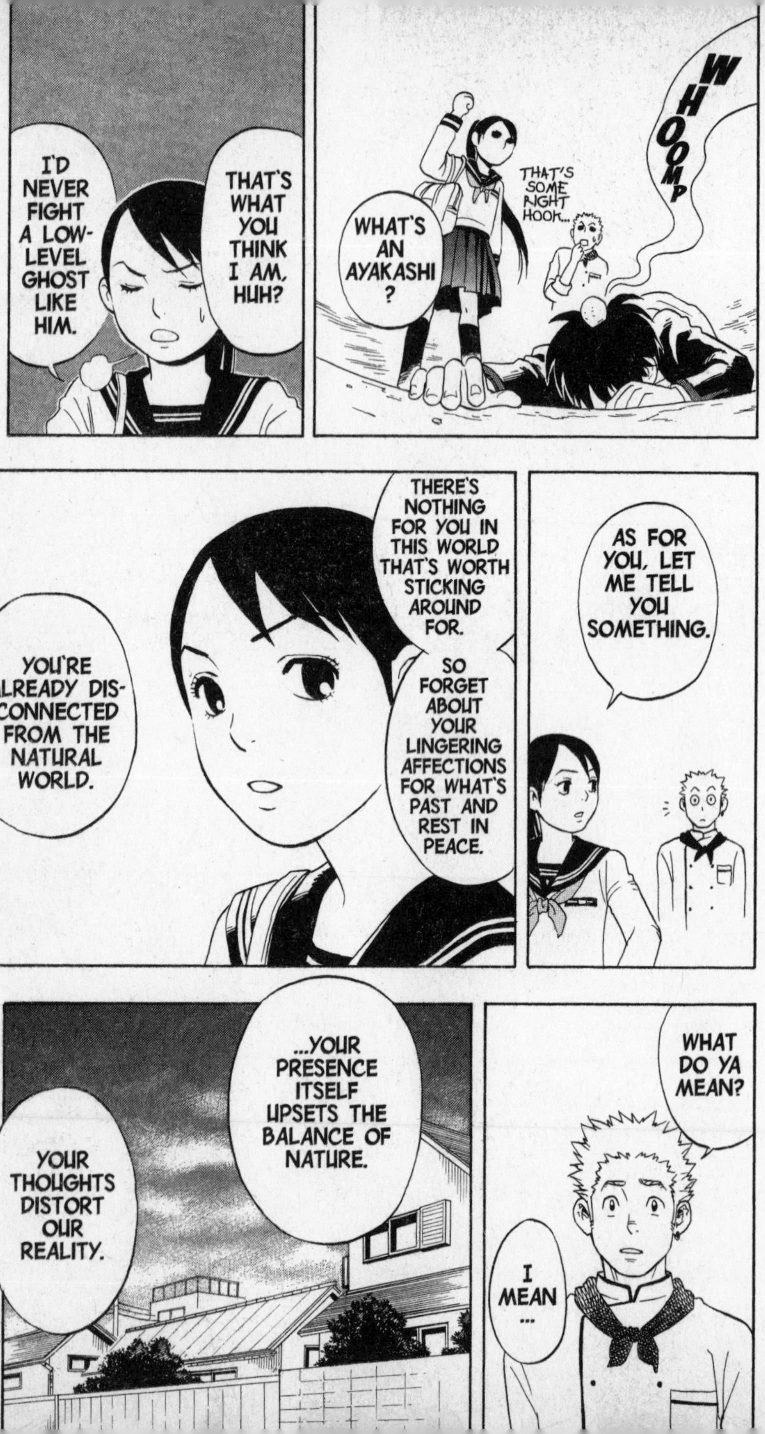
WHOOMP
THAT'S SOME RIGHT HOOK...
WHAT'S AN AYAKASHI?
THAT'S WHAT YOU THINK I AM, HUH?
I'D NEVER FIGHT A LOW-LEVEL GHOST LIKE HIM.
AS FOR YOU, LET ME TELL YOU SOMETHING.
THERE'S NOTHING FOR YOU IN THIS WORLD THAT'S WORTH STICKING AROUND FOR.
SO FORGET ABOUT YOUR LINGERING AFFECTIONS FOR WHAT'S PAST AND REST IN PEACE.
YOU'RE ALREADY DIS-CONNECTED FROM THE NATURAL WORLD.
WHAT DO YA MEAN?
I MEAN ...
...YOUR PRESENCE ITSELF UPSETS THE BALANCE OF NATURE.
YOUR THOUGHTS DISTORT OUR REALITY.

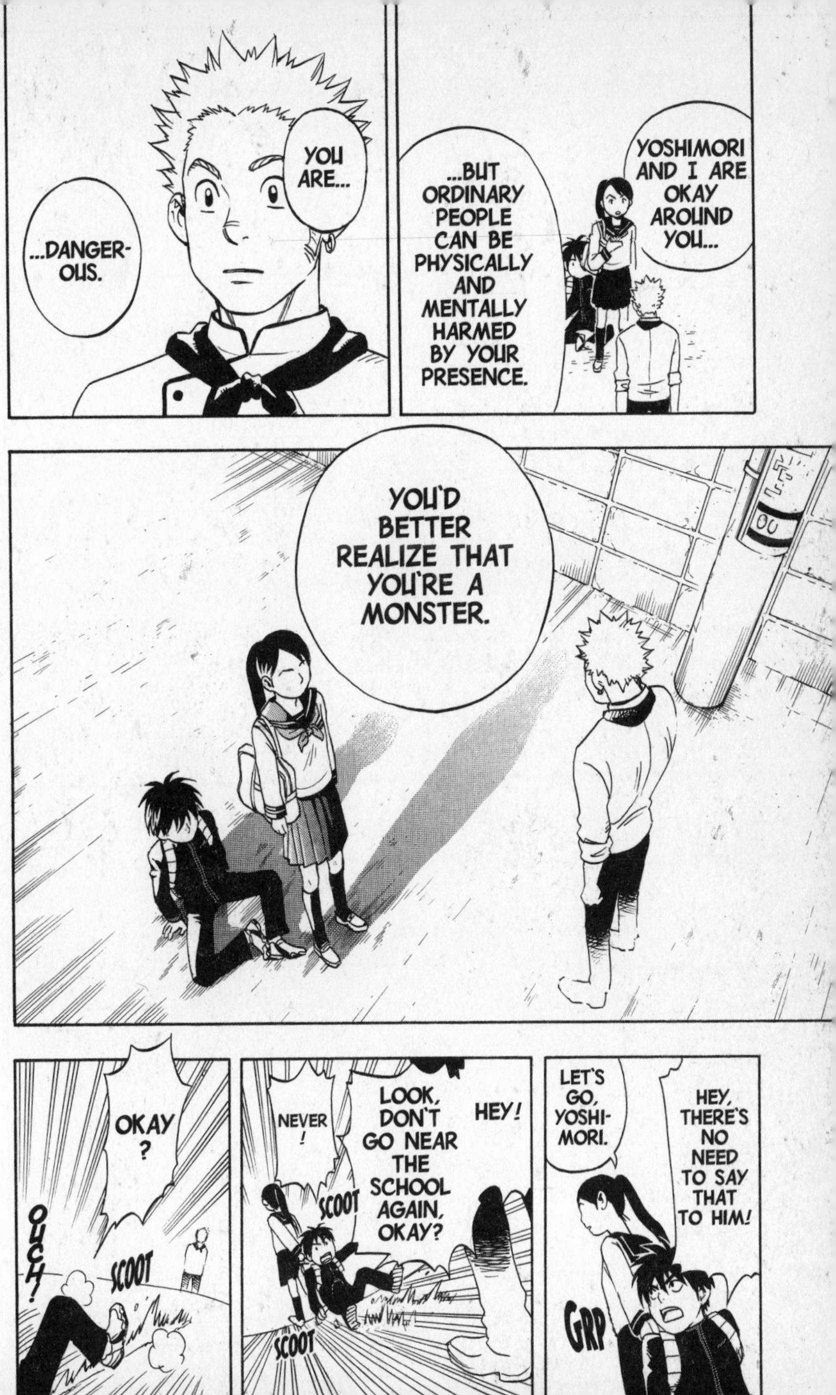
YOSHIMORI AND I ARE OKAY AROUND YOU...
...BUT ORDINARY PEOPLE CAN BE PHYSICALLY AND MENTALLY HARMED BY YOUR PRESENCE.
YOU ARE...
...DANGEROUS.
YOU'D BETTER REALIZE THAT YOU'RE A MONSTER.
HEY, THERE'S NO NEED TO SAY THAT TO HIM!
LET'S GO, YOSHIMORI.
GRP
HEY!
LOOK, DON'T GO NEAR THE SCHOOL AGAIN, OKAY?
NEVER!
SCOOT
SCOOT
OKAY?
OUCH!
SCOOT

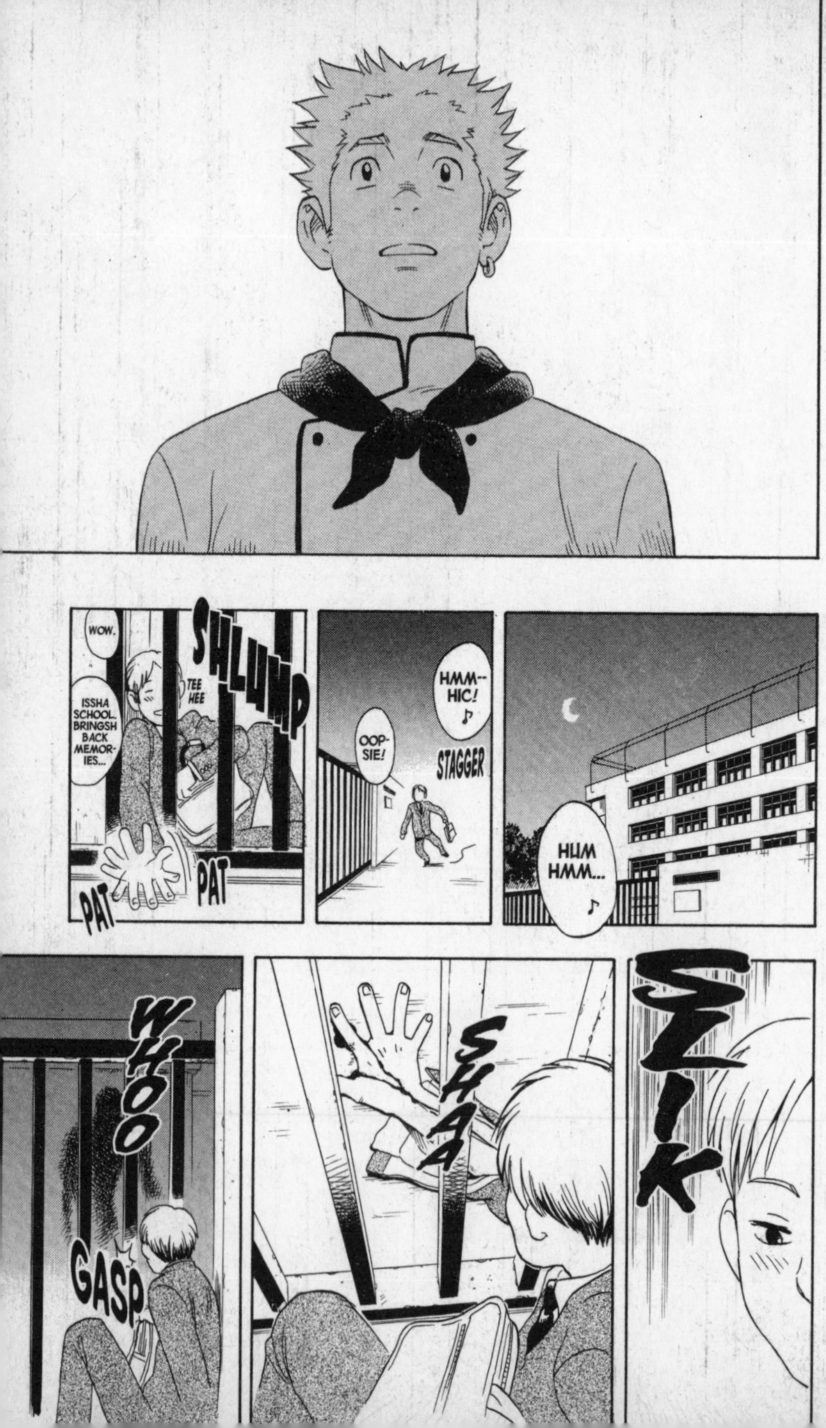
HUM HMM... ♪
HMM-- HIC! ♪
OOP-SIE!
STAGGER
WOW.
SHLUMP
TEE HEE
ISSHA SCHOOL. BRINGSH BACK MEMORIES...
PAT
PAT
SHAA
WHOO
GASP

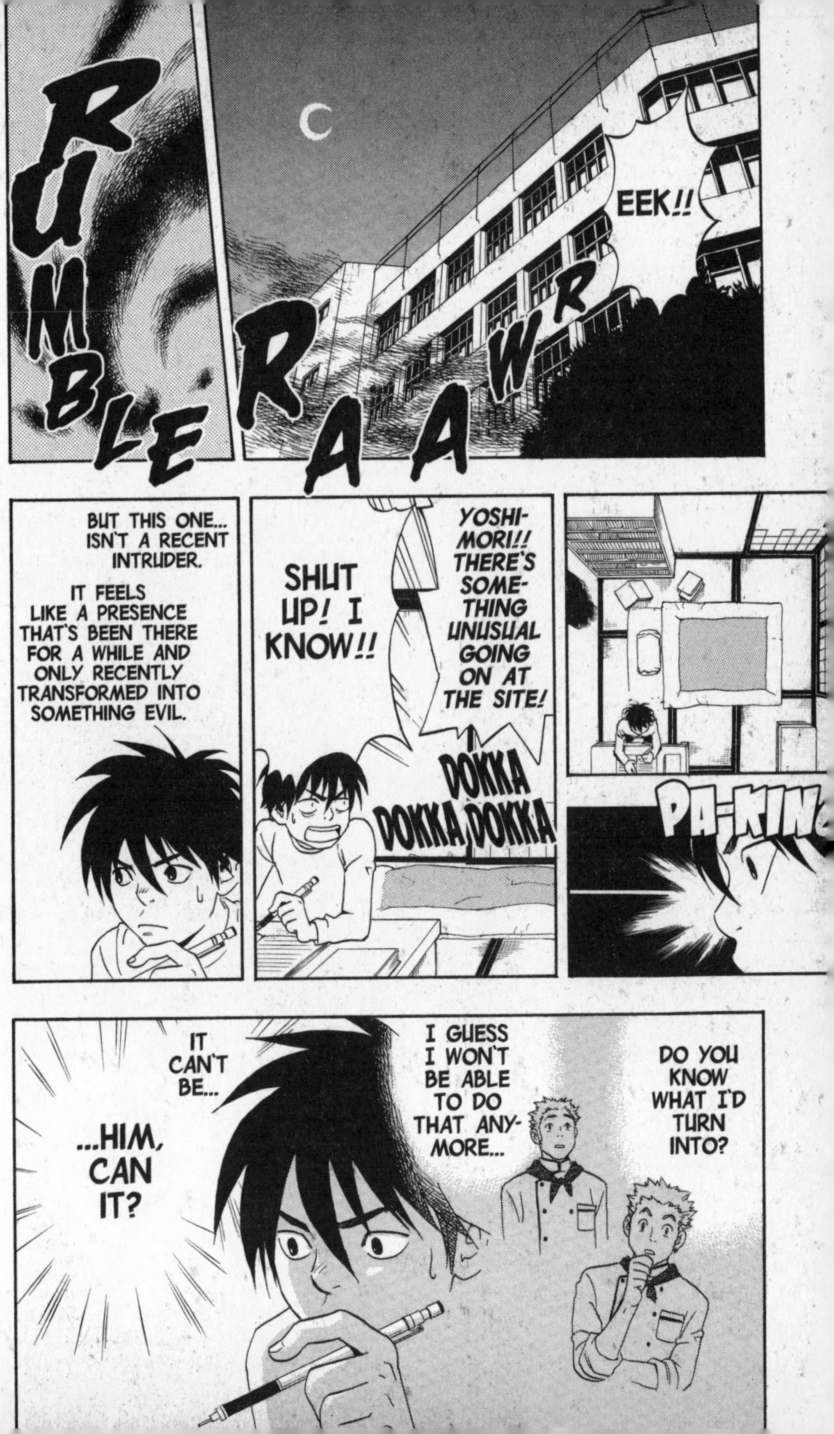
EEK!!
RAAAWR
RUMBLE
PA-KIN
YOSHI-MORI!! THERE'S SOME-THING UNUSUAL GOING ON AT THE SITE!
SHUT UP! I KNOW!!
DOKKA DOKKA DOKKA
BUT THIS ONE... ISN'T A RECENT INTRUDER.
IT FEELS LIKE A PRESENCE THAT'S BEEN THERE FOR A WHILE AND ONLY RECENTLY TRANSFORMED INTO SOMETHING EVIL.
DO YOU KNOW WHAT I'D TURN INTO?
I GUESS I WON'T BE ABLE TO DO THAT ANY-MORE...
IT CAN'T BE...
...HIM, CAN IT?

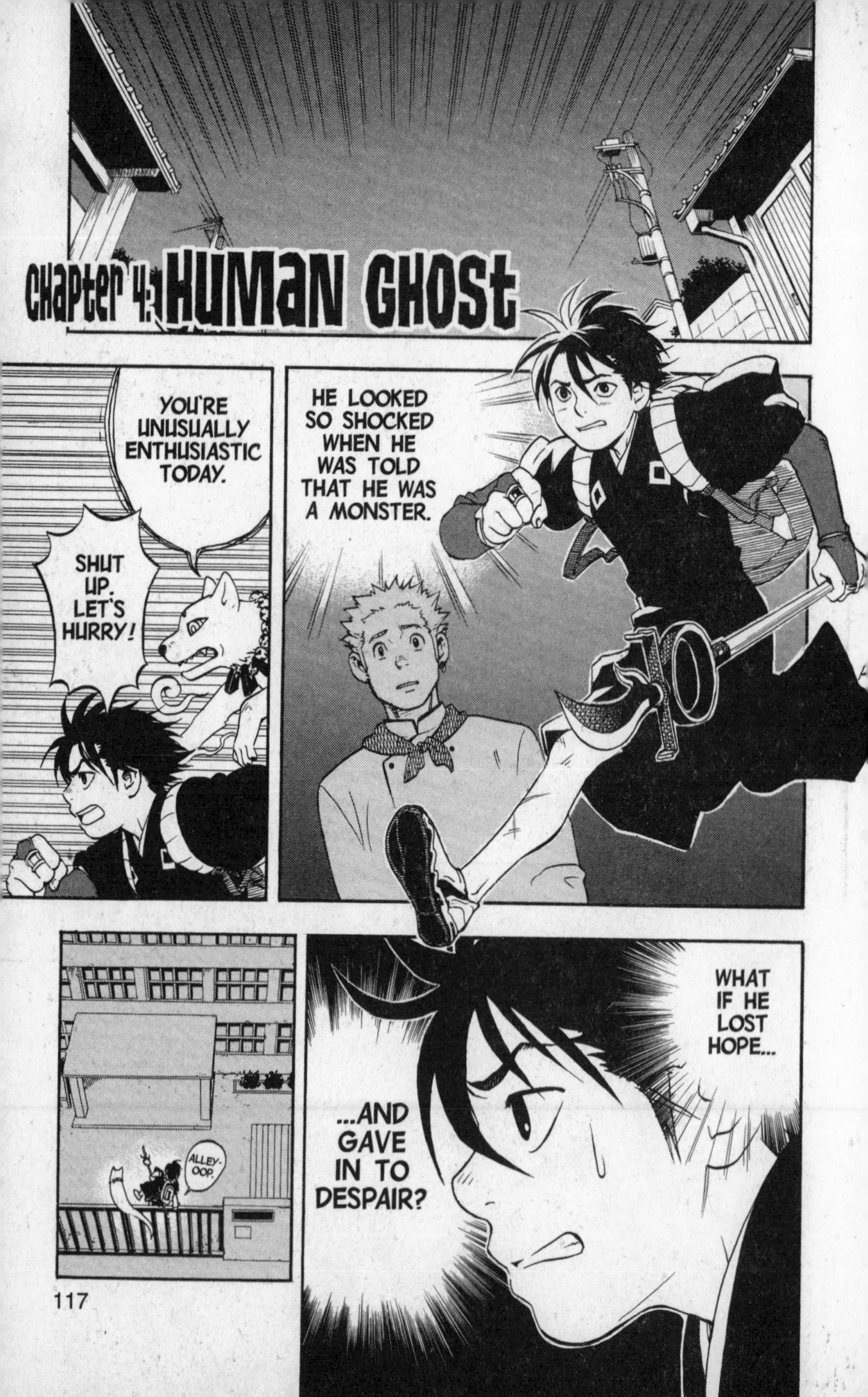
Chapter 4: Human Ghost
HE LOOKED SO SHOCKED WHEN HE WAS TOLD THAT HE WAS A MONSTER.
YOU'RE UNUSUALLY ENTHUSIASTIC TODAY.
SHUT UP. LET'S HURRY!
WHAT IF HE LOST HOPE...
...AND GAVE IN TO DESPAIR?
ALLEY-OOP.

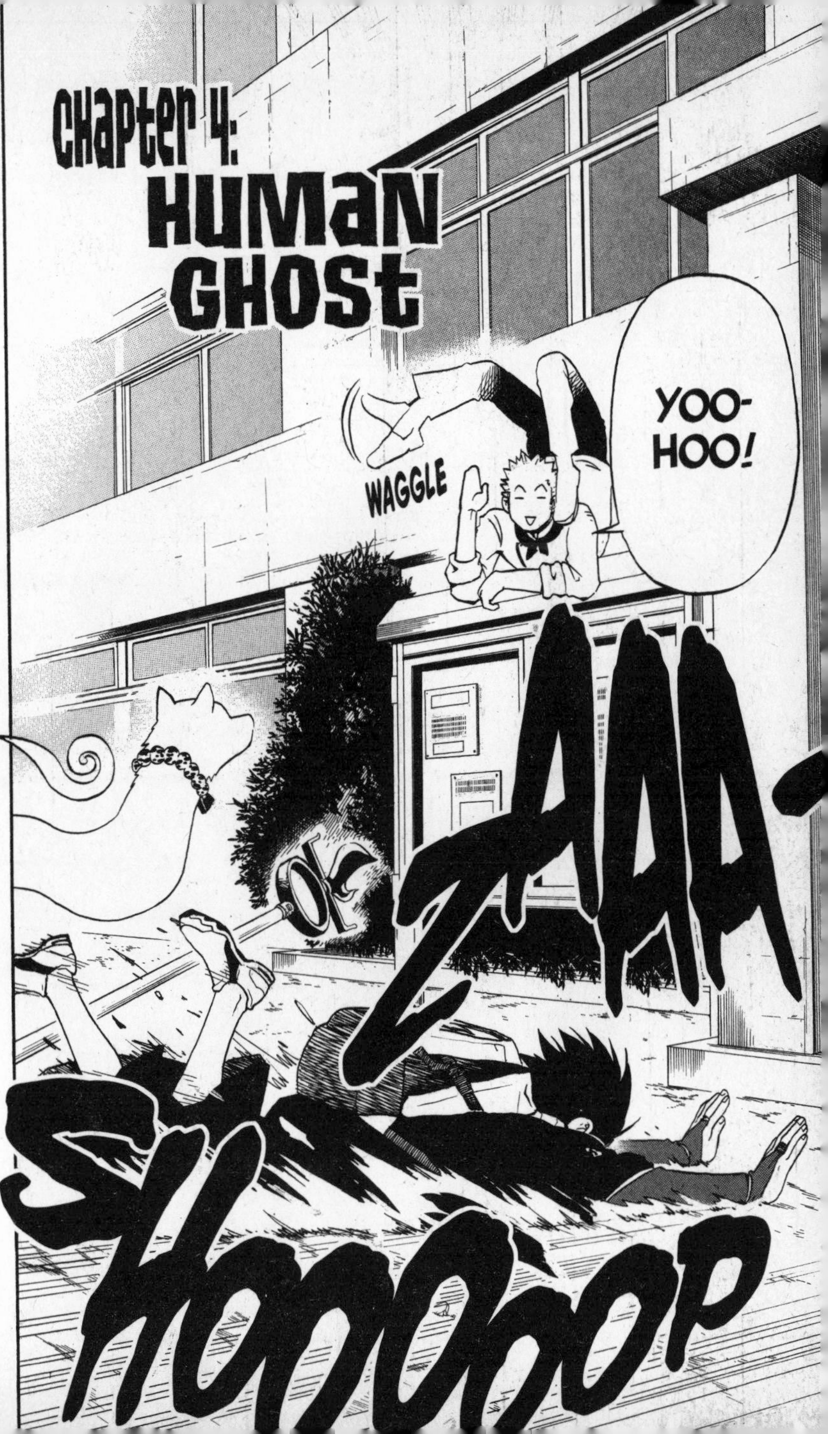
Chapter 4:
Human Ghost
YOO-HOO!
WAGGLE
ZAAA
SHOOOOP

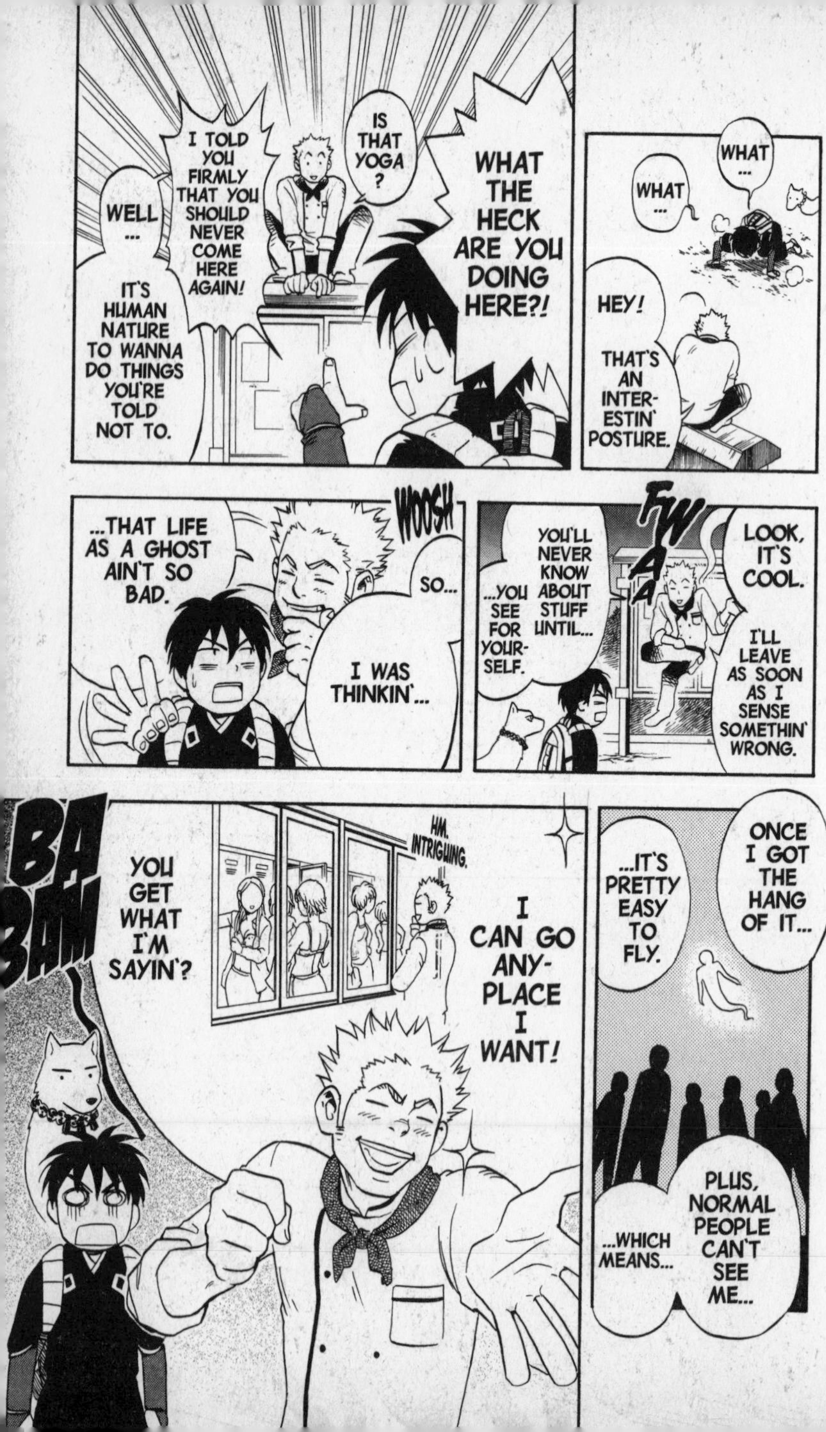
WHAT ...
WHAT ...
HEY!
THAT'S AN INTER-ESTIN' POSTURE.
WHAT THE HECK ARE YOU DOING HERE?!
IS THAT YOGA?
I TOLD YOU FIRMLY THAT YOU SHOULD NEVER COME HERE AGAIN!
WELL ...
IT'S HUMAN NATURE TO WANNA DO THINGS YOU'RE TOLD NOT TO.
LOOK, IT'S COOL.
I'LL LEAVE AS SOON AS I SENSE SOMETHIN' WRONG.
FWAA
YOU'LL NEVER KNOW ABOUT STUFF UNTIL...
...YOU SEE FOR YOUR-SELF.
WOOSH
SO...
I WAS THINKIN'...
...THAT LIFE AS A GHOST AIN'T SO BAD.
ONCE I GOT THE HANG OF IT...
...IT'S PRETTY EASY TO FLY.
PLUS, NORMAL PEOPLE CAN'T SEE ME...
...WHICH MEANS...
I CAN GO ANY-PLACE I WANT!
HM. INTRIGUING.
YOU GET WHAT I'M SAYIN'?
BA BAM

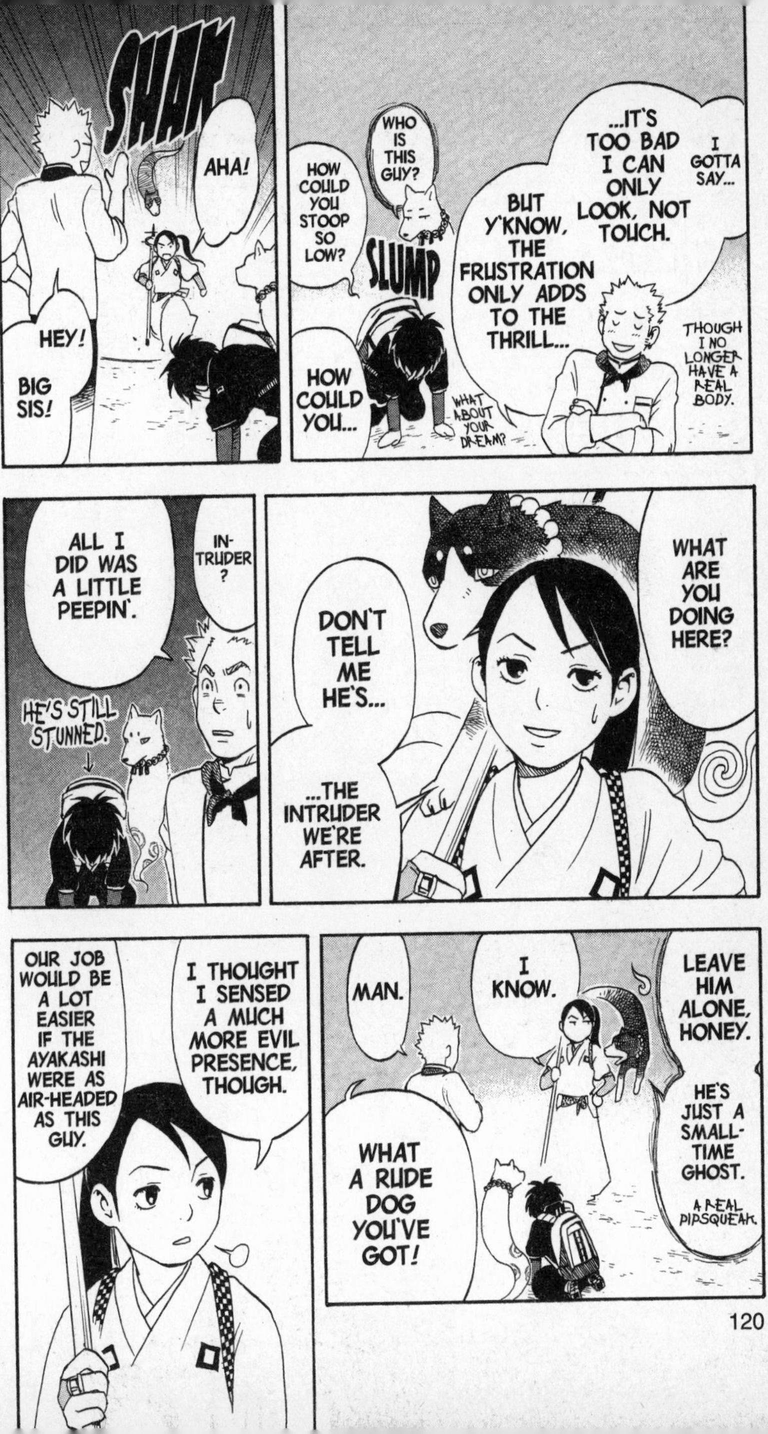
I GOTTA SAY...
...IT'S TOO BAD I CAN ONLY LOOK, NOT TOUCH.
BUT Y'KNOW, THE FRUSTRATION ONLY ADDS TO THE THRILL...
THOUGH I NO LONGER HAVE A REAL BODY.
WHO IS THIS GUY?
HOW COULD YOU STOOP SO LOW?
SLUMP
HOW COULD YOU...
WHAT ABOUT YOUR DREAM?
SHAK
AHA!
HEY! BIG SIS!
WHAT ARE YOU DOING HERE?
DON'T TELL ME HE'S...
...THE INTRUDER WE'RE AFTER.
IN-TRUDER?
ALL I DID WAS A LITTLE PEEPIN'.
HE'S STILL STUNNED.
LEAVE HIM ALONE, HONEY.
HE'S JUST A SMALL-TIME GHOST.
A REAL PIPSQUEAK.
I KNOW.
MAN.
WHAT A RUDE DOG YOU'VE GOT!
I THOUGHT I SENSED A MUCH MORE EVIL PRESENCE, THOUGH.
OUR JOB WOULD BE A LOT EASIER IF THE AYAKASHI WERE AS AIR-HEADED AS THIS GUY.

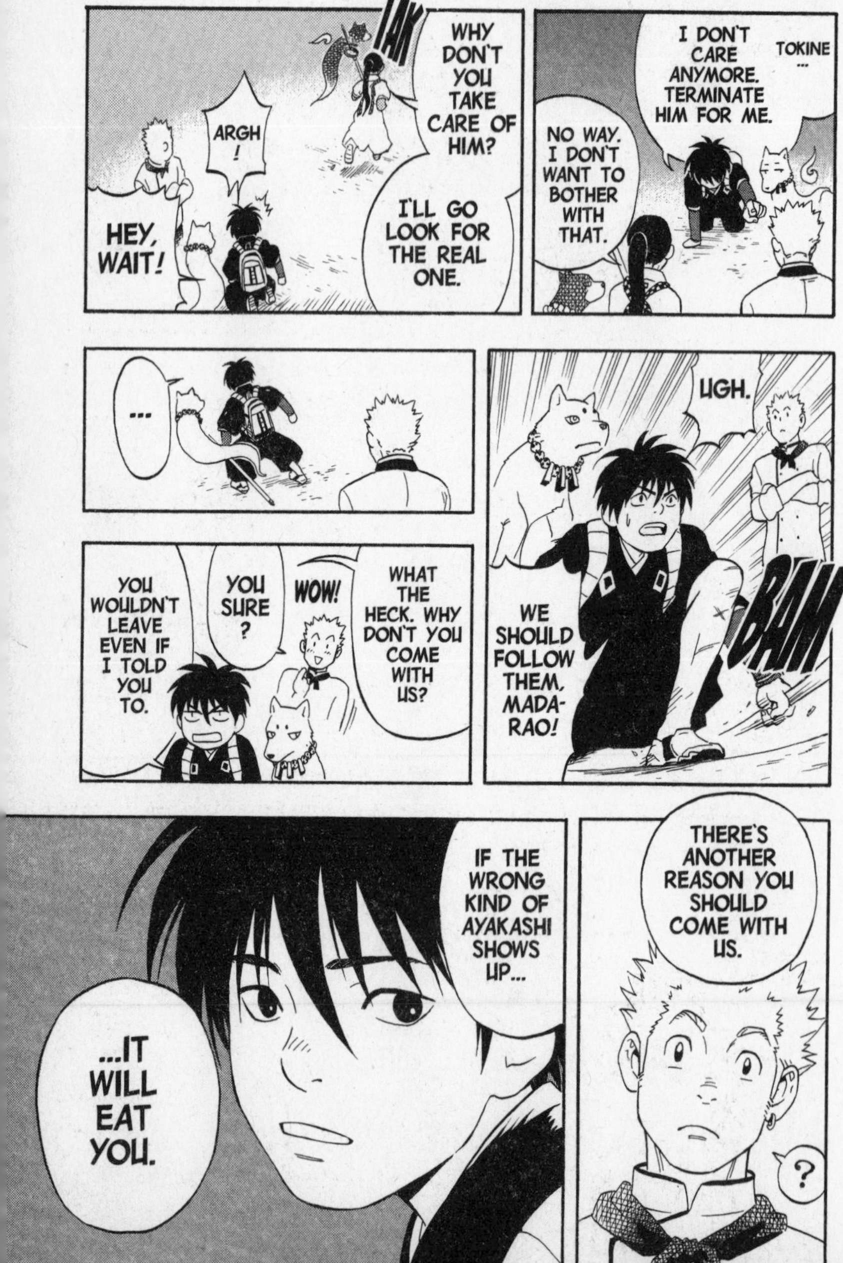
I DON'T CARE ANYMORE. TERMINATE HIM FOR ME.
TOKINE...
NO WAY. I DON'T WANT TO BOTHER WITH THAT.
TAK
WHY DON'T YOU TAKE CARE OF HIM?
I'LL GO LOOK FOR THE REAL ONE.
ARGH!
HEY, WAIT!
UGH.
BAM
WE SHOULD FOLLOW THEM, MADARAO!
...
WHAT THE HECK. WHY DON'T YOU COME WITH US?
WOW!
YOU SURE?
YOU WOULDN'T LEAVE EVEN IF I TOLD YOU TO.
THERE'S ANOTHER REASON YOU SHOULD COME WITH US.
?
IF THE WRONG KIND OF AYAKASHI SHOWS UP...
...IT WILL EAT YOU.

H T A

H T A

H T A

WOULD YOU TWO STOP JABBERING?!

THIS ISN'T A GAME!

THIS IS GETTIN' IN- TENSE!

YOU REALLY ARE A MARTIAL- ARTS GUY!

HOLY CRUD.

I CAN'T CONCEN- TRATE!!

DAK

GRR R R

DAK DAK DAK

DAK

OLD OBJECTS WITH VERY STRONG SPIRITS CAN OCCASIONALLY BECOME AYAKASHI...

AN UM- BRELLA

...BUT SUCH OBJECTS RARELY TURN UP HERE.

AN UMBRELLA GHOST.

AN ANCIENT EXAMPLE.

RATHER, IT'S AS IF WHATEVER IT IS BECAME EVIL ONLY AFTER ARRIVING.

I'M ALMOST CERTAIN THAT THIS IS A GHOST.

AYAKASHI, UNLIKE GHOSTS, ARE BASICALLY EVIL FROM THE GET-GO.

IT DOESN'T FEEL LIKE SOMETHING THAT WAS ALREADY EVIL ENTERED HERE.

TONIGHT'S PREY ISN'T AN AYA- KASHI!

I CAN'T HELP IT! I'VE NEVER SEEN AN AYA- KASHI!

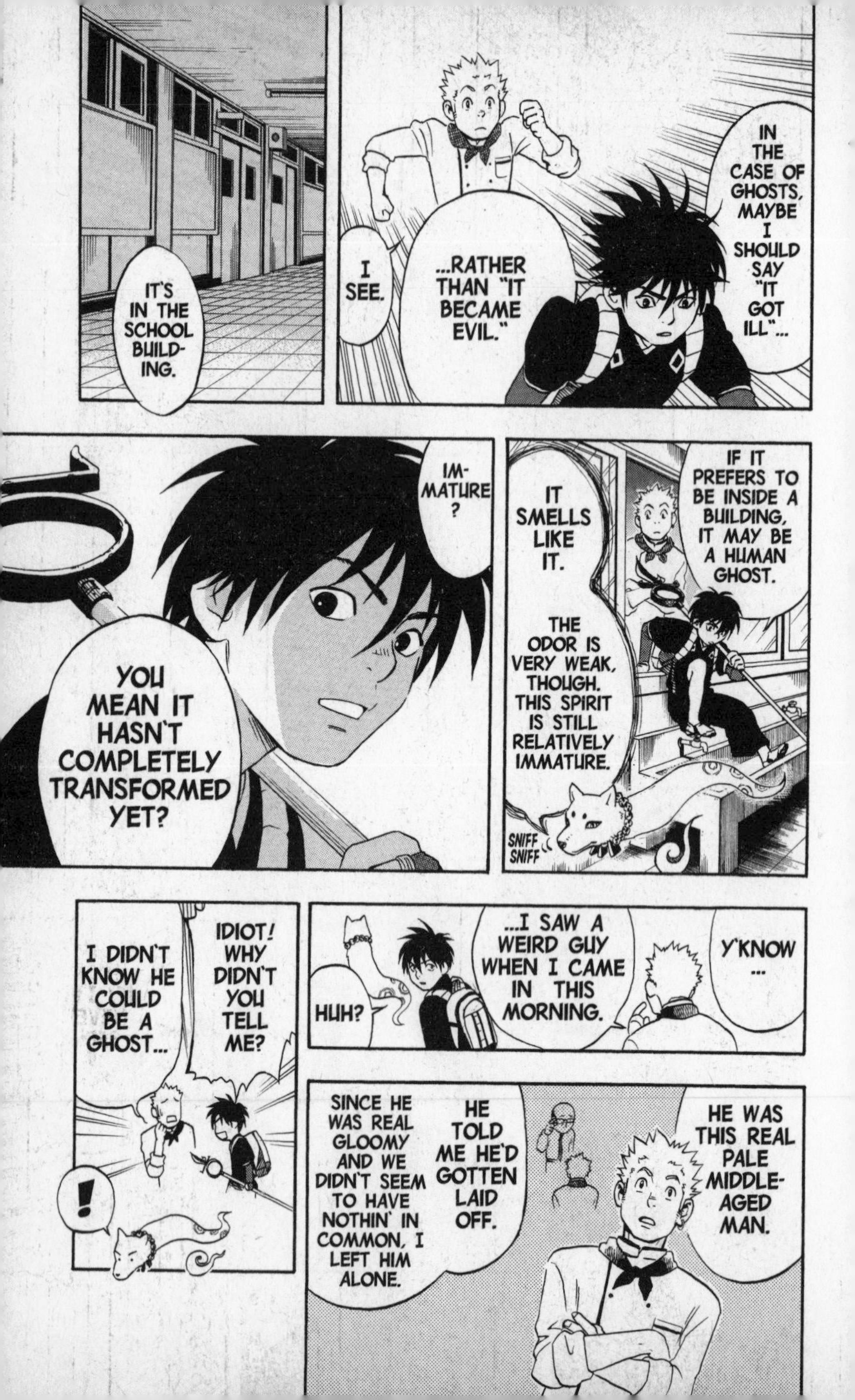
IN THE CASE OF GHOSTS, MAYBE I SHOULD SAY "IT GOT ILL"...
...RATHER THAN "IT BECAME EVIL."
I SEE.
IT'S IN THE SCHOOL BUILD-ING.
IF IT PREFERS TO BE INSIDE A BUILDING, IT MAY BE A HUMAN GHOST.
IT SMELLS LIKE IT.
THE ODOR IS VERY WEAK, THOUGH. THIS SPIRIT IS STILL RELATIVELY IMMATURE.
SNIFF SNIFF
IM-MATURE?
YOU MEAN IT HASN'T COMPLETELY TRANSFORMED YET?
Y'KNOW...
...I SAW A WEIRD GUY WHEN I CAME IN THIS MORNING.
HUH?
HE WAS THIS REAL PALE MIDDLE-AGED MAN.
HE TOLD ME HE'D GOTTEN LAID OFF.
SINCE HE WAS REAL GLOOMY AND WE DIDN'T SEEM TO HAVE NOTHIN' IN COMMON, I LEFT HIM ALONE.
IDIOT! WHY DIDN'T YOU TELL ME?
I DIDN'T KNOW HE COULD BE A GHOST...
!

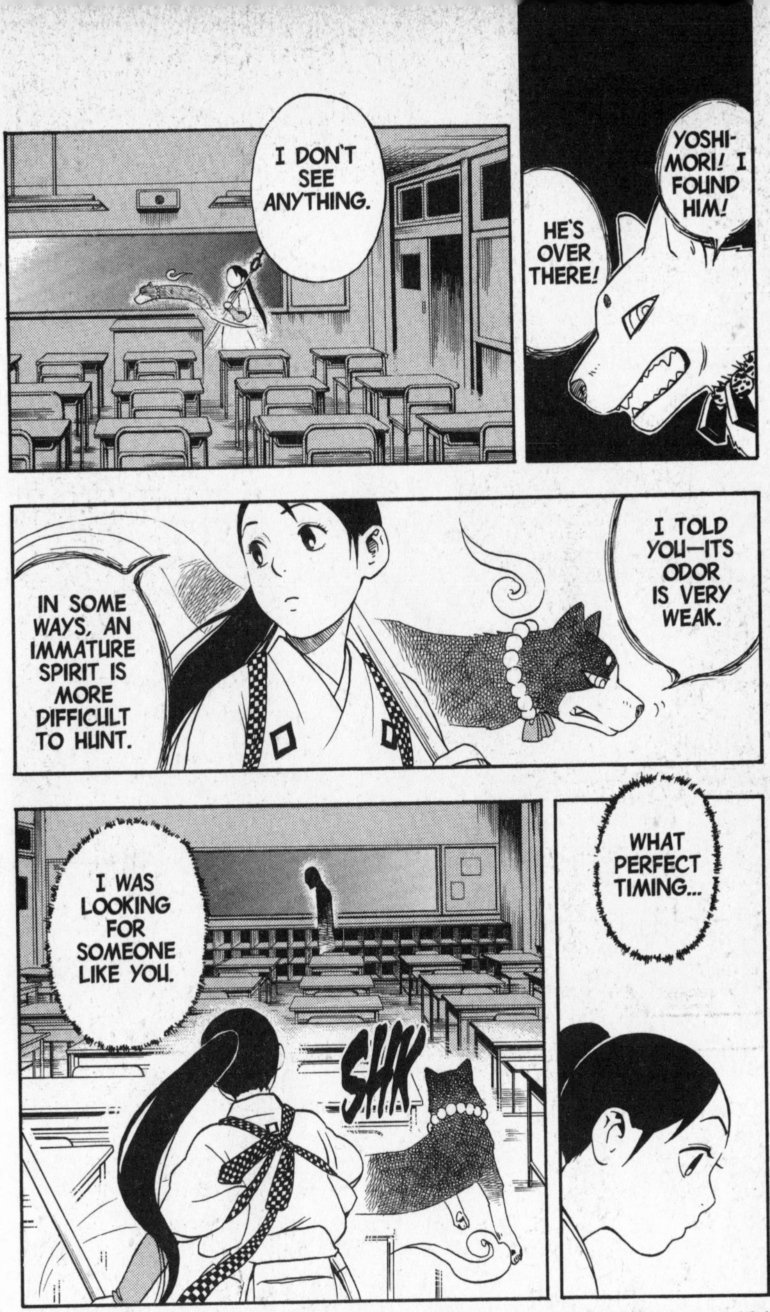
YOSHI-MORI! I FOUND HIM!
HE'S OVER THERE!
I DON'T SEE ANYTHING.
I TOLD YOU—ITS ODOR IS VERY WEAK.
IN SOME WAYS, AN IMMATURE SPIRIT IS MORE DIFFICULT TO HUNT.
WHAT PERFECT TIMING...
I WAS LOOKING FOR SOMEONE LIKE YOU.
SHK

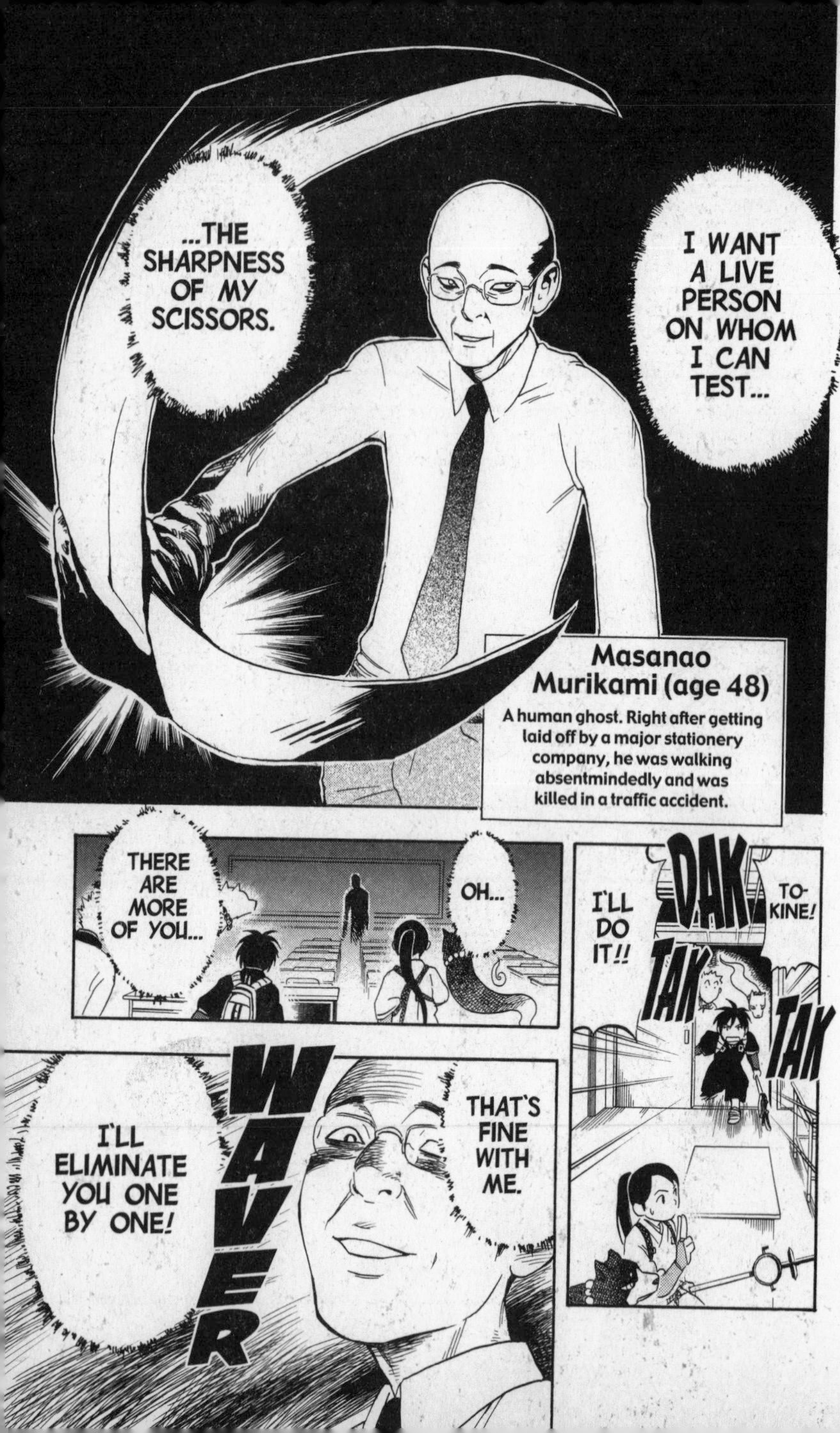
I WANT A LIVE PERSON ON WHOM I CAN TEST...
...THE SHARPNESS OF MY SCISSORS.
Masanao Murikami (age 48)
A human ghost. Right after getting laid off by a major stationery company, he was walking absentmindedly and was killed in a traffic accident.
OH...
THERE ARE MORE OF YOU...
THAT'S FINE WITH ME.
WAVER
I'LL ELIMINATE YOU ONE BY ONE!
TO-KINE!
DAK
I'LL DO IT!!
TAK
TAK

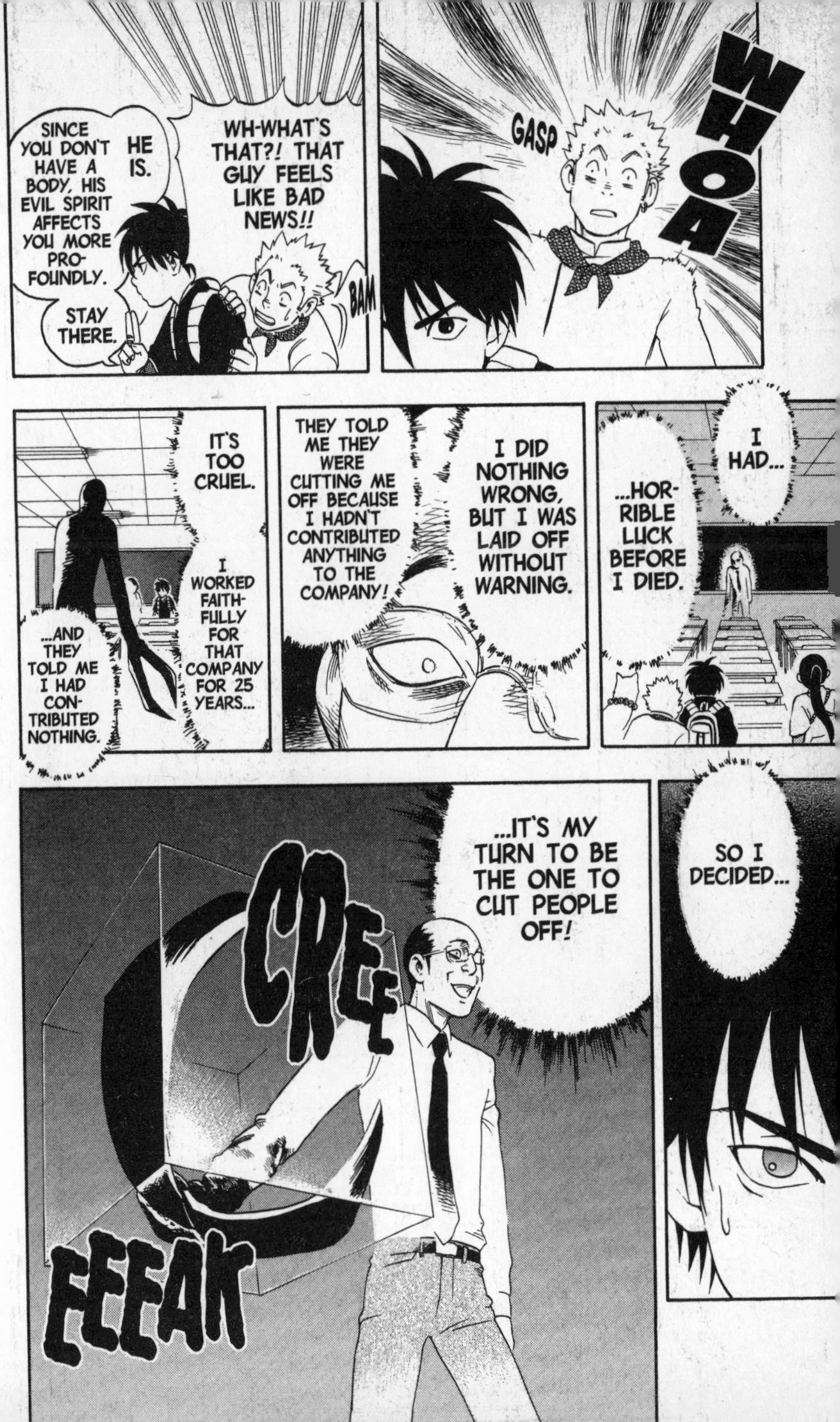
WHOA
GASP
WH-WHAT'S THAT?! THAT GUY FEELS LIKE BAD NEWS!!
HE IS.
SINCE YOU DON'T HAVE A BODY, HIS EVIL SPIRIT AFFECTS YOU MORE PRO-FOUNDLY.
BAM
STAY THERE.
I HAD...
...HOR-RIBLE LUCK BEFORE I DIED.
I DID NOTHING WRONG, BUT I WAS LAID OFF WITHOUT WARNING.
THEY TOLD ME THEY WERE CUTTING ME OFF BECAUSE I HADN'T CONTRIBUTED ANYTHING TO THE COMPANY!
IT'S TOO CRUEL.
I WORKED FAITH-FULLY FOR THAT COMPANY FOR 25 YEARS...
...AND THEY TOLD ME I HAD CON-TRIBUTED NOTHING.
SO I DECIDED...
...IT'S MY TURN TO BE THE ONE TO CUT PEOPLE OFF!
CREE
EEEAK

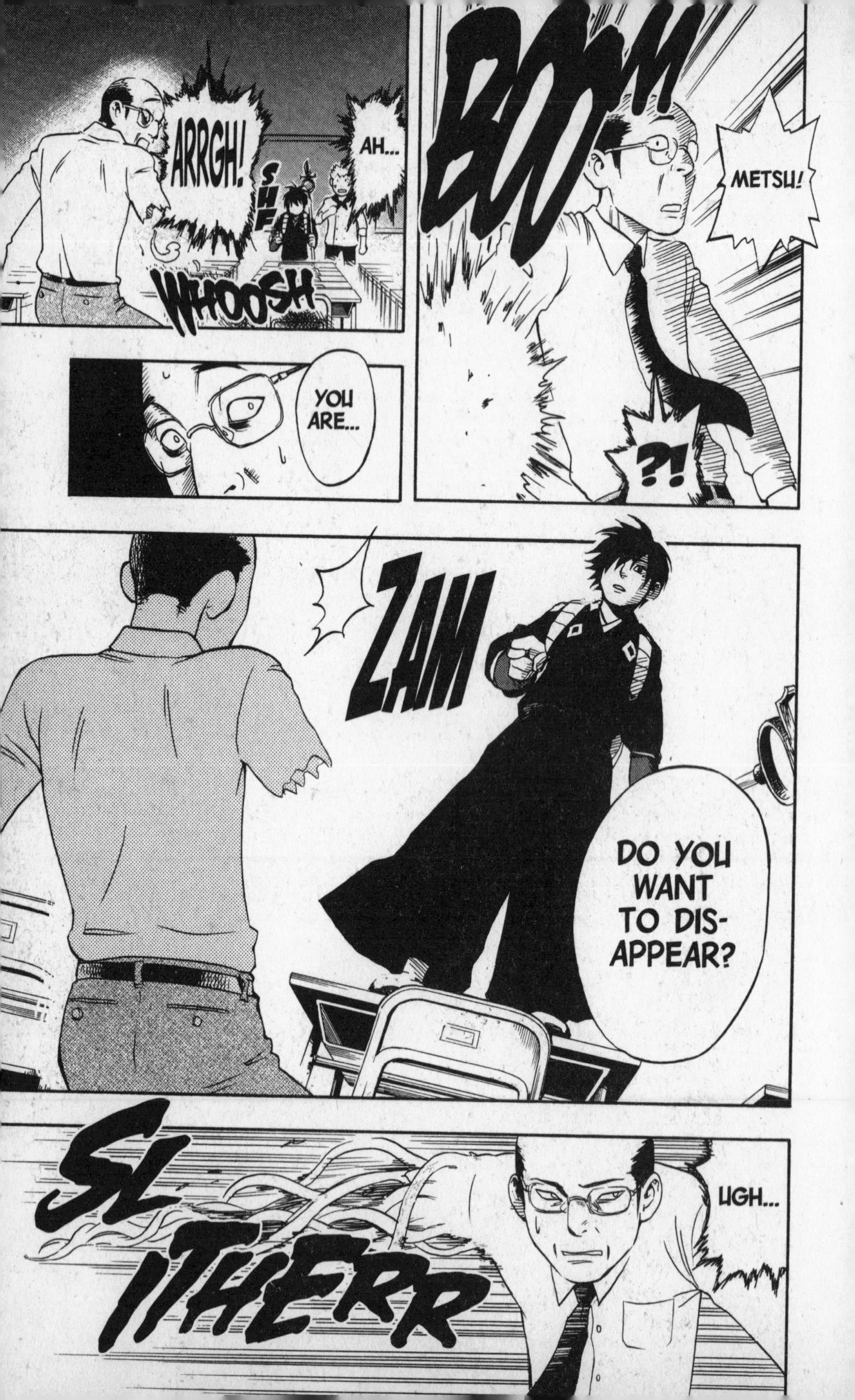
METSU!
BOOM
?!
AH...
ARRGH!
SHF
WHOOSH
YOU ARE...
DO YOU WANT TO DIS- APPEAR?
ZAM
UGH...
SL ITHERR

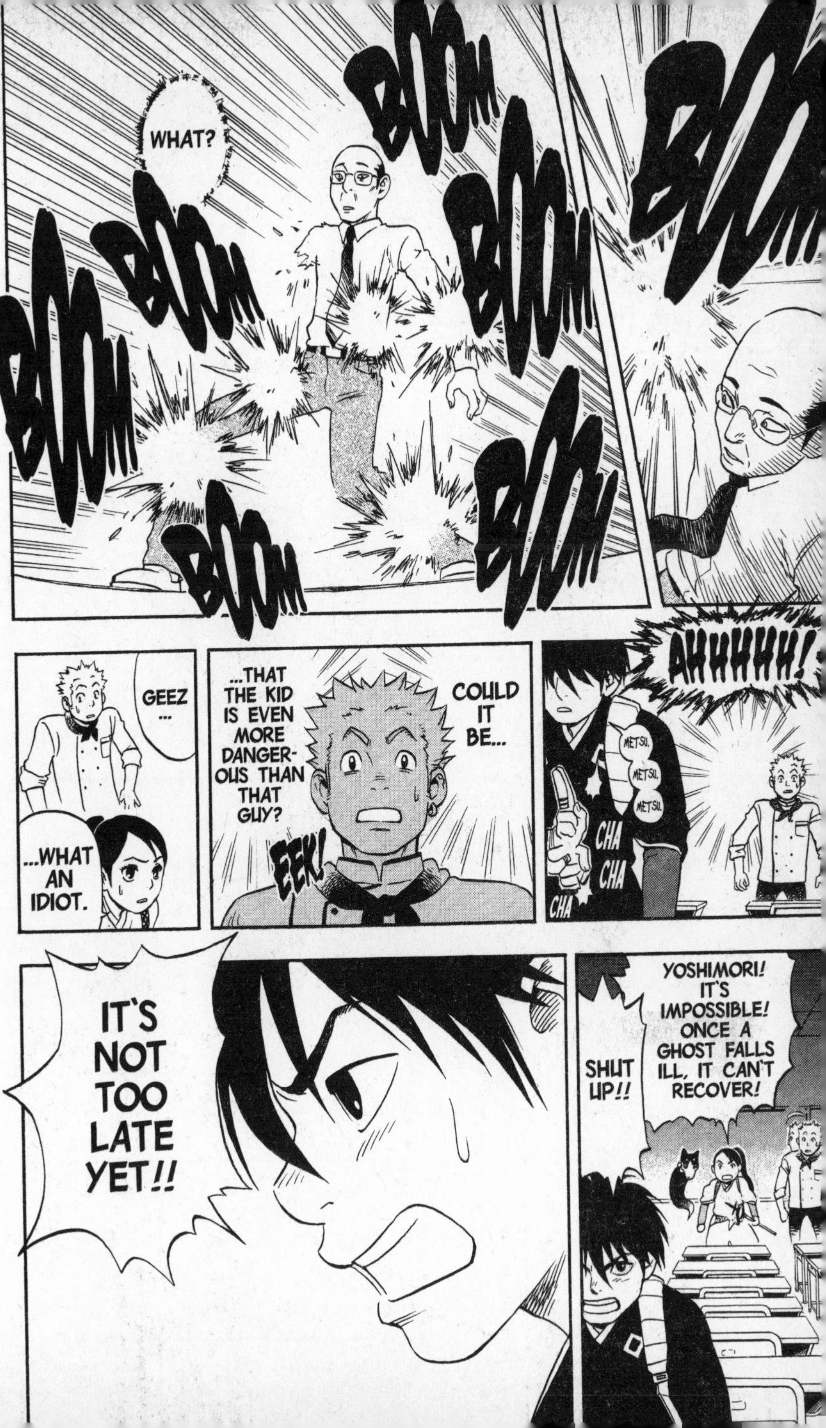
BOOM
WHAT?
BOOM
BOOM
BOOM
BOOM
BOOM
BOOM
BOOM
AHHHHH!
METSU.
METSU.
METSU.
CHA
CHA
CHA
COULD IT BE...
...THAT THE KID IS EVEN MORE DANGEROUS THAN THAT GUY?
EEK!
GEEZ...
...WHAT AN IDIOT.
YOSHIMORI! IT'S IMPOSSIBLE! ONCE A GHOST FALLS ILL, IT CAN'T RECOVER!
SHUT UP!!
IT'S NOT TOO LATE YET!!

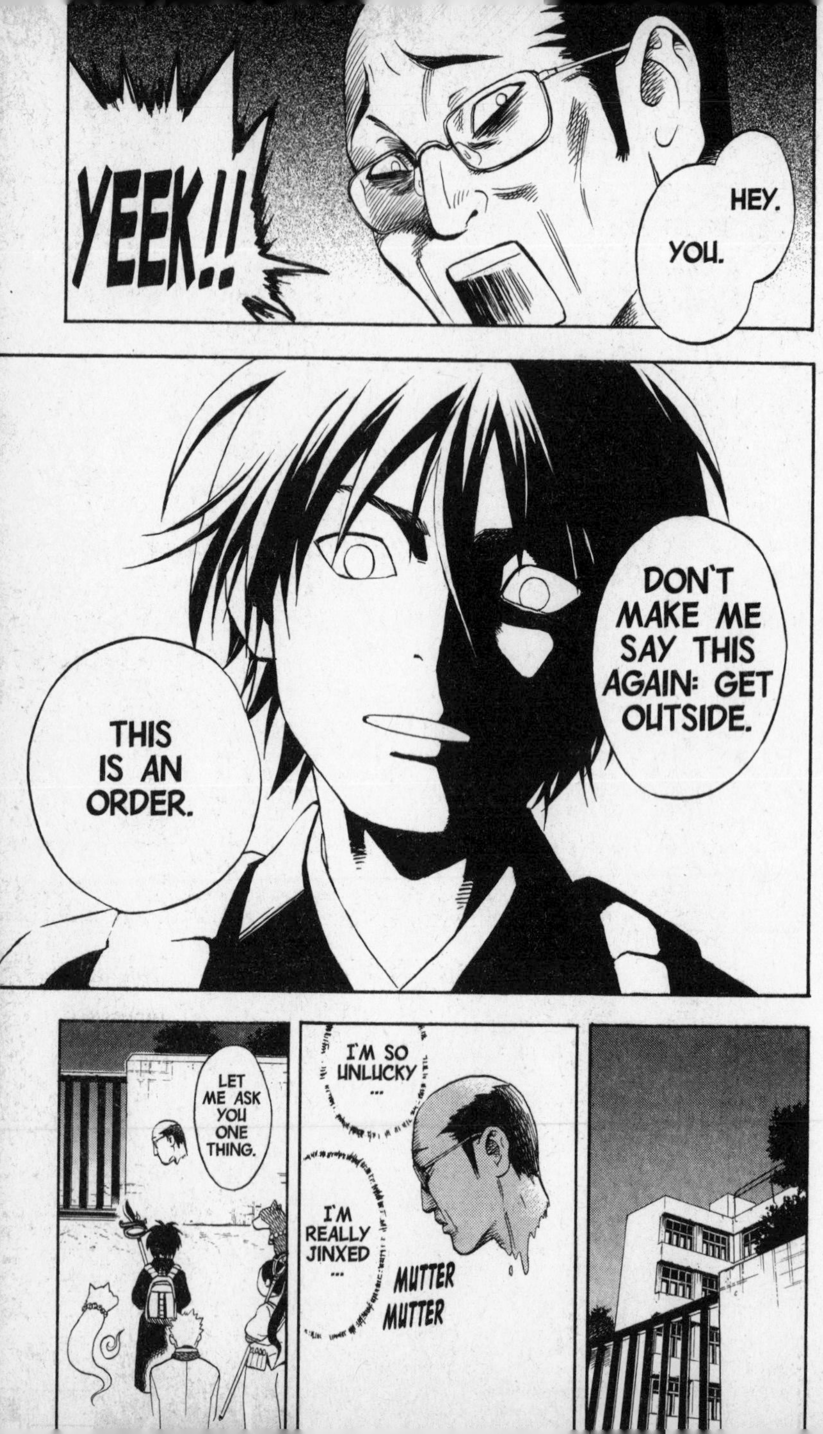
HEY.
YOU.
YEEK!!
DON'T MAKE ME SAY THIS AGAIN: GET OUTSIDE.
THIS IS AN ORDER.
I'M SO UNLUCKY...
I'M REALLY JINXED...
MUTTER MUTTER
LET ME ASK YOU ONE THING.

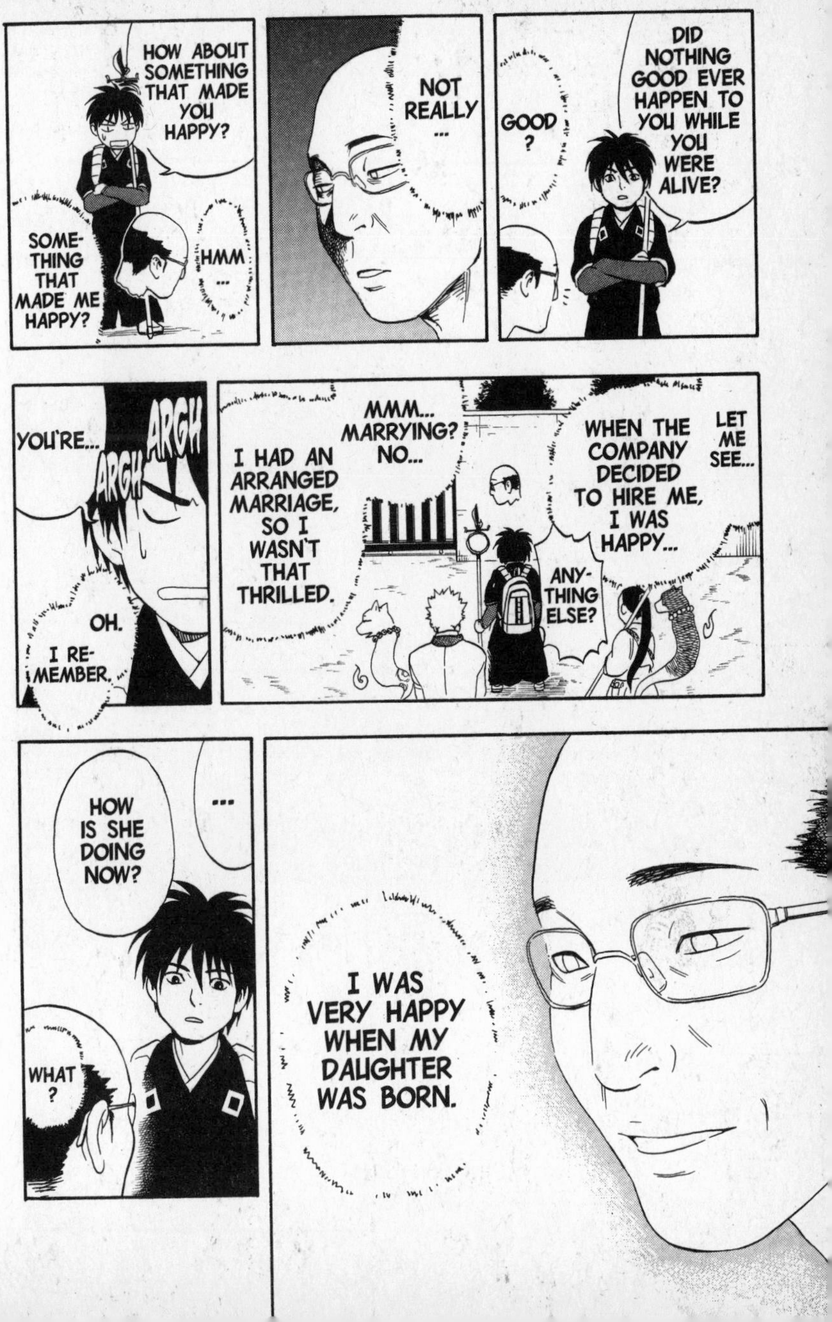
DID NOTHING GOOD EVER HAPPEN TO YOU WHILE YOU WERE ALIVE?
GOOD?
NOT REALLY...
HOW ABOUT SOMETHING THAT MADE YOU HAPPY?
HMM...
SOMETHING THAT MADE ME HAPPY?
LET ME SEE...
WHEN THE COMPANY DECIDED TO HIRE ME, I WAS HAPPY...
ANYTHING ELSE?
MMM... MARRYING? NO...
I HAD AN ARRANGED MARRIAGE, SO I WASN'T THAT THRILLED.
ARGH
ARGH
YOU'RE...
OH. I REMEMBER.
I WAS VERY HAPPY WHEN MY DAUGHTER WAS BORN.
...
HOW IS SHE DOING NOW?
WHAT?

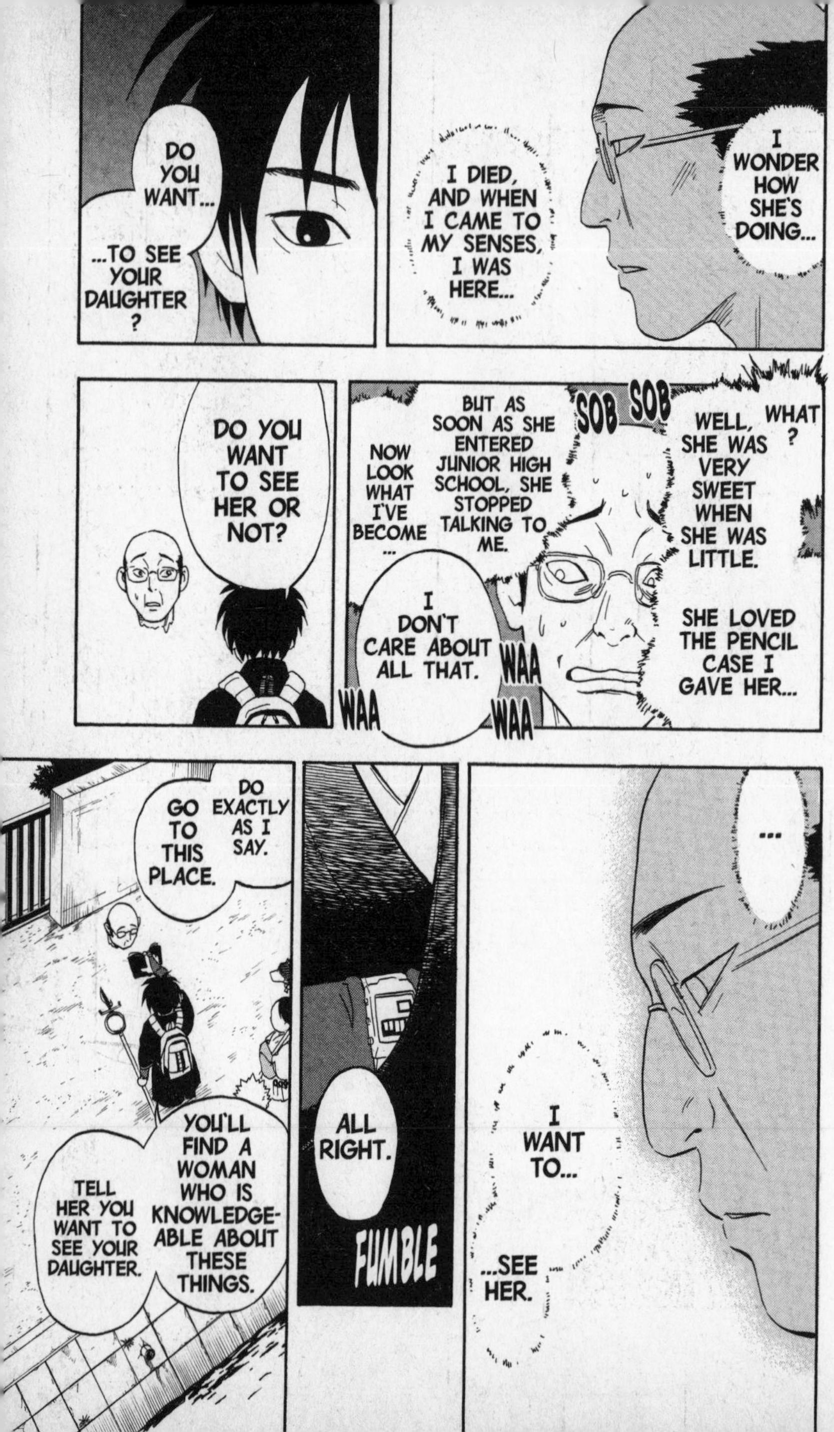
I WONDER HOW SHE'S DOING...
I DIED, AND WHEN I CAME TO MY SENSES, I WAS HERE...
DO YOU WANT...
...TO SEE YOUR DAUGHTER?
WHAT?
WELL, SHE WAS VERY SWEET WHEN SHE WAS LITTLE.
SHE LOVED THE PENCIL CASE I GAVE HER...
SOB SOB
BUT AS SOON AS SHE ENTERED JUNIOR HIGH SCHOOL, SHE STOPPED TALKING TO ME.
NOW LOOK WHAT I'VE BECOME...
I DON'T CARE ABOUT ALL THAT.
WAA WAA WAA
DO YOU WANT TO SEE HER OR NOT?
...
I WANT TO...
...SEE HER.
ALL RIGHT.
FUMBLE
DO EXACTLY AS I SAY.
GO TO THIS PLACE.
YOU'LL FIND A WOMAN WHO IS KNOWLEDGE-ABLE ABOUT THESE THINGS.
TELL HER YOU WANT TO SEE YOUR DAUGHTER.

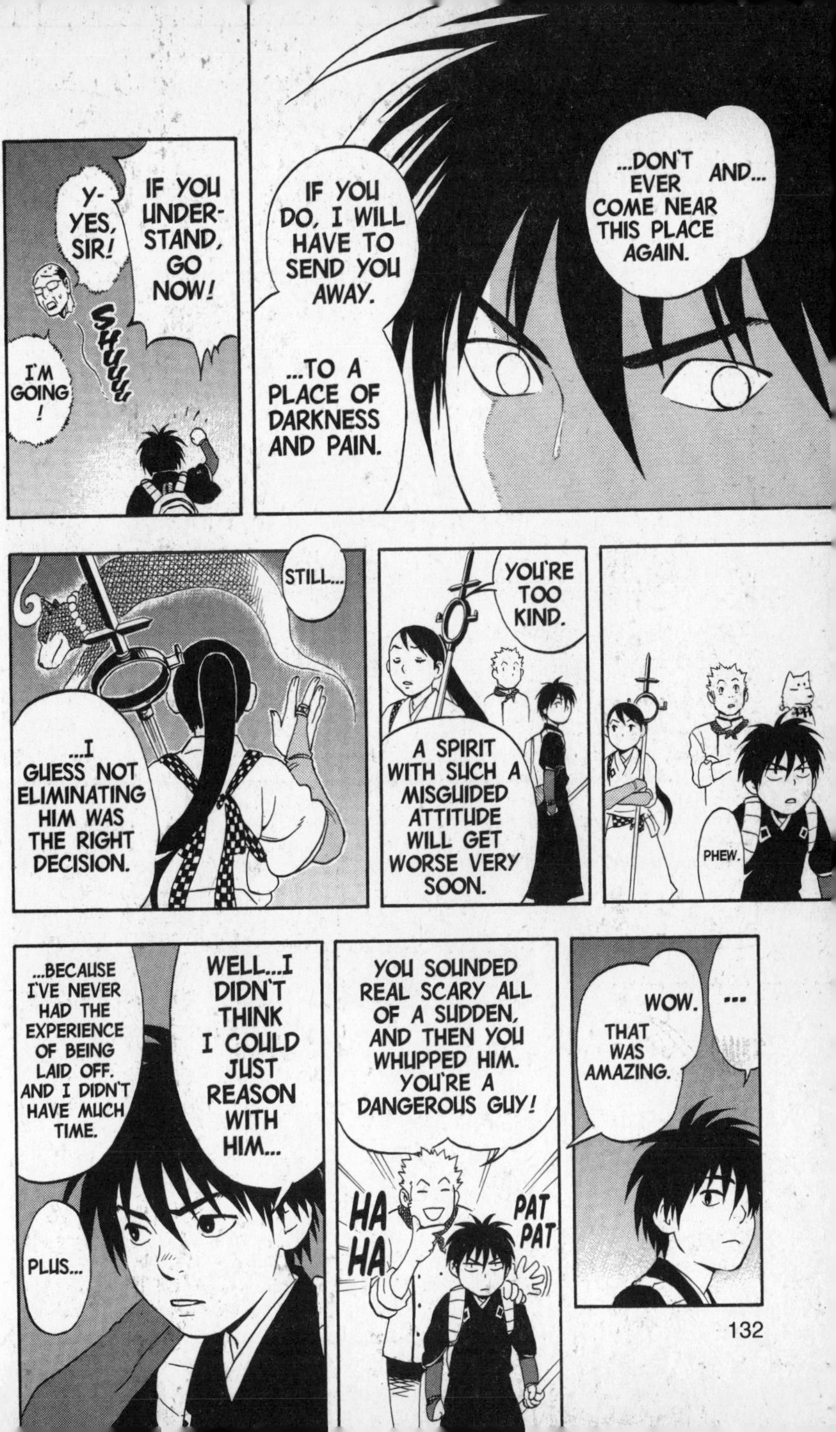
AND...
...DON'T EVER COME NEAR THIS PLACE AGAIN.
IF YOU DO, I WILL HAVE TO SEND YOU AWAY.
...TO A PLACE OF DARKNESS AND PAIN.
IF YOU UNDERSTAND, GO NOW!
Y-YES, SIR!
SHUUUU
I'M GOING!
PHEW.
YOU'RE TOO KIND.
A SPIRIT WITH SUCH A MISGUIDED ATTITUDE WILL GET WORSE VERY SOON.
STILL...
...I GUESS NOT ELIMINATING HIM WAS THE RIGHT DECISION.
...
WOW. THAT WAS AMAZING.
YOU SOUNDED REAL SCARY ALL OF A SUDDEN, AND THEN YOU WHUPPED HIM. YOU'RE A DANGEROUS GUY!
HA HA
PAT PAT
WELL...I DIDN'T THINK I COULD JUST REASON WITH HIM...
...BECAUSE I'VE NEVER HAD THE EXPERIENCE OF BEING LAID OFF. AND I DIDN'T HAVE MUCH TIME.
PLUS...

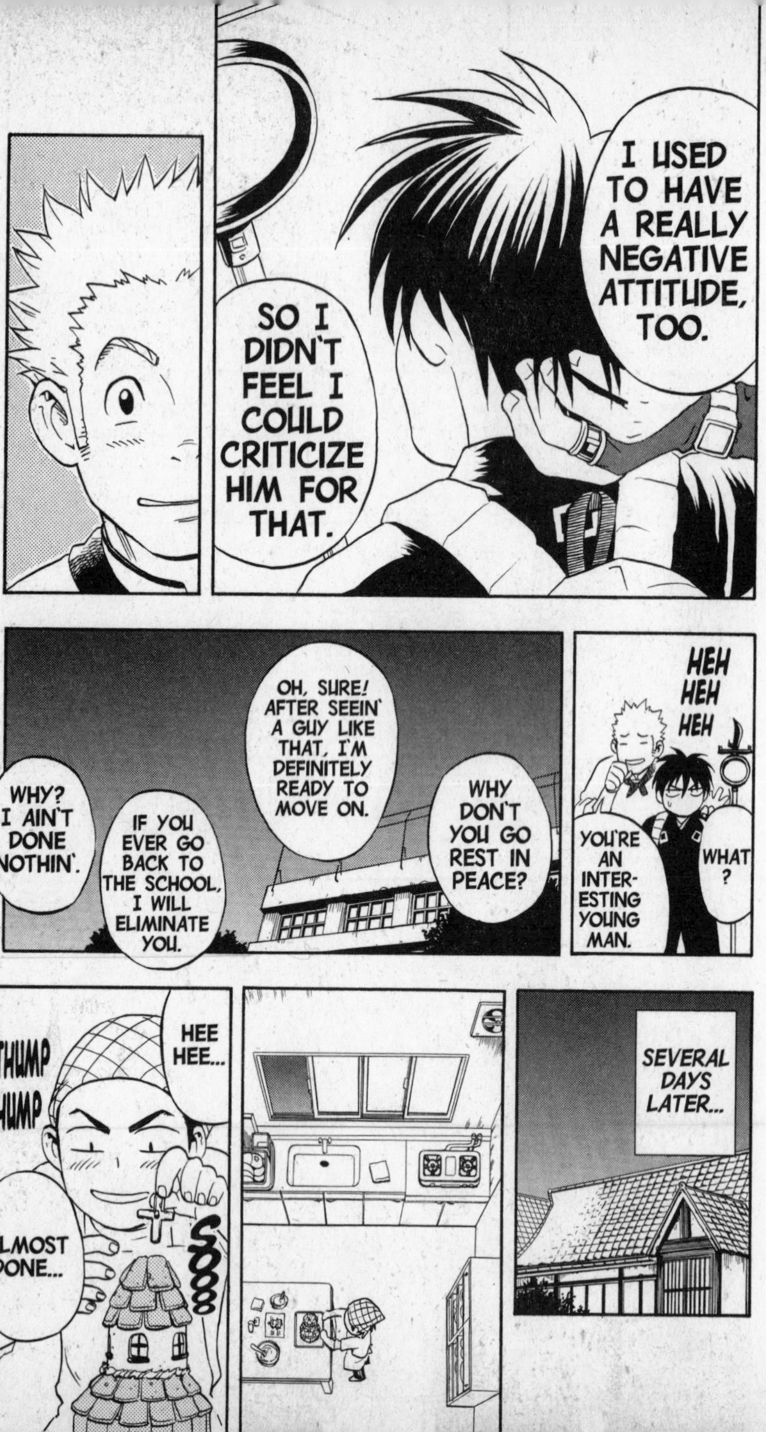
I USED TO HAVE A REALLY NEGATIVE ATTITUDE, TOO.
SO I DIDN'T FEEL I COULD CRITICIZE HIM FOR THAT.
HEH HEH HEH
YOU'RE AN INTER-ESTING YOUNG MAN.
WHAT ?
WHY DON'T YOU GO REST IN PEACE?
OH, SURE! AFTER SEEIN' A GUY LIKE THAT, I'M DEFINITELY READY TO MOVE ON.
IF YOU EVER GO BACK TO THE SCHOOL, I WILL ELIMINATE YOU.
WHY? I AIN'T DONE NOTHIN'.
SEVERAL DAYS LATER...
HEE HEE...
THUMP THUMP
ALMOST DONE...
SOOOO

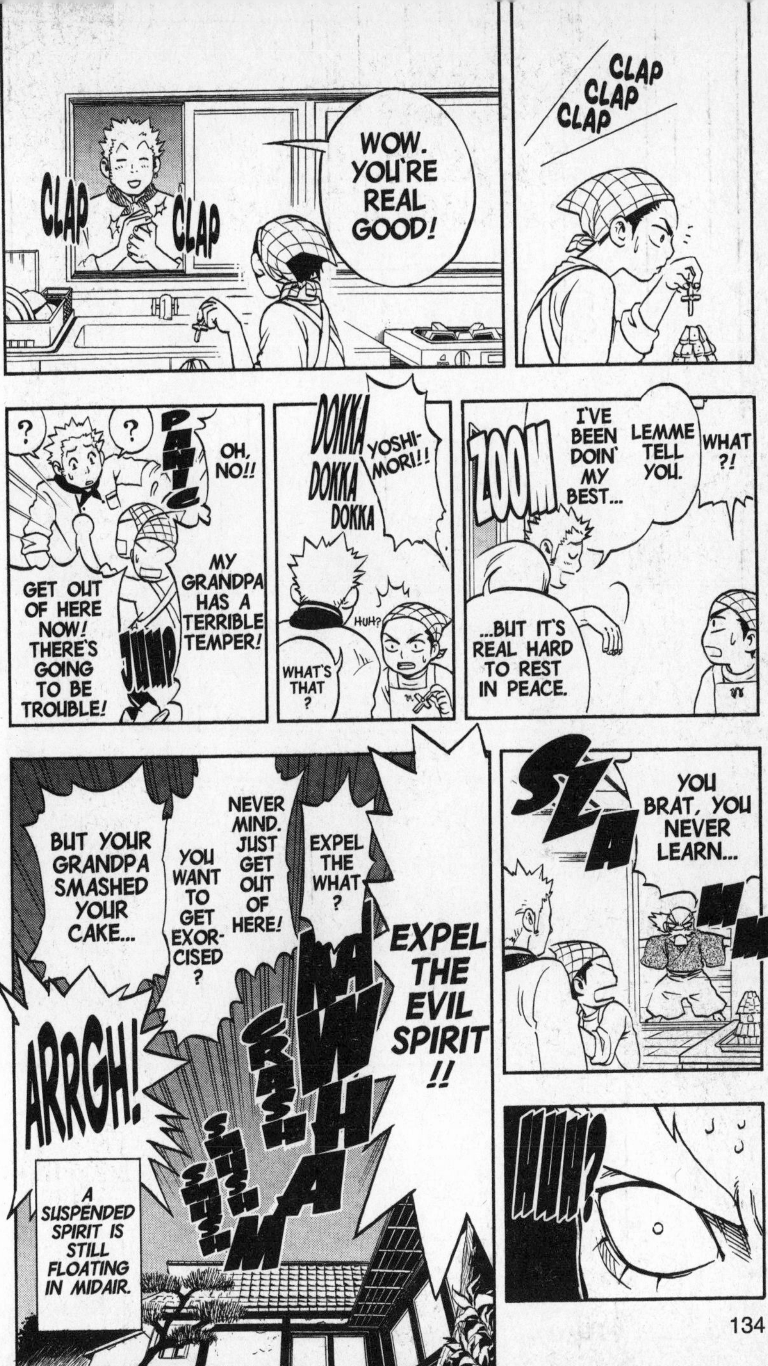
CLAP
CLAP
CLAP
CLAP
CLAP
WOW. YOU'RE REAL GOOD!
WHAT?!
LEMME TELL YOU.
I'VE BEEN DOIN' MY BEST...
ZOOM
...BUT IT'S REAL HARD TO REST IN PEACE.
YOSHI-MORI!!
DOKKA DOKKA DOKKA
HUH?
WHAT'S THAT?
OH, NO!!
PANIC
?
?
MY GRANDPA HAS A TERRIBLE TEMPER!
GET OUT OF HERE NOW! THERE'S GOING TO BE TROUBLE!
JUMP
YOU BRAT, YOU NEVER LEARN...
HUH?
EXPEL THE EVIL SPIRIT!!
EXPEL THE WHAT?
NEVER MIND. JUST GET OUT OF HERE!
YOU WANT TO GET EXOR-CISED?
BUT YOUR GRANDPA SMASHED YOUR CAKE...
WHAM
CRASH
ARRGH!
A SUSPENDED SPIRIT IS STILL FLOATING IN MIDAIR.

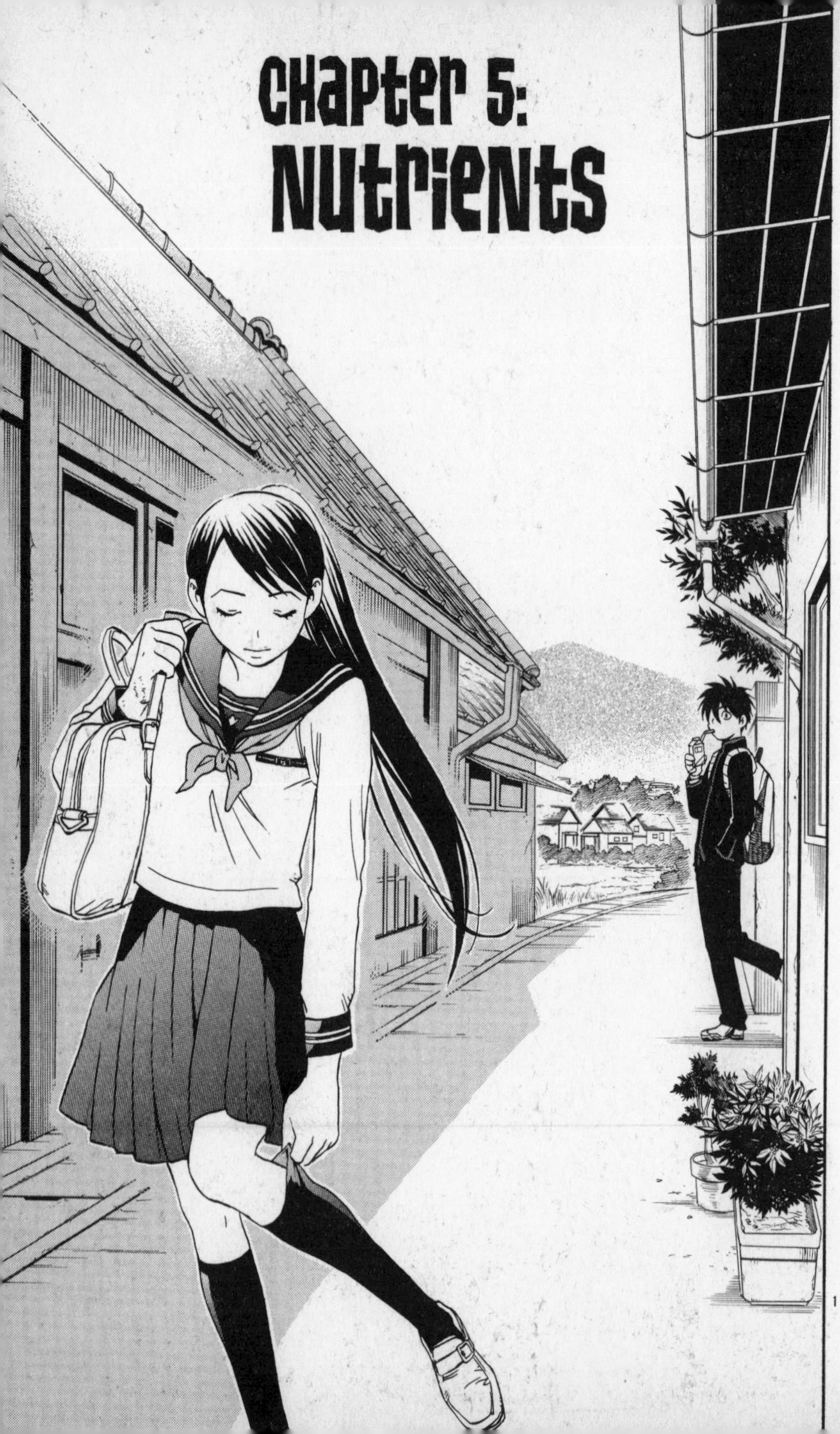
Chapter 5:
Nutrients

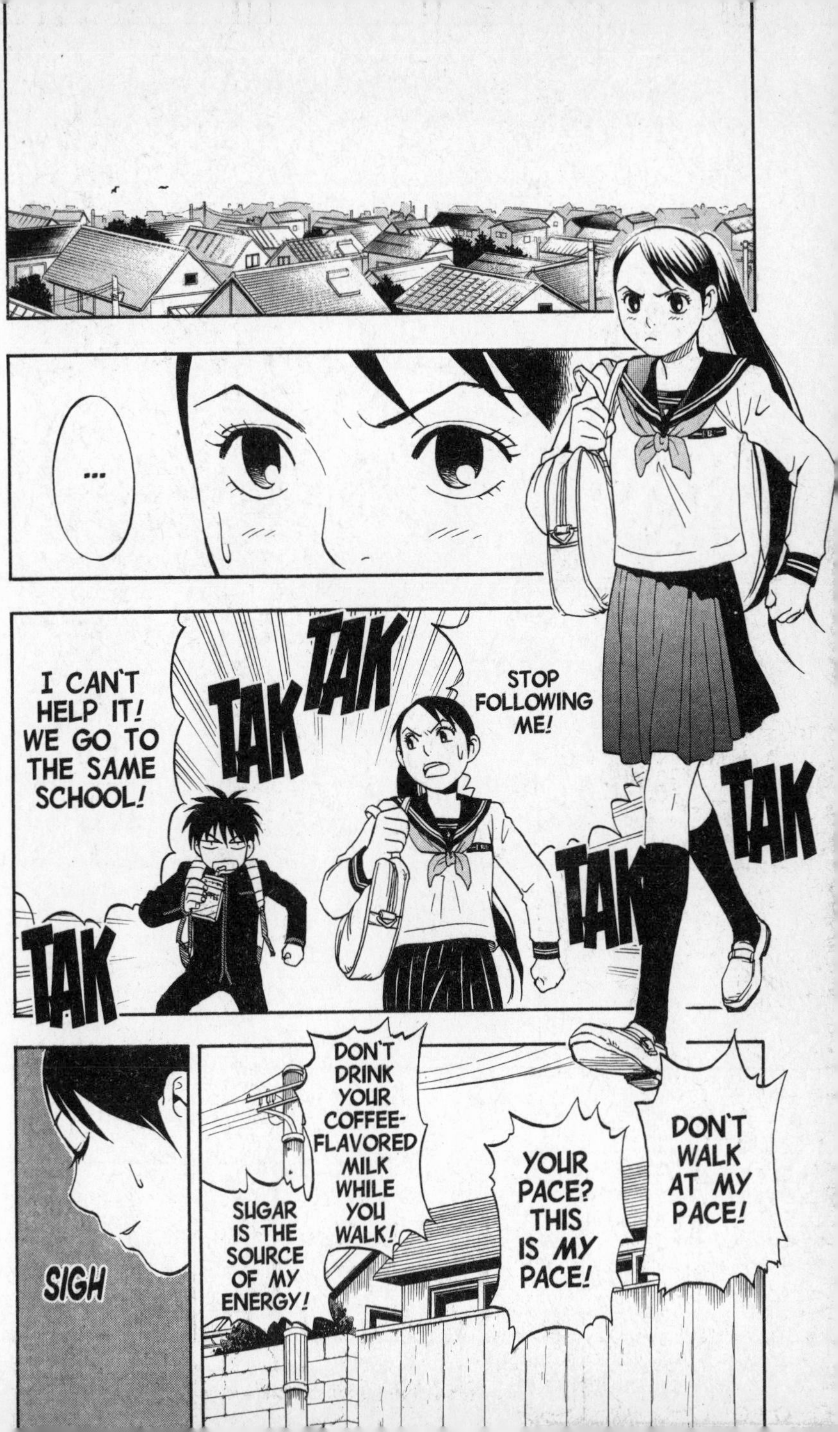
...
TAK
TAK
STOP FOLLOWING ME!
TAK
TAK
I CAN'T HELP IT! WE GO TO THE SAME SCHOOL!
TAK
DON'T WALK AT MY PACE!
YOUR PACE? THIS IS MY PACE!
DON'T DRINK YOUR COFFEE-FLAVORED MILK WHILE YOU WALK!
SUGAR IS THE SOURCE OF MY ENERGY!
SIGH

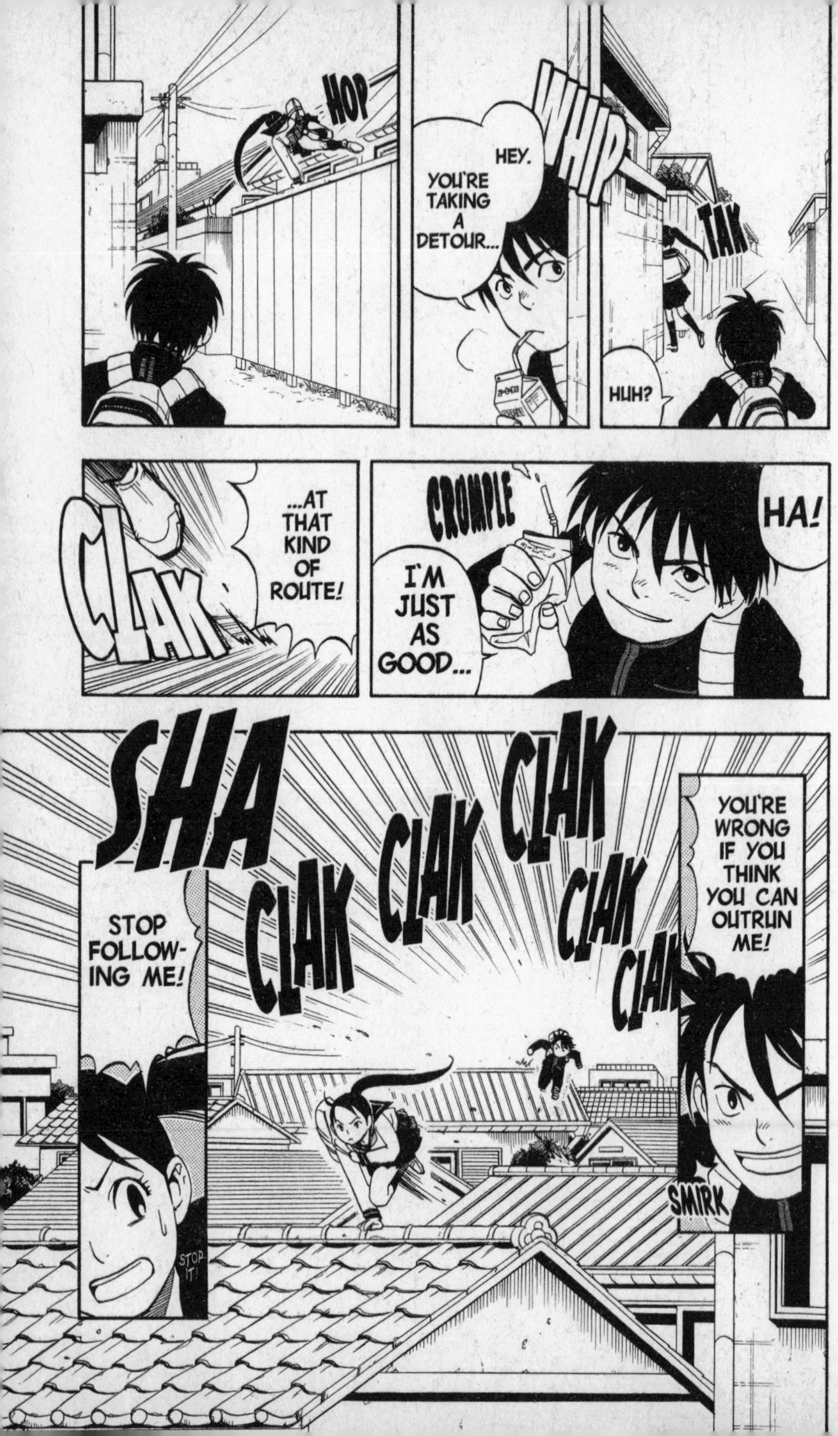
TAK
HUH?
WHIP
HEY.
YOU'RE TAKING A DETOUR...
HOP
HA!
I'M JUST AS GOOD...
CROMPLE
...AT THAT KIND OF ROUTE!
CLAK
YOU'RE WRONG IF YOU THINK YOU CAN OUTRUN ME!
SMIRK
CLAK
CLAK
CLAK
CLAK
CLAK
SHA
STOP FOLLOW-ING ME!
STOP IT!

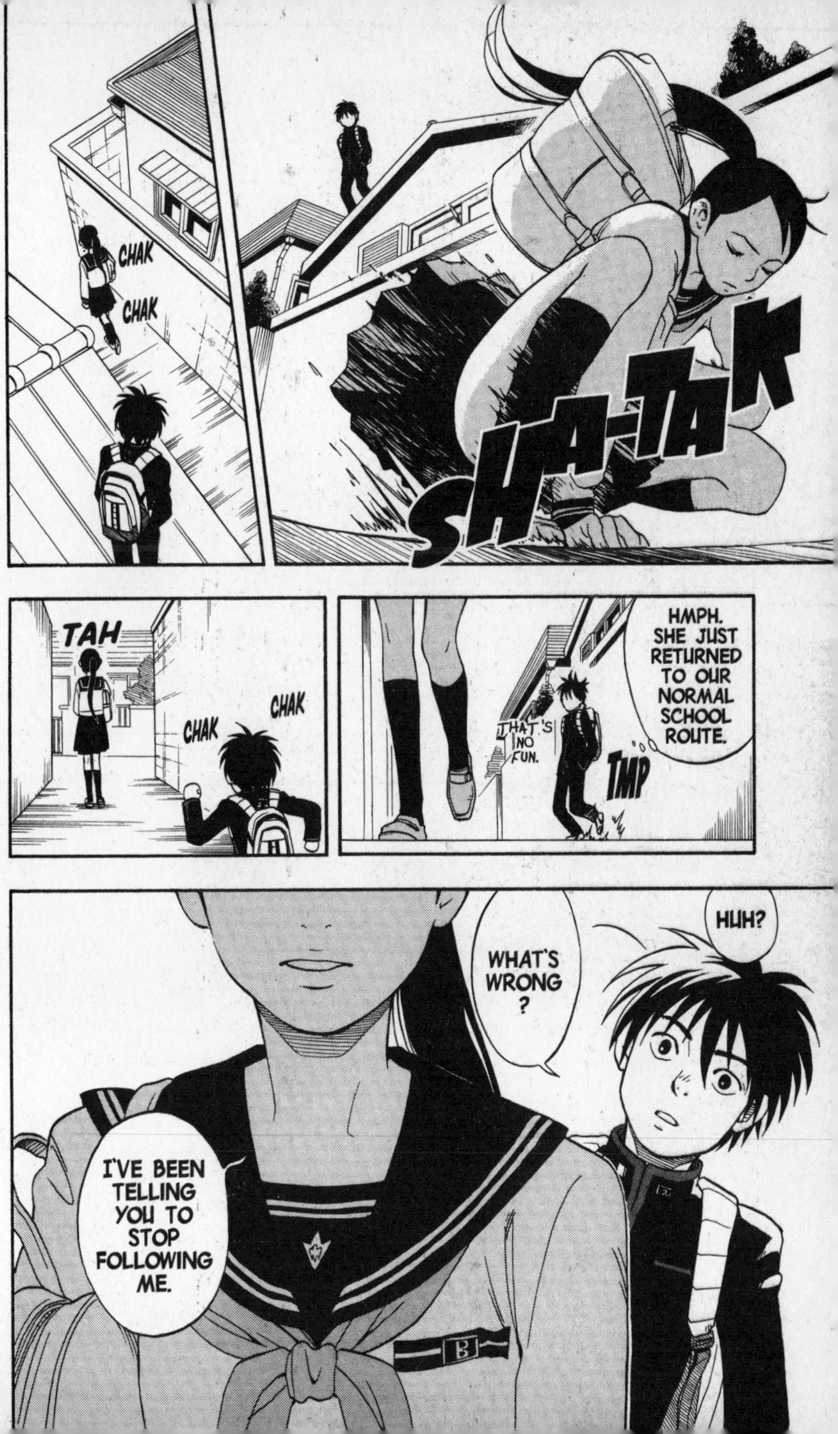
SHA-TAK
CHAK
CHAK
HMPH. SHE JUST RETURNED TO OUR NORMAL SCHOOL ROUTE.
TMP
THAT'S NO FUN.
TAH
CHAK
CHAK
HUH?
WHAT'S WRONG ?
I'VE BEEN TELLING YOU TO STOP FOLLOWING ME.

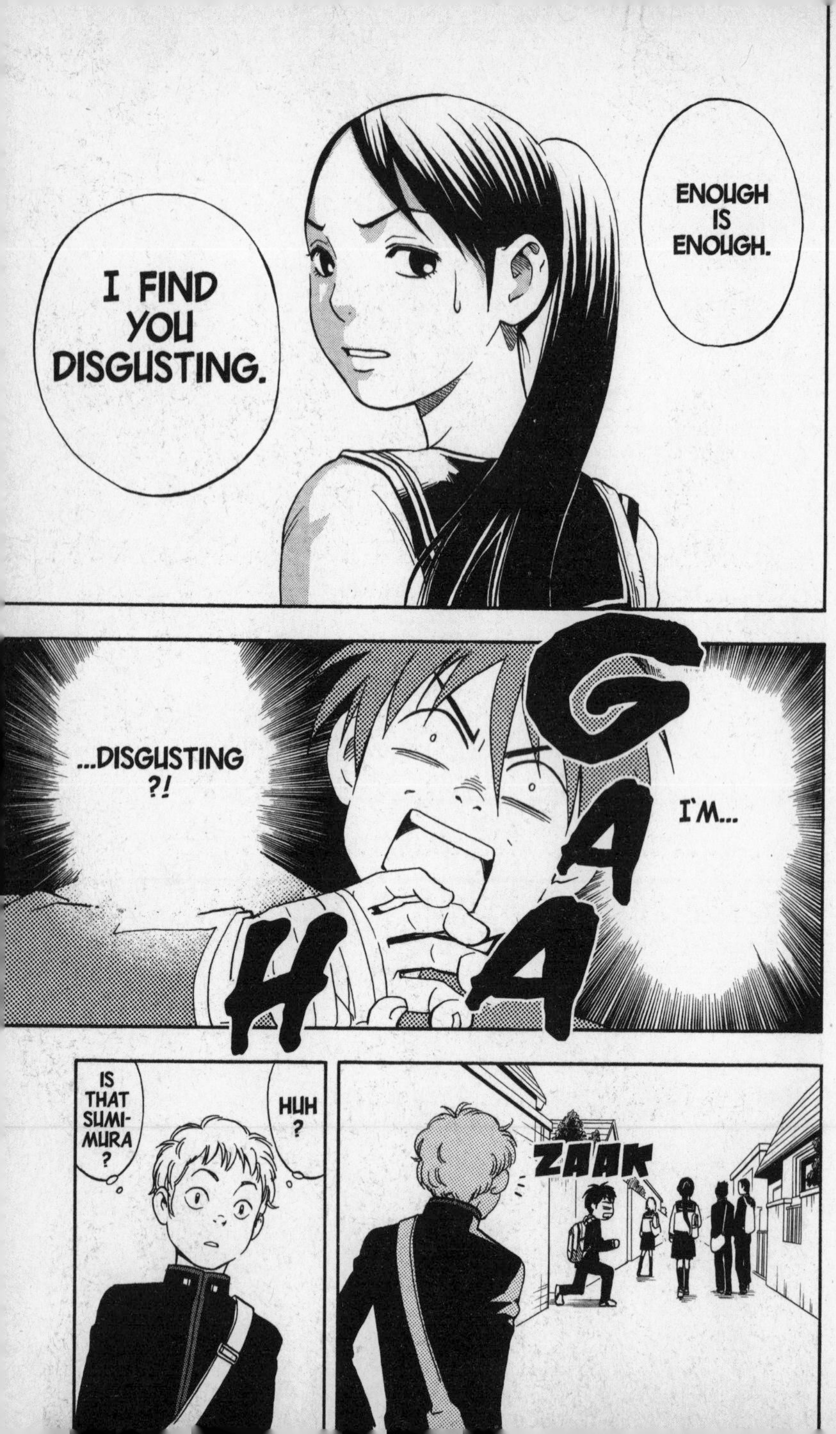
ENOUGH IS ENOUGH.
I FIND YOU DISGUSTING.
I'M...
GAAH
...DISGUSTING ?!
ZAAK
HUH ?
IS THAT SUMI-MURA ?

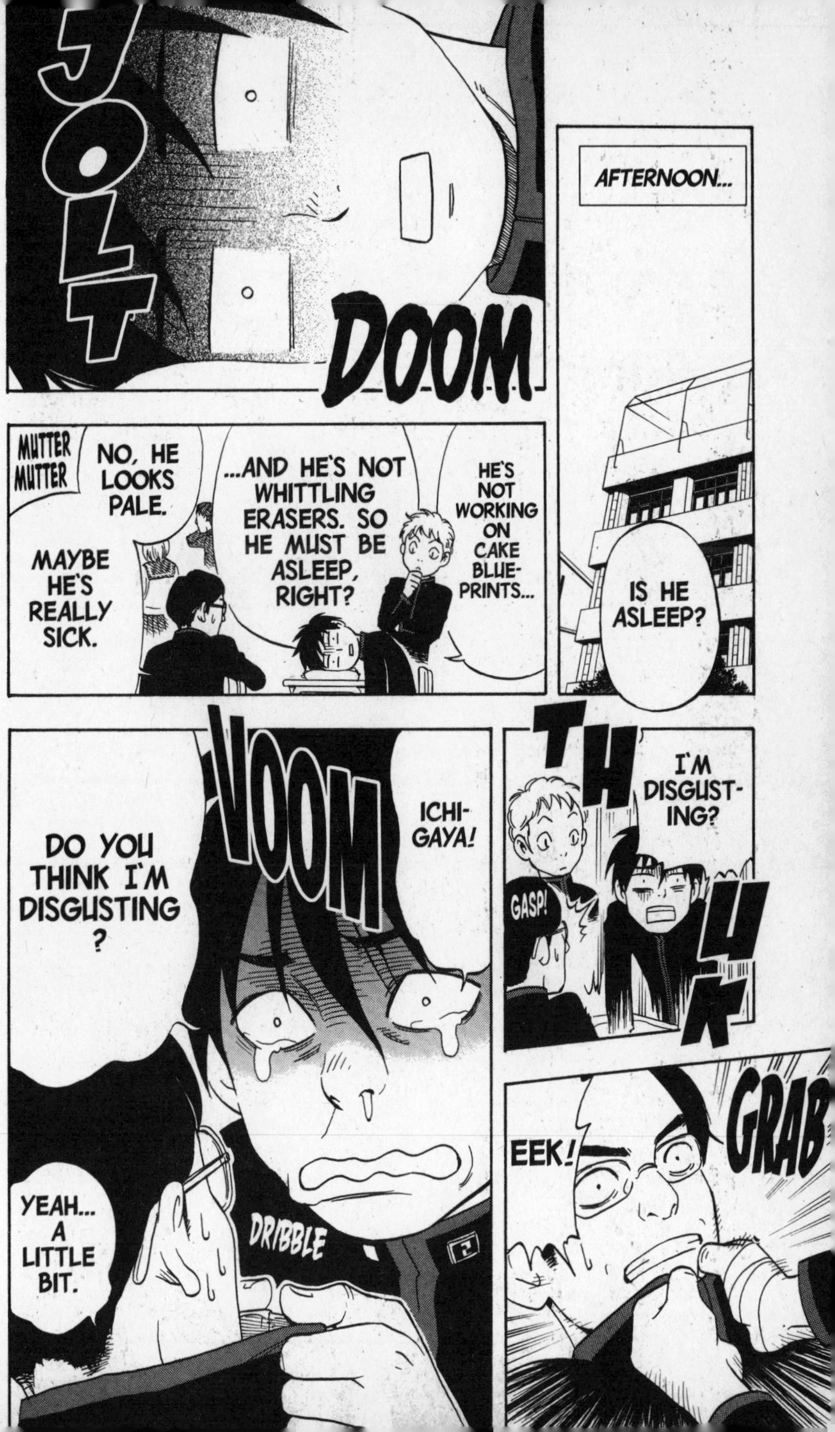
AFTERNOON...
IS HE ASLEEP?
HE'S NOT WORKING ON CAKE BLUE-PRINTS...
...AND HE'S NOT WHITTLING ERASERS. SO HE MUST BE ASLEEP, RIGHT?
NO, HE LOOKS PALE.
MUTTER MUTTER
MAYBE HE'S REALLY SICK.
JOLT
DOOM
TH
I'M DISGUST-ING?
GASP!
UNK
EEK!
GRAB
VOOM
ICHI-GAYA!
DO YOU THINK I'M DISGUSTING ?
DRIBBLE
YEAH... A LITTLE BIT.

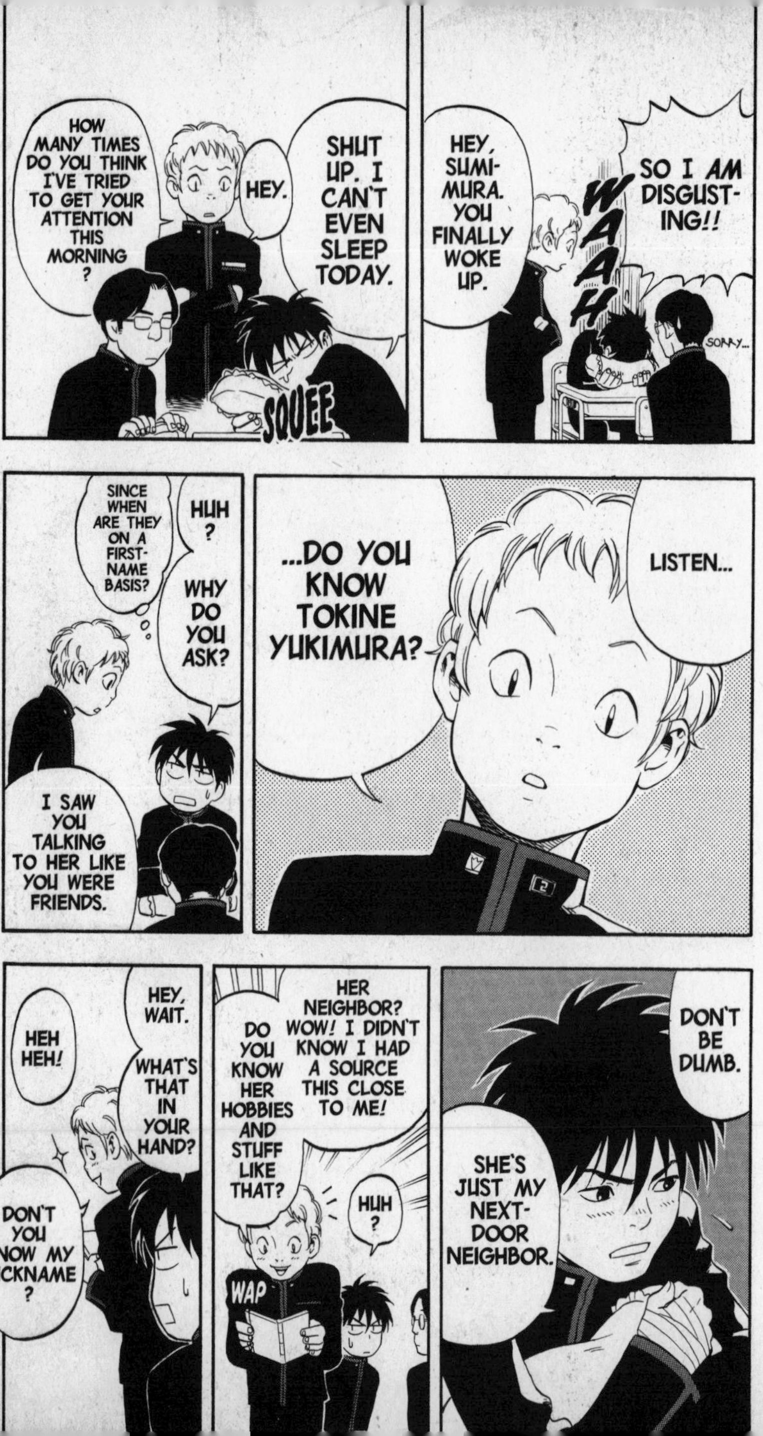
SO I AM DISGUSTING!!
WAAAH
HEY, SUMIMURA. YOU FINALLY WOKE UP.
SORRY...
SHUT UP. I CAN'T EVEN SLEEP TODAY.
HEY.
HOW MANY TIMES DO YOU THINK I'VE TRIED TO GET YOUR ATTENTION THIS MORNING?
SQUEE
LISTEN...
...DO YOU KNOW TOKINE YUKIMURA?
HUH? WHY DO YOU ASK?
SINCE WHEN ARE THEY ON A FIRST-NAME BASIS?
I SAW YOU TALKING TO HER LIKE YOU WERE FRIENDS.
DON'T BE DUMB.
SHE'S JUST MY NEXT-DOOR NEIGHBOR.
HER NEIGHBOR? WOW! I DIDN'T KNOW I HAD A SOURCE THIS CLOSE TO ME!
DO YOU KNOW HER HOBBIES AND STUFF LIKE THAT?
HUH?
WAP
HEY, WAIT. WHAT'S THAT IN YOUR HAND?
HEH HEH!
DON'T YOU KNOW MY NICKNAME?

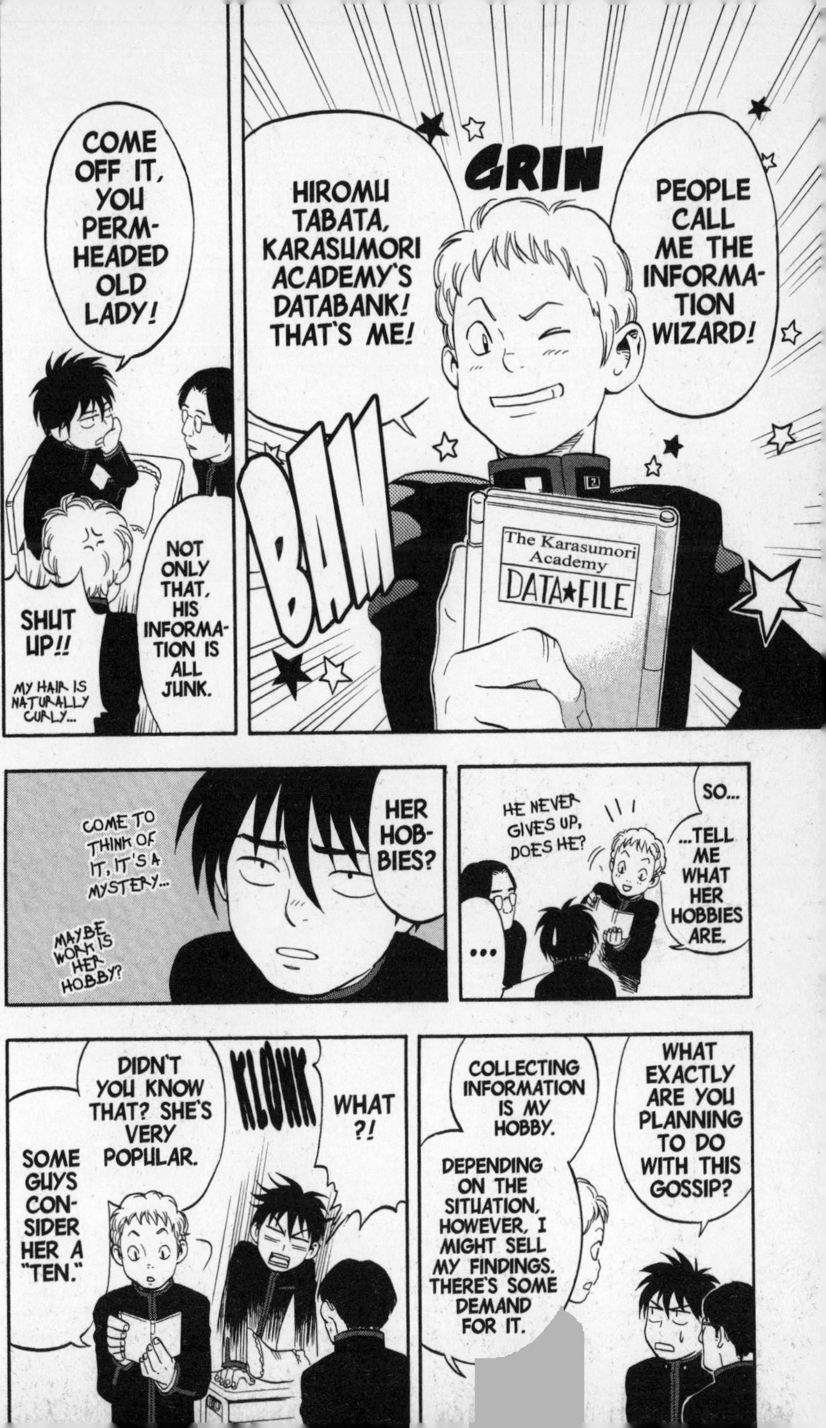
PEOPLE CALL ME THE INFORMATION WIZARD!
GRIN
HIROMU TABATA, KARASUMORI ACADEMY'S DATABANK! THAT'S ME!
The Karasumori Academy DATA★FILE
BAM
COME OFF IT, YOU PERM-HEADED OLD LADY!
NOT ONLY THAT, HIS INFORMATION IS ALL JUNK.
SHUT UP!!
MY HAIR IS NATURALLY CURLY...
SO...
...TELL ME WHAT HER HOBBIES ARE.
HE NEVER GIVES UP, DOES HE?
...
HER HOBBIES?
COME TO THINK OF IT, IT'S A MYSTERY...
MAYBE WORK IS HER HOBBY?
WHAT EXACTLY ARE YOU PLANNING TO DO WITH THIS GOSSIP?
COLLECTING INFORMATION IS MY HOBBY.
DEPENDING ON THE SITUATION, HOWEVER, I MIGHT SELL MY FINDINGS. THERE'S SOME DEMAND FOR IT.
WHAT ?!
KLONK
DIDN'T YOU KNOW THAT? SHE'S VERY POPULAR.
SOME GUYS CONSIDER HER A "TEN."

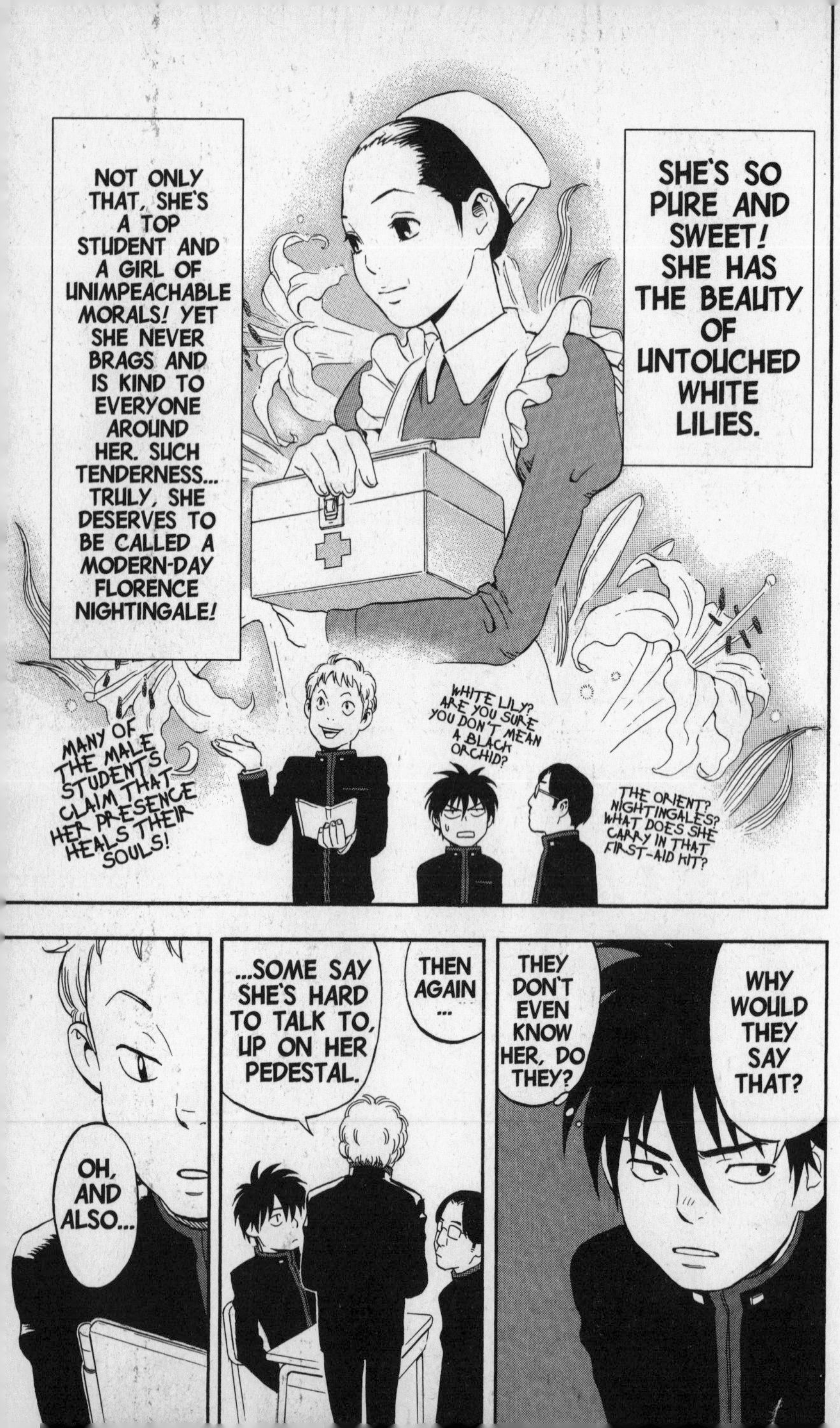
SHE'S SO PURE AND SWEET! SHE HAS THE BEAUTY OF UNTOUCHED WHITE LILIES.
NOT ONLY THAT, SHE'S A TOP STUDENT AND A GIRL OF UNIMPEACHABLE MORALS! YET SHE NEVER BRAGS AND IS KIND TO EVERYONE AROUND HER. SUCH TENDERNESS... TRULY, SHE DESERVES TO BE CALLED A MODERN-DAY FLORENCE NIGHTINGALE!
THE ORIENT? NIGHTINGALES? WHAT DOES SHE CARRY IN THAT FIRST-AID KIT?
WHITE LILY? ARE YOU SURE YOU DON'T MEAN A BLACK ORCHID?
MANY OF THE MALE STUDENTS CLAIM THAT HER PRESENCE HEALS THEIR SOULS!
WHY WOULD THEY SAY THAT?
THEY DON'T EVEN KNOW HER, DO THEY?
THEN AGAIN...
...SOME SAY SHE'S HARD TO TALK TO, UP ON HER PEDESTAL.
OH, AND ALSO...

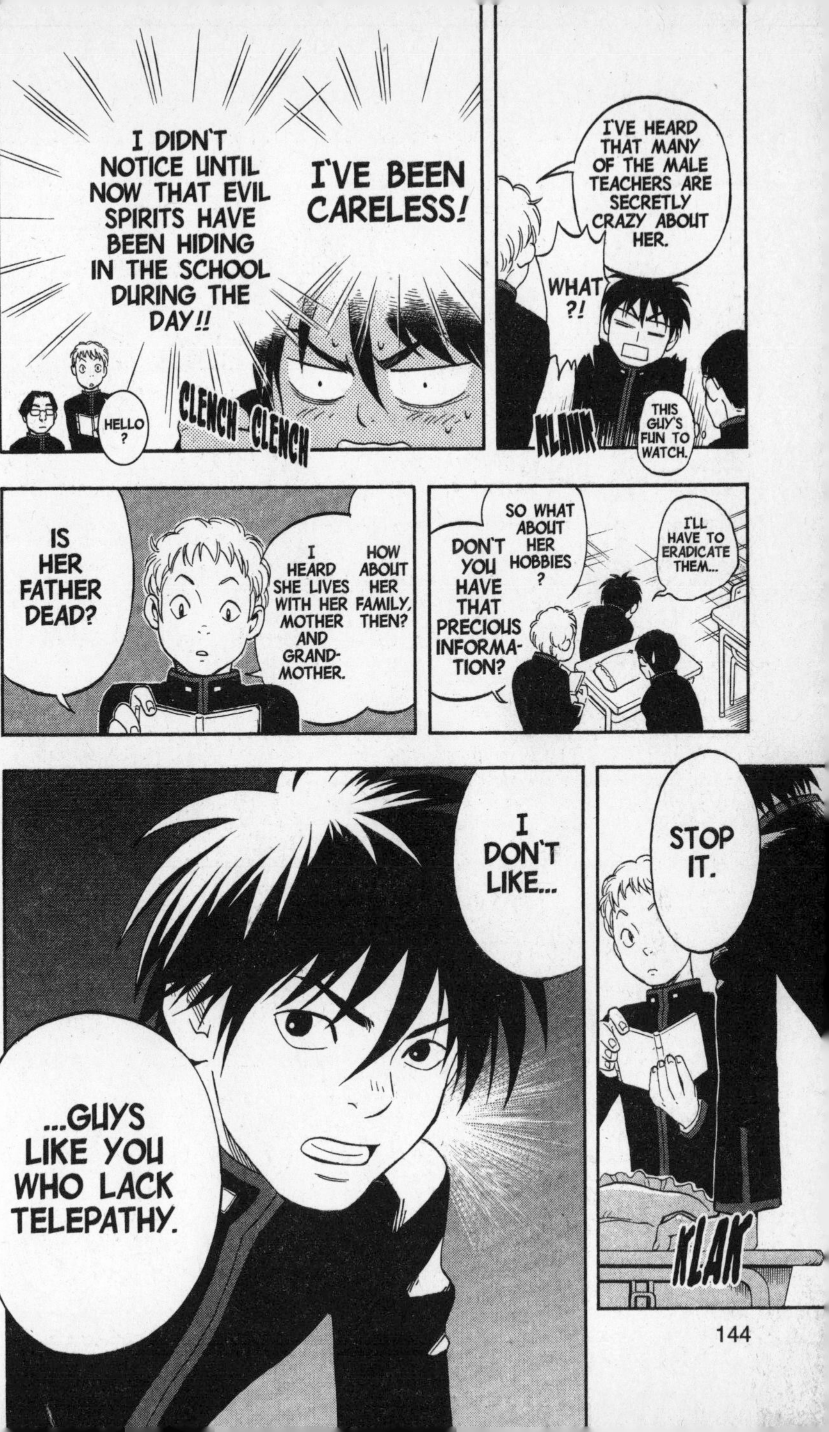
I'VE HEARD THAT MANY OF THE MALE TEACHERS ARE SECRETLY CRAZY ABOUT HER.
WHAT?!
KLANK
THIS GUY'S FUN TO WATCH.
I'VE BEEN CARELESS!
I DIDN'T NOTICE UNTIL NOW THAT EVIL SPIRITS HAVE BEEN HIDING IN THE SCHOOL DURING THE DAY!!
CLENCH CLENCH
HELLO?
I'LL HAVE TO ERADICATE THEM...
SO WHAT ABOUT HER HOBBIES?
DON'T YOU HAVE THAT PRECIOUS INFORMATION?
HOW ABOUT HER FAMILY, THEN?
I HEARD SHE LIVES WITH HER MOTHER AND GRAND-MOTHER.
IS HER FATHER DEAD?
STOP IT.
KLAK
I DON'T LIKE...
...GUYS LIKE YOU WHO LACK TELEPATHY.

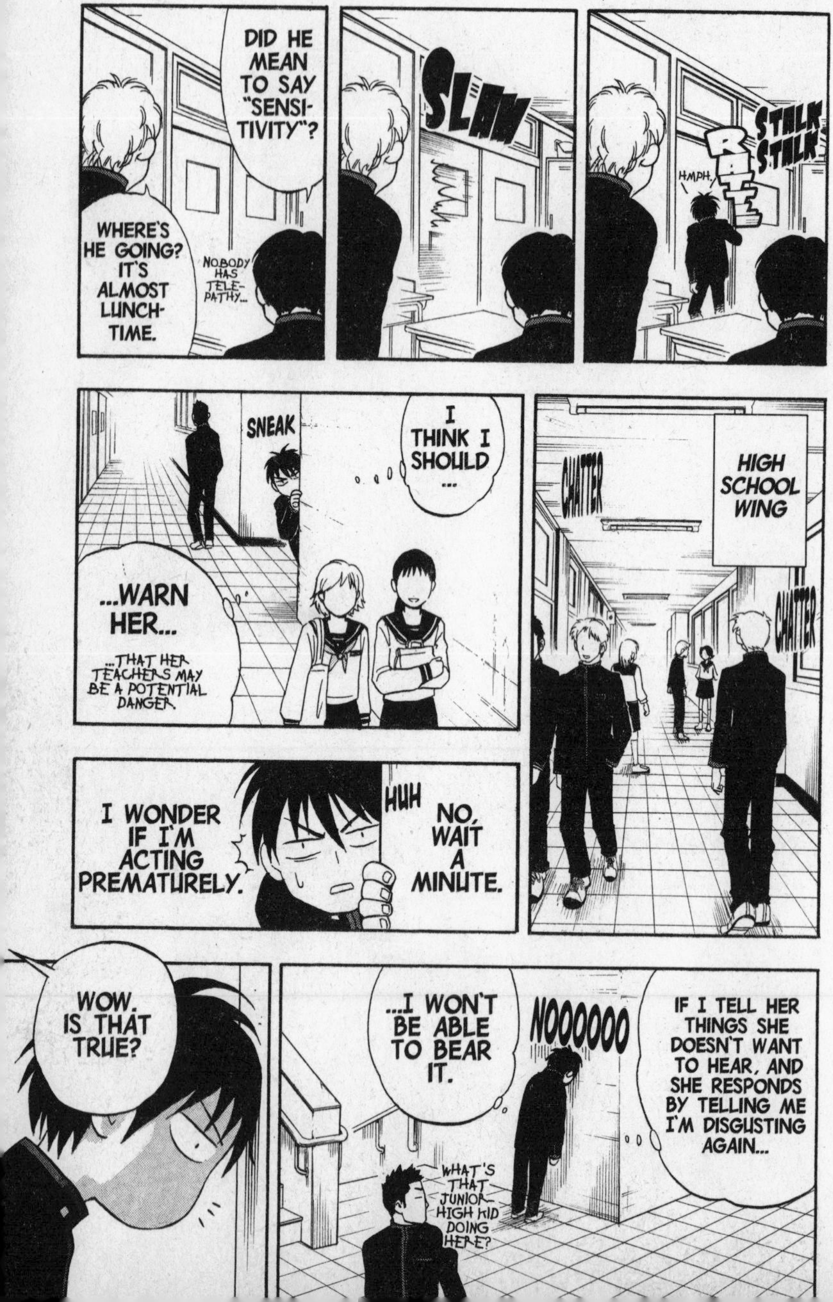
STALK STALK
RATTLE
HMPH.
SLAM
DID HE MEAN TO SAY "SENSITIVITY"?
WHERE'S HE GOING? IT'S ALMOST LUNCHTIME.
NOBODY HAS TELEPATHY...
HIGH SCHOOL WING
CHATTER
CHATTER
I THINK I SHOULD ...
...WARN HER...
...THAT HER TEACHERS MAY BE A POTENTIAL DANGER.
SNEAK
NO, WAIT A MINUTE.
HUH
I WONDER IF I'M ACTING PREMATURELY.
IF I TELL HER THINGS SHE DOESN'T WANT TO HEAR, AND SHE RESPONDS BY TELLING ME I'M DISGUSTING AGAIN...
NOOOOOO
...I WON'T BE ABLE TO BEAR IT.
WHAT'S THAT JUNIOR HIGH KID DOING HERE?
WOW. IS THAT TRUE?

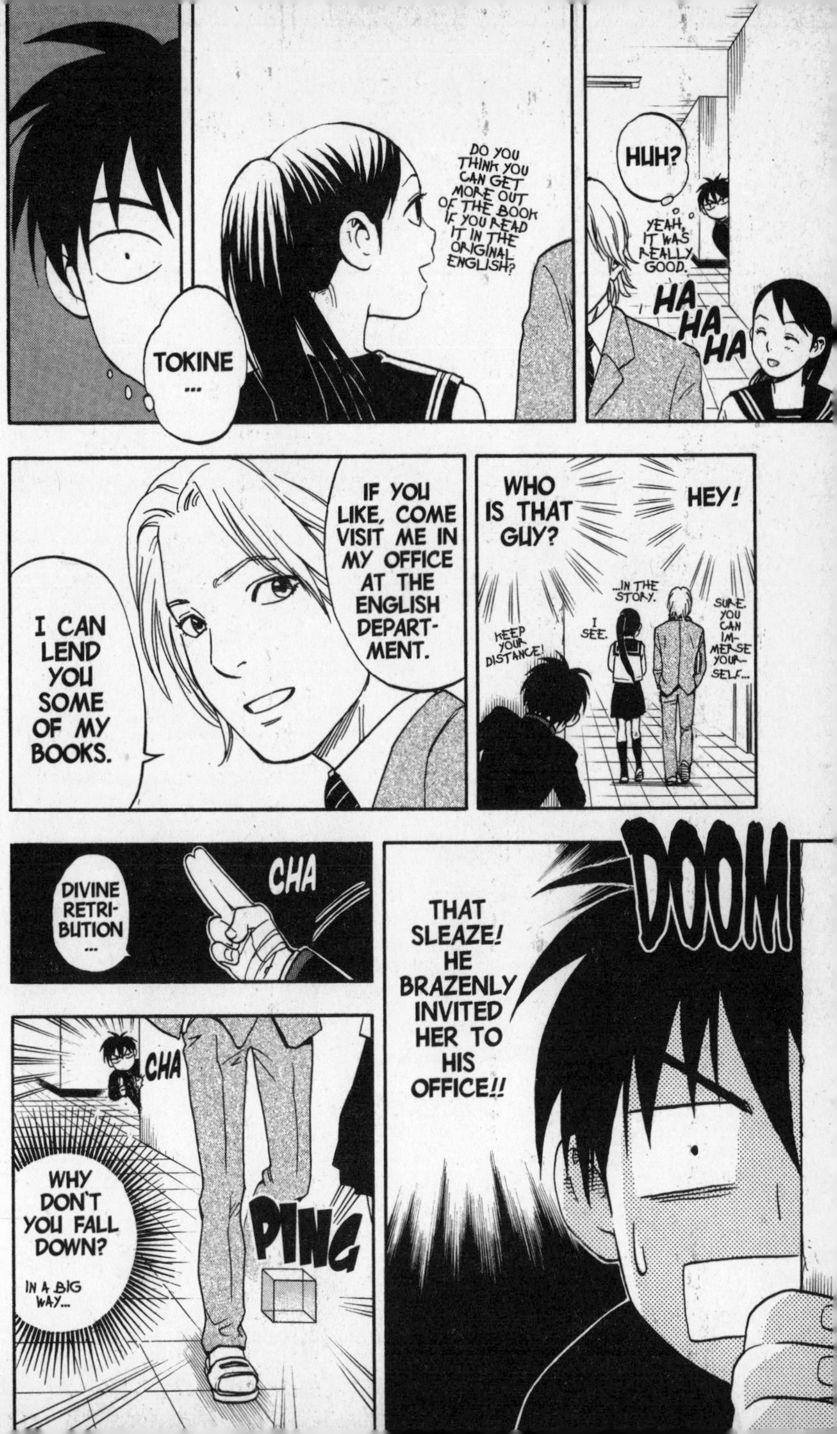
HUH?
YEAH, IT WAS REALLY GOOD.
HA HA HA
DO YOU THINK YOU CAN GET MORE OUT OF THE BOOK IF YOU READ IT IN THE ORIGINAL ENGLISH?
TOKINE ...
HEY!
WHO IS THAT GUY?
SURE. YOU CAN IM-MERSE YOUR-SELF...
...IN THE STORY.
I SEE.
KEEP YOUR DISTANCE!
IF YOU LIKE, COME VISIT ME IN MY OFFICE AT THE ENGLISH DEPART-MENT.
I CAN LEND YOU SOME OF MY BOOKS.
DOOM
THAT SLEAZE! HE BRAZENLY INVITED HER TO HIS OFFICE!!
CHA
DIVINE RETRI-BUTION ...
CHA
WHY DON'T YOU FALL DOWN?
IN A BIG WAY...
PING

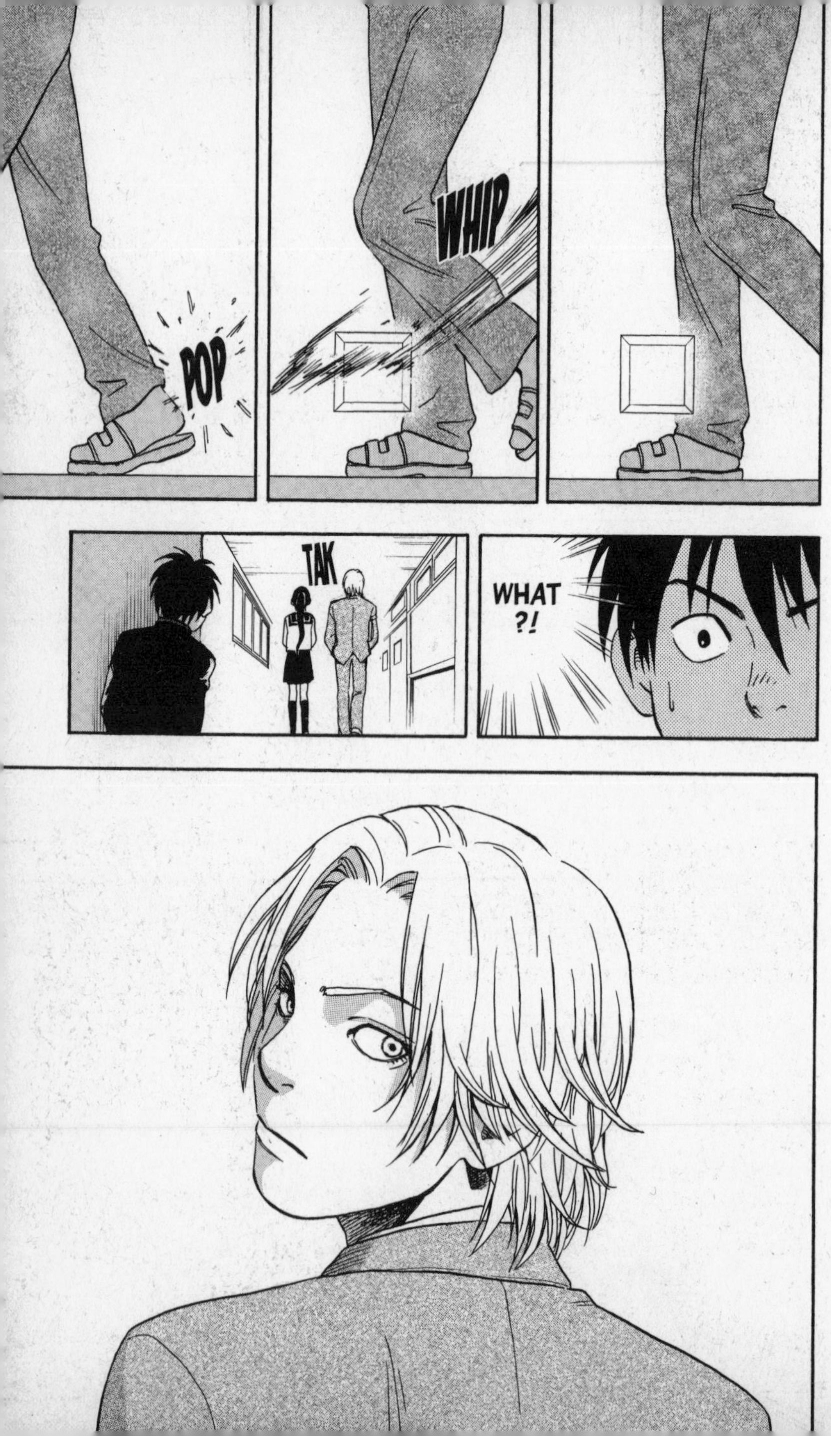
WHIP
POP
WHAT ?!
TAK

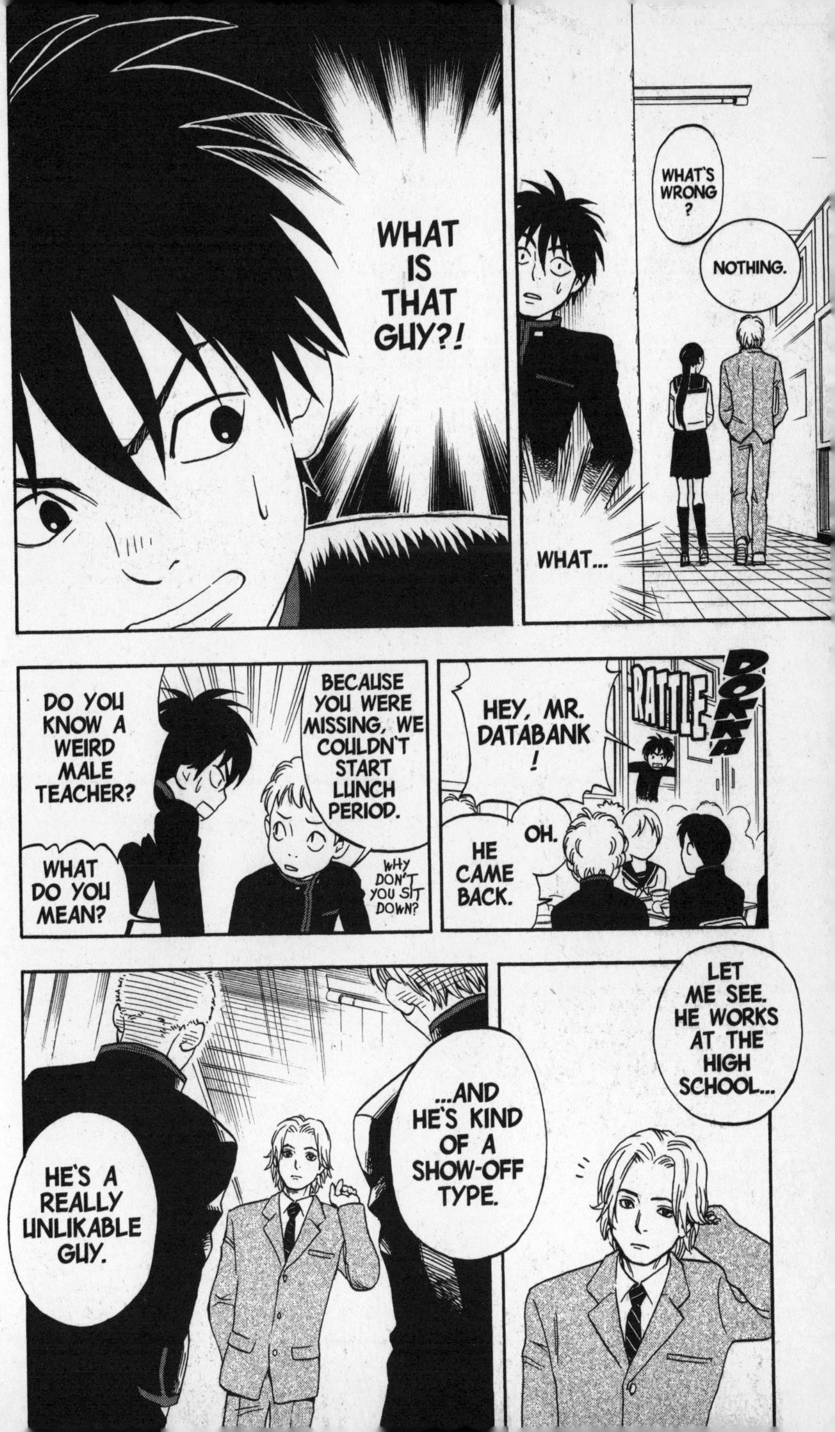
WHAT'S WRONG?
NOTHING.
WHAT...
WHAT IS THAT GUY?!
RATTLE
DOKA
HEY, MR. DATABANK!
OH.
HE CAME BACK.
BECAUSE YOU WERE MISSING, WE COULDN'T START LUNCH PERIOD.
DO YOU KNOW A WEIRD MALE TEACHER?
WHAT DO YOU MEAN?
WHY DON'T YOU SIT DOWN?
LET ME SEE. HE WORKS AT THE HIGH SCHOOL...
...AND HE'S KIND OF A SHOW-OFF TYPE.
HE'S A REALLY UNLIKABLE GUY.

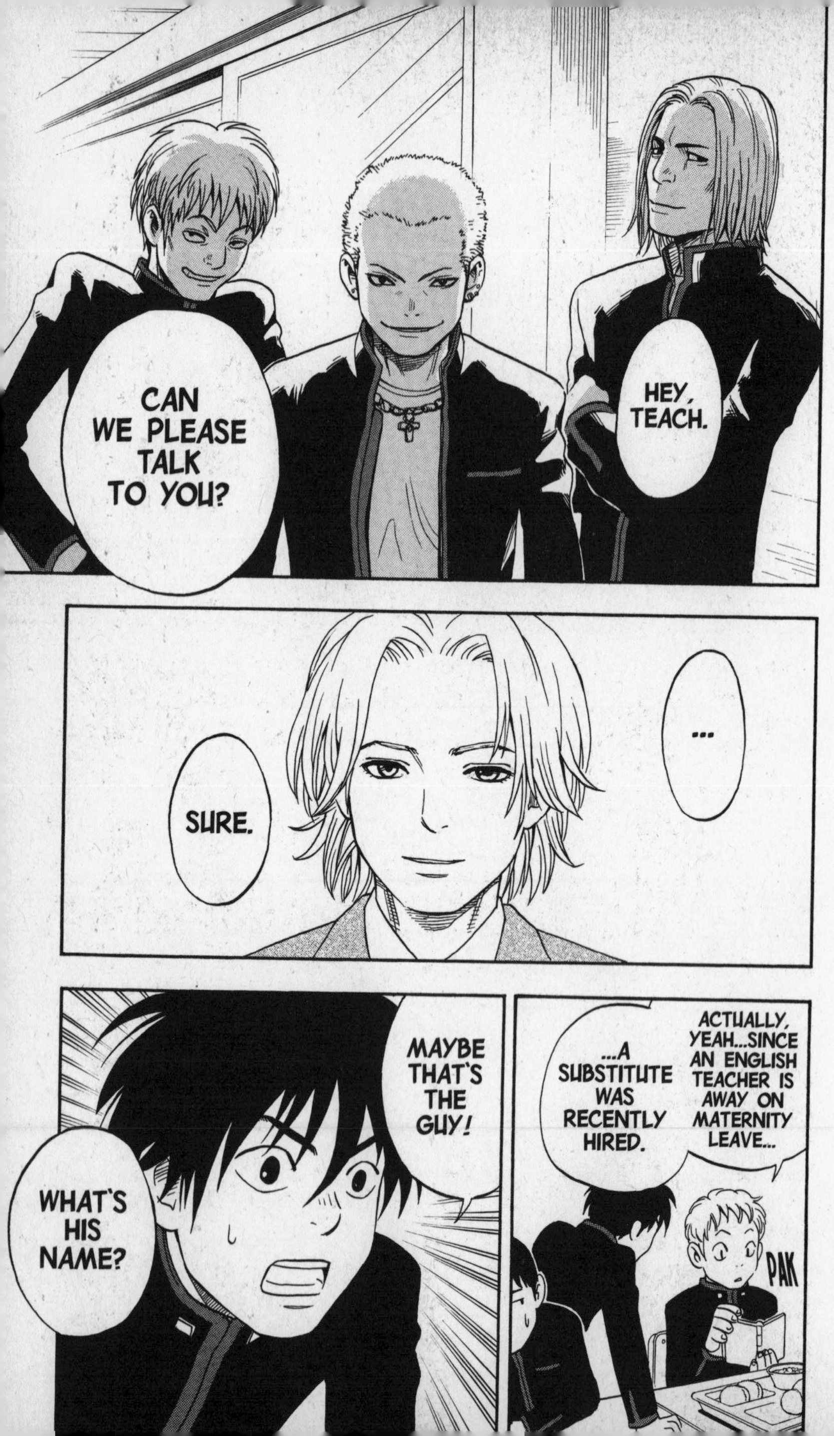
HEY, TEACH.
CAN WE PLEASE TALK TO YOU?
...
SURE.
ACTUALLY, YEAH...SINCE AN ENGLISH TEACHER IS AWAY ON MATERNITY LEAVE...
...A SUBSTITUTE WAS RECENTLY HIRED.
PAK
MAYBE THAT'S THE GUY!
WHAT'S HIS NAME?

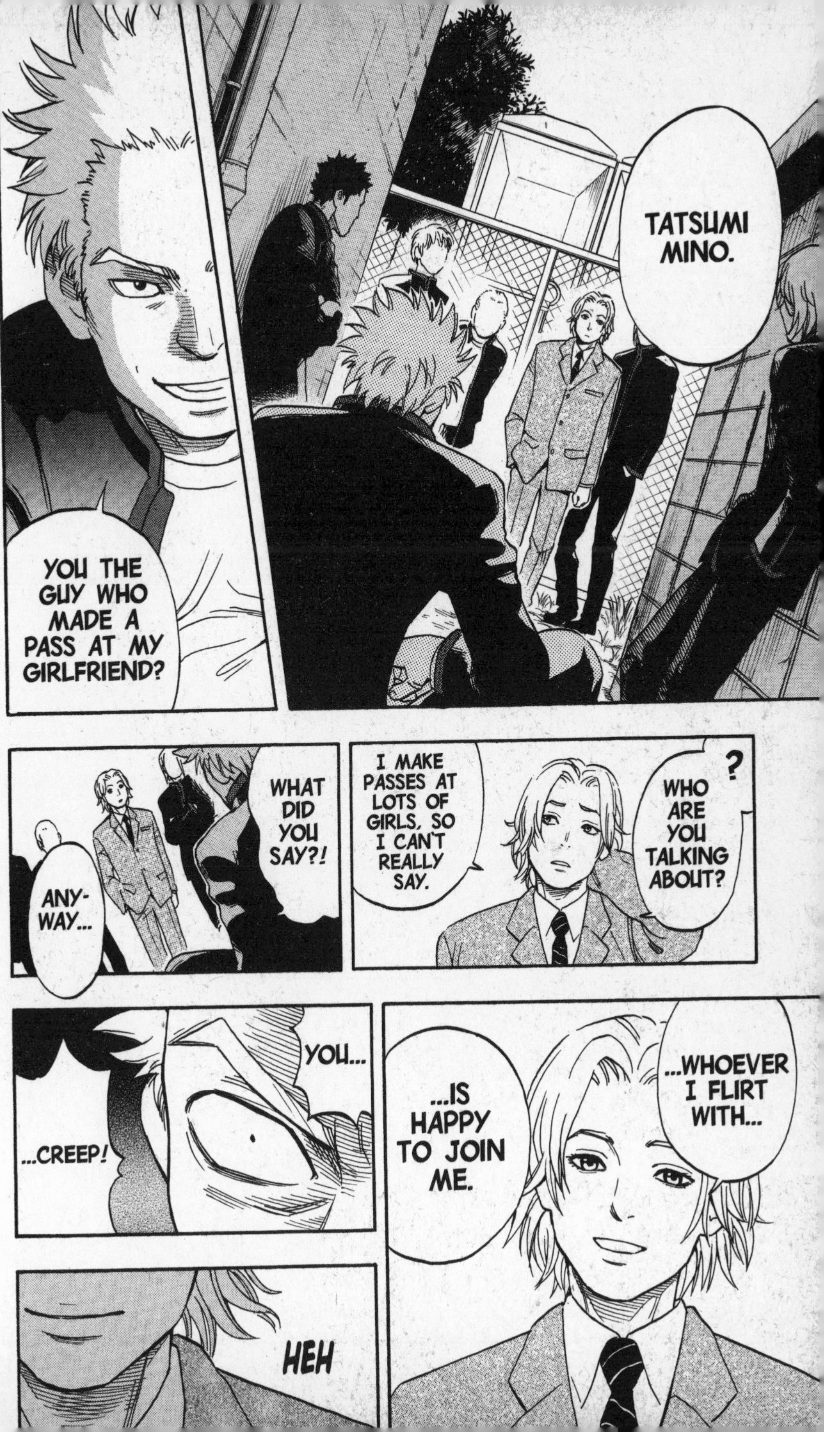
TATSUMI MINO.
YOU THE GUY WHO MADE A PASS AT MY GIRLFRIEND?
?
WHO ARE YOU TALKING ABOUT?
I MAKE PASSES AT LOTS OF GIRLS, SO I CAN'T REALLY SAY.
WHAT DID YOU SAY?!
ANY-WAY...
...WHOEVER I FLIRT WITH...
...IS HAPPY TO JOIN ME.
YOU...
...CREEP!
HEH

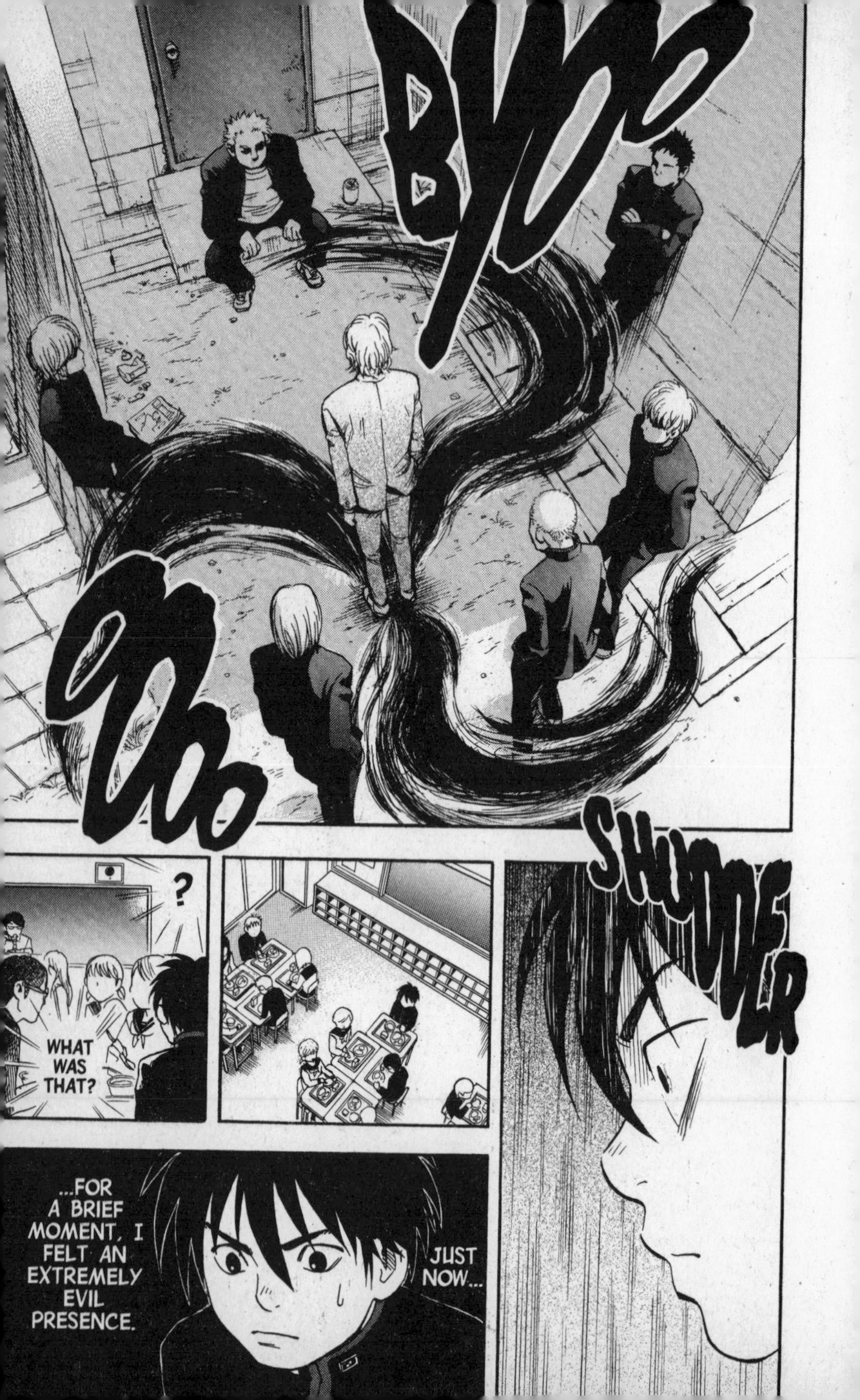
SHUDDER
?
WHAT WAS THAT?
JUST NOW...
...FOR A BRIEF MOMENT, I FELT AN EXTREMELY EVIL PRESENCE.

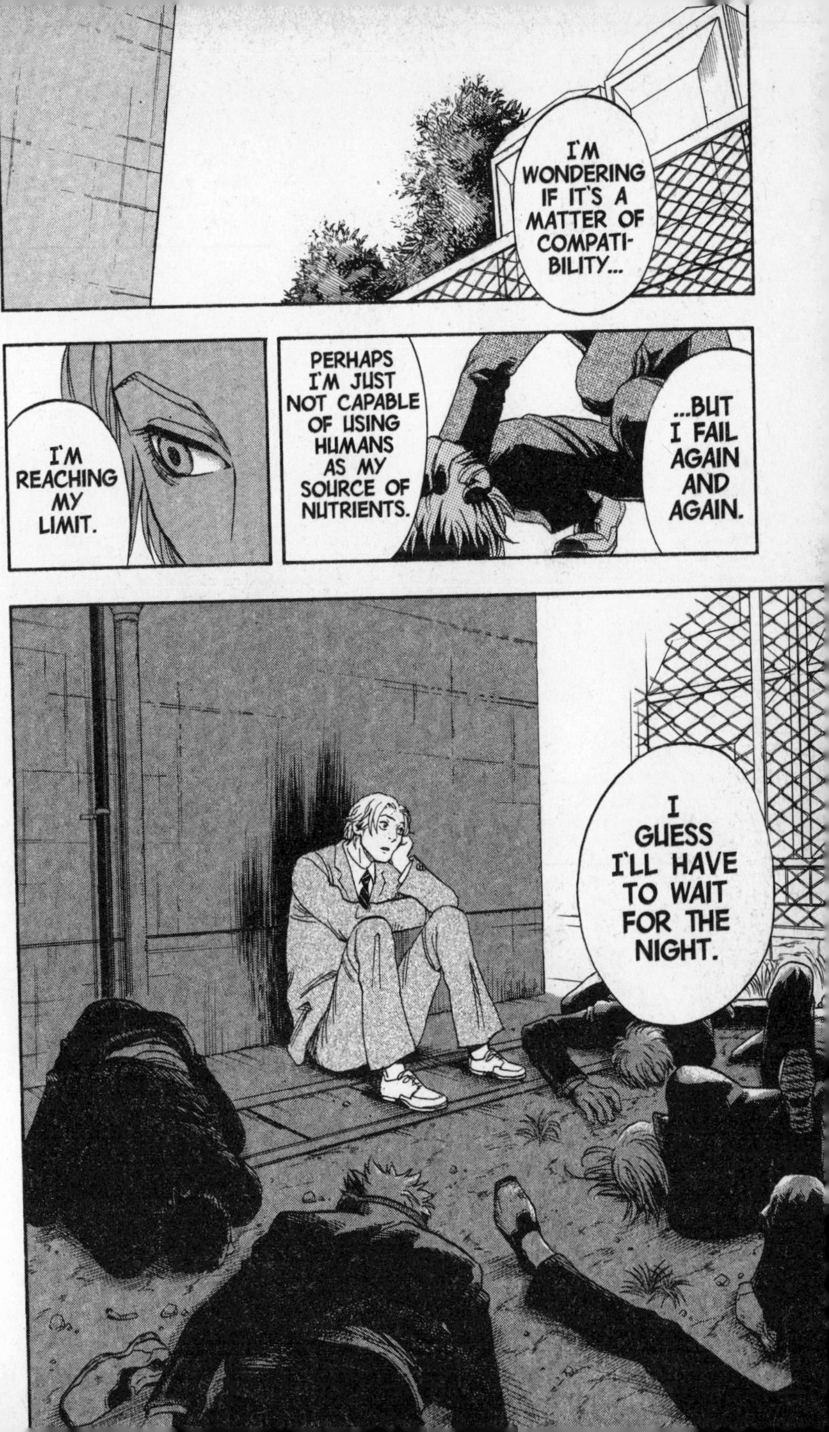
I'M WONDERING IF IT'S A MATTER OF COMPATI-BILITY...
...BUT I FAIL AGAIN AND AGAIN.
PERHAPS I'M JUST NOT CAPABLE OF USING HUMANS AS MY SOURCE OF NUTRIENTS.
I'M REACHING MY LIMIT.
I GUESS I'LL HAVE TO WAIT FOR THE NIGHT.

Chapter 6: A Dangerous Man

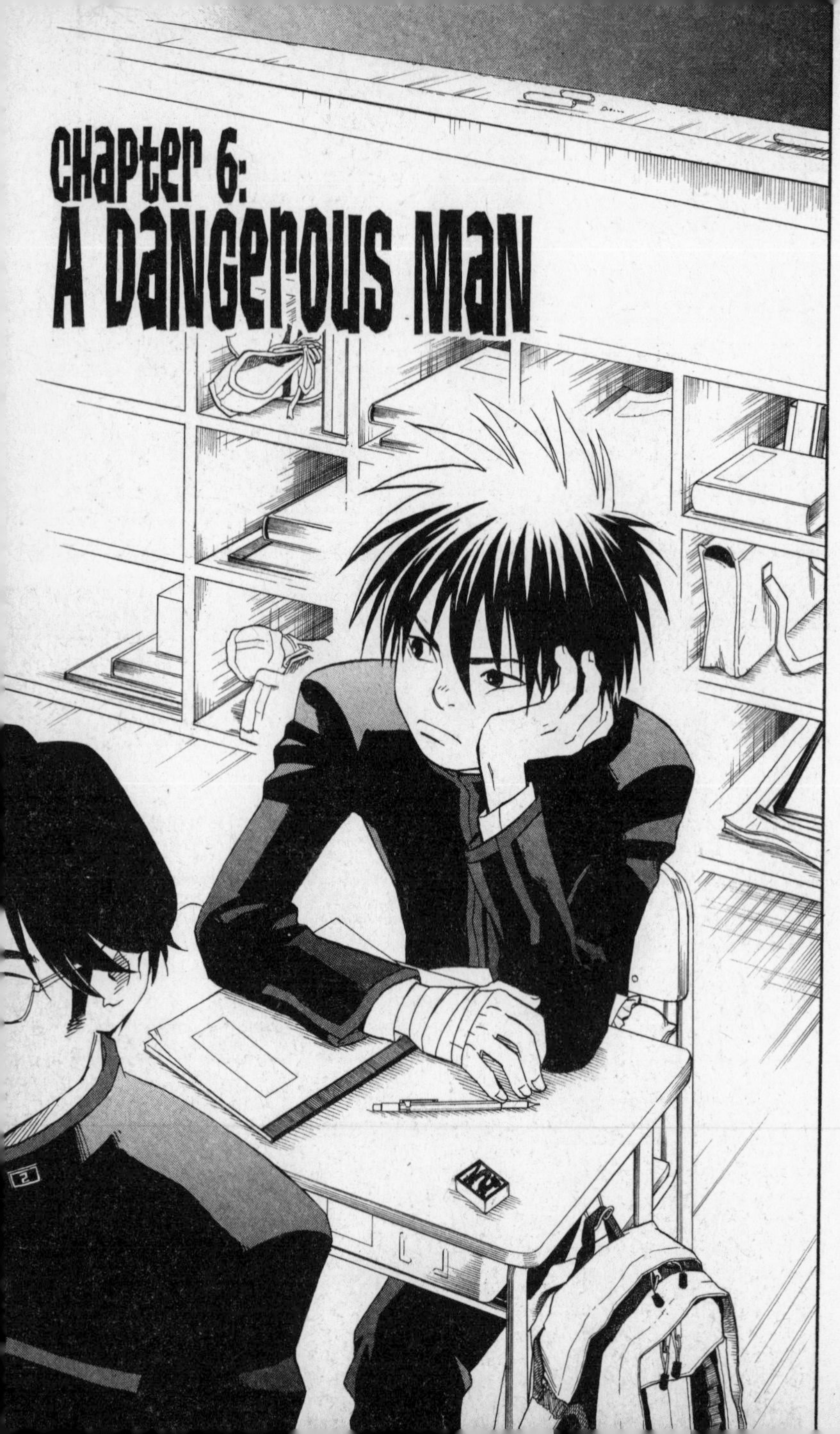

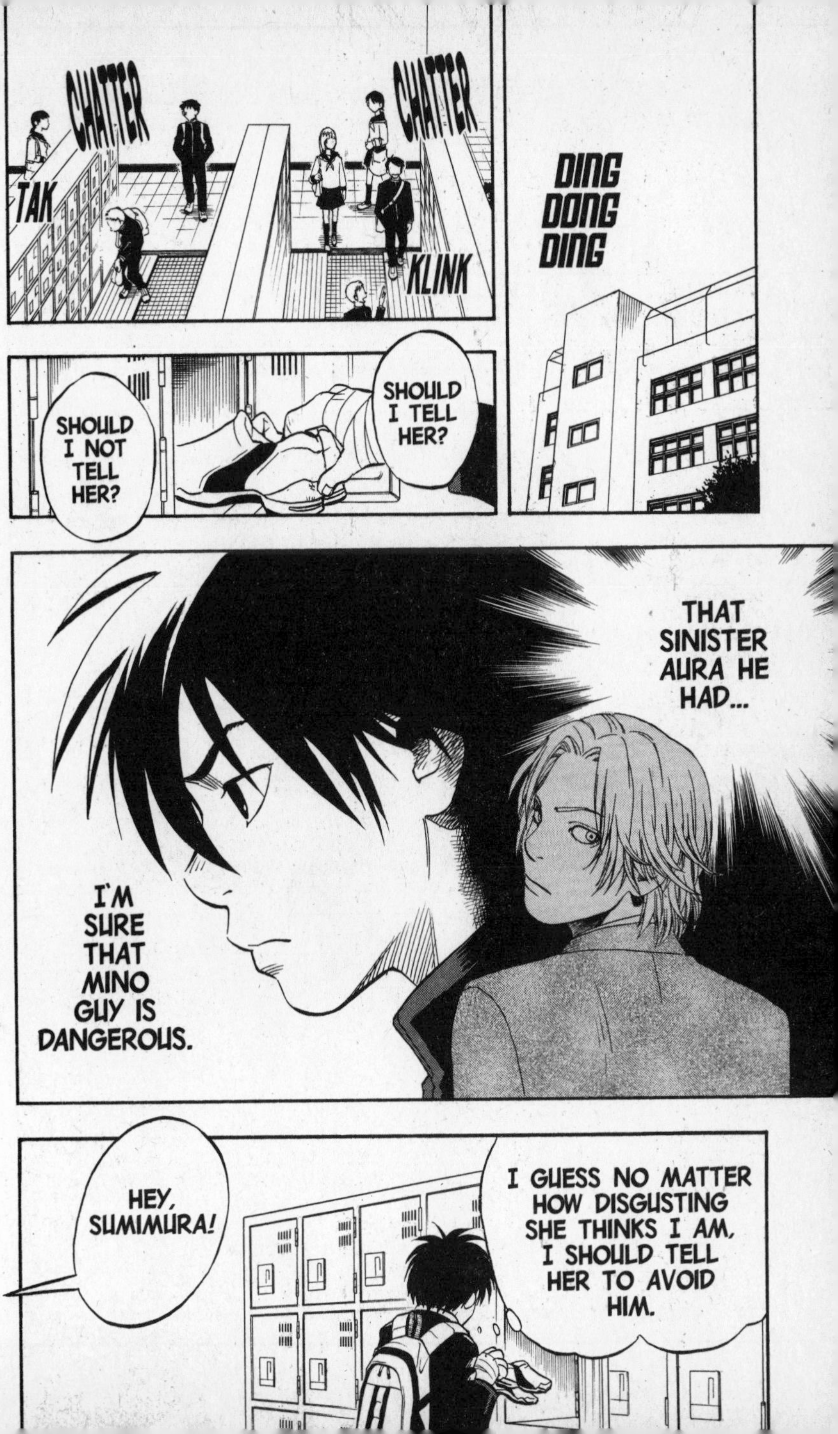
DING DONG DING
CHATTER
KLINK
CHATTER
TAK
SHOULD I TELL HER?
SHOULD I NOT TELL HER?
THAT SINISTER AURA HE HAD...
I'M SURE THAT MINO GUY IS DANGEROUS.
I GUESS NO MATTER HOW DISGUSTING SHE THINKS I AM, I SHOULD TELL HER TO AVOID HIM.
HEY, SUMIMURA!

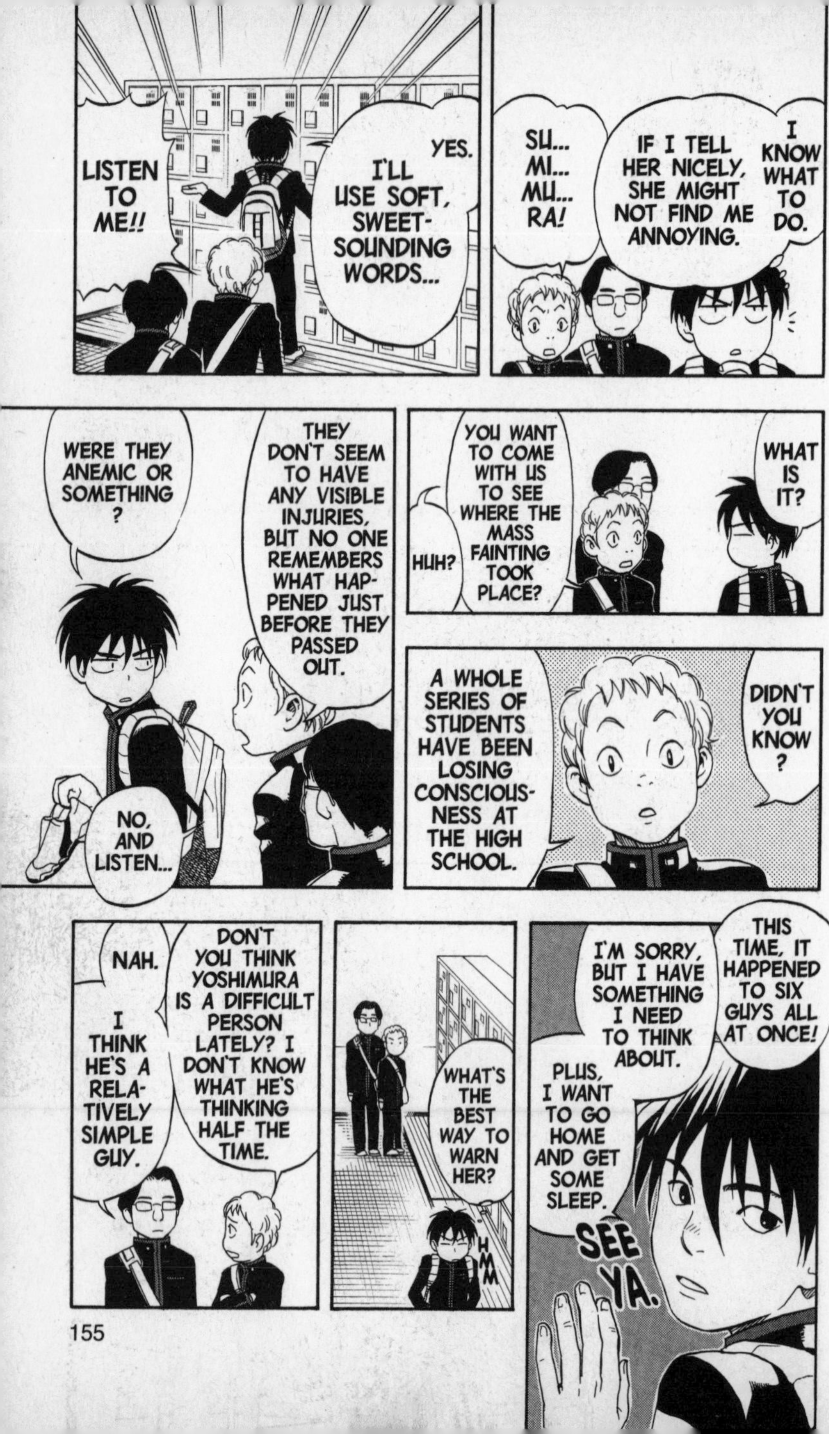
I KNOW WHAT TO DO.
IF I TELL HER NICELY, SHE MIGHT NOT FIND ME ANNOYING.
SU... MI... MU... RA!
YES. I'LL USE SOFT, SWEET-SOUNDING WORDS...
LISTEN TO ME!!
WHAT IS IT?
YOU WANT TO COME WITH US TO SEE WHERE THE MASS FAINTING TOOK PLACE?
HUH?
DIDN'T YOU KNOW?
A WHOLE SERIES OF STUDENTS HAVE BEEN LOSING CONSCIOUSNESS AT THE HIGH SCHOOL.
THEY DON'T SEEM TO HAVE ANY VISIBLE INJURIES, BUT NO ONE REMEMBERS WHAT HAPPENED JUST BEFORE THEY PASSED OUT.
WERE THEY ANEMIC OR SOMETHING?
NO, AND LISTEN...
THIS TIME, IT HAPPENED TO SIX GUYS ALL AT ONCE!
I'M SORRY, BUT I HAVE SOMETHING I NEED TO THINK ABOUT.
PLUS, I WANT TO GO HOME AND GET SOME SLEEP.
SEE YA.
WHAT'S THE BEST WAY TO WARN HER?
HMM
DON'T YOU THINK YOSHIMURA IS A DIFFICULT PERSON LATELY? I DON'T KNOW WHAT HE'S THINKING HALF THE TIME.
NAH.
I THINK HE'S A RELATIVELY SIMPLE GUY.

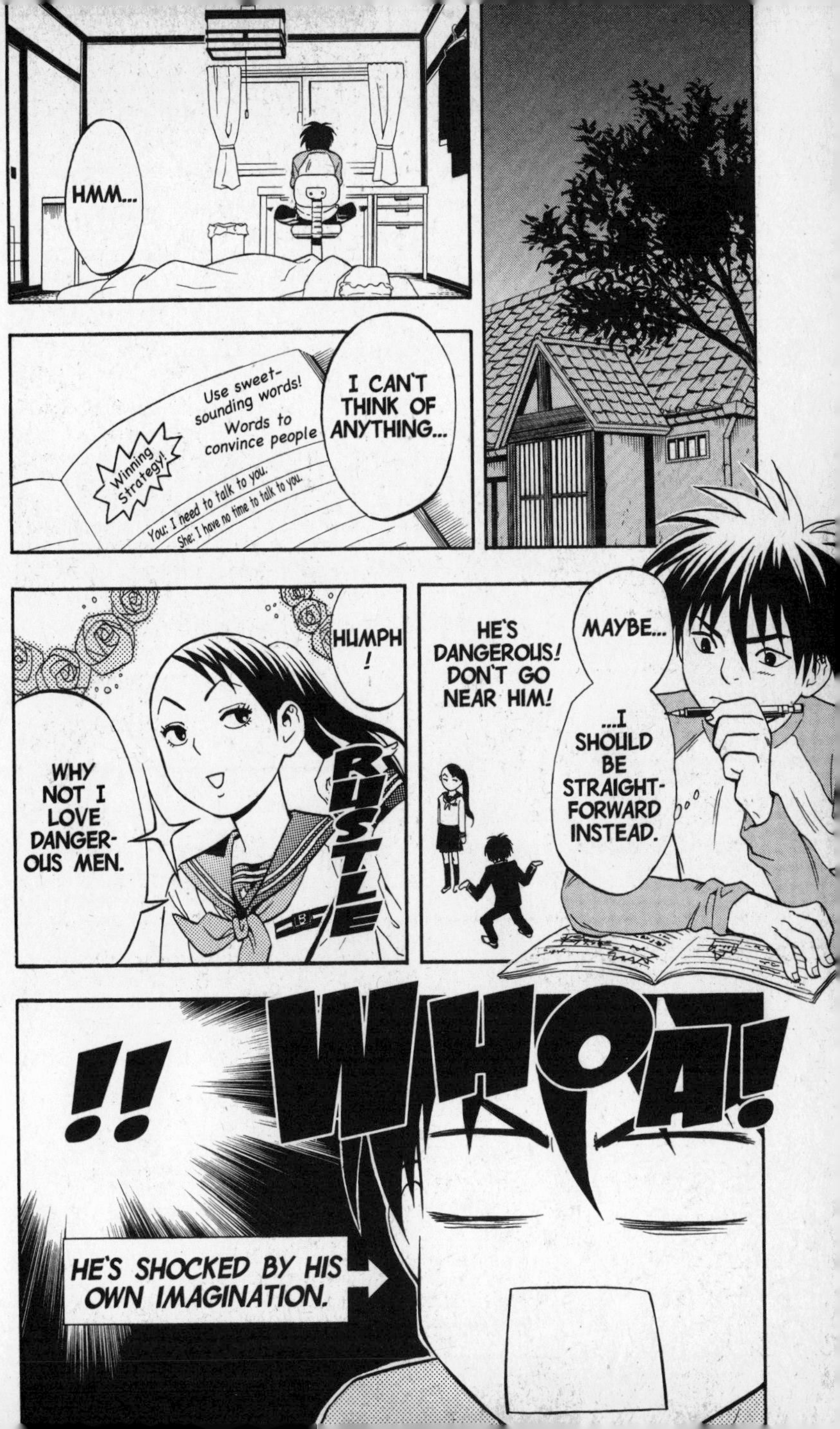
HMM...
I CAN'T THINK OF ANYTHING...
Use sweet-sounding words! Words to convince people
Winning Strategy!
You: I need to talk to you.
She: I have no time to talk to you.
MAYBE...
...I SHOULD BE STRAIGHT-FORWARD INSTEAD.
HE'S DANGEROUS! DON'T GO NEAR HIM!
HUMPH!
RUSTLE
WHY NOT I LOVE DANGER-OUS MEN.
WHOA!
!!
HE'S SHOCKED BY HIS OWN IMAGINATION.

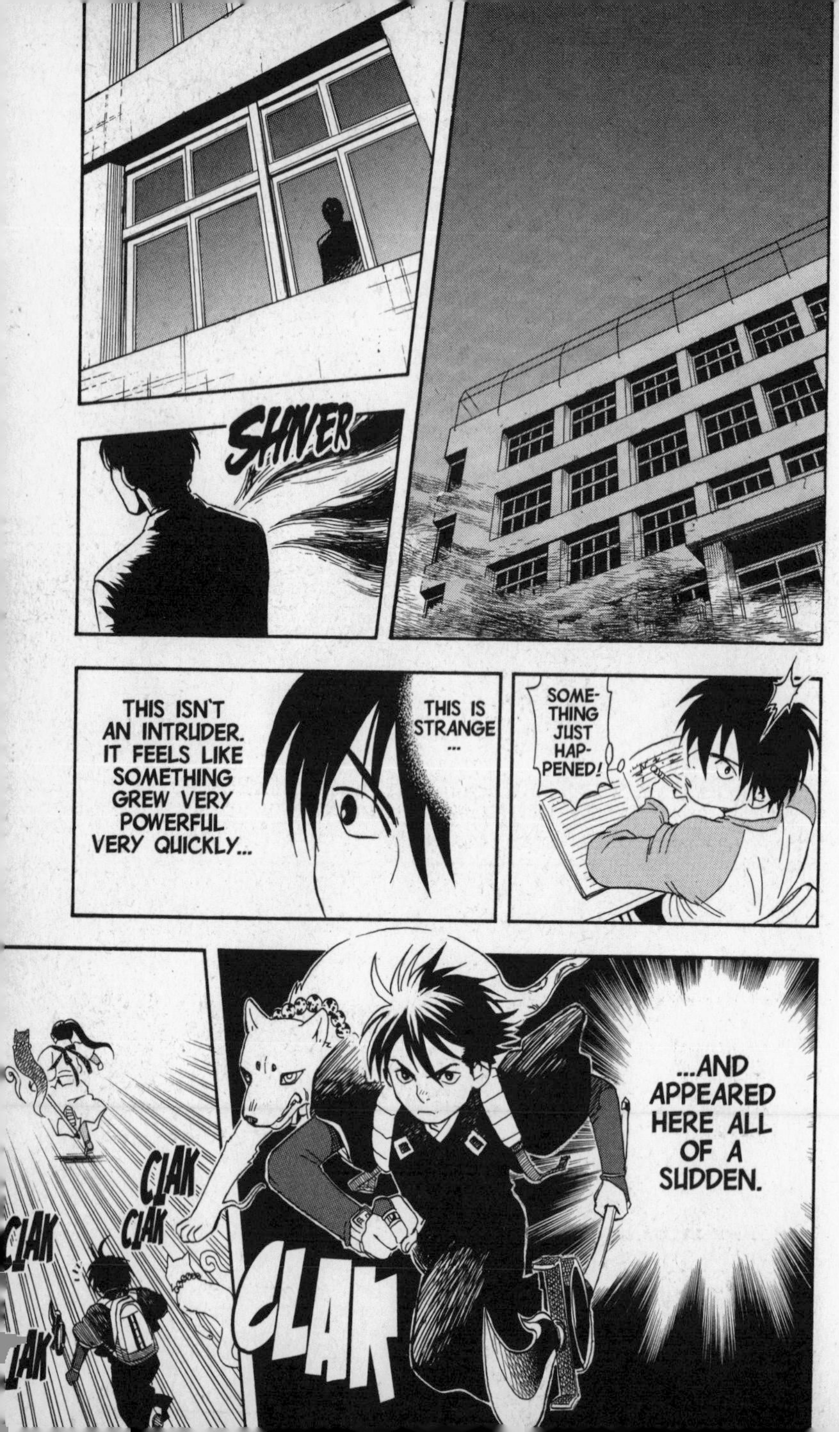
SHIVER
SOMETHING JUST HAPPENED!
THIS IS STRANGE...
THIS ISN'T AN INTRUDER. IT FEELS LIKE SOMETHING GREW VERY POWERFUL VERY QUICKLY...
...AND APPEARED HERE ALL OF A SUDDEN.
CLAK
CLAK
CLAK
CLAK
LAK

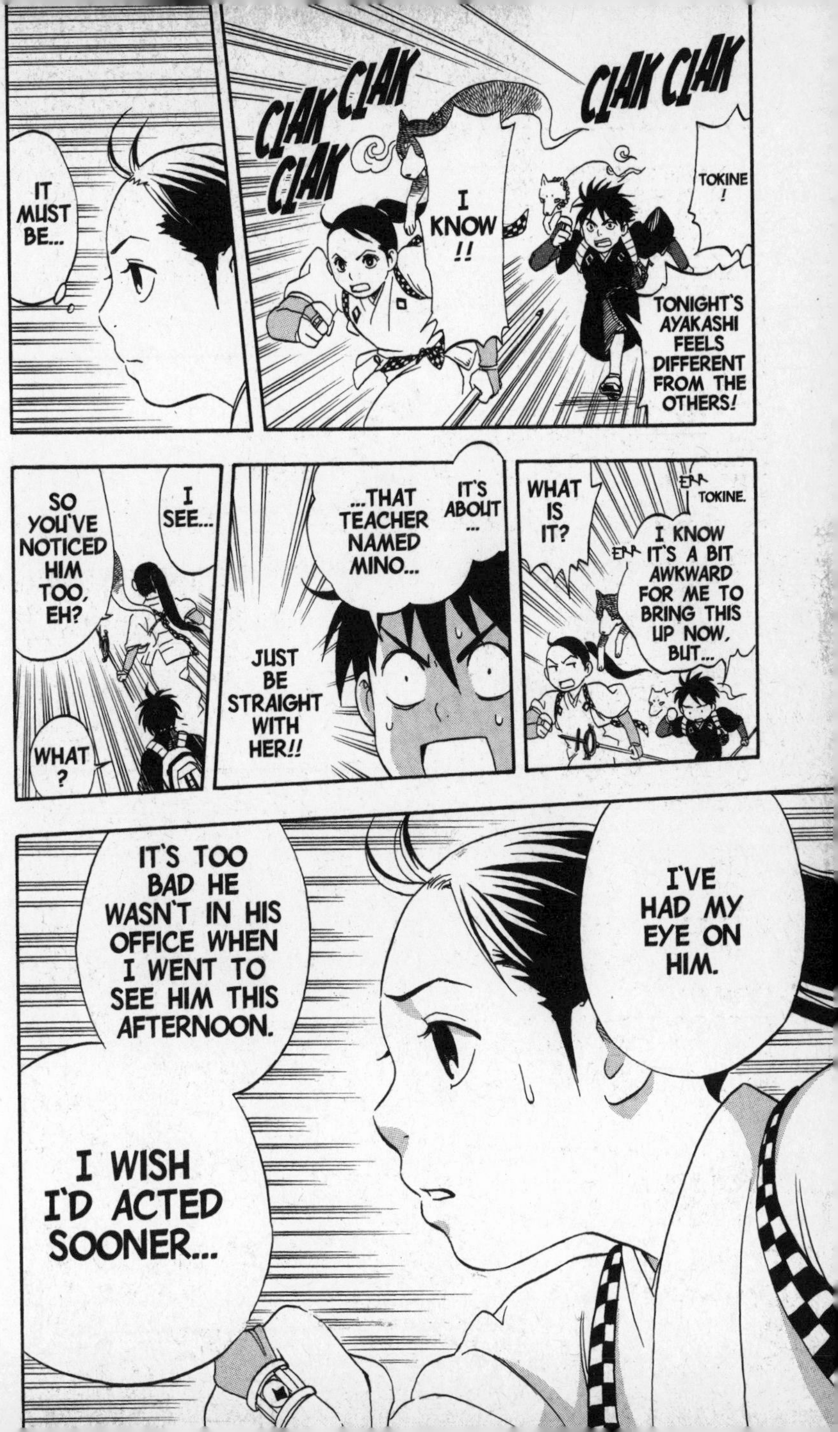
CLAK CLAK
TOKINE!
TONIGHT'S AYAKASHI FEELS DIFFERENT FROM THE OTHERS!
CLAK CLAK CLAK
I KNOW!!
IT MUST BE...
ERR TOKINE.
WHAT IS IT?
ERR I KNOW IT'S A BIT AWKWARD FOR ME TO BRING THIS UP NOW, BUT...
IT'S ABOUT...
...THAT TEACHER NAMED MINO...
JUST BE STRAIGHT WITH HER!!
I SEE...
SO YOU'VE NOTICED HIM TOO, EH?
WHAT?
I'VE HAD MY EYE ON HIM.
IT'S TOO BAD HE WASN'T IN HIS OFFICE WHEN I WENT TO SEE HIM THIS AFTERNOON.
I WISH I'D ACTED SOONER...

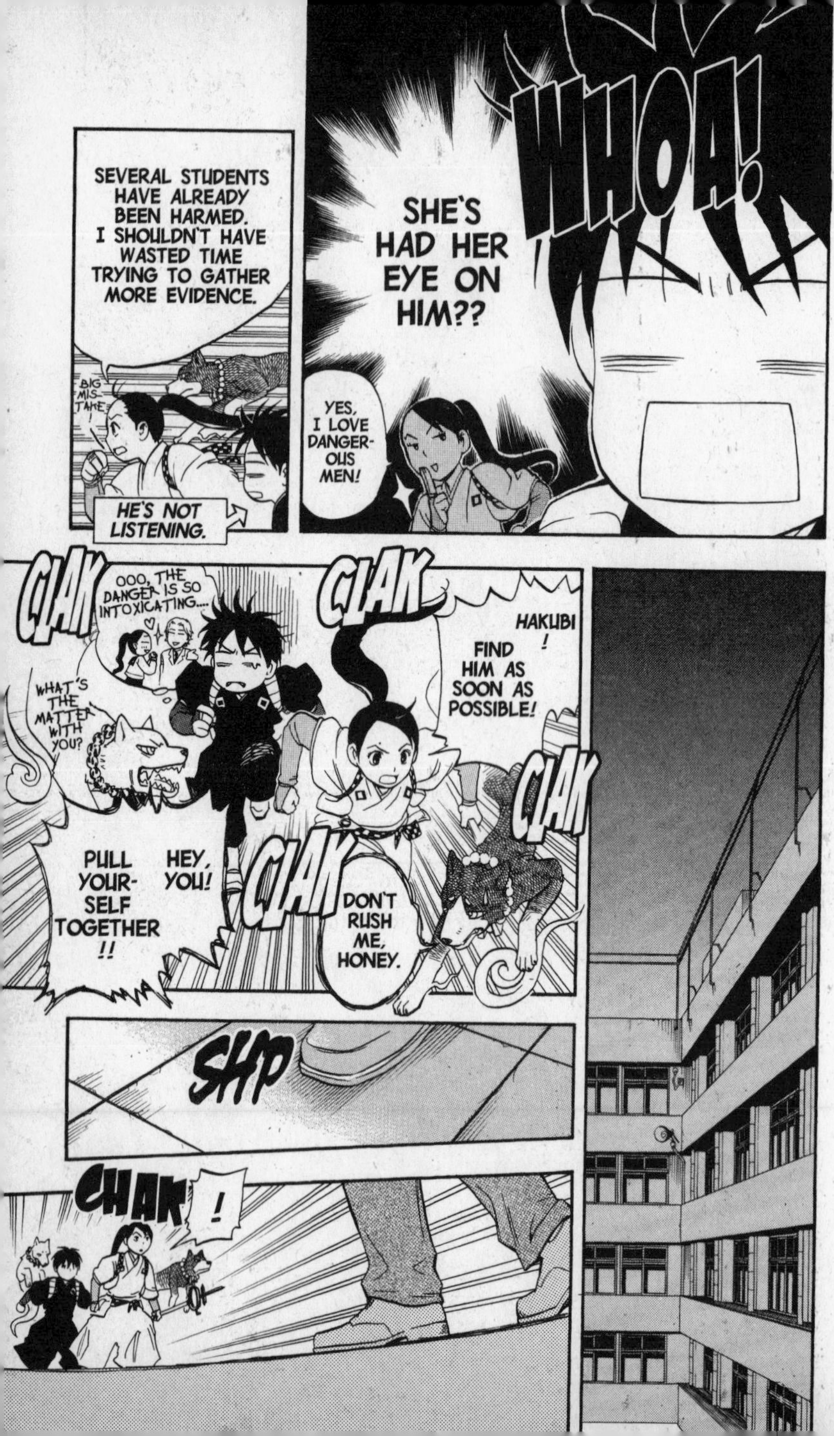
WHOA!
SHE'S HAD HER EYE ON HIM??
YES, I LOVE DANGEROUS MEN!
SEVERAL STUDENTS HAVE ALREADY BEEN HARMED. I SHOULDN'T HAVE WASTED TIME TRYING TO GATHER MORE EVIDENCE.
BIG MISTAKE!
HE'S NOT LISTENING.
CLAK
HAKUBI! FIND HIM AS SOON AS POSSIBLE!
CLAK
OOO, THE DANGER IS SO INTOXICATING....
WHAT'S THE MATTER WITH YOU?
CLAK
HEY, YOU!
PULL YOURSELF TOGETHER!!
CLAK
DON'T RUSH ME, HONEY.
SHP
CHAK!

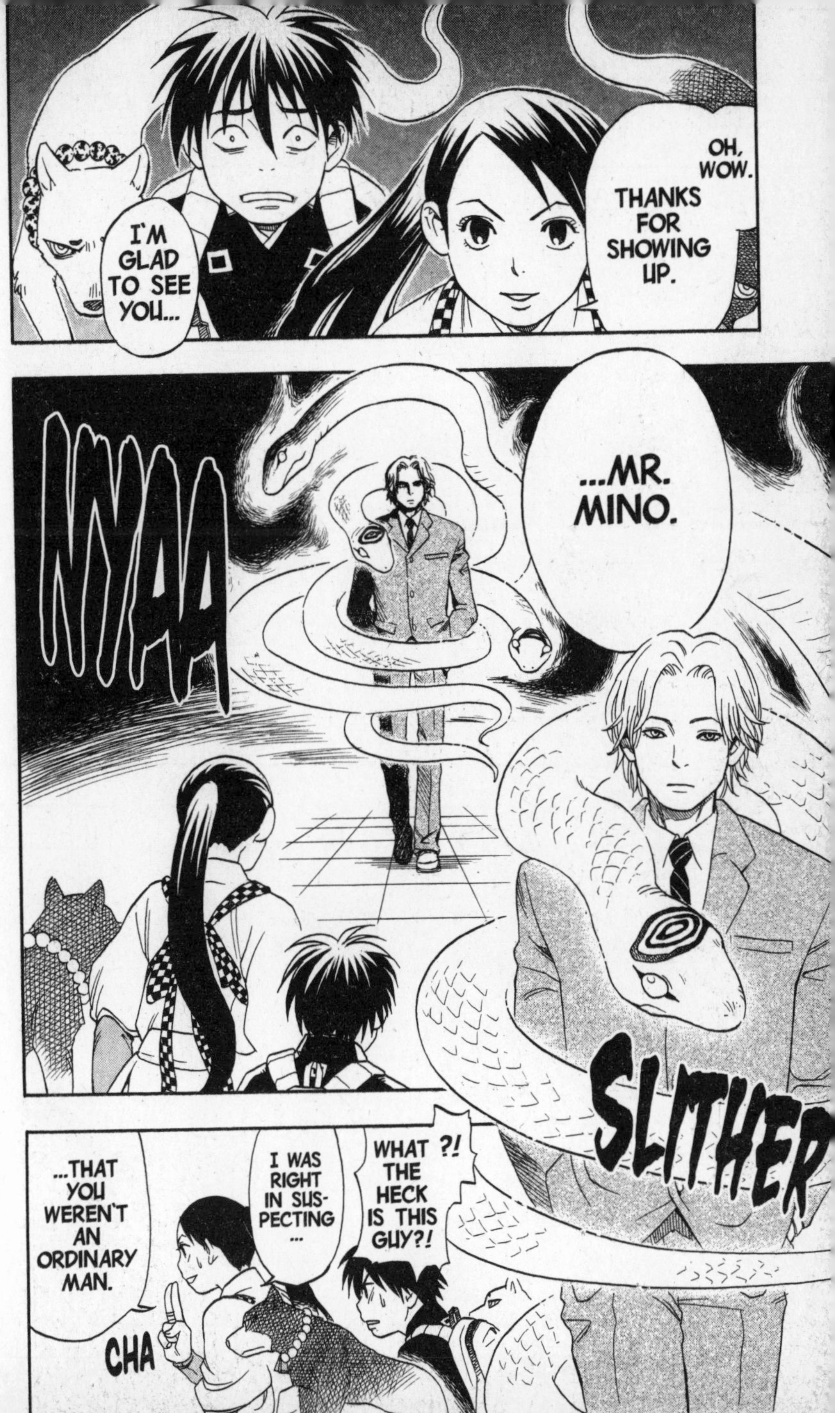
OH, WOW. THANKS FOR SHOWING UP.
I'M GLAD TO SEE YOU...
...MR. MINO.
NYAA
SLITHER
WHAT?! THE HECK IS THIS GUY?!
I WAS RIGHT IN SUS-PECTING...
...THAT YOU WEREN'T AN ORDINARY MAN.
CHA

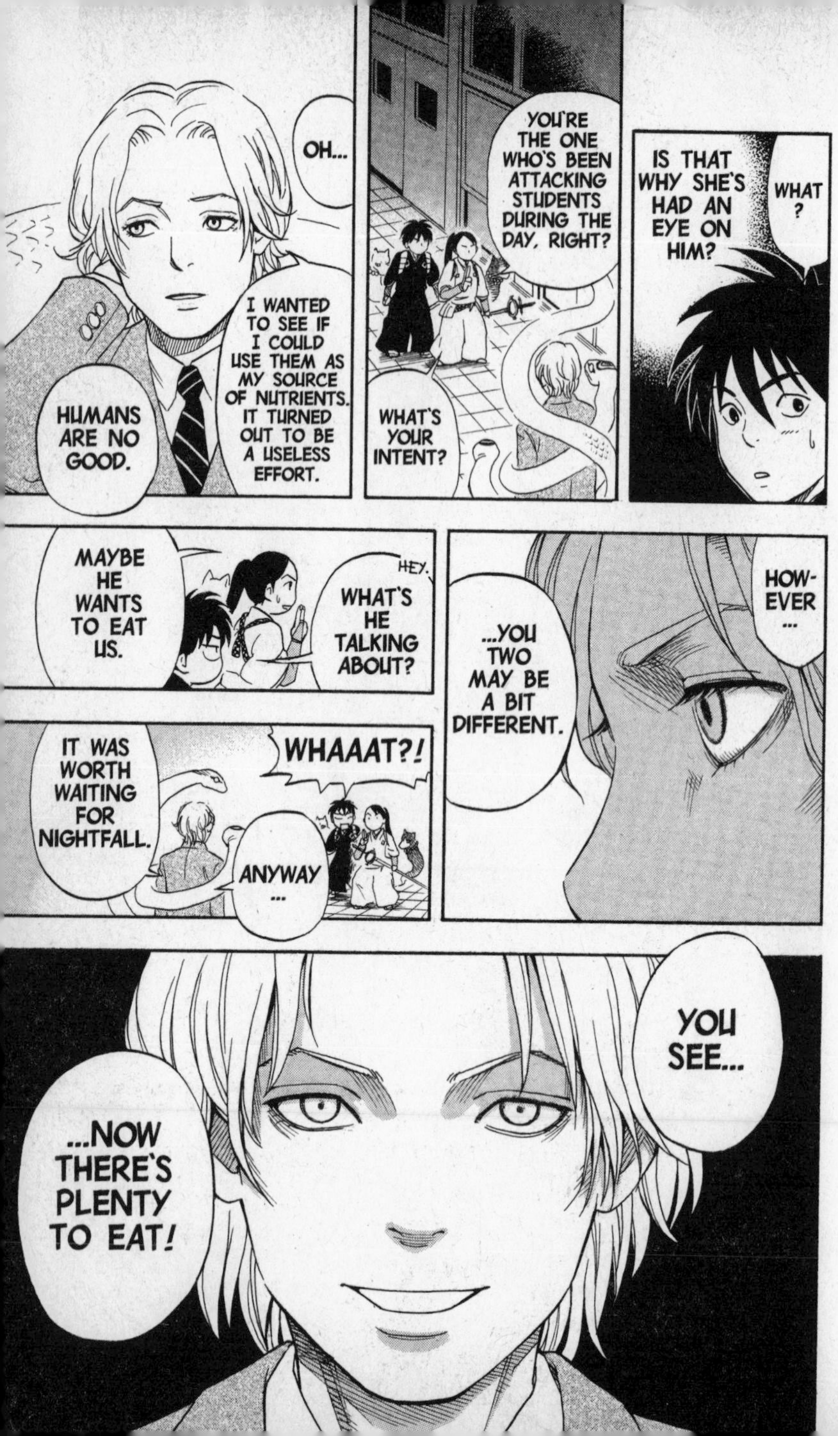
WHAT ?
IS THAT WHY SHE'S HAD AN EYE ON HIM?
YOU'RE THE ONE WHO'S BEEN ATTACKING STUDENTS DURING THE DAY, RIGHT?
WHAT'S YOUR INTENT?
OH...
I WANTED TO SEE IF I COULD USE THEM AS MY SOURCE OF NUTRIENTS. IT TURNED OUT TO BE A USELESS EFFORT.
HUMANS ARE NO GOOD.
HOW-EVER...
...YOU TWO MAY BE A BIT DIFFERENT.
HEY.
WHAT'S HE TALKING ABOUT?
MAYBE HE WANTS TO EAT US.
ANYWAY...
IT WAS WORTH WAITING FOR NIGHTFALL.
WHAAAT?!
YOU SEE...
...NOW THERE'S PLENTY TO EAT!

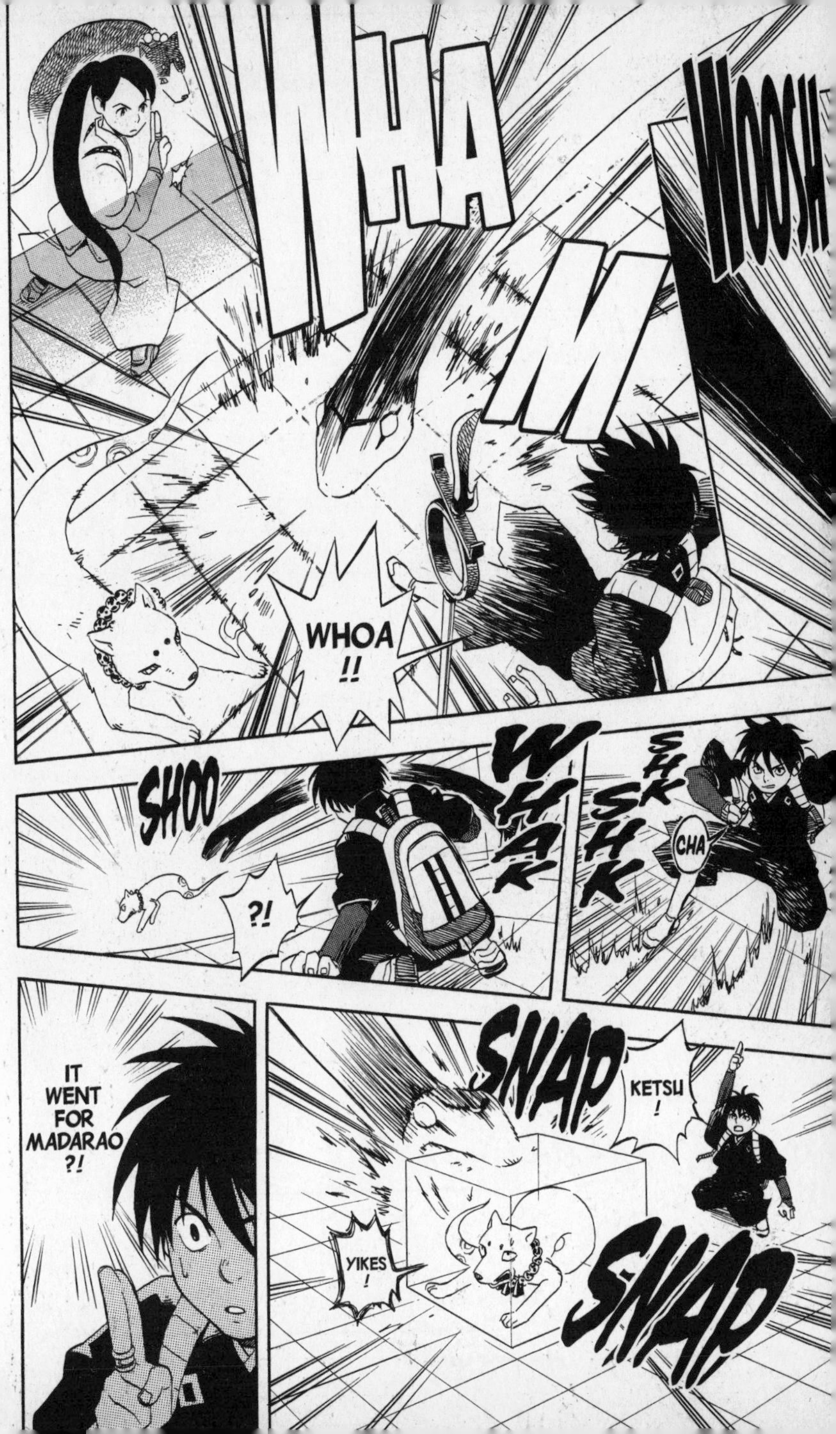
WOOSH
WHAM
WHOA !!
SHK SHK
CHA
WHAK
SHOO
?!
KETSU !
SNAP
SNAP
YIKES !
IT WENT FOR MADARAO ?!

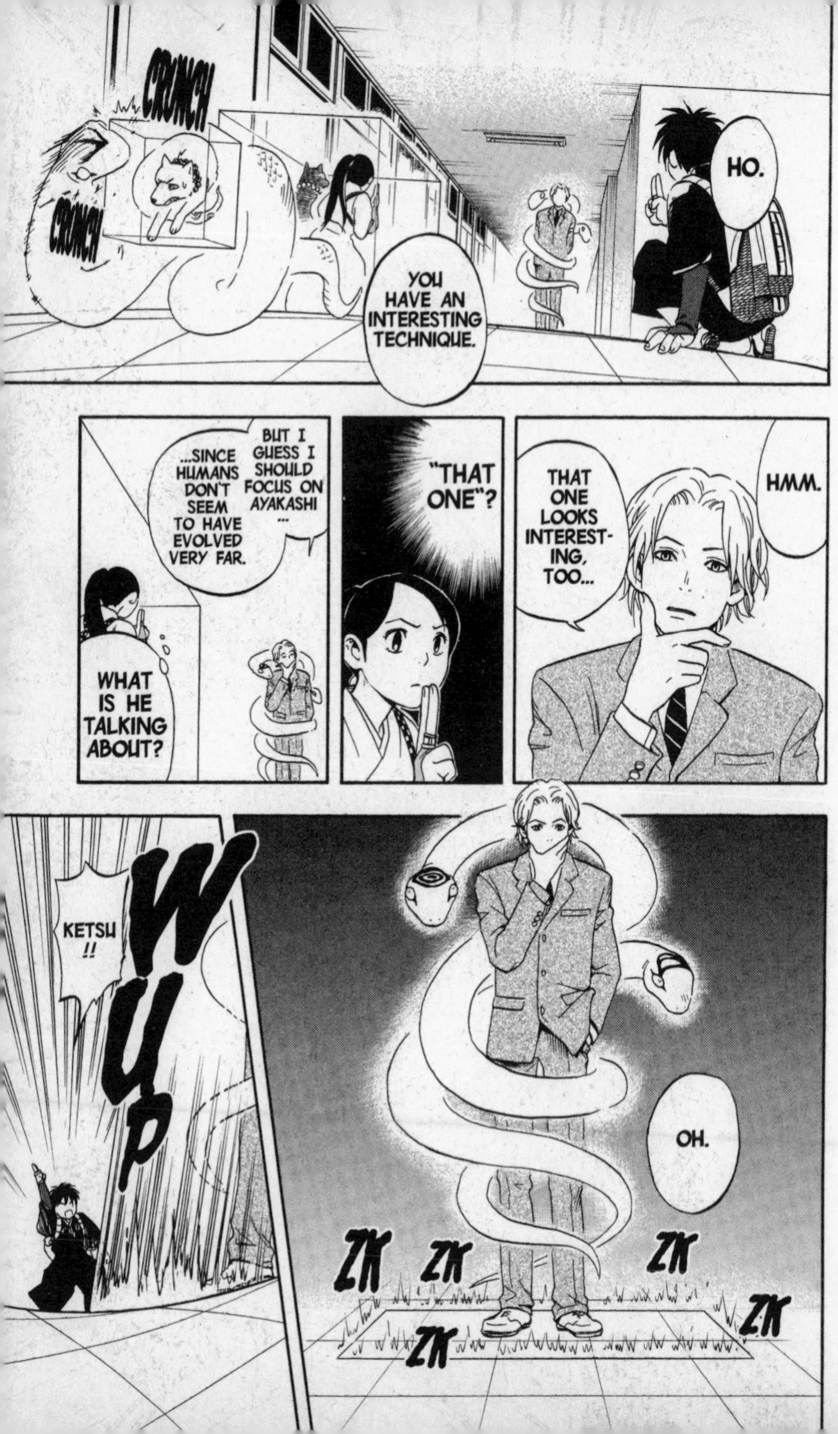
HO.
YOU HAVE AN INTERESTING TECHNIQUE.
CRUNCH
CRUNCH
HMM.
THAT ONE LOOKS INTERESTING, TOO...
"THAT ONE"?
BUT I GUESS I SHOULD FOCUS ON AYAKASHI...
...SINCE HUMANS DON'T SEEM TO HAVE EVOLVED VERY FAR.
WHAT IS HE TALKING ABOUT?
OH.
ZK ZK ZK ZK ZK
WUP
KETSU!!

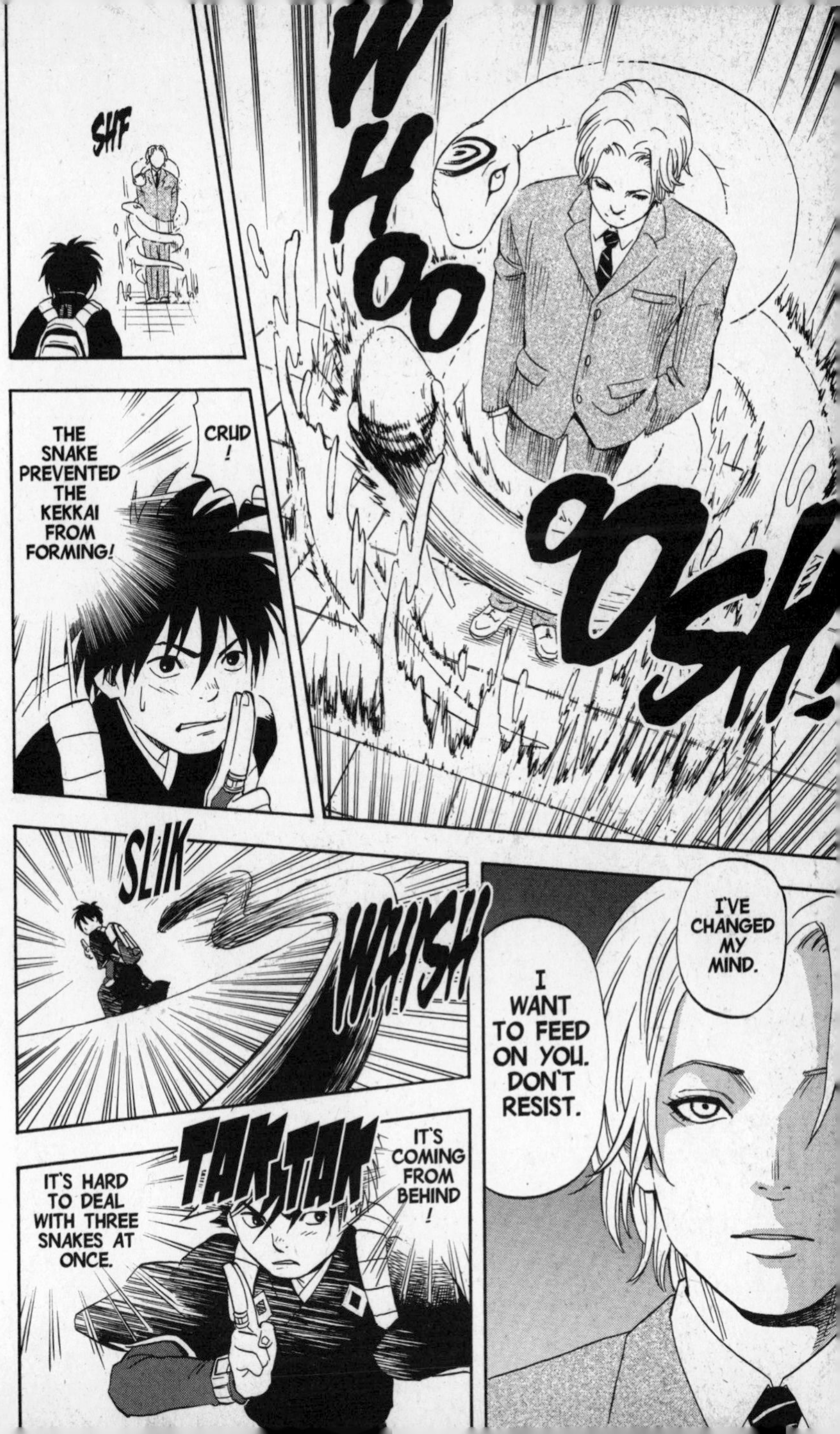
WHOOOOSH!!
SHF
CRUD!
THE SNAKE PREVENTED THE KEKKAI FROM FORMING!
I'VE CHANGED MY MIND.
I WANT TO FEED ON YOU. DON'T RESIST.
SLIK
WHISH
TAK TAK
IT'S COMING FROM BEHIND!
IT'S HARD TO DEAL WITH THREE SNAKES AT ONCE.

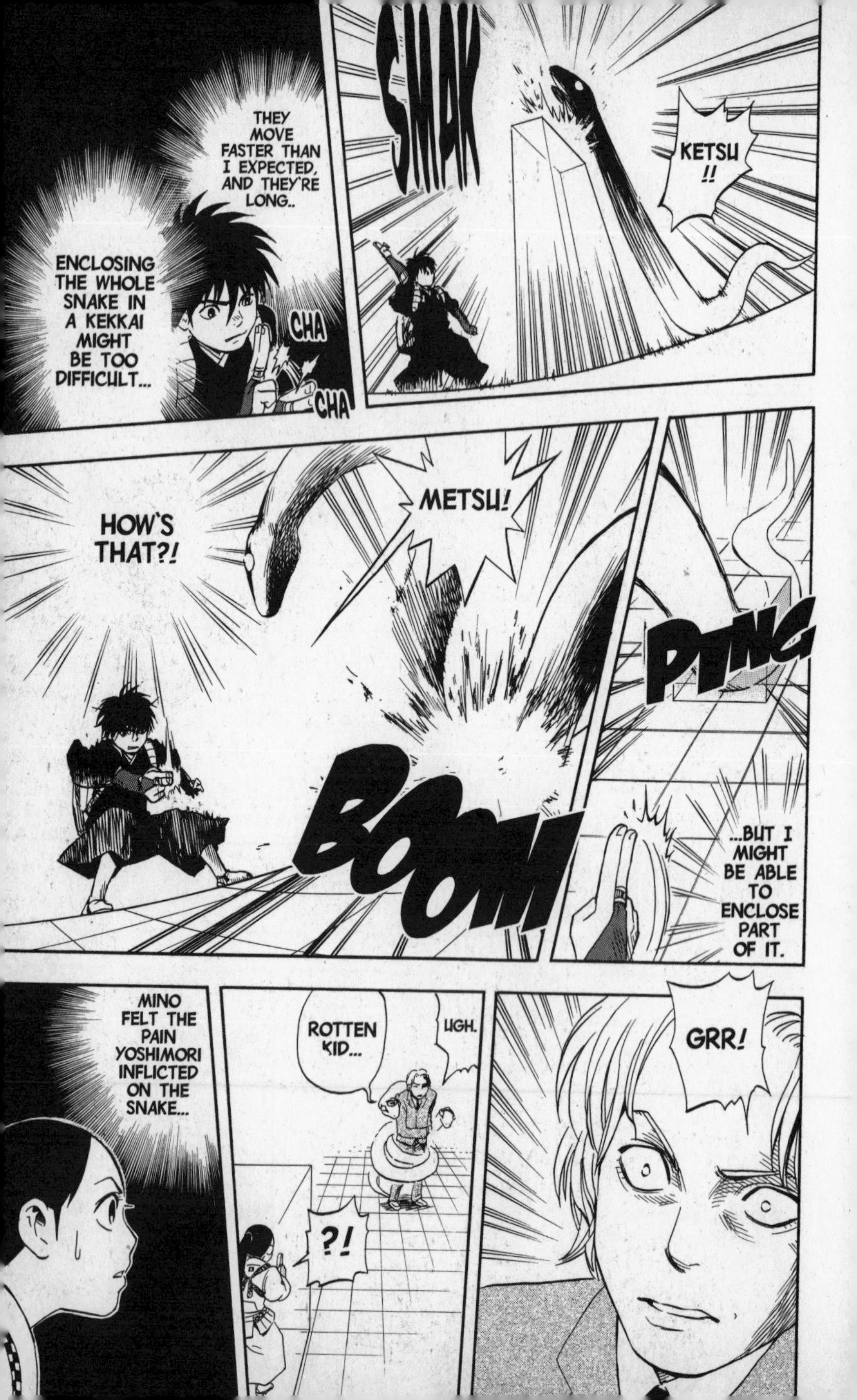
SHAK
KETSU !!
THEY MOVE FASTER THAN I EXPECTED, AND THEY'RE LONG..
ENCLOSING THE WHOLE SNAKE IN A KEKKAI MIGHT BE TOO DIFFICULT...
CHA
CHA
PING
...BUT I MIGHT BE ABLE TO ENCLOSE PART OF IT.
METSU!
HOW'S THAT?!
BOOM
GRR!
UGH.
ROTTEN KID...
?!
MINO FELT THE PAIN YOSHIMORI INFLICTED ON THE SNAKE...

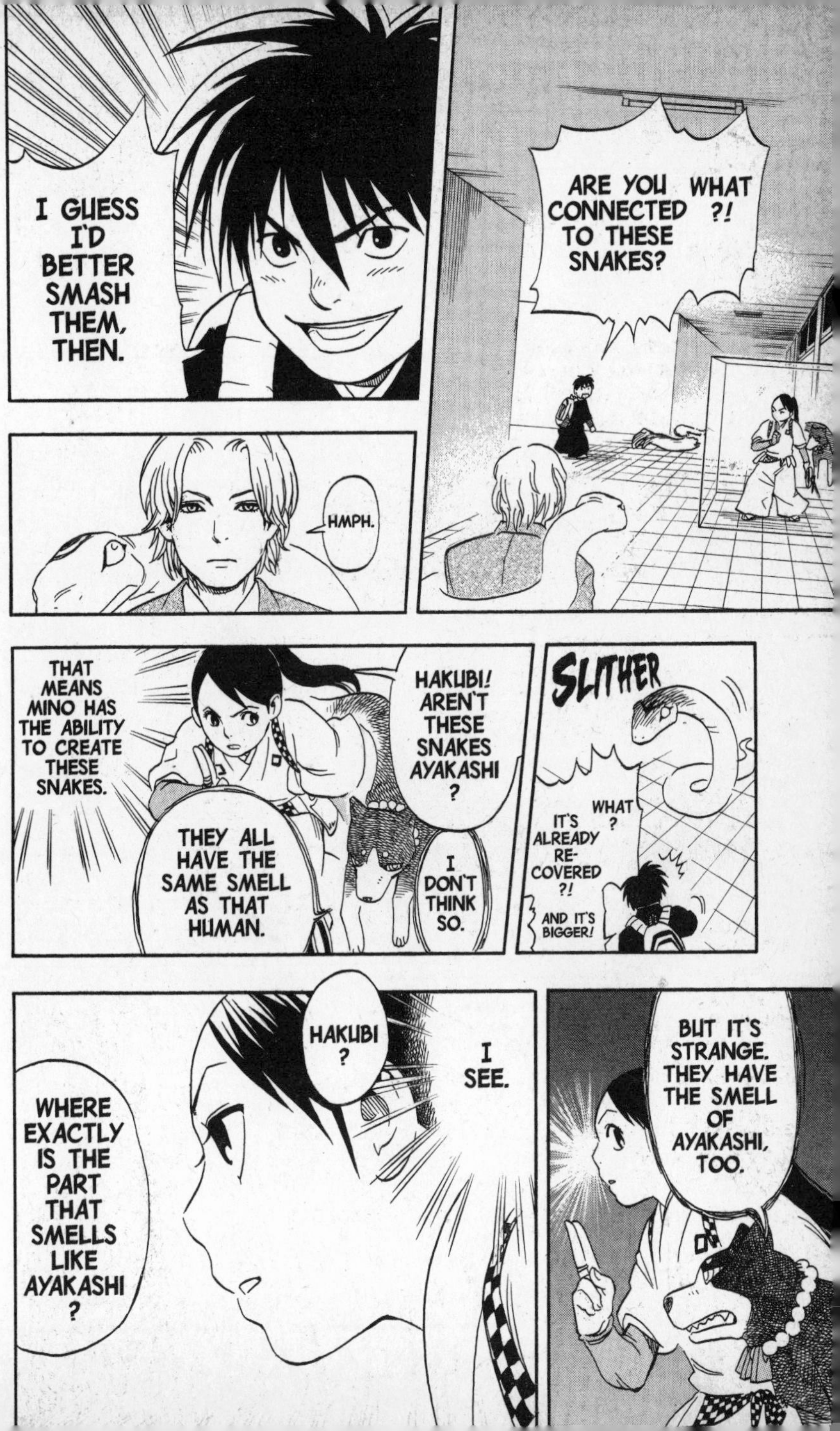
WHAT ?!
ARE YOU CONNECTED TO THESE SNAKES?
I GUESS I'D BETTER SMASH THEM, THEN.
HMPH.
SLITHER
WHAT ?
IT'S ALREADY RE-COVERED ?!
AND IT'S BIGGER!
HAKUBI! AREN'T THESE SNAKES AYAKASHI ?
I DON'T THINK SO.
THEY ALL HAVE THE SAME SMELL AS THAT HUMAN.
THAT MEANS MINO HAS THE ABILITY TO CREATE THESE SNAKES.
BUT IT'S STRANGE. THEY HAVE THE SMELL OF AYAKASHI, TOO.
I SEE.
HAKUBI ?
WHERE EXACTLY IS THE PART THAT SMELLS LIKE AYAKASHI ?

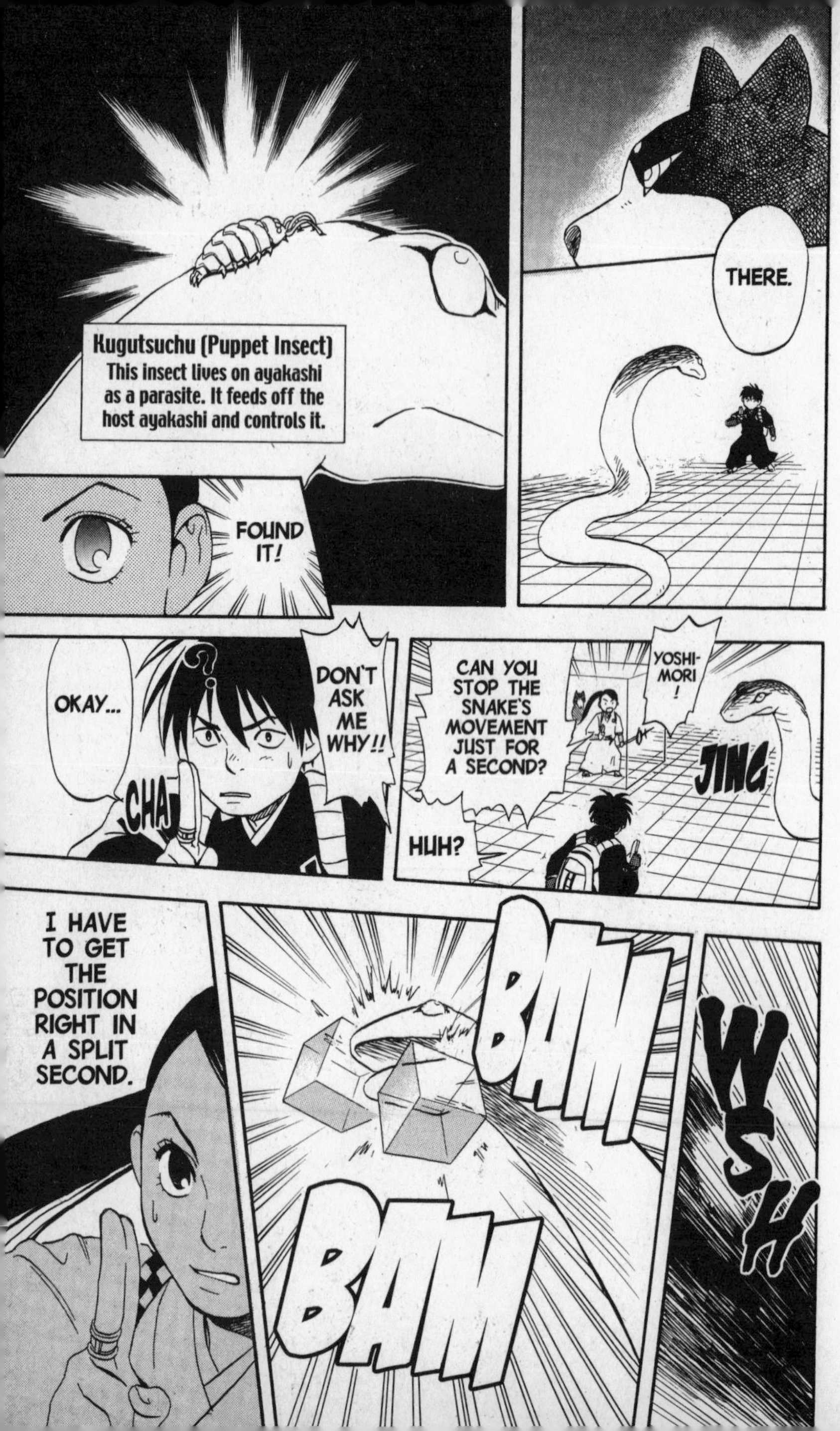
THERE.
Kugutsuchu (Puppet Insect)
This insect lives on ayakashi as a parasite. It feeds off the host ayakashi and controls it.
FOUND IT!
YOSHI-MORI!
CAN YOU STOP THE SNAKE'S MOVEMENT JUST FOR A SECOND?
JING
HUH?
DON'T ASK ME WHY!!
OKAY...
CHA
WSH
BAM
BAM
I HAVE TO GET THE POSITION RIGHT IN A SPLIT SECOND.

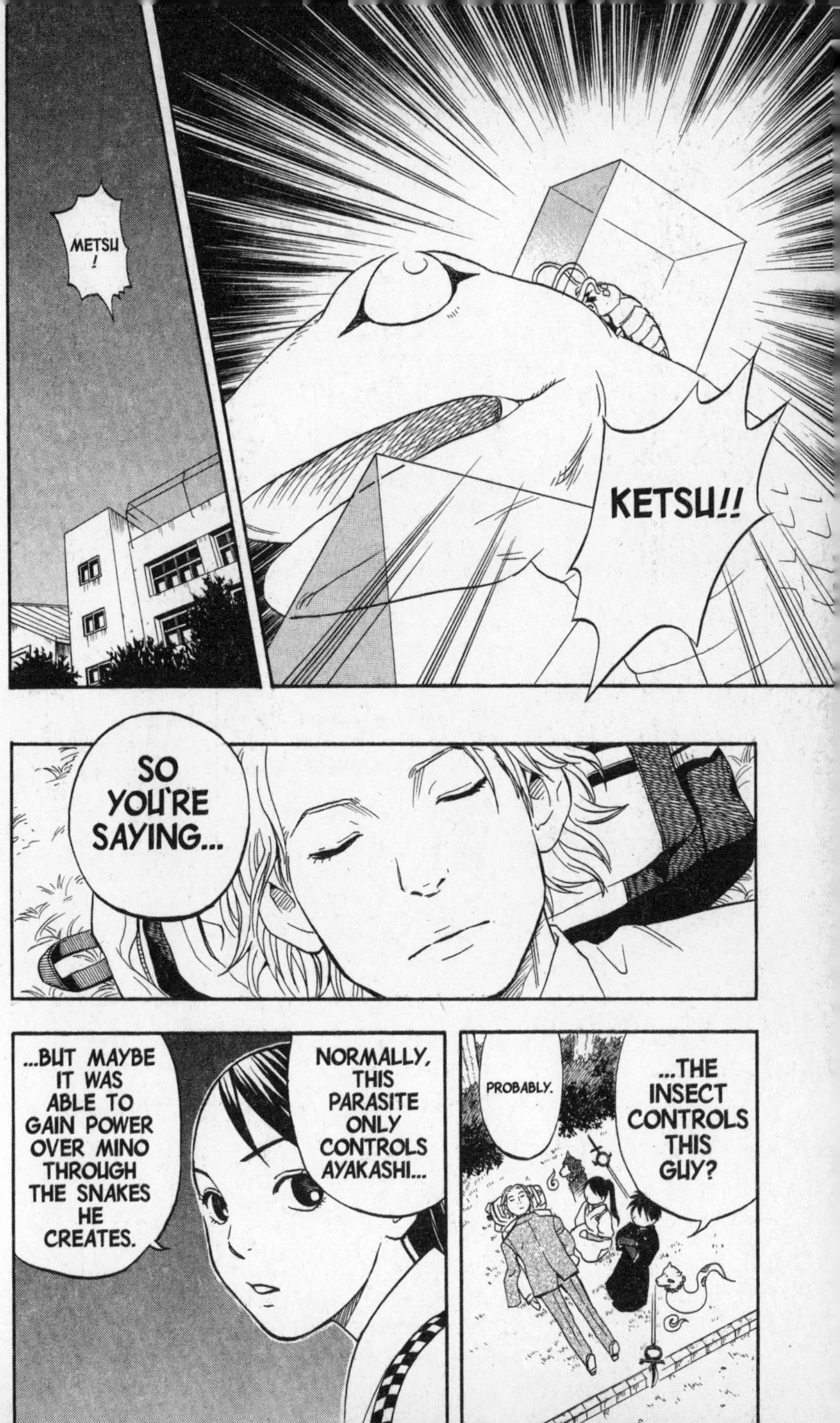
KETSU!!
METSU!
SO YOU'RE SAYING...
...THE INSECT CONTROLS THIS GUY?
PROBABLY.
NORMALLY, THIS PARASITE ONLY CONTROLS AYAKASHI...
...BUT MAYBE IT WAS ABLE TO GAIN POWER OVER MINO THROUGH THE SNAKES HE CREATES.

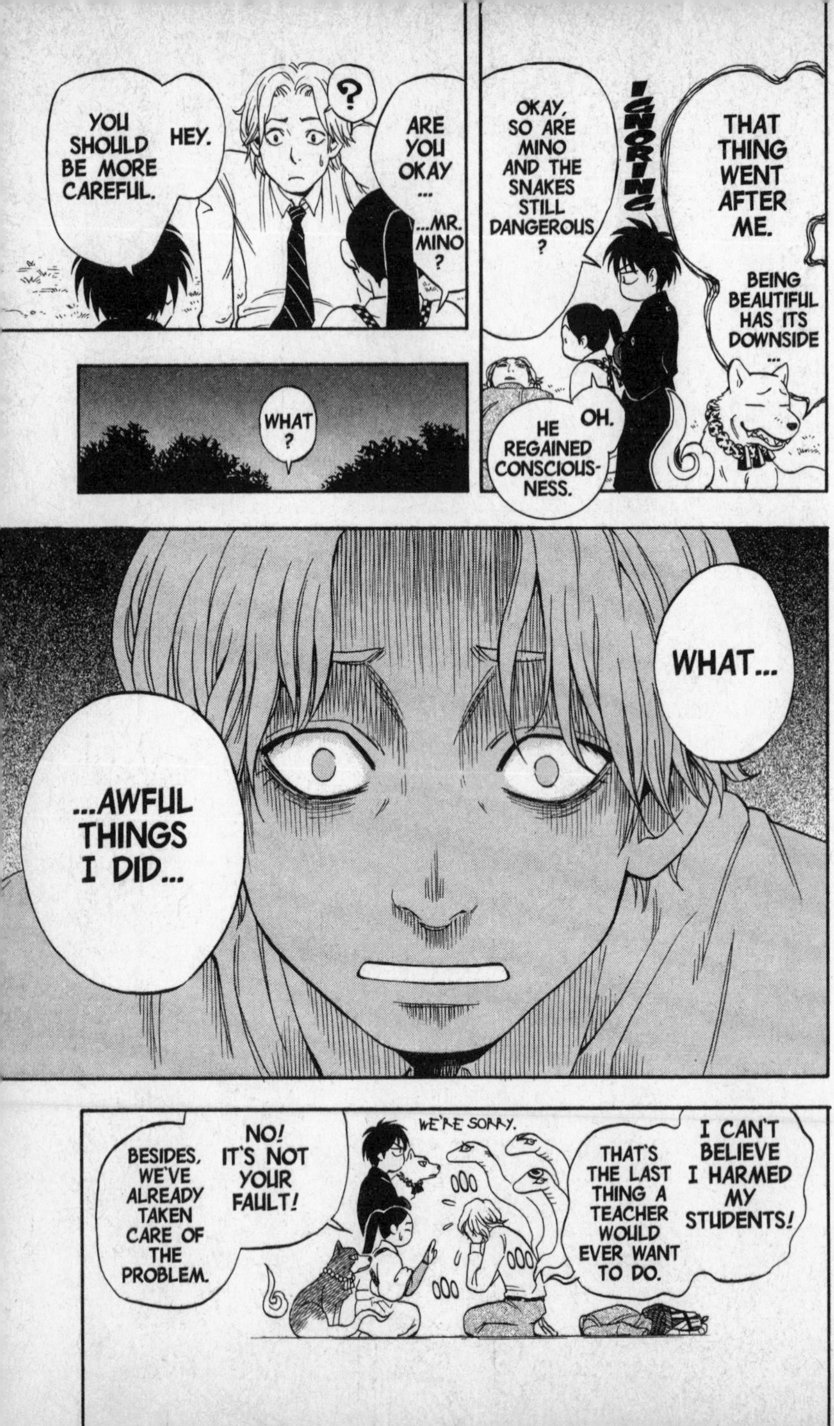
THAT THING WENT AFTER ME.
BEING BEAUTIFUL HAS ITS DOWNSIDE ...
IGNORING
OKAY, SO ARE MINO AND THE SNAKES STILL DANGEROUS?
OH. HE REGAINED CONSCIOUSNESS.
ARE YOU OKAY ... ...MR. MINO?
?
HEY.
YOU SHOULD BE MORE CAREFUL.
WHAT?
WHAT...
...AWFUL THINGS I DID...
I CAN'T BELIEVE I HARMED MY STUDENTS!
THAT'S THE LAST THING A TEACHER WOULD EVER WANT TO DO.
WE'RE SORRY.
NO! IT'S NOT YOUR FAULT!
BESIDES, WE'VE ALREADY TAKEN CARE OF THE PROBLEM.

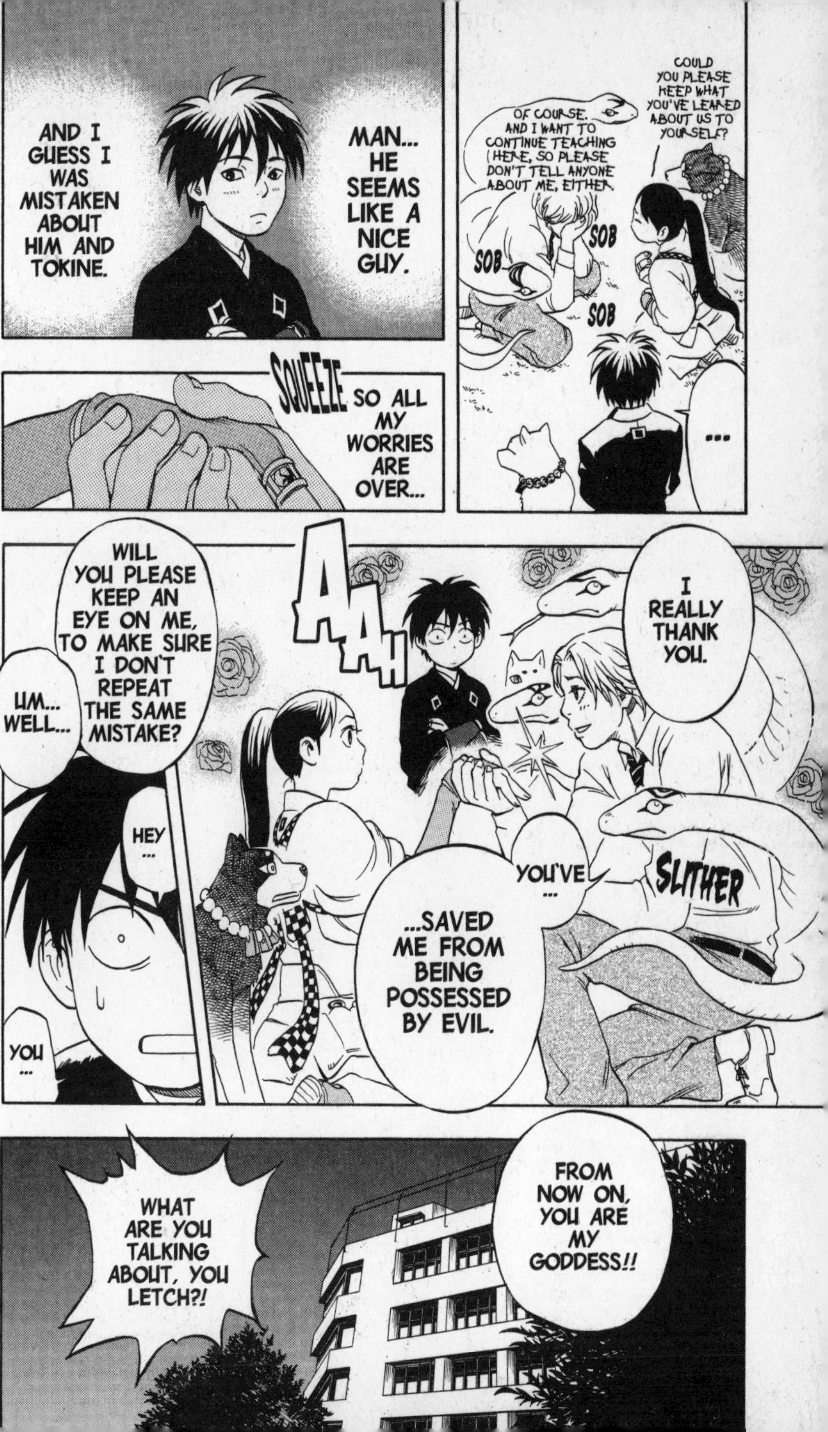
COULD YOU PLEASE KEEP WHAT YOU'VE LEARED ABOUT US TO YOURSELF?
OF COURSE. AND I WANT TO CONTINUE TEACHING HERE, SO PLEASE DON'T TELL ANYONE ABOUT ME, EITHER.
SOB
SOB
SOB
...
MAN... HE SEEMS LIKE A NICE GUY.
AND I GUESS I WAS MISTAKEN ABOUT HIM AND TOKINE.
SQUEEZE
SO ALL MY WORRIES ARE OVER...
AAAH
I REALLY THANK YOU.
YOU'VE...
...SAVED ME FROM BEING POSSESSED BY EVIL.
SLITHER
WILL YOU PLEASE KEEP AN EYE ON ME, TO MAKE SURE I DON'T REPEAT THE SAME MISTAKE?
UM... WELL...
HEY...
YOU...
FROM NOW ON, YOU ARE MY GODDESS!!
WHAT ARE YOU TALKING ABOUT, YOU LETCH?!

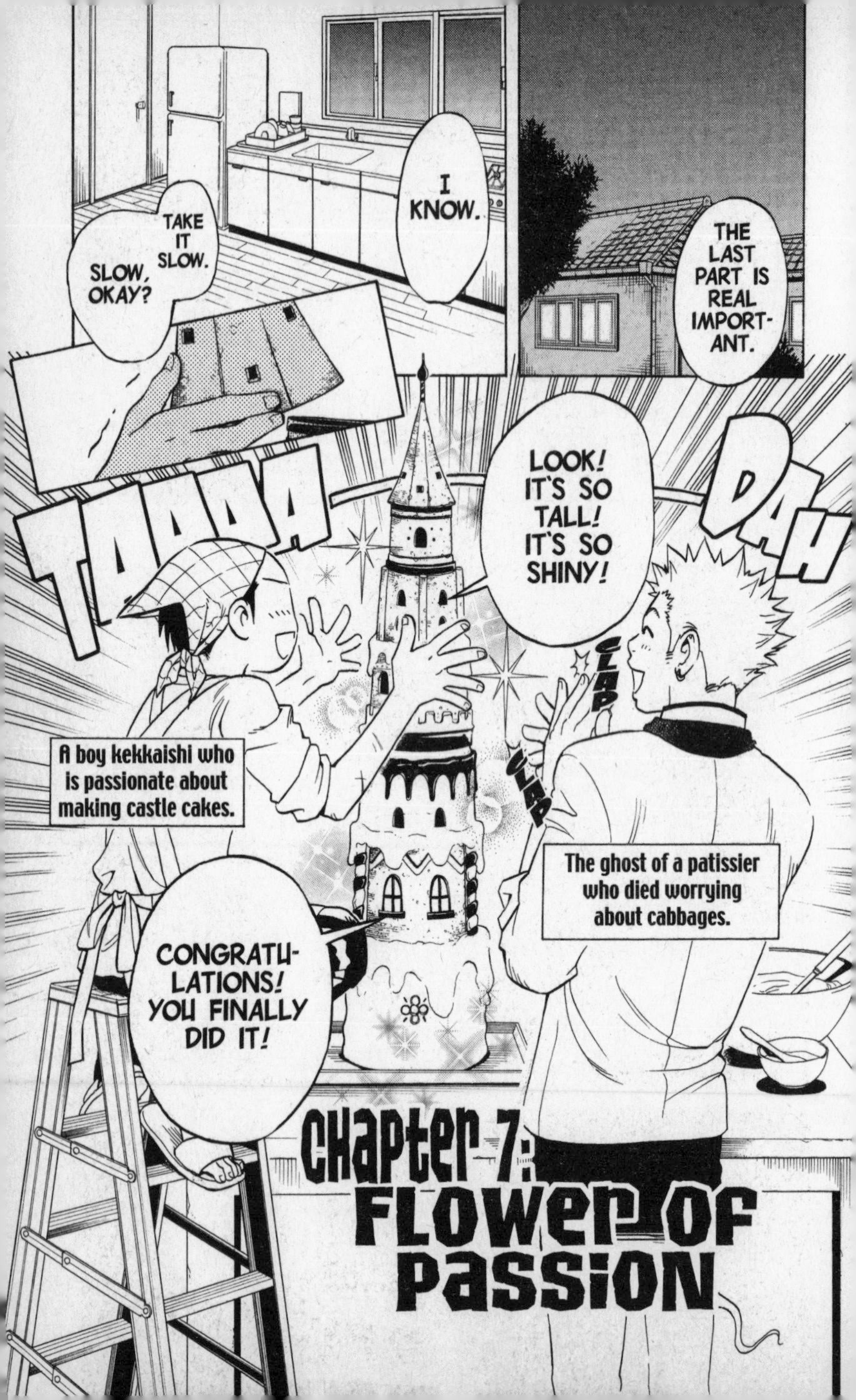
THE LAST PART IS REAL IMPORTANT.
I KNOW.
TAKE IT SLOW.
SLOW, OKAY?
TADAA
DAH
LOOK! IT'S SO TALL! IT'S SO SHINY!
CLAP
CLAP
A boy kekkaishi who is passionate about making castle cakes.
The ghost of a patissier who died worrying about cabbages.
CONGRATULATIONS! YOU FINALLY DID IT!
CHAPTER 7: FLOWER OF PASSION

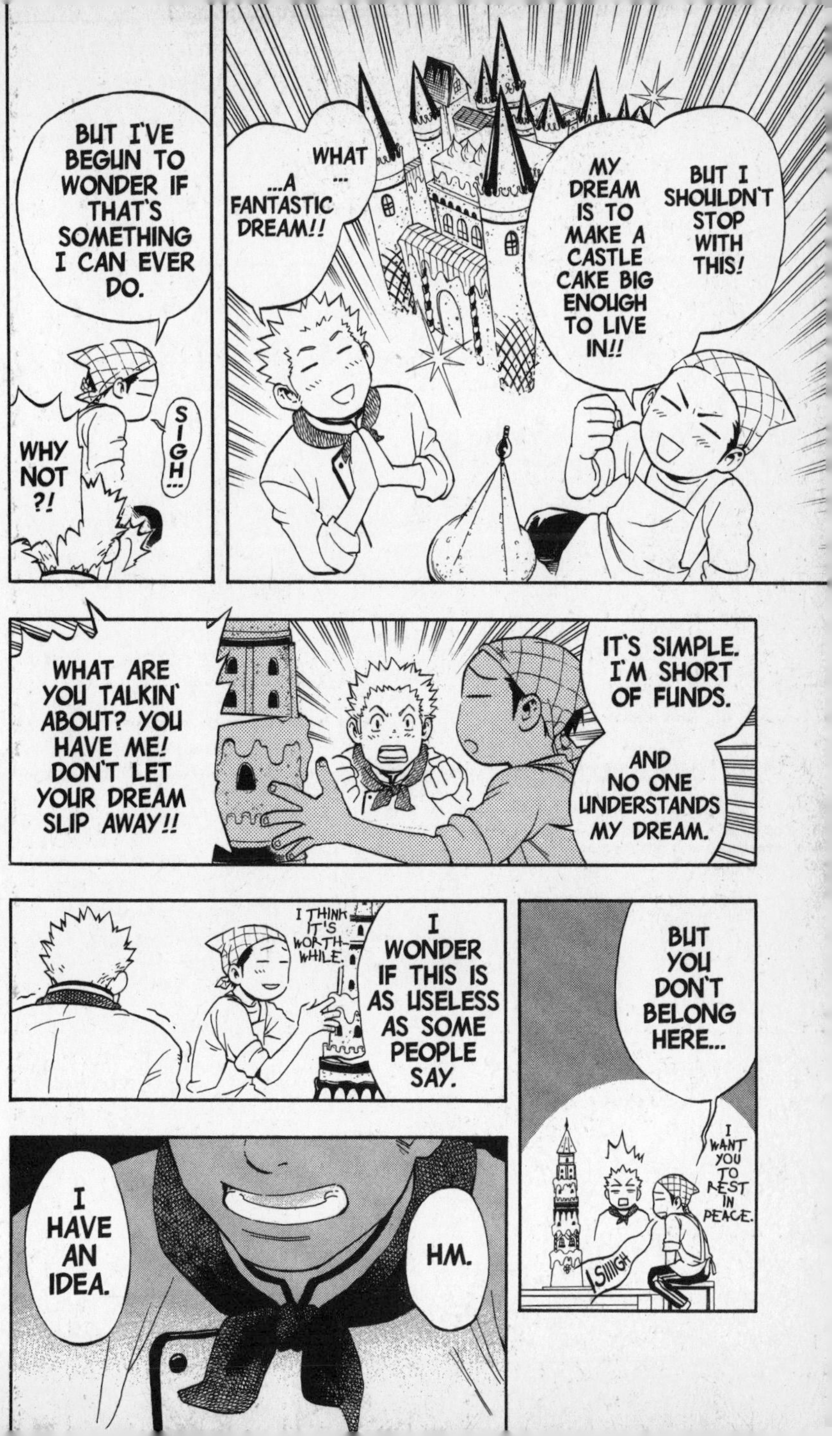
BUT I SHOULDN'T STOP WITH THIS!
MY DREAM IS TO MAKE A CASTLE CAKE BIG ENOUGH TO LIVE IN!!
WHAT ... ...A FANTASTIC DREAM!!
BUT I'VE BEGUN TO WONDER IF THAT'S SOMETHING I CAN EVER DO.
SIGH...
WHY NOT?!
IT'S SIMPLE. I'M SHORT OF FUNDS.
AND NO ONE UNDERSTANDS MY DREAM.
WHAT ARE YOU TALKIN' ABOUT? YOU HAVE ME! DON'T LET YOUR DREAM SLIP AWAY!!
I WONDER IF THIS IS AS USELESS AS SOME PEOPLE SAY.
I THINK IT'S WORTHWHILE.
BUT YOU DON'T BELONG HERE...
I WANT YOU TO REST IN PEACE.
SIIIIGH
HM.
I HAVE AN IDEA.

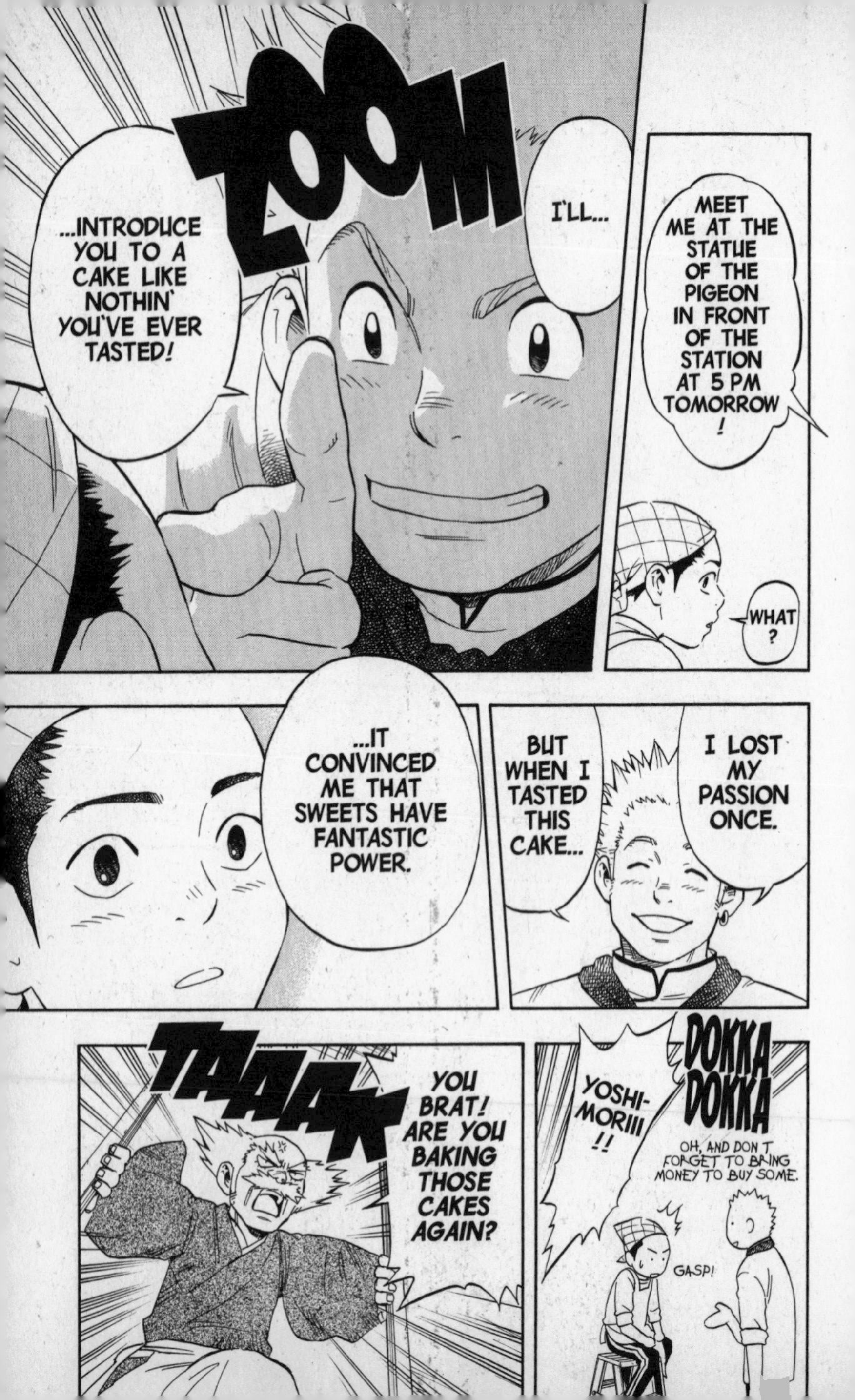
I'LL...
...INTRODUCE YOU TO A CAKE LIKE NOTHIN' YOU'VE EVER TASTED!
ZOOM
MEET ME AT THE STATUE OF THE PIGEON IN FRONT OF THE STATION AT 5 PM TOMORROW!
WHAT?
I LOST MY PASSION ONCE.
BUT WHEN I TASTED THIS CAKE...
...IT CONVINCED ME THAT SWEETS HAVE FANTASTIC POWER.
DOKKA DOKKA
YOSHI-MORIII!!
OH, AND DON'T FORGET TO BRING MONEY TO BUY SOME.
GASP!
TAAAK
YOU BRAT! ARE YOU BAKING THOSE CAKES AGAIN?

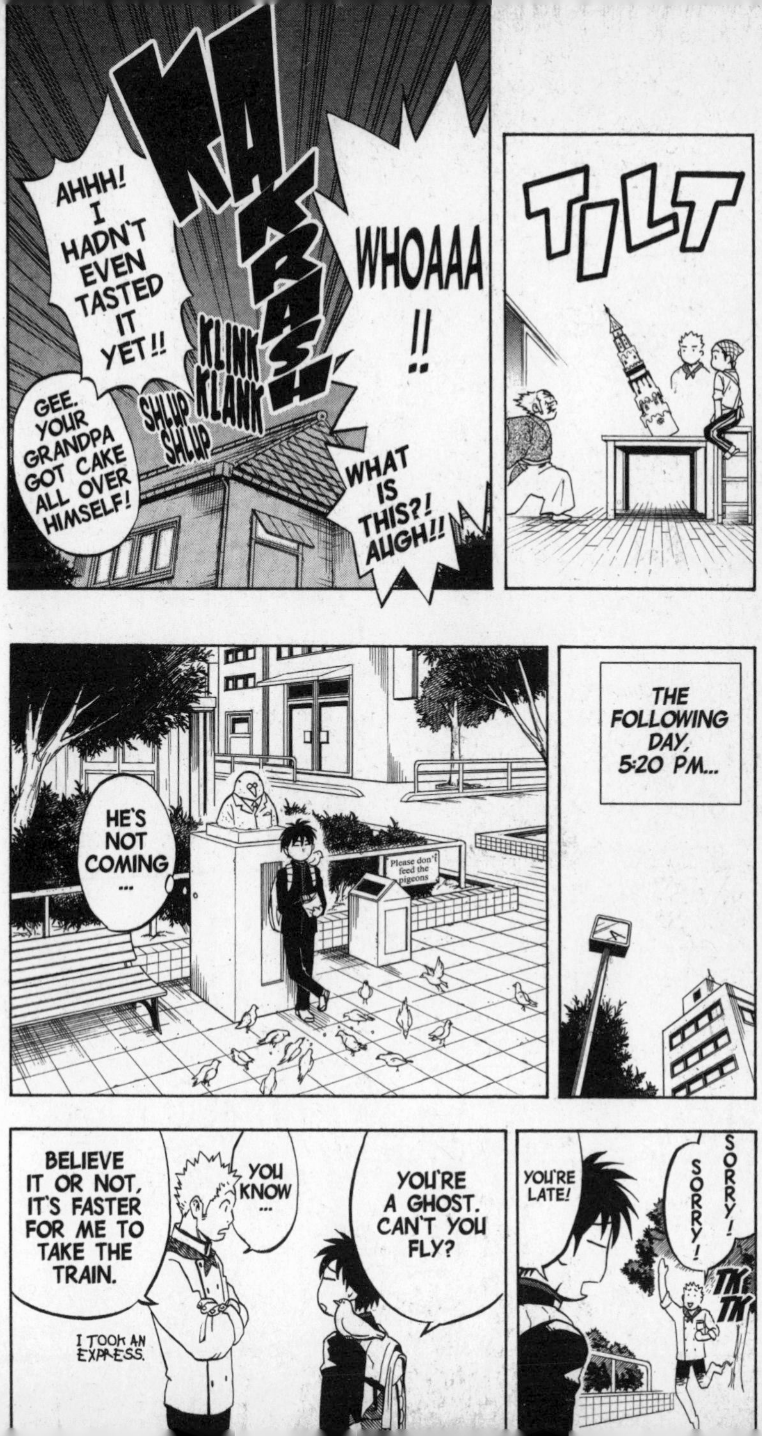
TILT
WHOAAA!!
KA-KRASH
AHHH! I HADN'T EVEN TASTED IT YET!!
KLINK KLANK
SHLUP SHLUP
WHAT IS THIS?! AUGH!!
GEE. YOUR GRANDPA GOT CAKE ALL OVER HIMSELF!
THE FOLLOWING DAY, 5:20 PM...
Please don't feed the pigeons
HE'S NOT COMING...
SORRY! SORRY!
YOU'RE LATE!
TK TK
YOU'RE A GHOST. CAN'T YOU FLY?
YOU KNOW...
BELIEVE IT OR NOT, IT'S FASTER FOR ME TO TAKE THE TRAIN.
I TOOK AN EXPRESS.

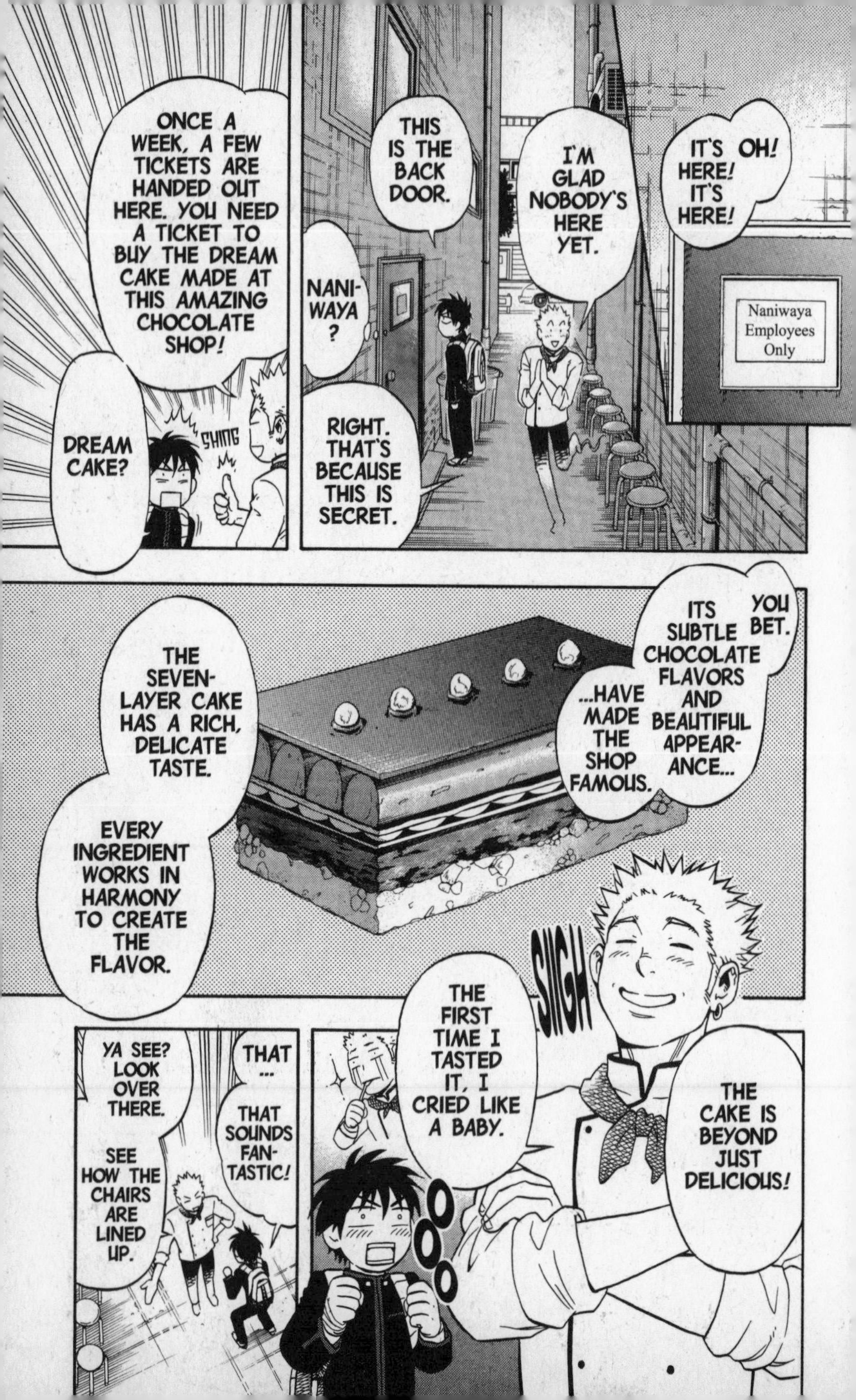
OH!
IT'S HERE! IT'S HERE!
Naniwaya Employees Only
I'M GLAD NOBODY'S HERE YET.
THIS IS THE BACK DOOR.
NANI-WAYA?
RIGHT. THAT'S BECAUSE THIS IS SECRET.
ONCE A WEEK, A FEW TICKETS ARE HANDED OUT HERE. YOU NEED A TICKET TO BUY THE DREAM CAKE MADE AT THIS AMAZING CHOCOLATE SHOP!
SHING
DREAM CAKE?
YOU BET.
ITS SUBTLE CHOCOLATE FLAVORS AND BEAUTIFUL APPEAR-ANCE...
...HAVE MADE THE SHOP FAMOUS.
THE SEVEN-LAYER CAKE HAS A RICH, DELICATE TASTE.
EVERY INGREDIENT WORKS IN HARMONY TO CREATE THE FLAVOR.
SIGH
THE CAKE IS BEYOND JUST DELICIOUS!
THE FIRST TIME I TASTED IT, I CRIED LIKE A BABY.
THAT... THAT SOUNDS FAN-TASTIC!
YA SEE? LOOK OVER THERE.
SEE HOW THE CHAIRS ARE LINED UP.

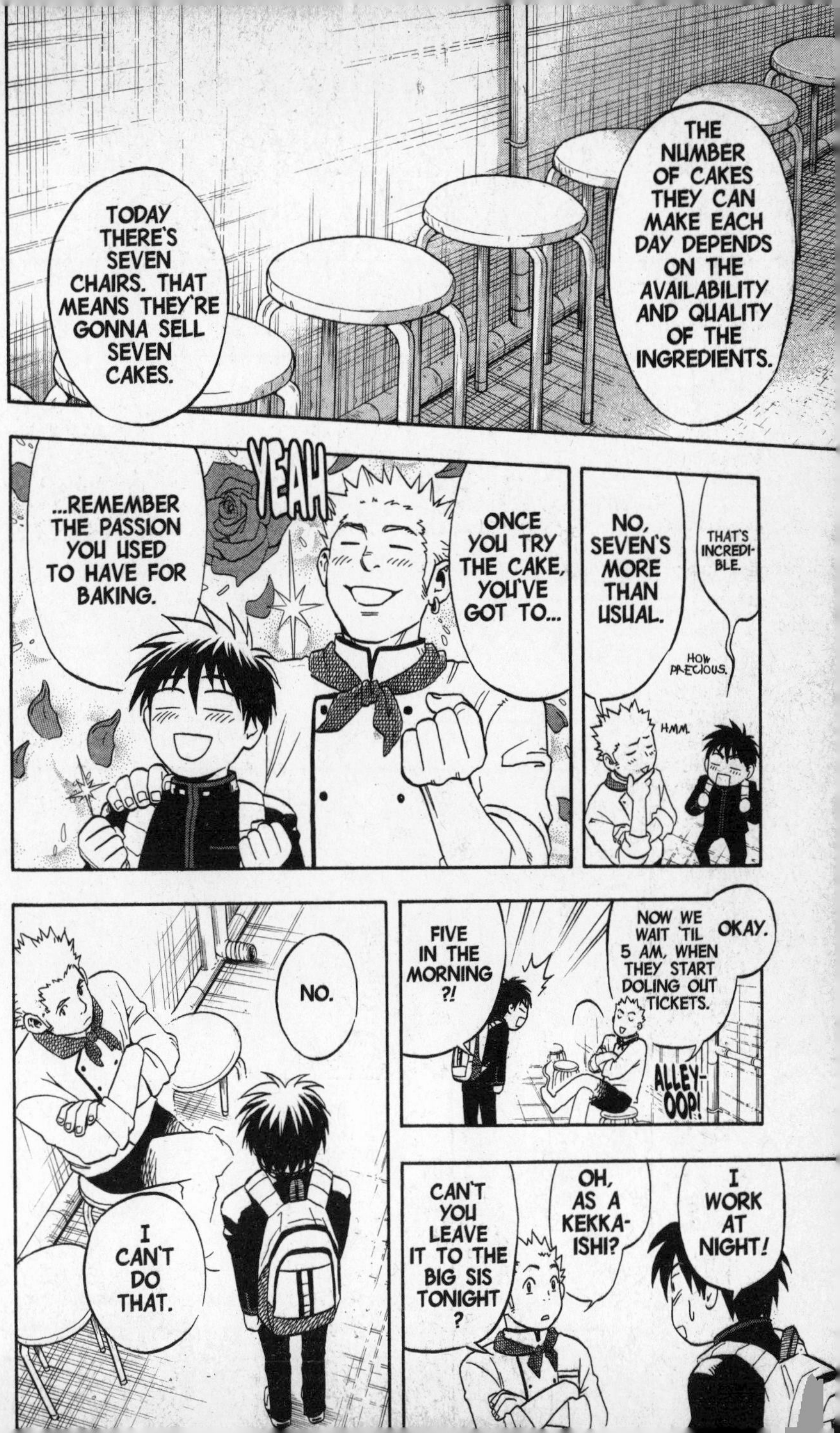
THE NUMBER OF CAKES THEY CAN MAKE EACH DAY DEPENDS ON THE AVAILABILITY AND QUALITY OF THE INGREDIENTS.
TODAY THERE'S SEVEN CHAIRS. THAT MEANS THEY'RE GONNA SELL SEVEN CAKES.
THAT'S INCREDI-BLE.
NO, SEVEN'S MORE THAN USUAL.
HOW PRECIOUS.
HMM.
ONCE YOU TRY THE CAKE, YOU'VE GOT TO...
YEAH
...REMEMBER THE PASSION YOU USED TO HAVE FOR BAKING.
OKAY.
NOW WE WAIT 'TIL 5 AM, WHEN THEY START DOLING OUT TICKETS.
ALLEY-OOP!
FIVE IN THE MORNING ?!
I WORK AT NIGHT!
OH, AS A KEKKA-ISHI?
CAN'T YOU LEAVE IT TO THE BIG SIS TONIGHT ?
NO.
I CAN'T DO THAT.

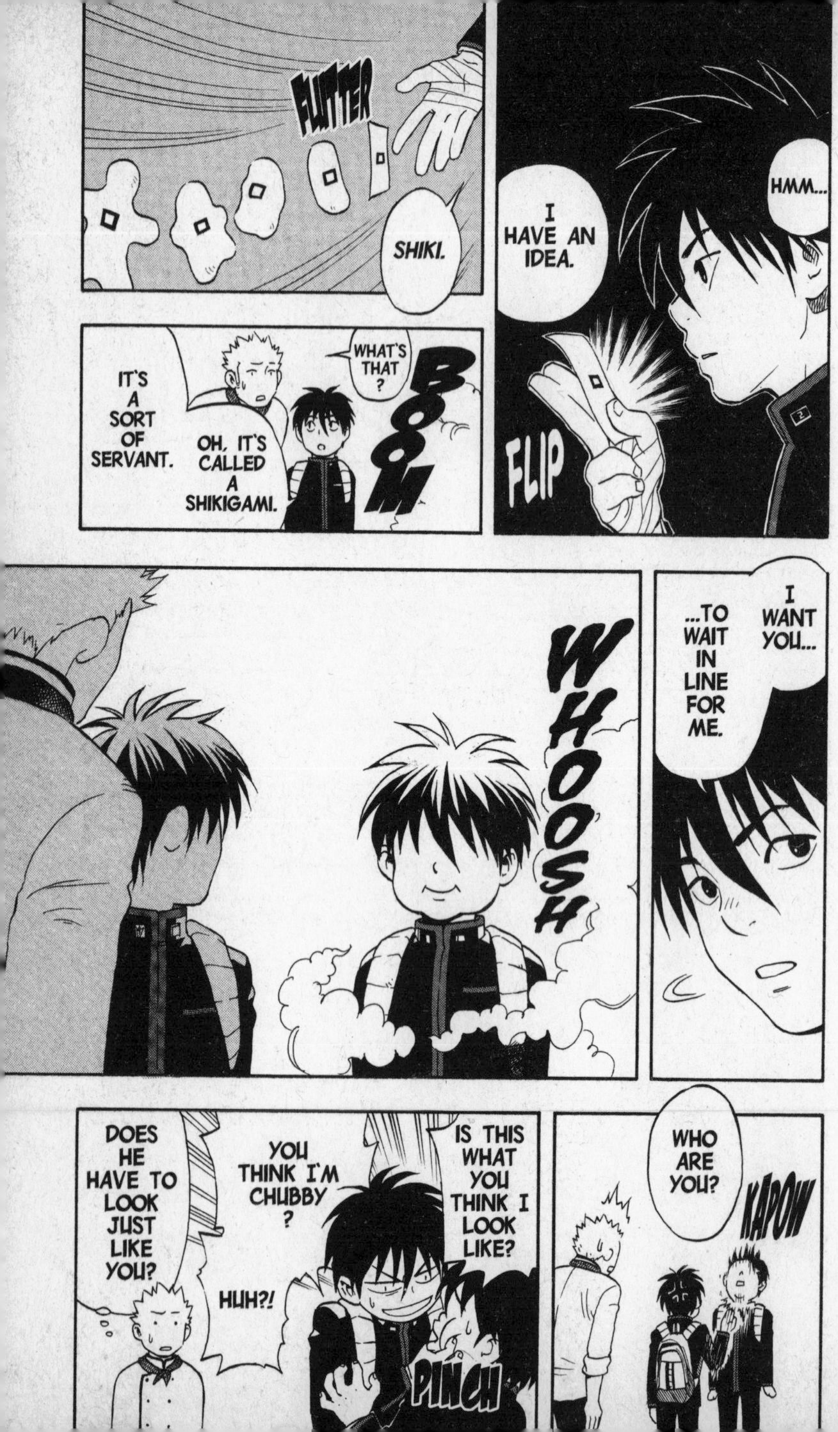
HMM...
I HAVE AN IDEA.
FLIP
FLUTTER
SHIKI.
WHAT'S THAT?
BOOM
OH, IT'S CALLED A SHIKIGAMI.
IT'S A SORT OF SERVANT.
I WANT YOU...
...TO WAIT IN LINE FOR ME.
WHOOOSH
WHO ARE YOU?
KAPOW
IS THIS WHAT YOU THINK I LOOK LIKE?
YOU THINK I'M CHUBBY?
HUH?!
PINCH
DOES HE HAVE TO LOOK JUST LIKE YOU?

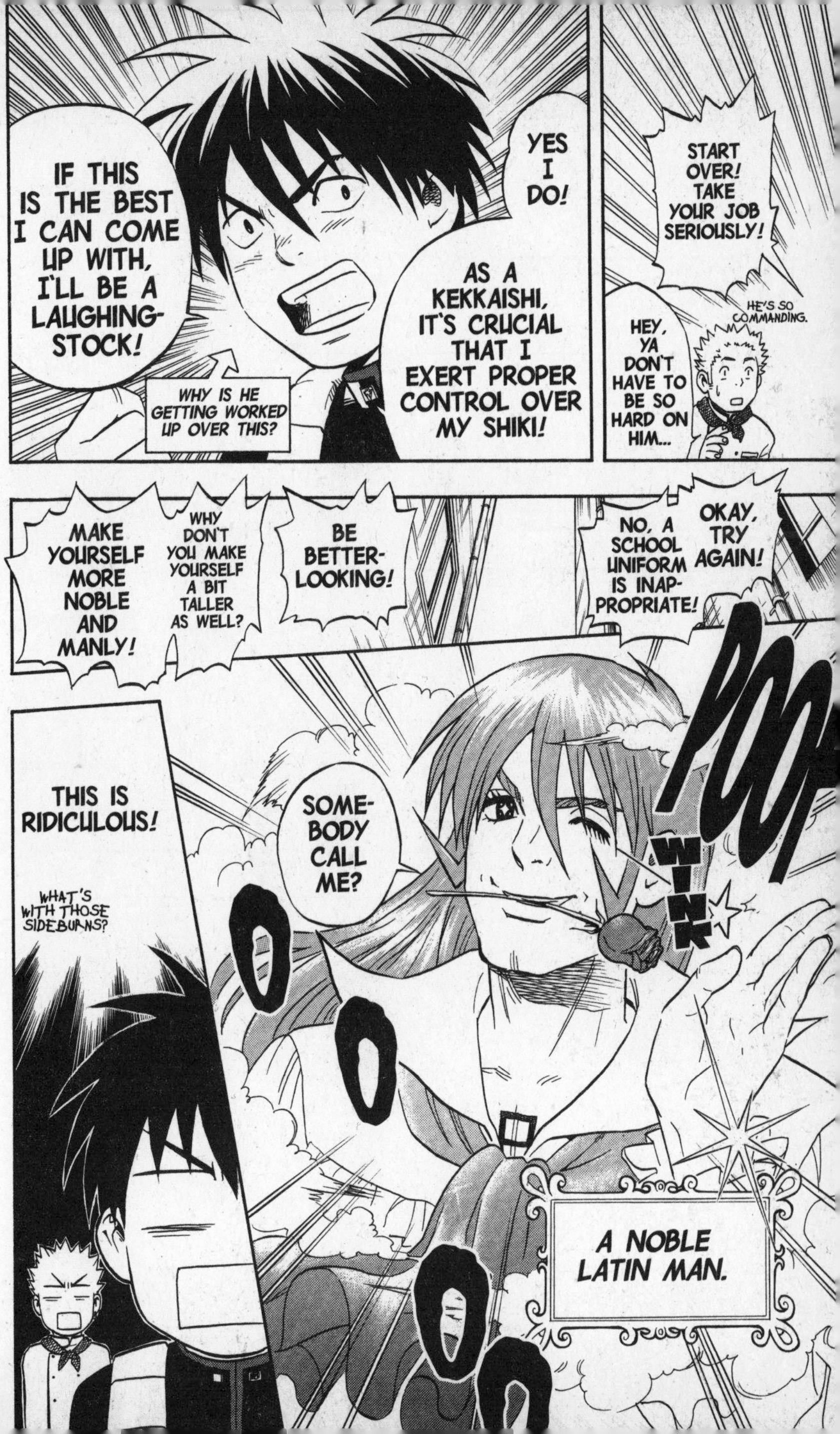
START OVER! TAKE YOUR JOB SERIOUSLY!
HE'S SO COMMANDING.
HEY, YA DON'T HAVE TO BE SO HARD ON HIM...
YES I DO!
AS A KEKKAISHI, IT'S CRUCIAL THAT I EXERT PROPER CONTROL OVER MY SHIKI!
IF THIS IS THE BEST I CAN COME UP WITH, I'LL BE A LAUGHING-STOCK!
WHY IS HE GETTING WORKED UP OVER THIS?
OKAY, TRY AGAIN!
NO, A SCHOOL UNIFORM IS INAP-PROPRIATE!
BE BETTER-LOOKING!
WHY DON'T YOU MAKE YOURSELF A BIT TALLER AS WELL?
MAKE YOURSELF MORE NOBLE AND MANLY!
POOF
WINK
SOME-BODY CALL ME?
A NOBLE LATIN MAN.
THIS IS RIDICULOUS!
WHAT'S WITH THOSE SIDEBURNS?

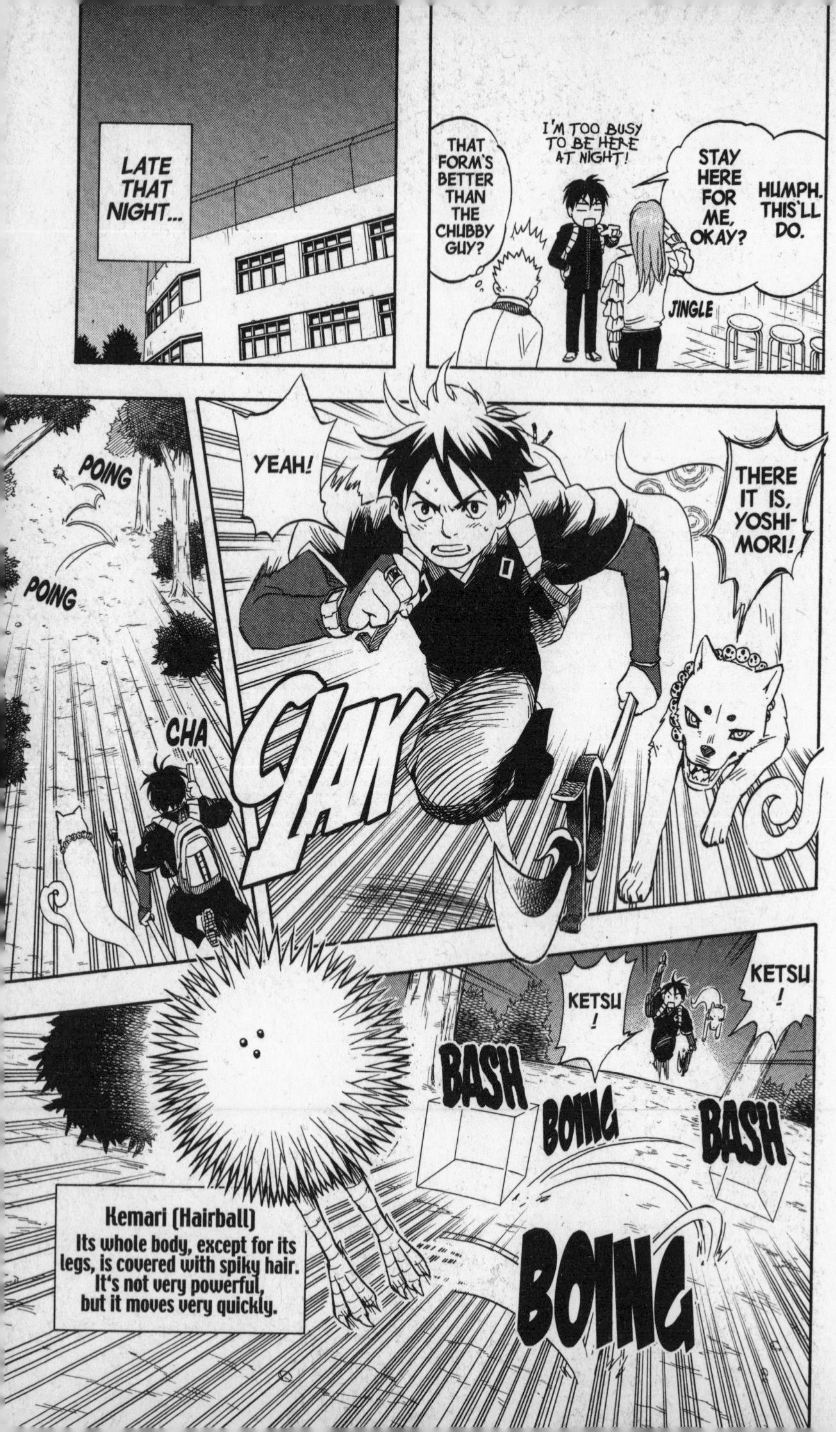
HUMPH. THIS'LL DO.
STAY HERE FOR ME, OKAY?
I'M TOO BUSY TO BE HERE AT NIGHT!
THAT FORM'S BETTER THAN THE CHUBBY GUY?
JINGLE
LATE THAT NIGHT...
THERE IT IS, YOSHIMORI!
YEAH!
CLAK
POING
POING
CHA
KETSU!
KETSU!
BASH
BOING
BASH
BOING
Kemari (Hairball)
Its whole body, except for its legs, is covered with spiky hair. It's not very powerful, but it moves very quickly.

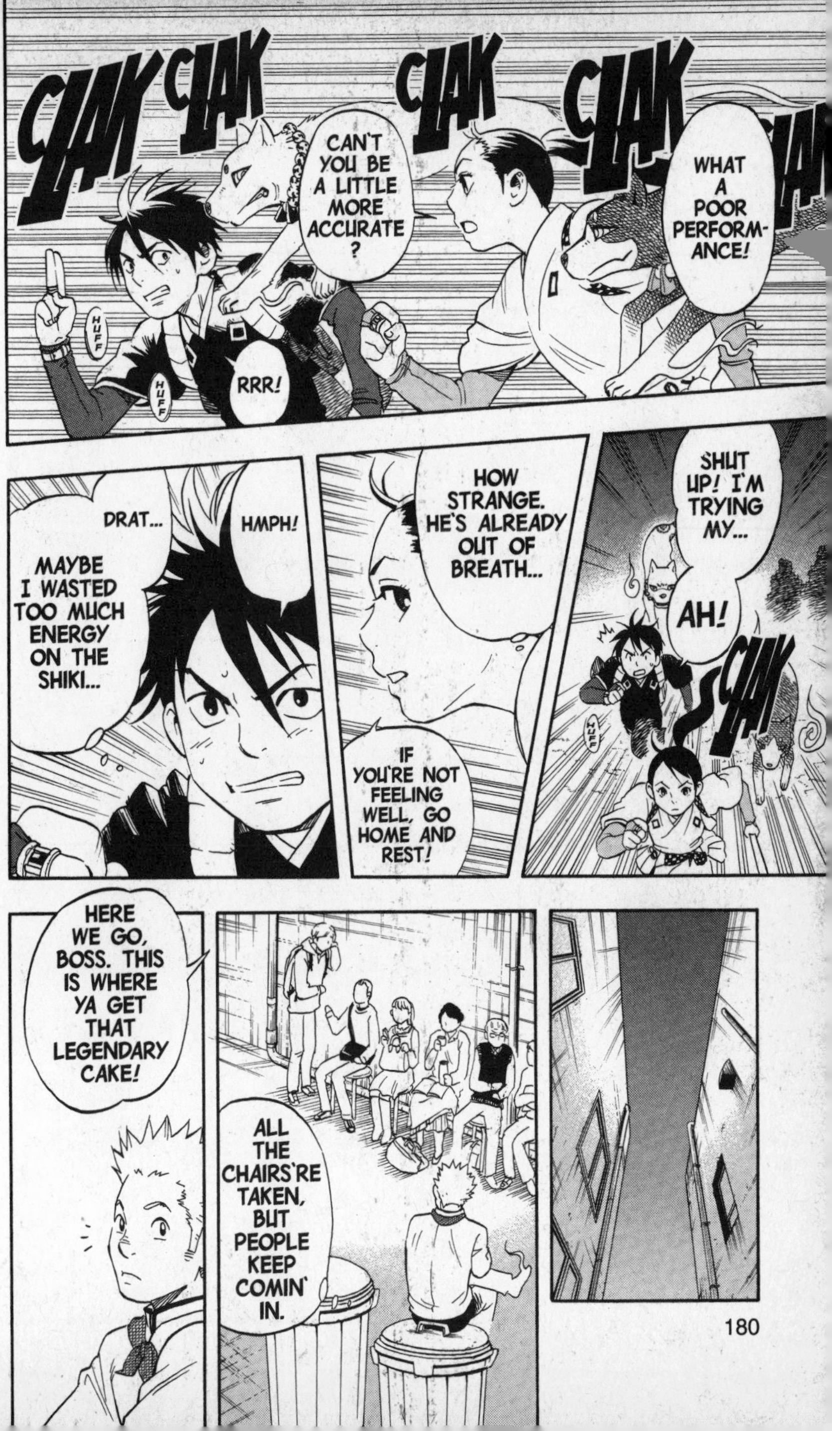
CIAK
WHAT A POOR PERFORMANCE!
CIAK
CIAK
CAN'T YOU BE A LITTLE MORE ACCURATE?
CIAK
CIAK
RRR!
HUFF
HUFF
SHUT UP! I'M TRYING MY...
AH!
CIAK
HUFF
HOW STRANGE. HE'S ALREADY OUT OF BREATH...
IF YOU'RE NOT FEELING WELL, GO HOME AND REST!
HMPH!
DRAT...
MAYBE I WASTED TOO MUCH ENERGY ON THE SHIKI...
ALL THE CHAIRS'RE TAKEN, BUT PEOPLE KEEP COMIN' IN.
HERE WE GO, BOSS. THIS IS WHERE YA GET THAT LEGENDARY CAKE!

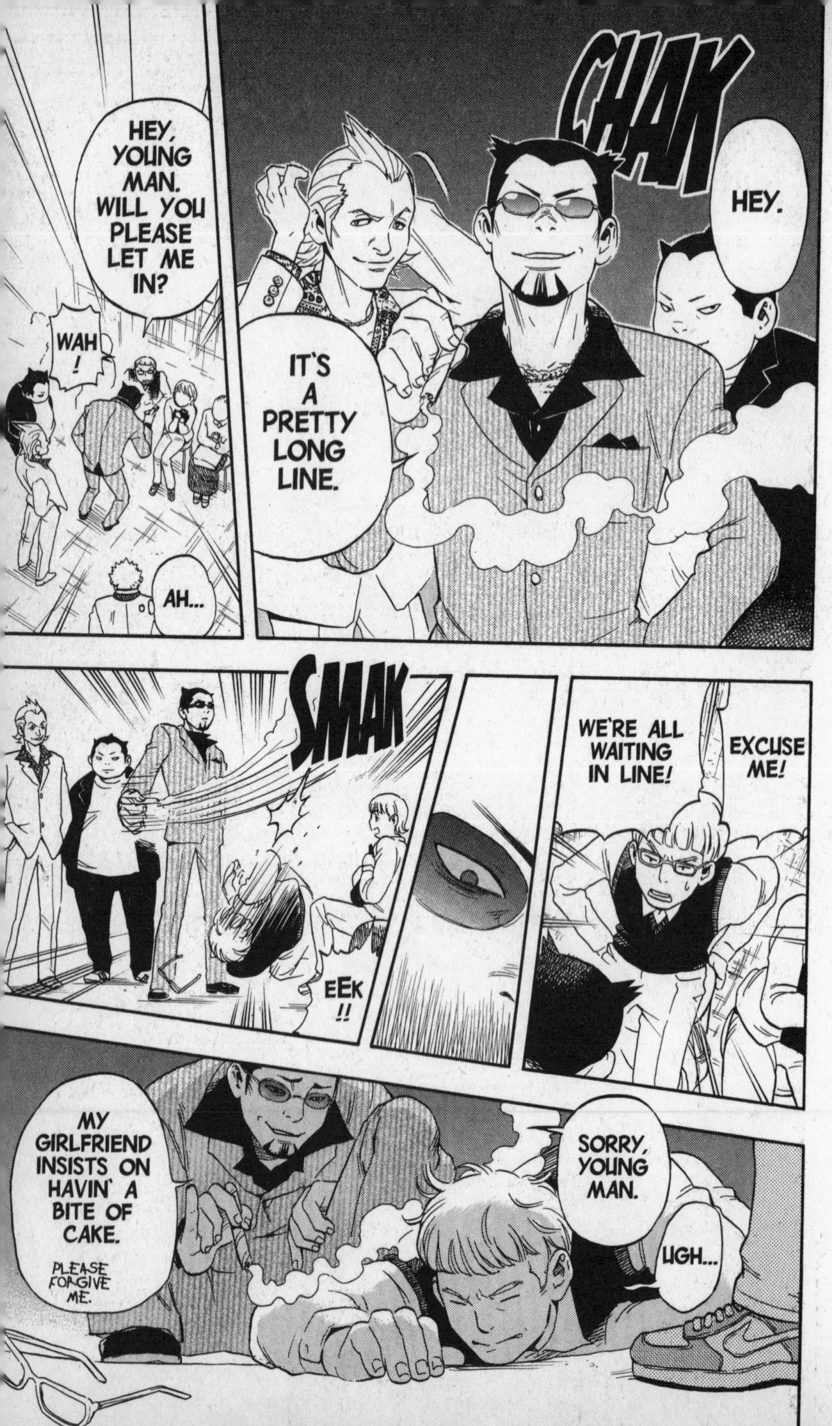
CHAK
HEY.
IT'S A PRETTY LONG LINE.
HEY, YOUNG MAN. WILL YOU PLEASE LET ME IN?
WAH!
AH...
EXCUSE ME!
WE'RE ALL WAITING IN LINE!
SMAK
EEK!!
SORRY, YOUNG MAN.
UGH...
MY GIRLFRIEND INSISTS ON HAVIN' A BITE OF CAKE.
PLEASE FORGIVE ME.

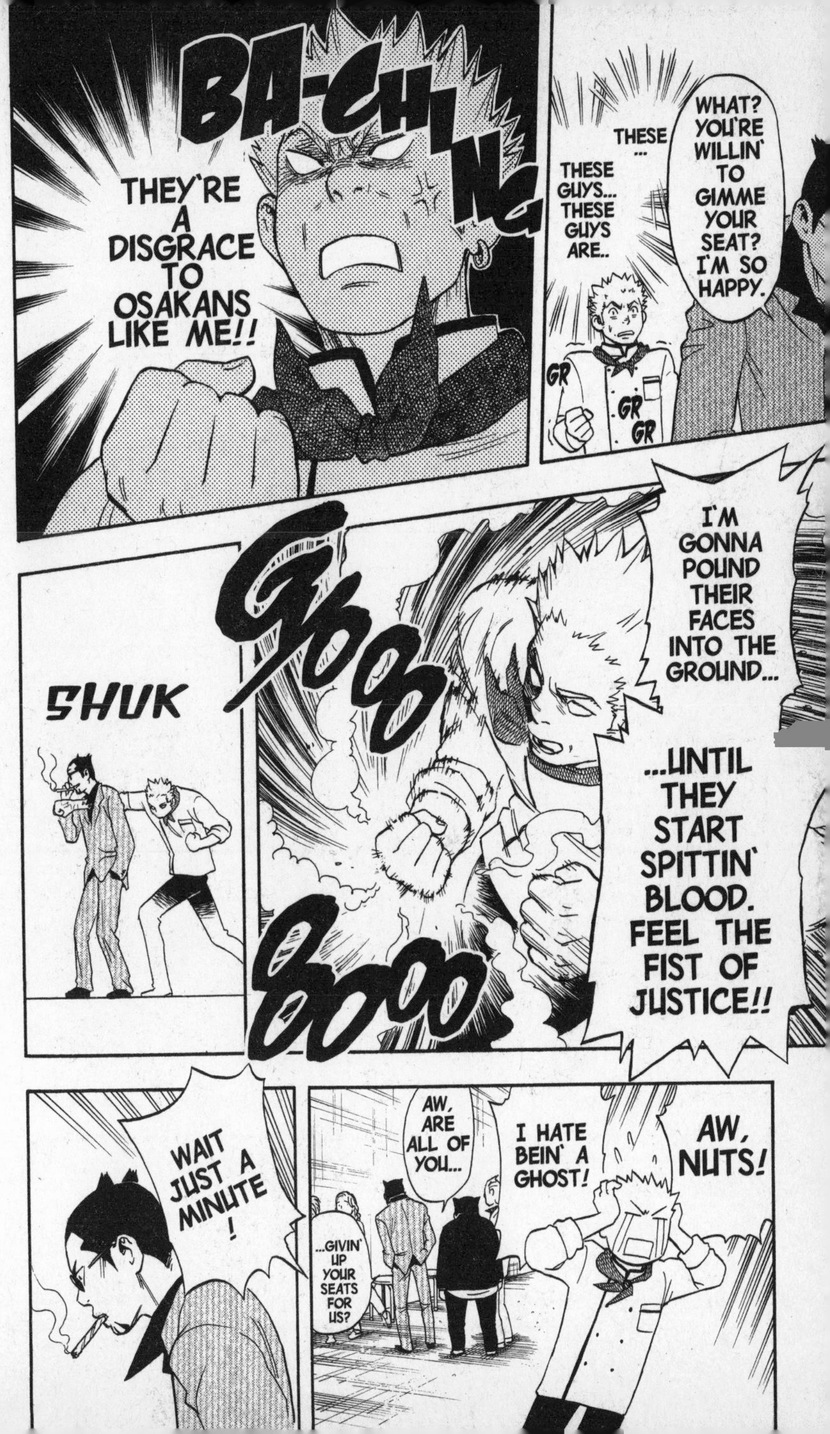
WHAT? YOU'RE WILLIN' TO GIMME YOUR SEAT? I'M SO HAPPY.
THESE ...
THESE GUYS... THESE GUYS ARE..
GR GR GR
BA-CHING
THEY'RE A DISGRACE TO OSAKANS LIKE ME!!
I'M GONNA POUND THEIR FACES INTO THE GROUND...
...UNTIL THEY START SPITTIN' BLOOD. FEEL THE FIST OF JUSTICE!!
SHUK
AW, NUTS!
I HATE BEIN' A GHOST!
AW, ARE ALL OF YOU...
...GIVIN' UP YOUR SEATS FOR US?
WAIT JUST A MINUTE!

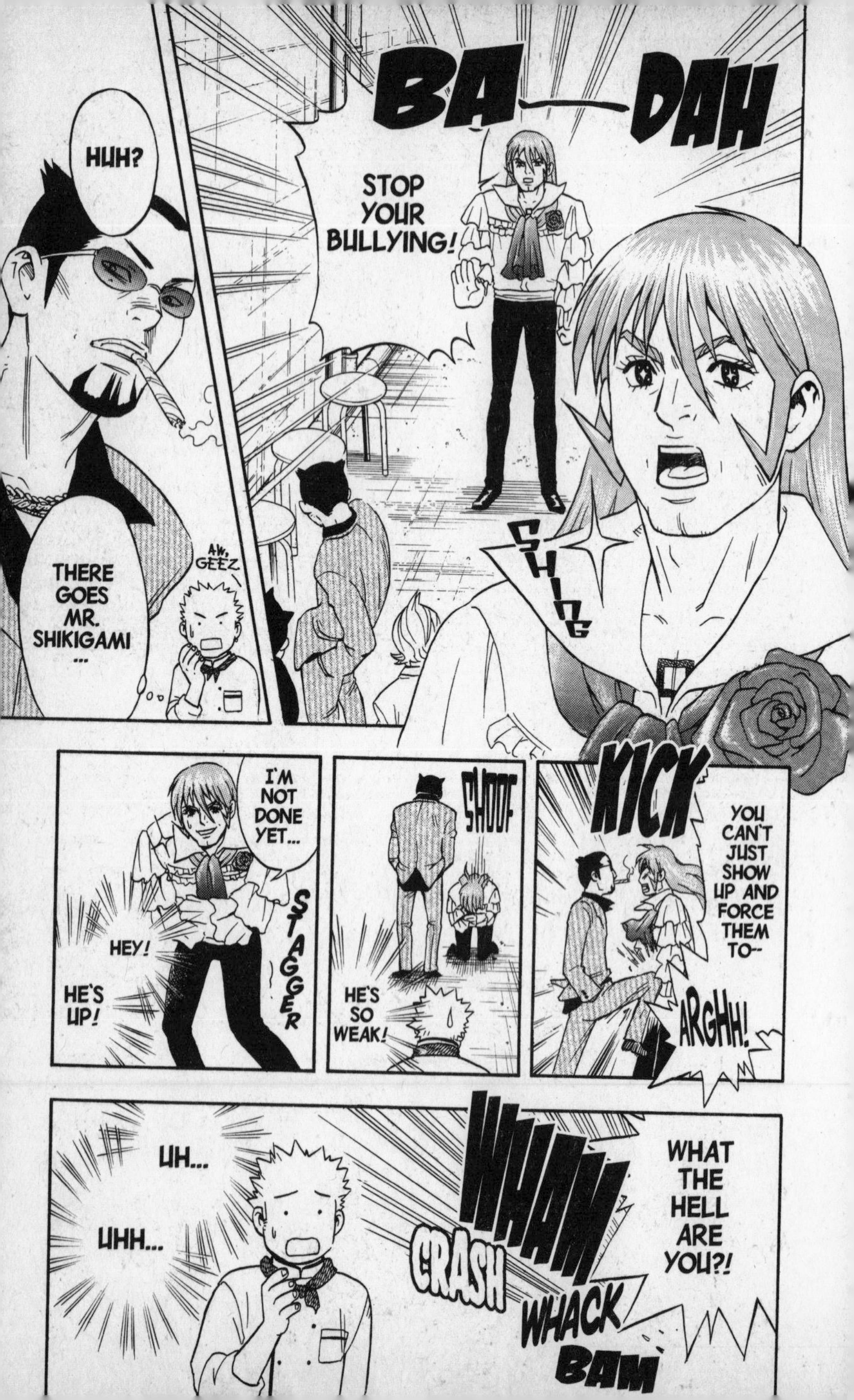
BA—DAH
STOP YOUR BULLYING!
SHING
HUH?
THERE GOES MR. SHIKIGAMI ...
AW, GEEZ.
KICK
YOU CAN'T JUST SHOW UP AND FORCE THEM TO--
ARGHH!
SHOOF
HE'S SO WEAK!
I'M NOT DONE YET...
STAGGER
HEY!
HE'S UP!
WHAM
WHAT THE HELL ARE YOU?!
CRASH
WHACK
BAM
UH...
UHH...

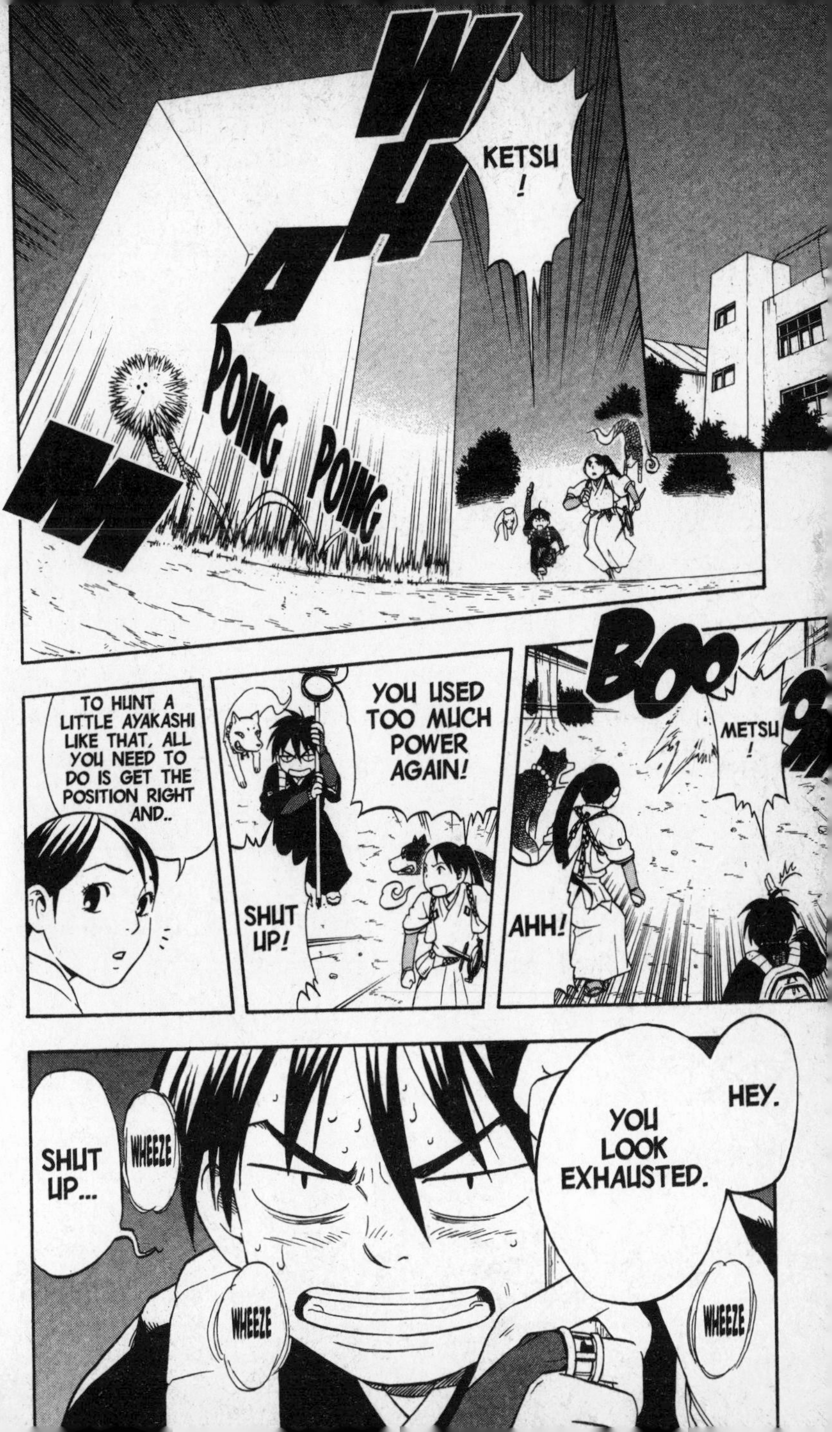
KETSU!
WHAM
POING
POING
BOO
METSU!
AHH!
YOU USED TOO MUCH POWER AGAIN!
SHUT UP!
TO HUNT A LITTLE AYAKASHI LIKE THAT, ALL YOU NEED TO DO IS GET THE POSITION RIGHT AND..
HEY.
YOU LOOK EXHAUSTED.
WHEEZE
SHUT UP...
WHEEZE
WHEEZE

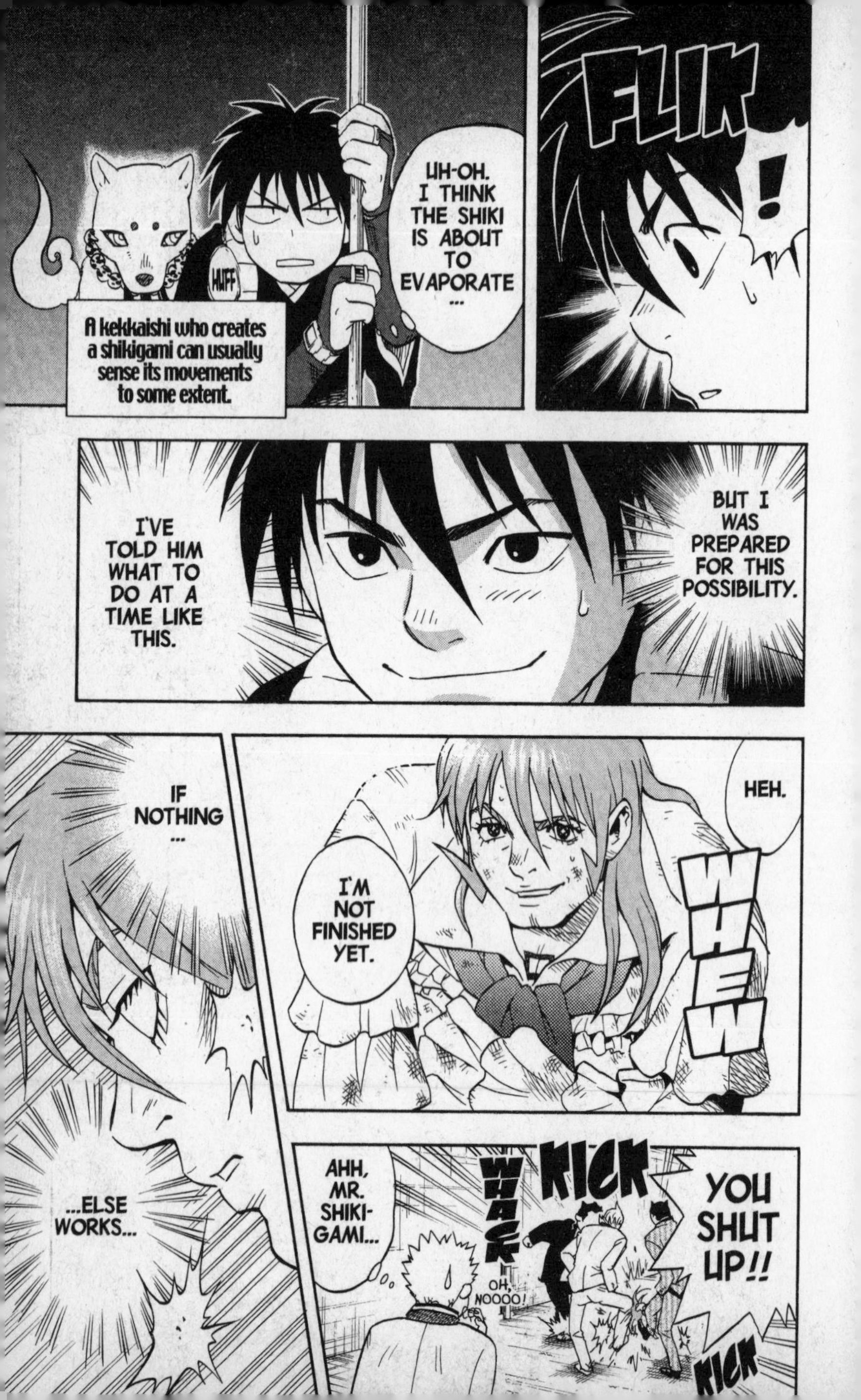
FLIR
!
UH-OH. I THINK THE SHIKI IS ABOUT TO EVAPORATE...
HUFF
A kekkaishi who creates a shikigami can usually sense its movements to some extent.
BUT I WAS PREPARED FOR THIS POSSIBILITY.
I'VE TOLD HIM WHAT TO DO AT A TIME LIKE THIS.
HEH.
WHEW
I'M NOT FINISHED YET.
KICK
YOU SHUT UP!!
WHACK
OH, NOOOO!
AHH, MR. SHIKI-GAMI...
KICK
IF NOTHING...
...ELSE WORKS...

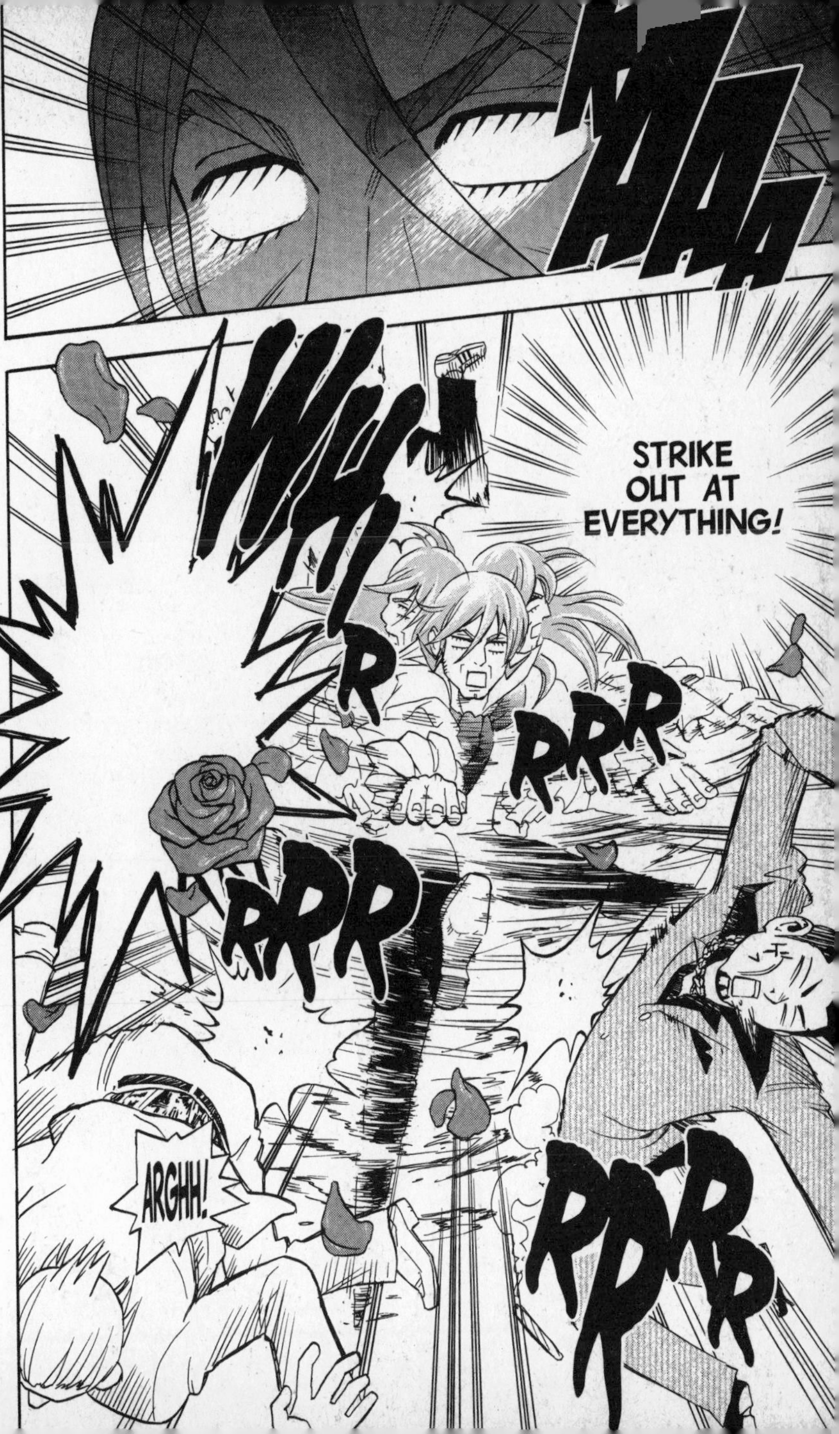
STRIKE OUT AT EVERYTHING!
ARGHH!

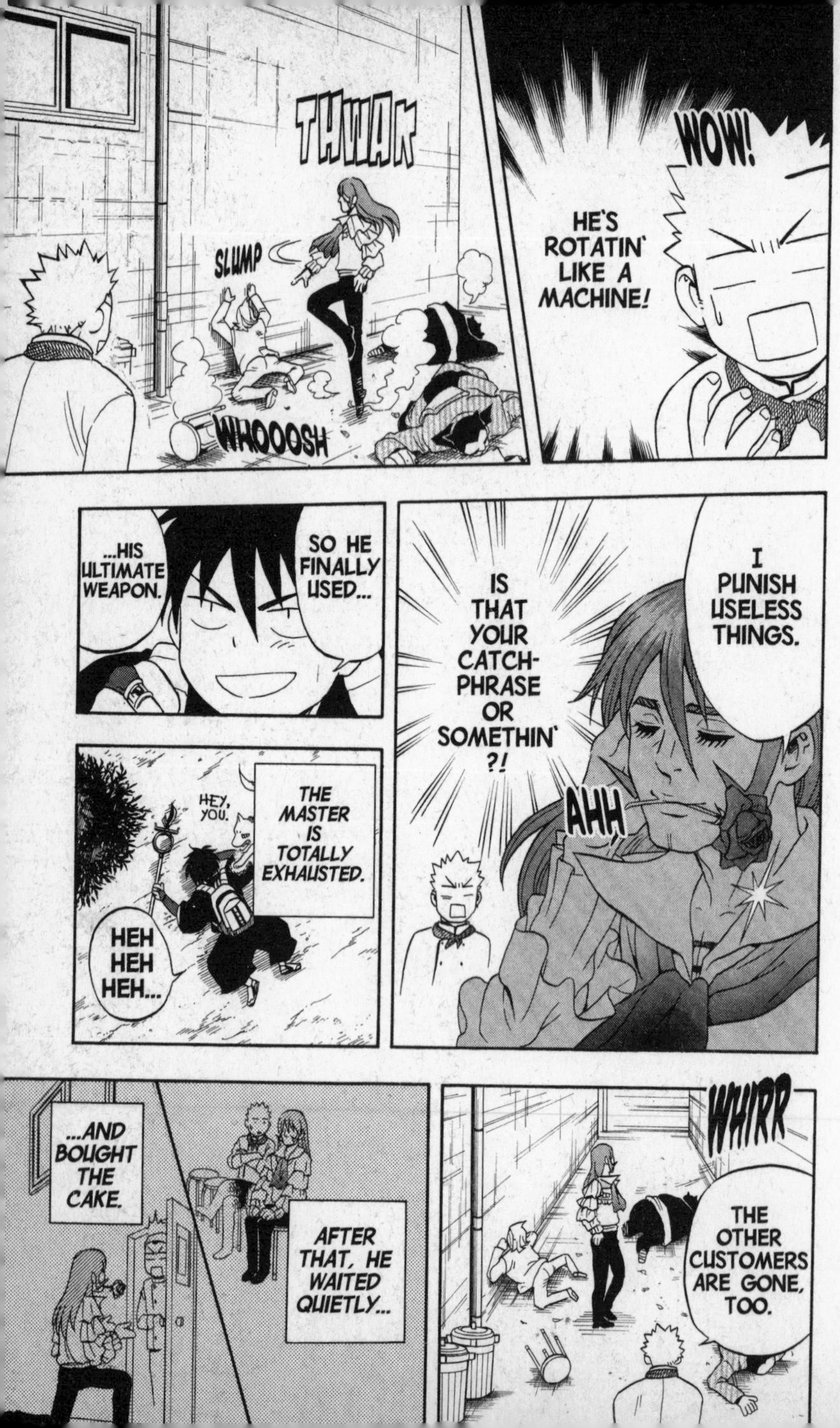
WOW!
HE'S ROTATIN' LIKE A MACHINE!
THWAK
SLUMP
WHOOOSH
I PUNISH USELESS THINGS.
IS THAT YOUR CATCH-PHRASE OR SOMETHIN'?!
AHH
SO HE FINALLY USED...
...HIS ULTIMATE WEAPON.
THE MASTER IS TOTALLY EXHAUSTED.
HEY, YOU.
HEH HEH HEH...
WHIRR
THE OTHER CUSTOMERS ARE GONE, TOO.
AFTER THAT, HE WAITED QUIETLY...
...AND BOUGHT THE CAKE.

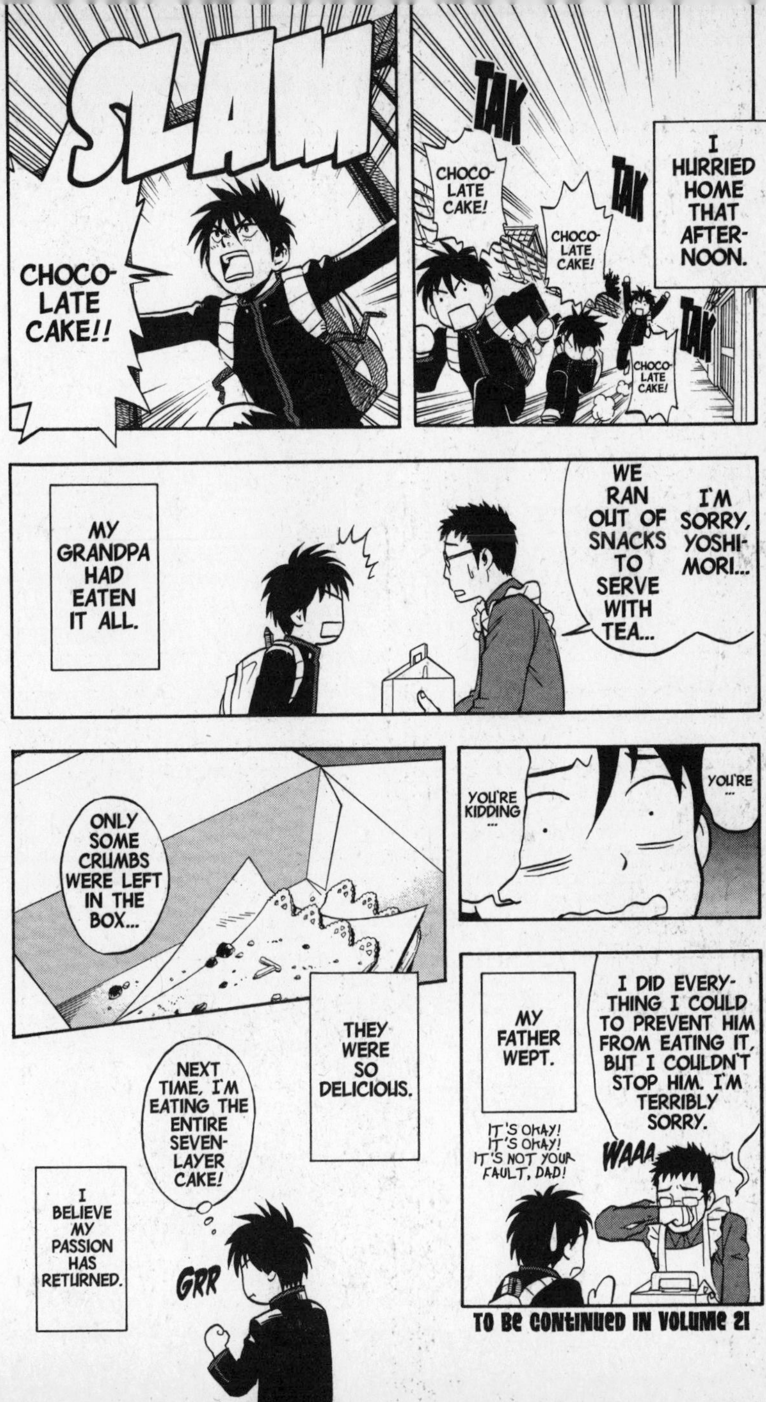
I HURRIED HOME THAT AFTERNOON.
TAK
CHOCOLATE CAKE!
TAK
CHOCOLATE CAKE!
TAK
CHOCOLATE CAKE!
SLAM
CHOCOLATE CAKE!!
I'M SORRY, YOSHIMORI...
WE RAN OUT OF SNACKS TO SERVE WITH TEA...
MY GRANDPA HAD EATEN IT ALL.
YOU'RE...
YOU'RE KIDDING...
ONLY SOME CRUMBS WERE LEFT IN THE BOX...
I DID EVERYTHING I COULD TO PREVENT HIM FROM EATING IT, BUT I COULDN'T STOP HIM. I'M TERRIBLY SORRY.
MY FATHER WEPT.
WAAA
IT'S OKAY! IT'S OKAY! IT'S NOT YOUR FAULT, DAD!
THEY WERE SO DELICIOUS.
NEXT TIME, I'M EATING THE ENTIRE SEVEN-LAYER CAKE!
GRR
I BELIEVE MY PASSION HAS RETURNED.
TO BE CONTINUED IN VOLUME 21

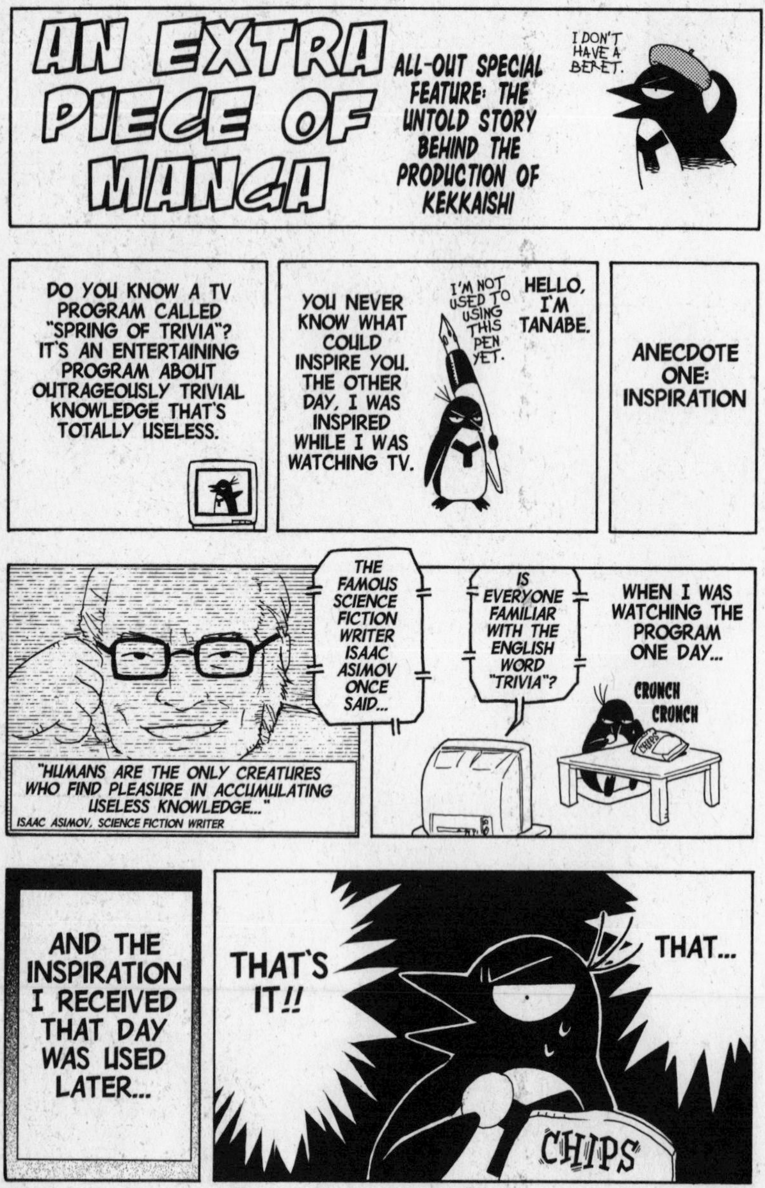
AN EXTRA PIECE OF MANGA
ALL-OUT SPECIAL FEATURE: THE UNTOLD STORY BEHIND THE PRODUCTION OF KEKKAISHI
I DON'T HAVE A BERET.
ANECDOTE ONE: INSPIRATION
HELLO, I'M TANABE.
I'M NOT USED TO USING THIS PEN YET.
YOU NEVER KNOW WHAT COULD INSPIRE YOU. THE OTHER DAY, I WAS INSPIRED WHILE I WAS WATCHING TV.
DO YOU KNOW A TV PROGRAM CALLED "SPRING OF TRIVIA"? IT'S AN ENTERTAINING PROGRAM ABOUT OUTRAGEOUSLY TRIVIAL KNOWLEDGE THAT'S TOTALLY USELESS.
WHEN I WAS WATCHING THE PROGRAM ONE DAY...
CRUNCH
CRUNCH
CHIPS
IS EVERYONE FAMILIAR WITH THE ENGLISH WORD "TRIVIA"?
THE FAMOUS SCIENCE FICTION WRITER ISAAC ASIMOV ONCE SAID...
"HUMANS ARE THE ONLY CREATURES WHO FIND PLEASURE IN ACCUMULATING USELESS KNOWLEDGE..."
ISAAC ASIMOV, SCIENCE FICTION WRITER
THAT...
THAT'S IT!!
CHIPS
AND THE INSPIRATION I RECEIVED THAT DAY WAS USED LATER...

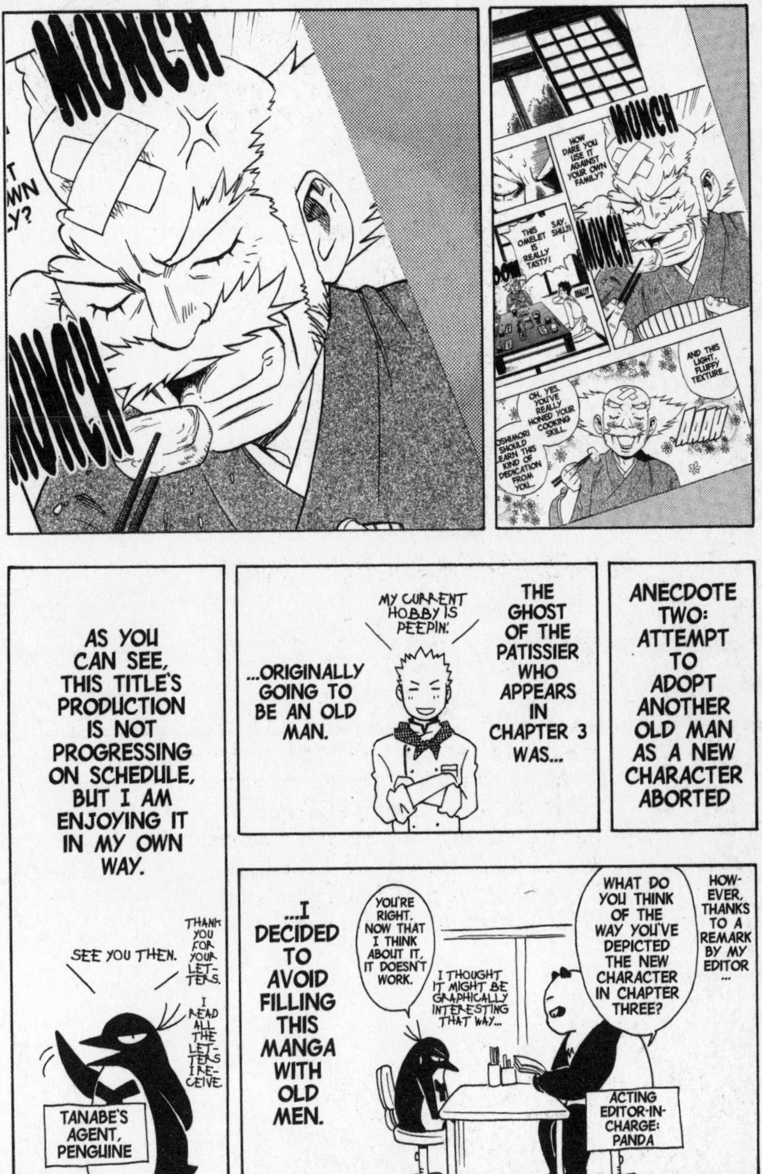
MUNCH
HOW DARE YOU USE IT AGAINST YOUR OWN FAMILY?
SAY, SHUJI!
THIS OMELET IS REALLY TASTY!
MUNCH
AND THIS LIGHT, FLUFFY TEXTURE...
OH, YES. YOU'VE REALLY HONED YOUR COOKING SKILL.
YOSHIMORI SHOULD LEARN THIS KIND OF DEDICATION FROM YOU...
AAAH
MUNCH
MUNCH
ANECDOTE TWO: ATTEMPT TO ADOPT ANOTHER OLD MAN AS A NEW CHARACTER ABORTED
THE GHOST OF THE PATISSIER WHO APPEARS IN CHAPTER 3 WAS...
MY CURRENT HOBBY IS PEEPIN'.
...ORIGINALLY GOING TO BE AN OLD MAN.
HOWEVER, THANKS TO A REMARK BY MY EDITOR...
WHAT DO YOU THINK OF THE WAY YOU'VE DEPICTED THE NEW CHARACTER IN CHAPTER THREE?
ACTING EDITOR-IN-CHARGE: PANDA
I THOUGHT IT MIGHT BE GRAPHICALLY INTERESTING THAT WAY...
YOU'RE RIGHT. NOW THAT I THINK ABOUT IT, IT DOESN'T WORK.
...I DECIDED TO AVOID FILLING THIS MANGA WITH OLD MEN.
AS YOU CAN SEE, THIS TITLE'S PRODUCTION IS NOT PROGRESSING ON SCHEDULE, BUT I AM ENJOYING IT IN MY OWN WAY.
THANK YOU FOR YOUR LETTERS.
I READ ALL THE LETTERS I RECEIVE.
SEE YOU THEN.
TANABE'S AGENT, PENGUINE

I want to be a dashing fellow.

Skating

MESSAGE FROM YELLOW TANABE

When I was a kid, I didn't know the word *kekkai* ("protective ward"), but my friends and I used to play a game in which we pretended that we could create invisible walls. We'd declare, "I stretched the barrier from here to there!" If someone stepped into that barrier, ignoring a friend's declaration, he'd be given the cold shoulder as if he'd done something insensitive. I feel it is far more difficult to undo a *kekkai*, a barrier, than to create one.

KEKKAISHI

VOLUME 1
STORY AND ART BY YELLOW TANABE

English Adaptation/Shaenon Garrity
Translation/Yuko Sawada
Touch-up Art & Lettering/Stephen Dutro
Cover Design & Graphic Layout/Amy Martin
Editor/Megan Bates

Managing Editor/Annette Roman
Director of Production/Noboru Watanabe
Vice President of Publishing/Alvin Lu
Sr. Director of Acquisitions/Rika Inouye
Vice President of Sales & Marketing/Liza Coppola
Publisher/Hyoe Narita

© 2004 Yellow Tanabe/Shogakukan, Inc. First published by Shogakukan, Inc. in Japan as "Kekkaishi." New and adapted artwork and text © 2005 VIZ, LLC. The KEKKAISHI logo is a trademark of VIZ, LLC. All rights reserved. The stories, characters and incidents mentioned in this publication are entirely fictional.

No portion of this book may be reproduced or transmitted in any form or by any means without written permission from the copyright holders.

Printed in Canada

Published by VIZ, LLC
P.O. Box 77010
San Francisco, CA 94107

Action Edition
10 9 8 7 6 5 4 3 2 1
First printing, April 2005

PARENTAL ADVISORY
KEKKAISHI is rated T for Teen. Contains fantasy violence. Recommended for ages 13 and up.

www.viz.com

store.viz.com

Editor's Recommendations

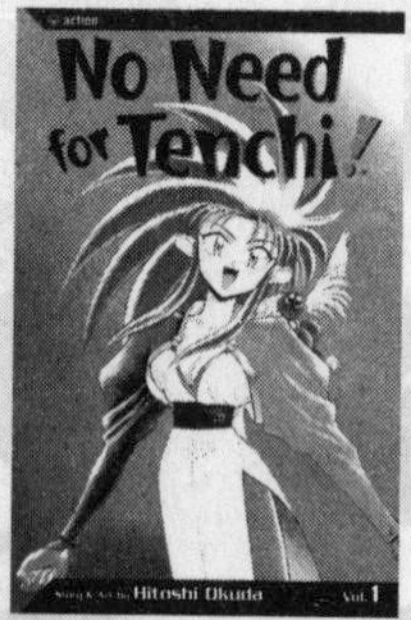
No Need for Tenchi!
Hitoshi Okuda
Vol. 1

© HITOSHI OKUDA 1994 © AIC/VAP•NTV

No Need for Tenchi!
The trouble and fun all began when ordinary teenager Tenchi Musaki inadvertently released the legendary demon Ryoko from his grandfather's shrine. Turned out Ryoko was actually a marooned space pirate! Since then, she's become Tenchi's unwanted houseguest, attracting a host of other troublemaking aliens!

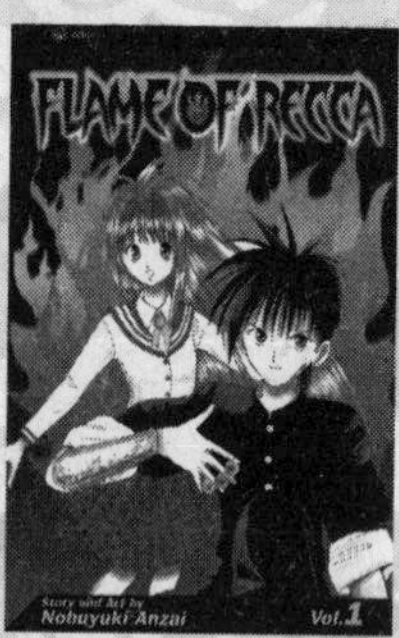
FLAME OF RECCA
Nobuyuki Anzai
Vol. 1

©1995 Nobuyuki Anzai/Shogakukan, Inc.

Flame of Recca
Recca Hanabishi, a regular high school kid who hopes one day to become a ninja, is thrown for a loop the day he meets a cute and mysterious girl named Yanagi. Suddenly, the teenager discovers he's had super-ninja secret powers all along. Recca, who can control fire, must learn how to navigate the esoteric world of ninja warriors.

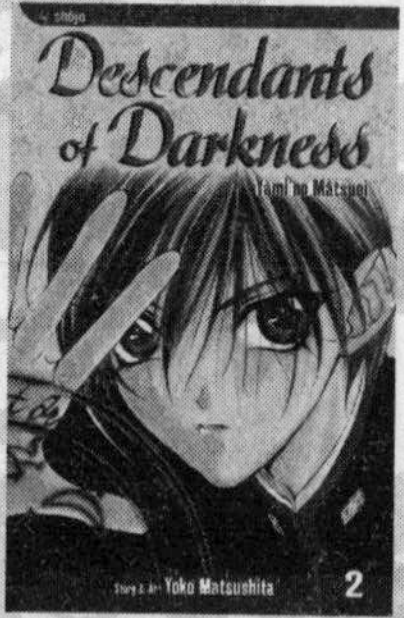
Descendants of Darkness
Yoko Matsushita
2

Yami no Matsuei © Yoko Matsushita 1996/HAKUSENSHA, Inc.

Descendants of Darkness
As a Guardian of Death, Asato Tsuzuki has a lot to think about. First of all, there are all those dead people. Someone's got to escort them safely to the afterlife. Then there's all that bureaucracy. It turns out that the affairs of death come with a lot of paperwork, budgetary concerns and endless busywork...

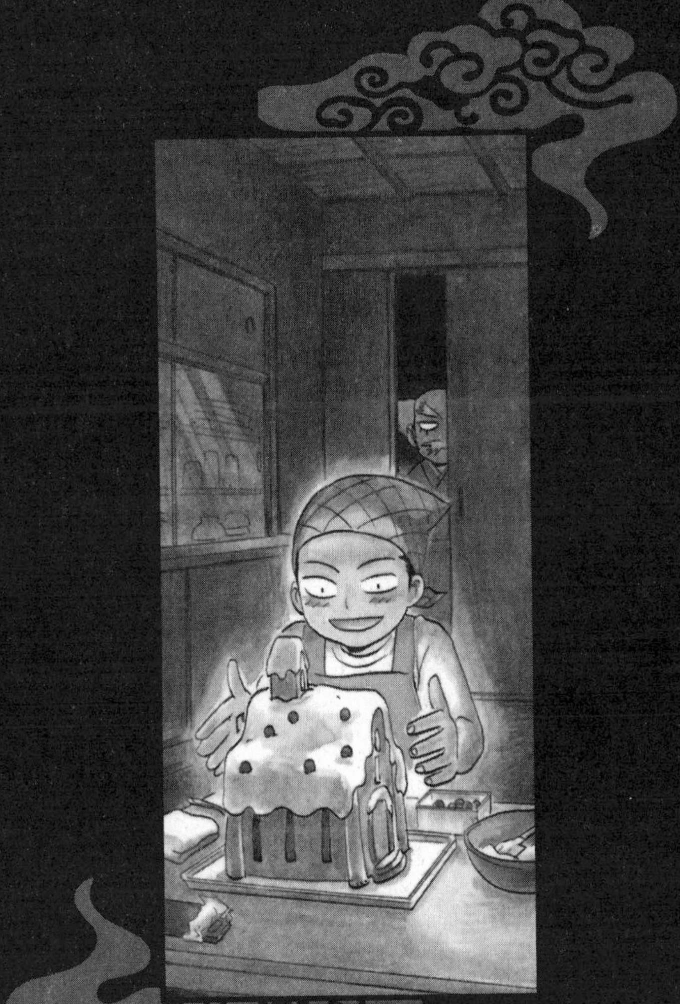

FULLMETAL ALCHEMIST

Breaking the Laws of Nature is a Serious Crime

Two brothers thought they could change nature with science, but Edward ended up with mechanical limbs and Alphonse's soul encased in a suit of armor. Forced to use his unique powers as a state alchemist, Edward must fight an evil force.

But nature has also created the Philosopher's Stone—a legendary artifact that will give its possessor immeasurable power. Does it hold the power to turn Edward and Alphonse back to normal?

only
$9⁹⁹

Story and art by
Hiromu Arakawa

1

Play the new game for
your PlayStation® 2
computer entertainment
system from

SQUARE ENIX.
www.square-enix.com
Published by Square Enix, Inc.

T TEEN
ESRB

Blood
Mild Language
Suggestive Themes
Violence

www.viz.com

*The manga inspiration for
the popular TV show—now
available in stores!*

NOT ALL LEGENDS ARE EXTINCT

Humans thought the wolves died off
two centuries ago in this bleak post-
apocalyptic wasteland. But some
survivors lurk among the humans
by mentally cloaking their animal bodies.
One white wolf, Kiba, scours the land
for the scent of the Lunar Flower
that will lead them all to Paradise...

Only $9.99!

STORY BY
BONES, Keiko Nobumoto

ART BY
Toshitsugu Iida

Start your graphic novel
collection today!

action

FRESH FROM JAPAN
日本最新

www.viz.com

© 2003 TOSHITSUGU IIDA and BONES • KEIKO NOBUMOTO/BV/KODANSHA LTD.

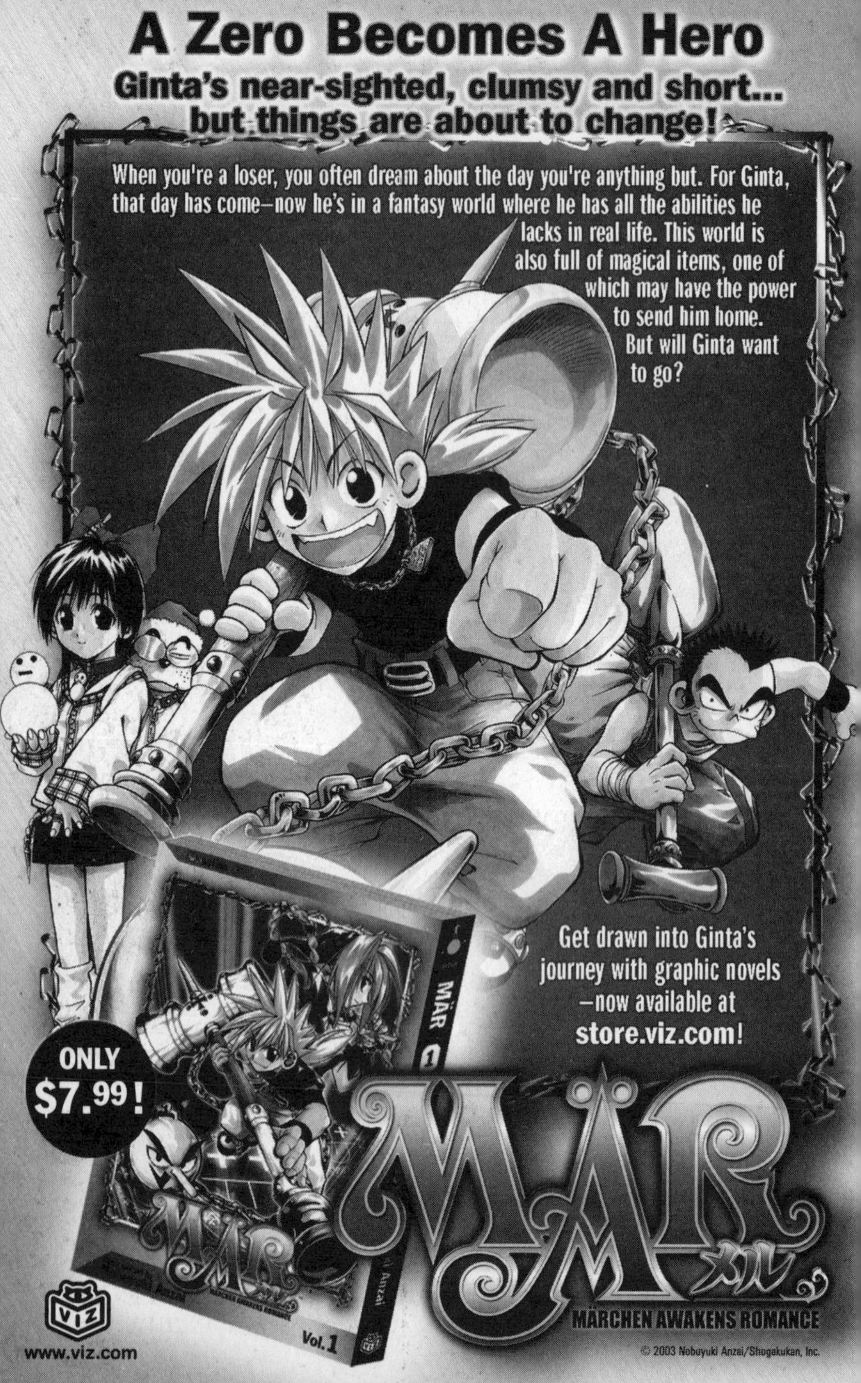
A Zero Becomes A Hero
Ginta's near-sighted, clumsy and short...
but things are about to change!
When you're a loser, you often dream about the day you're anything but. For Ginta, that day has come—now he's in a fantasy world where he has all the abilities he lacks in real life. This world is also full of magical items, one of which may have the power to send him home. But will Ginta want to go?
Get drawn into Ginta's journey with graphic novels —now available at store.viz.com!
ONLY $7.99!
MÄR
MÄRCHEN AWAKENS ROMANCE
VIZ
www.viz.com
© 2003 Nobuyuki Anzai/Shogakukan, Inc.

action

All New ACTION Graphic Novels!

The latest volumes now available at store.viz.com:

Fullmetal Alchemist, Vol. 1
Kekkaishi, Vol. 1
MÄR, Vol. 1
Battle Angel Alita, Vol. 9 (2nd ed)
Case Closed, Vol. 5
Cheeky Angel, Vol. 6
Excel Saga, Vol. 12
No Need for Tenchi!, Vol. 3 (2nd ed)
Ranma 1/2, Vol. 17 (2nd ed) *
Ranma 1/2, Vol. 18 (2nd ed) *
Ranma 1/2, Vol. 30 *

All books starting at $7.99!

* Also available on DVD from VIZ

www.viz.com

FULLMETAL ALCHEMIST © Hiromu Arakawa/SQUARE ENIX KEKKAISHI © 2004 Yellow Tanabe/Shogakukan, Inc.
MÄR © 2003 Nobuyuki Anzai/Shogakukan, Inc. GUNNM © 1991 by YUKITO KISHIRO/SHUEISHA Inc.
CASE CLOSED © 1994 Gosho Aoyama/Shogakukan, Inc. CHEEKY ANGEL © 1999 Hiroyuki Nishimori/Shogakukan, Inc.
EXCEL SAGA © 1997 Rikdo Koshi/SHONENGAHOSHA NO NEED FOR TENCHI! © HITOSHI OKUDA 1995 © AIC/VAP • NTV
RANMA 1/2 ©1988 Rumiko Takahashi/Shogakukan, Inc.

COMPLETE OUR SURVEY AND LET US KNOW WHAT YOU THINK!

☐ Please do NOT send me information about VIZ products, news and events, special offers, or other information.

☐ Please do NOT send me information from VIZ's trusted business partners.

Name: _____

Address: _____

City: _____ **State:** _____ **Zip:** _____

E-mail: _____

☐ Male ☐ Female **Date of Birth (mm/dd/yyyy):** ___ / ___ / ___ (Under 13? Parental consent required)

What race/ethnicity do you consider yourself? (please check one)

☐ Asian/Pacific Islander ☐ Black/African American ☐ Hispanic/Latino

☐ Native American/Alaskan Native ☐ White/Caucasian ☐ Other: _____

What VIZ product did you purchase? (check all that apply and indicate title purchased)

☐ DVD/VHS _____

☐ Graphic Novel _____

☐ Magazines _____

☐ Merchandise _____

Reason for purchase: (check all that apply)

☐ Special offer ☐ Favorite title ☐ Gift

☐ Recommendation ☐ Other _____

Where did you make your purchase? (please check one)

☐ Comic store ☐ Bookstore ☐ Mass/Grocery Store

☐ Newsstand ☐ Video/Video Game Store ☐ Other: _____

☐ Online (site: _____)

What other VIZ properties have you purchased/own? _____

_____

How many anime and/or manga titles have you purchased in the last year? How many were VIZ titles? (please check one from each column)

ANIME	MANGA	VIZ
☐ None	☐ None	☐ None
☐ 1-4	☐ 1-4	☐ 1-4
☐ 5-10	☐ 5-10	☐ 5-10
☐ 11+	☐ 11+	☐ 11+

I find the pricing of VIZ products to be: (please check one)

☐ Cheap ☐ Reasonable ☐ Expensive

What genre of manga and anime would you like to see from VIZ? (please check two)

☐ Adventure ☐ Comic Strip ☐ Science Fiction ☐ Fighting
☐ Horror ☐ Romance ☐ Fantasy ☐ Sports

What do you think of VIZ's new look?

☐ Love It ☐ It's OK ☐ Hate It ☐ Didn't Notice ☐ No Opinion

Which do you prefer? (please check one)

☐ Reading right-to-left
☐ Reading left-to-right

Which do you prefer? (please check one)

☐ Sound effects in English
☐ Sound effects in Japanese with English captions
☐ Sound effects in Japanese only with a glossary at the back

THANK YOU! Please send the completed form to:

NJW Research
42 Catharine St.
Poughkeepsie, NY 12601

KU-175-288

All information provided will be used for internal purposes only. We promise not to sell or otherwise divulge your information.

NO PURCHASE NECESSARY. Requests not in compliance with all terms of this form will not be acknowledged or returned. All submissions are subject to verification and become the property of VIZ, LLC. Fraudulent submission, including use of multiple addresses or P.O. boxes to obtain additional VIZ information or offers may result in prosecution. VIZ reserves the right to withdraw or modify any terms of this form. Void where prohibited, taxed, or restricted by law. VIZ will not be liable for lost, misdirected, mutilated, illegible, incomplete or postage-due mail. © 2003 VIZ, LLC. All Rights Reserved. VIZ, LLC, property titles, characters, names and plots therein under license to VIZ, LLC. All Rights Reserved.